07/08

UNIVERSITY OF WOLVERHAMPTON

Walsall Learning Centre
University of Wolverhampton
Gorway
Walsall WS1 3BD
Telephone: 0845 408 1631
Online renewals: www.wlv.ac.uk/lib/my account

23/3/11		

Telephone Renewals: 01902 321333 or 0845 408 1631
Please Return this item on or before the last date shown above.
Fines will be charged if items are returned late.
See tariff of fines displayed at the Counter.

PERFORMANCE ON THE EDGE

TRANSFORMATIONS OF CULTURE

JOHANNES BIRRINGER

continuum
LONDON • NEW YORK

First published in 2000 by
Continuum
11 York Road, London SE1 7NX
370 Lexington Avenue, New York NY 10017-6503

© Johannes Birringer 2000

Johannes Birringer has asserted his right under the Copyright, Designs and
Patents Act 1998, to be identified as the author of this work

British Library Cataloguing in Publication Data
A catalogue record for this book is available from the British Library

ISBN 0 485 00418 6   HB
0 8264 5779 7 PB

Library of Congress Cataloging-in-Publication Data
Birringer, Johannes H.
Performance on the edge: transformations of culture / Johannes Birringer
p. cm.
Includes index.
ISBN 0-485-00418-6 (alk. paper)
1. Performance art.   2. Artistic collaboration.   I. Title.
NX456.5.P38 B57 2000
700'.9'04—dc21   99-086429

Typeset by RefineCatch Limited, Bungay, Suffolk
Printed and bound in Great Britain by
Bookcraft (Bath) Ltd

LA FRONTERA ES LO UNICO QUE COMPARTIMOS.

ÜBER DIE GRENZE WEHT DER WIND
DIE HERBSTBLÄTTER
DER ERLAUBTEN ÜBERTRETUNG
INS ANDERLAND.
DAS ASYL DER SONNE
WIRD KÄLTER.

For Angeles

CONTENTS

LIST OF ILLUSTRATIONS

Front cover video stills: from *Lovers Fragments* and *Verschlossene Räume*, created by AlienNation Co./ Fantasielabor, 1995.

All video stills are taken from the productions, video works and rehearsals by members of AlienNation Co. and their collaborators. The production and exhibition photographs, unless otherwise indicated, are by Johannes Birringer.

ACKNOWLEDGMENTS

This book might have been a performance-film or multimedia installation, and many different communities would be invited on opening night to celebrate the work to which they have contributed. I thank all my colleagues in the Dance & Technology Online Network for their feedback, and I am very grateful to all those collaborators who helped me in the construction of the images in this book, and who gave me permission to intercut some of the visual narratives of our collective memory and physical interactions into the pages.

I am also grateful to the book's designers for their willingness to experiment with the textures of video stills, digital files, computer print-outs, and photographs. I am particularly grateful for the loyalty and support of my editor, Tristan Palmer, who believed in this project. The photographs of other exhibitions, films, and performances are reprinted with the permission of the artists whose work I encountered and reviewed. I am thankful to them. Several photographers, visual artists, and art galleries have been very generous in allowing me to use their photographs.

Some portions of the writings in this book have previously appeared in print or in my own video works. I thank the editors of *Performing Arts Journal*, *The Drama Review*, *Theater Topics*, *Gestos*, *Canadian Slavonic Papers*, and *Maska* for supporting my work-in-progress. Some fragments of the writing exist in other languages, and I have tried to translate them back into English. Some of my collaborators graciously helped me with transcriptions from the Slovene, Russian, Polish, Portuguese, and Spanish languages. My friends in East Germany were patient and forgiving when I did not always recognize the connotations of my divided mother tongue. Apropos of tongues: my favorite painting of Orpheus is by Cuban painter Tonel who depicts the complex relations between language and exile in a sardonic image, '*del artista bilingue*,' which shows two long, protruding tongues coming out of a head, one in the front, the other in the back. I think Paul Klee would have liked it. So, read my tongues. I should add that Kiss & Tell, the Canadian group of photographers/writers, came up with a sexy title for their collaboration: 'Her Tongue on My Theory.' Their photo-text essays are wonderfully inspirational.

During the six years of composing this book, much of my time was devoted to rehearsal workshops and productions. Finding the space to write, and to think through the body of material and experience, was made infinitely more pleasant in the company of those who shared similar concerns with me. We argued over the issues we confronted in the performances and the cross-cultural encounters, and the main metaphor for our dialogue, learnt from the practice of dance, is that of *contact improvisation*. It should be apparent that performance encompasses different styles based on contact. When I practice such contact improvisation, exercising the fullest consciousness of movement in and with my body, I realize that an alternative discourse might be required to overcome the rules of conventional scholarship or theory. We need a discourse that refuses to dislocate our physical and emotional experience and the processes of incorporation we live in the creative integration of the arts. New conceptualizations of/in performance are like new movement possibilities we learn by doing. While my debts will become apparent, I owe thanks to those colleagues in the university who have continued to support my deviations from various disciplinary streams. I would like to mention the late Robert Corrigan, Herbert Blau, Gautam Dasgupta, Josette Féral, Jeongwon Joe, George E. Marcus, Bonnie Marranca, Maria Teresa Marrero, Julian Olf, Henry M. Sayre, Richard Schechner, Elena Siemens, Carol Simpson Stern, Nena Torres, and Heiner Weidmann.

There are many others who have contributed significantly to the errant process of my working in different locations, and who offered me opportunities to conduct artistic research or participate in cultural projects. They will recognize the occasions of their vital contribution in the text. This will be particularly evident in those scenes that re-create conversations and collaborative rehearsals. I owe so much to my artistic mentors, collaborators, and students that I want to acknowledge their presence in my life. Strong and lasting friendships with David Caton, Richard Stout, Melissa Noble, Diana and Carlos Glandt, Graciella Poppi, Elba Baños and Malcolm Munro, Clarissa Guidry, Isabelle Ganz, Tonya Borisov, Yiannis Efstathiou, Gabriela Villegas, Tania Bothelo and Gilberto Neto, Hans Staartjes, Laura Steckler, Christopher Steele, Joanna and Allen Pasternak gave me spiritual sustenance in Houston. Susan Bianconi, Iris Carulli, Renato Miceli, Elise Kermani, Sara Chazen, Barbara Mensch, Ivor Miller, Idania Díaz Gonzáles, Donna Drewes, and the Cleary family were generous comrades who gave me shelter and inspiration in New York City, New Haven, and Boston. Juan Villegas, Lillian Manzor-Coats, Alicia del Campo, Silvia Pellarollo and their co-conspirators in the Irvine Hispanic Theater Research Group invited me into their Latin American/Latino/Chicano theater research network in southern California. I owe thanks to the Performance Studies and Theater departments at Northwestern University for letting me convert teaching into experimental labs and off-shore production workshops. I will always remember the students who chose to take risks and work with us in spite of the general, aggravating prejudice against performance art, and art-process in general, that informs the liberal humanism of institutions claiming to be pluralist yet anxiously defending disciplinary centeredness. A lot of decentering remains to be done.

At other times I visited performance festivals, workshops, and conferences, and I am grateful for generous invitations to present work and exchange ideas at events organized by Scott deLahunta and Ric Allsopp (Amsterdam), Carmen

Garrido (Barcelona), Janet Lansdale (University of Surrey), Virve Sutinen (Helsinki), Josette Féral (Montréal), Pia Kleber (Toronto), Uschi Schmidt-Fehringer (Saarbrücken), Chris Butler (Chichester), Uli Birringer (Eisenhüttenstadt), Attilio Caffarena (Genova), Nils Eichberg (Berlin), Tom Mulready (Cleveland), Tim Fiori and Mitchell Covic (Chicago), Jessica Kriesz (Copenhagen), Abdel Hernández, Surpik Angelini and George Marcus (Artists in Trance, Houston), and Wendy Watriss and Fred Baldwin (Houston). I would like to thank Kampnagel Fabrik Hamburg, TanzWerkstatt Berlin, Tanzwerkstatt Europa (Munich), and Europäische Werkstatt für Kunst und Kultur Hellerau (Dresden) for inviting me to their theater/dance festivals; Irena Staudohar and Polona Mertelj for arranging the 'Physical Theater' workshop in Ljubljana; the Union of Democratic Communications for inviting me to their workshop at the International School of Film & TV in Cuba; and Ivor Miller for introducing me to his friends and fellow *santeros* in Havana.

During studio visits, rehearsals, projects, and other occasions I learnt to appreciate the intensity and commitment of several artists who have left a deep impression on me; they include Pina Bausch and her company, Deborah Hay, Meredith Monk, Carolee Schneemann, Marina Abramović, Coco Fusco, Guillermo Gómez-Peña, Goran Dordević, James Luna, Tim Miller, Meg Stuart, Jutta Hell and Dieter Baumann (Tanztheater Rubato), Helmut Psotta and Grupo Chaclacayo, Michael Tracy, Melanie Lien Palm, Esther Parada, Bob Peters, Marlon Riggs, Nedko Solakov, Michael Tracy, Ela Troyano, Víctor Varela, and Zoran Masirević.

The passionate generosity of those artists, cultural workers, and families I met in Cuba, Slovenia, and East Germany has had the most visceral impact on my work. The collaborations and plans that evolved from these encounters have a certain utopian dimension that I hope to explore in my next films and writings. I am deeply indebted to their invitations and hospitality, and their challenges to my limited comprehension of borders and transcultural processes. Special thanks are due to Rosa Ileana Boudet, Vivian Martínes Tabares, Nara Mansur, Magaly Muguercia, Rigoberto López, Jorge Perugorría, Víctor Varela, and Mirtha and Guillermo Diaz Gonzáles in Havana and the members of La Jaula Abierta in Alamar; Eda Čufer, Marko Peljhan, Irena Štaudohar, Marko Košnik, Emil Hrvatin, Mojca Kumerdej, Naja Kos, Barbara Drnać, and Mateja Rebolj in Ljubljana; Anett Schauermann and the members of the Fantasielabor in Eisenhüttenstadt; Ute Pischtschan, Detlef Schneider, Julius Skowronek, Jo Siamon Salich, and the members of RU-IN in Dresden; and Uschi Schmidt-Fehringer, Leonie Quint, Ute Ritschel, Astrid Swift, and Frank Leimbach on the western border of Germany.

Finally, this book would not have been written without the exciting, nurturing, and contentious collaborations I experienced with the composers, musicians, performers, and visual artists who journeyed and worked with me on the productions of *AD MORTEM*, *Orpheus and Eurydike*, *From the Border*, *Lovers Fragments*, *Parsifal*, *La lógica que se cumple*, *LBLM*, *Before Night Falls*, *North by South*, *migbot*, and the *Parachute* cycle developed in various abandoned or inaccessible downtown locations after my return to Houston in 1997. I deeply appreciate the vitality and political commitment of those in our activist and alternative communities who have clarity of vision and are moving toward life, transforming it (as choreographer Anna Halprin would call the holistic quality of such process). I thank you all for exploring the creative ecstasies, perversions, and pitfalls of collective work, and for sharing your erotic energies with me. Some of you have taught me more about contemporary art and social relations than I could ever learn from cultural theories. I trust our 'AlienNation' company will make it into the next century: T.Weldon Anderson, Don Calledare, Patrick Clark, John Cook, Christina Giannelli, Steve Lafayette, Serena Lin, André Marquetti, Elaine Molinaro, Peter Mueller, Steve Paré, Tara Peters, Craig Roberts, Angeles Romero, Imma Sarries-Zgonc, Christy Singleton, Patricia Sotarello, Mariko Ventura, and Emmanuel Woodward.

My brothers and their families have always given me their support when I needed it, and my mother, in her great wisdom, lovingly refuses to believe in experimental theater. She has never seen my work, but I choreographed my *Parsifal* performance for her, knowing that she would have been my toughest audience. This book is dedicated to Angeles Romero whose poetry and dark sense of irony I would not ever want to miss in my life.

PREFACE

We work on the edge of time. Traditional writing formats of books on performance will perhaps soon be supplanted by experimental video-essays, CD-ROMS,
Internet publications, and interactive exhibitions. Almost all of my performances
and workshops have been documented audio-visually and displayed on my website, contrary to the myth that performance art cannot be recorded because it
lives in and for the moment. Most of my work was not created for a moment but
for various kinds of continuity. Some of these projects were composed as videos
without script or story-board, others were performed on the stage or in specific
sites or alternative spaces, and now we have scores that are then mediated again
in different constellations, exhibitions, and frameworks. All performance projects are interconnected, transforming experience. More recently, projects have
evolved that were prepared through email correspondence and designed for real
locations as well as for online webcasts. They assume their own electronic lives,
and my writings and reflections usually follow the practical work and the digital
or photographic scenarios that are created in the diachronic process.

While video and digital processing are becoming ever more important instruments of analytical reflection on our work in different cultural locations, they are
also independent and interdependent modes of creative production, intervening
into the performance work with the specific memory they record or construct of
the collaborations that are the physical basis for these pages. It will become
necessary to address the changes in our methods of composition effected by
interactive technologies at the turn of the century, as these technologies exceed
the limits of the physical and of performance. This book, however, does not
dwell much on virtual realities. It rests on the (shifting) ground of my bodily
understanding of interactivity, offering an account of my performance-journey
across several geographical borders and conceptual boundaries.

Performance on the Edge provides a particular kind of testimony of interaction
and collaboration in independent performance, dance theater, media art and
activism as I have experienced them throughout the 1990s. In one sense, the
book traces a personal path, which I begin to sketch in the Introduction, reliving
my visceral memories of a ritual event on the Rio Grande/Río Bravo in 1990, a
few months after the fall of the Berlin Wall. This event on the border, with its
burnt offering and ritual destruction of a cross dedicated to the living intersection of Latin and North America, triggered my subsequent return to Berlin and

my extended 'video archaeology' of Germany's internalized border, a conflicted mental map of divisive cultural and political notions of identity/identification.

In another sense, the *Border-Land* video project entered the transitional historical phase of the momentous revolutionary transformations affecting Central and Eastern Europe, and my awareness of these changes was increasingly shaped by local performances, workshops, encounters, and contact improvisations with others. In the three chapters which comprise the first half of the book, I offer a detailed account of these encounters and collaborations, including my crossing over into Cuba and a different space of post-revolutionary disillusionment.

Although *Performance on the Edge* was never intended to address the 'border discourse' so fashionably promoted in the field of cultural studies, it may implicitly question some of the terms of the debates on postmodern performance, and the disciplinary construct of academic 'performance studies,' as it traces its own pathways, failures, and revelations in transcultural collaboration with other artists and workers in the periphery of metropolitan theories and commodified grooves. In a very basic sense, it addresses the potential and feasibility of collaboration along different lines, not those of established models in the theater or film or recording industry, but those of experimental art and alternative media which are forever unfolding, changing, and fluid. Like the transcultural friendships that have evolved through my journeys and collaborations, experimental art by necessity needs to reinvent itself along the way, since the support systems for alternative culture, in the United States and elsewhere, have been very nearly dismantled, and virtual realities don't offer food and shelter.

One of the outcomes of workshops, productions, and the shooting-on-location for *Border-Land* was the formation of AlienNation Co. in 1993. Our international company became the vehicle for cooperation and site-specific projects in different locations chronicled in Chapter 1, 'After the Revolution,' and Chapter 2, 'Dialogues and Border Crossings.' These chapters also illuminate the narrative styles of reassemblage in the book, following the filmic principle of montage, with jump cuts, voice-overs, silent image passages, dialogues, and observations that might be performative or analytical or both. There are also repetitions that have to do with the rhythms of experience in the field of experimental performance whose rehearsals and creative processes distinguish it somewhat from ethnographic praxis and the anthropological impetus of 'rendering' the field notes. But since dance and contact improvisation, for example, suffer the reputation of being impermanent and ephemeral (and not collectable by museums and libraries), we need to emphasize the material effects of rehearsals and site-specific work and their vital relationship to everyday life. Transcultural collaboration always involves choreographic methods, and thus we collect movements, notations, videos, sounds, sketches, drawings, costumes, recipes, and reflections. We remember certain steps and always collect new ones.

Chronicling our performance, video and dance work in the Midwest, Texas, Holland, East Germany, Slovenia, Cuba, and on the borders of former Cold War divides and present North/Central American fault lines, *Performance on the Edge* collects dialogues about performance as process and physical *mudanzas* of contact, as emotional commitment to political activism and the reconstruction of community, as site-specific intervention into social and technological structures of abandonment, and as highly charged embodiments of erotic fantasies.

Working on the edges or outer limits of entrenched cultural constructs and artistic genres, these performance dialogues address the politics of community-oriented artmaking in an era marked by the AIDS crisis, cultural and racial polarization, warfare, separatism, and xenophobia. As I traveled eastward, away from Germany and its deceptively euphoric unification politics, the war broke out in former Yugoslavia. Soon I encountered refugees and artists from Bosnia, and a devastating exhibition: *Sarajevo: Witnesses of Existence*. I also met refugees from Peru, a group of visual artists who had left the Andes because their work had aroused the suspicion of the authorities. They fled the state's surveillance and military aggression against indigenous people, and their *Parsifal Prolog*, staged at the Hellerau Festpielhaus in East Germany, became the basis for a collaborative opera that investigates legacies of violence and cultural myths of redemption.

In Chapter 3, 'MAKROLAB: a Heterotopia,' I witness the construction of a counter-surveillance system by artists who realize that forceful aggression can be replaced by newer technological systems of information and control, which are totally indifferent to resistance, converting objects, events, and people into data. The MAKROLAB project challenges our assumptions about the relations between media and activism, bodily identities and virtual communities, technological imperatives and organic experiences of social processes.

The second part of the book offers critical meditations on contemporary cultural practice – ethnography, performance, international feminist and gay/lesbian visual art, film/video – from different angles that connect the multi-directional links in the book. In Chapter 4, 'The Transcultural Imaginary,' I examine cultural trade and the trading of concepts, both in the arts and in the social sciences, which affect our meeting with others and the perceptions of others. In re-evaluating the terms of such 'meeting grounds,' special attention is given to the economic processes within which cultural production and performance take place.

Chapter 5, 'La melancolía de la jaula,' collects evidence of cultural trade in some of the common frameworks of contemporary exhibition, namely film, theater, music and performance festivals. The chapter examines the presentation of Latin American/Latino art in the United States, and then changes location and interfaces with practitioners in Cuba, evoking some poignant echoes and ironies with regard to the cage and the melancholy (the loss of containment) discovered in Chapter 2.

Finally, the concluding chapter on *Lovers Fragments* excavates the personalized fantasies and imaginaries of performance artists in our company working close to the skin (the erotic) and equally close to the screens and phantasms of our cultural and sexual identities in a rehearsal of shared narratives. These narratives, unfinished and unredeemed, return us to the question of the ritual on the border river. The passion (and perverse pathos) of performance affects our awareness of differences that cannot be pierced. The living river does not know that it is a border or a myth, but it can be abused, polluted. Recovering a pattern or a rehearsal of intersecting narratives may produce the tools we need to break down the languages of containment and the false redemptions. Collaboration, I argue, is mostly an unaccommodated act of love. Our burnt offerings need witnesses of their existence. Our temporary workshops and the transitory communities they form are vital because they may not last, and therefore we have no time to waste, to camouflage and repress our experiences and creativities. Performance from the margins, this book claims, produces some of the most vibrant and resonant work in the cultural worlds, and transcultural productions must tell their site-specific stories even if these won't matter much to the global traffic in cultural domination.

Houston, March 1999

INTRODUCTION

During the Easter weekend of 1990 I participated in my first cross-over perform-ance on a literal border, the Rio Grande/Río Bravo. The event had consequences I was not aware of at the time, but this book will take account of them. My role was limited: I was both witness and filmmaker/recorder of the action, *The River Pierce: Sacrifice II, 13.4.90*, which consisted of a large gathering of invited parti-cipants in the small town of San Ygnacio and a ritual procession to the border followed by the burnt offering of a monumental ceremonial cross (*Cruz: La Pasión*) to the river that divides the South from the North. The event, in which more than a hundred people from Mexico and the United States took part, was choreographed and scripted by the artist Michael Tracy whose studio had been located in San Ygnacio for a number of years before he moved to central Mexico, to the other side. He had built the cross during a five-year period, 1982–7, and exhibited it as a sculptural object intended for its final destination as a 'burnt offering.'

Perhaps my role was less limited than I think now. I realized that my camera could record only the surface symbolism of the action, and I felt unable to act upon the ritual procedure that had been created. Yet I participated in the sequences of the whole event: the traveling and arrival, the meetings with the others, the preparations, the meals, the action, the conversations and medita-tions, the symposium that followed the day after the ritual event, the cooling down, the silence, and the departure. Half-way through the event I found out that there was an actual script, a kind of liturgical libretto and scenographic plan devised by Michael and modeled after the Via Dolorosa. A number of invited participants had quite precise roles in the ritual procession, whereas others had come mainly as witnesses or supporters. The filming of the action had in fact been assigned to a small camera team, and my own use of the camera was somewhat accidental; I became an extra, without clear directions as to what I was supposed to film, and Michael asked me to be as unobtrusive as possible. Perhaps this is what I mean by 'limited.' I was outside of the script, and in a certain sense I remained unpersuaded by the ritual. It affected me differently, without affect-ing me in such a way that I could have identified with its rhythms, symbolic structure, liturgies, and visual choreography, nor with its deliberate gesturing at the Passion and the Crucifixion. Thinking of it now, I believe I must have been

Figure 1 Sacrifice II, 13.4.90: The River Pierce. Michael Tracy's *Cruz: La Pasión* on mule driven cart has reached the river; children carrying Virgen image on the left; mud people preparing fire on the right. Performance action created Michael Tracy. San Ygnacio, 1990. Photo courtesy of the artist.

appalled at being confronted, after all these years, with the ceremonial trappings of my childhood Catholicism. Michael's performance aesthetic was confrontational, of course. We were not asked to re-enact a Christian ritual but to turn it inside out, to burn the symbol and exorcize the demons of piety. Michael's passion was intensely emotional and politically expressionist – it invoked a festering wound on the edge of our cultural consciousness. His liturgies demanded both physical involvement and an intellectual commitment to the ceremonial subversion, as it became gradually clear to us that the ritual did not invoke resurrection but turned into a baroque epitaph for a polluted river.

The border river, in this allegory, became the stage for a political ceremony in which we were asked to remember the social and political struggle between the United States and Latin America, and to reflect on the ongoing 'drama of two distinct cultures hemorrhaging into each other,' as Michael described it in his invitation. His metaphors of abjection and pollution, blood and sewage, added to the cruel plasticity of his cross sculpture, and many of us stood silently on the banks as we looked at the conflagration. We could not move.

There was something mortifying about the solemnity of the action. It was a valuable and disconcerting experience, and I tried to make sense of my conflicting emotions as I improvised shooting with my camera, unobtrusively capturing

Figure 2 Sacrifice II, 13.4.90: The River Pierce. The burning cross floats in the Rio Grande/Río Bravo. Performance action created by Michael Tracy. San Ygnacio, 1990. Photo courtesy of the artist.

the aesthetic form of this ritual. I felt trapped in the no man's land between performance and ritual, political demonstration and aesthetic masturbation. It was a suffocating experience, and at the same time I knew that the border ritual was less important than the concrete relationship to the border that each of us had to confront, to imagine, to create. It became more urgent to me to recognize what, and whom, was excluded by the ritual, and what, and whom, was served by the symbolism. Can we speak of the failure of ritual? Had I witnessed another paratheatrical avant-garde event that banked its political intentions on the perverse cult of primitivism? Or did the ritual in fact succeed in drawing attention to the predicament of aesthetic performance gesturing through the flames?

It took some time, but after the ritual had ended and the flames died down, Michael and a few others went out on the river to collect the ashes of the cross. Meanwhile the people who had come to meet at the border began to relate to each other, to exchange their reactions and their thinking, to become involved with each other's way of looking, remembering, and understanding. I became aware of some of the angry and confused townspeople who had not been invited to the ritual and suspected the worst from all those foreign artists who had descended upon their town's traditional Easter preparations. I began to argue with the Mexican artists about their perceptions of the 'polluted river,' and then met with some of the US activists in our group who worked as legal counselors for immigrants and refugees. A process had started that made us question our political and ideological positions *vis-à-vis* this place and this border. The river has two names. Different meanings and connotations attach themselves to these names, depending on our standpoints or investments. Our physical engagement in the ritual gave way to an ethical debate on social relations, on our existential sense of belonging or not belonging, our living on the border or outside the border.

We all move across spaces, we live in space-time of movement. We also inhabit certain locations in and for which we work, rebuilding our sense of self from the ashes of the bridges that burnt down. Many of us live in cultural exile. And you may argue that we all have certain rituals we enact or fail to even notice anymore because they have become second nature. Along with them, we may come to feel more strongly the spiritual yearnings in us that a detached and ever more cynical postmodernism seemed to have banished for good.

The event left its traces on my imagination and my growing awareness of borders and border cultures. Having lived in Texas for five years as a 'resident alien' without proper accreditation or work permit, I began to realize that my work as a performance artist was shifting its locations, broadening its assumptions and extending its underlying theory into other areas of cultural work. Those areas and testing grounds of performance, media, cultural activism and theory, near the end of the Reagan–Bush administrations, were becoming so heavily contested that someone coined the term 'culture wars' and began to collect the 'documents from the recent controversies in the arts,' almost as if it had become necessary to preserve the correspondences from the battle-lines.[1] The terms of the debate on the 'culture wars' seemed dictated by politicians, legislators, conservative publicists, and organizations that favored controls on public expression and thus nurtured an increasingly non-participatory democracy in the USA. The work of artists and educators, along with the expressions of many citizens of our diverse communities, became more conflicted and defensive as the 1990s wore on and social and economic disparities increased. The struggle for justice and equity, for freedom of expression and freedom of sexual preference, for better and more diversified education and health services, for a greater understanding and dialogue among cultures, and for the demise of discrimination, racism, sexism, and homophobia demanded new multicultural forms of grassroots political and community organizing.

The contested borderlines of inclusion and exclusion, or the arrangement and representation of 'identities,' thus gained a significance in the public expressions of the 1990s which I could not have anticipated as I ventured to explore the immediate cross-cultural contexts of my performance work in the late 1980s. By the time I left Texas and moved to Chicago, a few days before an actual war was to be waged in the Persian Gulf (as announced by ultimatum), it was too late to go back to any mode of aesthetic inquiry that did not take into account the fissures among cultures and the political implications of contemporary critical discourses on race, gender, ethnicity, and nation. Perhaps I should say my theoretical interest in postmodernism and the quibbles over aesthetic transgressions and appropriations had ended, more or less consciously, the moment I crossed the Río Bravo and watched the slow burning of the cross that drifted back and forth across the river. I did not wish to write another book on theater and postmodernism, even though my passion for performance keeps returning me to questions about the failures of our ritual practices. My new working term for the examination of the passion in such failures is 'collaboration.'

DANCING ON THE WALL, OR THE EUPHORIA OF PERFORMANCE

This book is a document of performance collaborations I experienced throughout the last ten years of the century. If there is a dimension of utopian thinking included in it, it rests in the practice and in the notion of art and action as a metaphor for living. Furthermore, at the point I started to collect these documents in 1991 I had already begun to prepare a series of projects that would allow or force me to scrutinize my own movement among different cultural spaces, as an emigrant who had grown up under the influence of European culture, its ideologies of art, and its modern myths of the avant-garde. When I was asked to write an editorial for a Houston newspaper on 10 November 1989, I assumed that global politics had changed with the fall of the Berlin Wall. My initial speculations on the accelerated collapse of the Cold War scenario were deeply pessimistic for reasons I am still seeking to work out in my mind and my memory. As a matter of personal irony, I had just completed a video-documentary, *Memories of the Revolution*, but those 'memories' were in fact staged as public spectacles of entertainment in Houston during the 1989 International Festival, proffering a superficial consumerist commemoration of the French Revolution, 200 years after. My sarcasm regarding the function of such staged memory in the faceless urban deserts of Houston took a bitter turn when I began to think about the repercussions of the dancing on the crumbled Berlin Wall. I didn't quite trust the dance even though I could sense the euphoria.

I feel that it is impossible for us to grasp 'history,' the passage of time and of momentous events, except emotionally, viscerally, as it sometimes happens when we witness a powerful performance we don't understand but for its bodily and affective impact on us. One problem in this case was that I was watching the dance on television; its virtuality became an obsession that I have tried to examine, in a number of ways, in subsequent performance experiments that explore the relations between our physical movement and connection in time and space, and our mediated and electronically processed movement, our life as images, our monitoring of our bodies and desires.

The fall of the Berlin Wall kindled an excitement and a hope for a different future that was ineluctably mixed up, not with a sense of loss, as later turned out to be the case for many nostalgic citizens of the former real-existing socialism, but with a fearful concern for the processes of negotiation and border-crossing that lay ahead of the Europe that appeared to reconstruct itself from the ashes of its 'post'-war confrontations. This phoenix began to throw its deep shadows on the next few years.

It was time to collect ashes. In the summer of 1990 I returned to Berlin and to the remains of the Wall that had divided the East from the West. I began an 'archaeological' video project (*Border-Land*) in the Berlin *Todesstreifen*, the so-called death-zone or no man's land of the dismantled border wall. I had decided to film the same locations in Berlin and along the East German–Polish border for a duration of five years, seeking to create a thick description of the physical and ideological transformations in the border zones of the reunited Germanies. In the following years, trying to experience and learn from the revolutionary changes in Central and Eastern Europe, I traveled not only along the East German border but into Poland, Hungary, Czechoslovakia, and Yugoslavia at the very time when the collapse of the Soviet Union became imminent and the war between Serbia and Croatia broke out, followed by the Serbian attack against Bosnia.

During the continually evolving phases of the video-documentary process, I also began to utilize the found and constructed footage in the collaborative performance work I created with ensemble members, artists and fellow researchers in East Germany, Slovenia, Cuba, and the USA. The encounters and dialogues with artists and cultural workers in Slovenia and Cuba began in 1993–4, after a small performance and film festival I helped to create in Chicago. It was during the rehearsal process for this festival, titled 'From the Border,' that I met José David, Andre Marquetti, Zoran Masirević, Avanthi Meduri, Elaine Molinaro, Juan Pedro, Marko Peljhan, Tara Peters, Imma Sarries-Zgonc, Patricia Sotarello, Nena Torres, Kukuli Velarde, Mariko Ventura, Mirtes Zwierzynski, and many others who helped to build an independent network of cultural communication and exchange. I consider my evolving itinerary – from Chicago to Central and Eastern Europe to Latin America – a very organic process of exploring the actual implications of former, new, or still existing borders, political and psychic divisions, transitions and blockades.

During this process some of us founded an ensemble, 'AlienNation Co.,' that worked together in producing research and media/performances, but also functioned as a conceptual structure of operations for projects that did not necessarily take place in one location nor need to be identified with the same members. Our sometimes quite dispersed company recognizes 'alienation' as a preface to the experience of working together, belonging, and belonging outside. Inevitably, we live the proliferation of imaginary border spaces and try to meet, whenever possible, in our intermediary collaborations. There is always uncertainty about the collective identity of the group, and more recently I have come to think that the group wouldn't exist except for its evolving, changing desire to find time to acknowledge the need to touch and share and breathe the energy of creative collaboration, and to find space in-between the entrapments we often experience in the daily grind of our lives.

As a cross-cultural process, our work improvises and rehearses complex, often contradictory performance and media strategies, while our emphasis is on the social interaction and the exchange of different ways of transforming materials, techniques, recipes, artistic sensibilities, and political positions. It would be presumptuous to claim that a single person could write a theory of performance-as-collaboration. Rather, this book seeks to trace the spirit and the material effects of collaborations I have participated in, and it thus partakes of the work of others, depending on the exchanges we were able to arrange and live in our work. Sometimes such work is also initiated by cultural events, exhibitions, workshops, political actions, and personal conflicts, and it will therefore be forever indebted to the critical experiences that arise from physical encounters, emotional relationships, and intellectual desires. There is a decisive erotic and euphoric dimension in all of these, and I will return to it near the end of the book, hoping that the energy to collaborate on performances will always exceed my effort to write something down.

The experience of forming an international performance group helped me to reflect on possible forms of belonging or not belonging that are not subject to constricted or generalizable notions of an intrinsic identity, national, cultural, or other. The issue of 'alien nation' (I prefer the German word *Anderland*, which doesn't properly exist but makes sense as a construct for certain fantasies of communities and 'the land') surfaces in the work of collaboration, of course, since we spend a good deal of time translating, learning each other's languages of practice and imagination, making contact with each other's bodily vocabularies, movements, and boundaries. Performing such translations I often find myself at a loss, almost as if no rehearsal can ever be taken for granted since the rituals of physical and mental preparation may have to be quickly adopted to a new situation, changed, reinvented, or abandoned. This happens when you don't stay in one place and within a specific discipline of training, and although performance artists sometimes get accused of a certain lack of discipline, I think it's actually the opposite phenomenon. Traveling across the borders of familiar methods and structures of belonging requires concentration and a radical passion for improvisation as the scores and libretti keep breaking down.

In this work we do a lot of reassembling, and there is no safe autonomy of the exercises. I trust this book will not serve as a guide to *training*, although I recommend a healthy dose of contact improvisation and a concentrated awareness of body-mind and physical-spiritual consciousness. The details of some of the improvisations will become clearer when I address the contexts of performance. (And I won't go into the failure of academic programs that pretend to teach 'embodied practice' or implement integrated arts curricula.) But we improvise within the limits of our imagination, and what I find so encouraging and exciting about the practice of collaboration is the necessarily constant struggle to welcome the widening range of the unexpected, the unpredictable, and the transformative experience. Regardless of the difficulties, there often appears the sudden strange beauty of the unexpected or the unthinkable, and this perverse beauty links art and sex in ways that may be improper to acknowledge in the academic world or the puritanical cosmos upheld by conservatives against all the odds in our profane popular cultures. The excitement of creativity comes from those moments, as in good sex, when we may lose control or realize, during the play of experimentation, that the boundaries drawn by rules and the demarcations of difference can unexpectedly shift, and thus change our relationship to perceived or projected identity. Our creativity in performance also depends on our physical awareness and critical sensitivity toward the media with which we translate each other's ideas, movements, and images, and although the creative process draws on what we know, there are no rules that could protect us from the pressures of the social worlds in which we encounter the fearfulness and violence of transformation. In a sense, what I am addressing here are the limits of the aesthetic, the limits of the protection of forms.

Images and thoughts that began to develop in *Border-Land* and haunted me over the next few years were affected by an immediate and palpable sense of the collapse of several Communist regimes, the collapse of the political utopia of socialism, and the unpredictable transformations of the political and cultural geographies in the East. These transformations will have a crucial influence on the organization of a new, united Europe; they also foreshadow and overshadow the precarious balancing act, on the edge of the abyss, that one experiences in Cuban society during its current 'Special Period' and its increasingly conflicted relationship to the North (the USA) and its exiled-Cuban communities.

In a sense, we all live in a 'special period' of growing tensions and very mixed-up emotions about our identities, our nationhood, and our citizenship in communities at the end of the century. Mexican performance artist Maris Bustamante, in her provocative *Naftaperformances*, speaks of the 'end of the century syndrome,' but her comments on our *fin de siècle* are thoroughly sarcastic and also prophetic (Chapter 5). NAFTA or the European Union are constructions, imaginary communities, forged by powerful economic interests and corporate alliances that have very little regard for the welfare of the people. Bustamante claims that she enjoys the 'terror of the dying borders,' since it is a new challenge to discover what it means to be an 'intercontinental artist.' But the terror, first of all, is very real. I will return to this terror in Chapter 5, on '*La melancolía de la jaula.*'

The specter of a reunified Germany began to loom large in my work, because already in 1991 I could observe the new strains and stresses created by the transborder migration of refugees and the conflicts over questions of asylum, and the status of refugees and immigrant minorities, in a multicultural society which hasn't learnt to include 'alien' histories and other languages into its democratic pedagogy. The entire question of citizenship in the new Europe is a volcano, and all political elections from now on will be shadowed by contests over belonging and not belonging. We are nowhere near the 'end of history,' nor have we witnessed the 'triumph of the West,' and the 'universalization of Western liberal democracy as the final form of human government,' as Francis Fukuyama proclaimed.[2] The 'New World Order,' announced by the USA's president before the relentless US intervention in the Persian Gulf, looked very much like the familiar one we knew. The imperial demonstration of US military and technological superiority in the Gulf War created a destructive spectacle which, in its colonialist dimension, indirectly exploited the economic and political weakness of the

Soviet Union and the so-called Third World to set an example. But who was teaching whom? In whose interest was the high-tech destruction choreographed?

I mention the Gulf War crisis because the invasion of Iraq was preceded by a familiar political ploy to exert pressure on 'the other': the ultimatum. Many of us felt rendered impotent by the structure of the ultimatum as we watched time running out and negotiations failing to take place, and by the time we took to the streets to protest the war it was too late. A strange and paradoxical patriotic fervor had seized the populace in the USA, and a huge international television audience logged on to the spectacle of high-tech warfare and the official media-sponsored version of events, a version which gave preference to hyperreal computer animations of precision-bombing over the very real deaths of civilians (the so-called 'collateral damage').

Within the simulacra of war games technology, performance effects matter and the fantasies of feedback mechanisms substitute for truth-claims that have referential bearing. As the ultimatum ran out, I happened to be teaching my first performance art class at Northwestern University, having arrived in Chicago a few days earlier. I remember vividly that one of the students performed a seven-minute piece in which he asked us to sit close to him and watch him as he set the clock and waited for time to run out while ceremonially preparing the knife with which he was going to cut his wrist. Not a word was spoken, and we had a little time to think about the relations between performance art and the real, about violence, self-inflicted pain, and the structure of complicity that had been set up. If this was a voluntary and demonstrative performance act, why would we interfere, breaking the conventions of 'illusion' that rule the theater even if performance art or body art has professed an anti-theatrical bias? If this was a real act and not an illusion, would we applaud the courage, savor the shock value, and grant the performer his right to take responsibility?

The ethical dilemma that underlies the degraded and debilitating socio-cultural and political conditions in the postmodern world gains clarity in such moments when we become aware of the the violence of the ultimatum and the ideological complicity that exists and is internalized in deference to roles that seem scripted in advance. This is another dance, a dance of complicity. It does not elicit euphoria but freezes us.

Whether we feel capable of wrenching the knife out of the hand, and of resisting the widespread indifference or cynical acquiescence to conventions, normative regimes, and interests of capital that script the roles, becomes a matter of becoming subjects critically aware of having a choice. To act otherwise and explore the ethical conflict in all its consequences that affect us means to question not only the laws (or The Law, as the Lacanians would say in reference to paternal laws and prohibitions) but also the repetitions and rehearsals through which we organize time and being, our bodies, genders, fantasies, experiences, and our representations of the world and our location in it. To speak of 'location,' in reference to politics, returns us to the dilemma of borders, to their paradoxical constructions of sites of difference, contact, inclusion, exclusion, crossing and transmission.

'Border-work,' as you will see the term used, is simply meant to indicate *processes of negotiation*. I will neither offer a global theory nor dwell on disciplinary concerns too much, since my performance work and critical writing are not dependent on my having to identify any allegiance to a discipline, least of all to the emerging field of 'performance studies.' Perhaps I can say this, in the late 1990s, almost in retrospect after having taught performance practice and theory in situations where the pressures of institutional identification reflected precisely the political and economic regimes that independent performance/art and cultural practices sought to dislodge, expose, shift, or undermine. The study of borders – and of the border police – grants particular insights not only into the nexus of power/knowledge but, more immediately, into the practice of choice-making itself. Such choice-making, addressed as an ethical challenge above, is perennially involved in any form of creative production, and this book is above all about diverse approaches to performance and art, media and activism as cultural strategies of *squatting*, i.e. temporarily and improperly occupying a contested space in the presence of the Law that seeks to define and demarcate the (e)state of ownership. You can't squat alone, and therefore I include conversations and dialogues with collaborators in this book.

The processes of negotiation are physical. I will speak as much as I can about my body, and the physical and emotional involvement in the work that I have explored with my collaborators, and the book will begin, near the end, to sketch an ethics of eros which is, above all, an attempt to describe the fantasies and contingencies of *collaboration* in performance work. Collaboration is a form of complicity, too, and only too rarely discussed among artists and scholars alike. In fact, I would argue that we lack a performance theory of interdisciplinary collaboration altogether, and I hope to make a contribution to these concerns of collective work or of coalitions that affect our performance practice as well as our active engagement in cultural politics. On the other hand, in the first two chapters I seek to trace those metaphors of 'the border' that became more specific and localized in the course of the projects I briefly introduced above. In using techniques of the body and studying the technological formation of bodies in contexts of cross-cultural production, performance contributes – particularly in its underassimilated ways – to the current articulation of 'border experience' (marginalized, minority, queer cultures), the critique of marginalization (cf. *Criticism in the Borderlands* and *Barrios and Borderlands*), and the vision of a new engaged, liberatory, multicultural education (border pedagogy or 'teaching to transgress,' as bell hooks suggests).[3]

When I started to work on my *Border-Land* video project in 1990, I could not foresee that the trope of the 'border' would gain such currency in the next few years. Nor is it comforting to claim that performance art or independent media art, however notorious some of the arresting images became during the NEA/censorship controversies in the USA, was and will remain marginal in the arena of transnational commodity culture. Marginality, as we have seen in the increasing academic output of cultural theories, has gained a market value; it has of course also proven useful for museum exhibitions and the curatorial fashion industry. Throughout my writings and dialogues, I try to remain conscious of the claims to marginality connected with the border, and with queer, feminist, subcultural, and non-Western liberationist theories and practices, as they intersect with my work and my own privileged marginal role as border-crosser.[4] You will no doubt remain skeptical of the various positions and border locations addressed here, realizing that the performance work and its rehearsals and emotional experiences cannot be textualized or recuperated without loss.

In the sense in which I emphasize the process of border-work, I imply that its ethics and politics of marginality rely on a continuing, inconclusive praxis of collaboration that does not serve academic or commercial interests and reproducible norms. Recording our performances rarely means distributing them commercially; we have failed to enter the market of world music or pop transculture. If the 'objects' of performance in these writings serve any purpose at all, it is to raise questions about their temporary movement-across, their crossings and stumblings, their dissolution and reappearance, their improper and unaccommodated gestures and, sometimes, their abject relationships to the Law. Performance art questions authority, and its disservice incorporates utopian energies.

PERFORMANCE ON THE EDGE OF THE STATE

In the third chapter I will discuss the notion of 'heterotopia' with regard to an artistic-scientific project (MAKROLAB) initiated by Slovene artist Marko Peljhan. This project examines the flow of transnational communications and the uncertain legality of performing counter-surveillance on the edges of art and aesthetic territory. The return to the law of the state has itself become problematic and improbably fraught with contradictions, as we see nation-state power erode and transnational corporate management maximize profits by freely crossing national borders. As with the free and unregulated flow of information in the Internet, the transmission of world commodity culture has been appropriated by transnational corporations that administer global production and consumption, generating new margins of the transnational class, namely a huge underclass of surplus labor everywhere: the unemployed, the underemployed, the homeless, the sick, and the displaced. In the language of the Internet: non-users, people without access.

In the context of this globalization and economic integration, the non-users and the displaced in various world diasporas experience the lack of protection by the declining nation-states. Disaffection from the state and its institutions is explosively on the rise, and the erosion of national coherence has contributed to the religious antagonisms, fundamentalisms, neo-ethnic and separatist conflicts and movements in the former Soviet Union, Yugoslavia, Czechoslovakia, India, Canada, Spain, Turkey, Algeria, Afghanistan, etc. In the USA, this disaffection has contributed to further social and racial polarizations, enabling the rise of the reactionary right. Economic anxiety and the demand for democratization and indigenous self-government in their specific region (challenging the idea of

Mexican national identity and of integrationalist ideology) motivated the Chiapas rebellion in 1994. Disconcerting analogies have opened up between the instabilities in the Middle East, with the stumbling delays of the Israeli–Palestinian peace accords, and the ethnic rivalries in Eastern and Central Europe. The aggressive Serbian war against Bosnia's multinational, cosmopolitan, and pluralist society, and most recently against the ethnic Albanians in Kosovo, has taken a disastrous course, humiliating Western diplomacy and policy debates while a genocide was taking place in plain view.

The explosive brutality of such aggression overshadows the less overt social and cultural crisis produced by West Germany's internal colonization of its 'other' half, its *Anderland*. But this colonization is a striking example of the transitions of political and cultural identities in a post-Communist Europe already afflicted by regional and ethnic separatisms, and the racist discriminations in response to migration and to minorities treated as migrants. In the context of disparate postcolonial cultural nationalisms in Latin America, Africa, Asia, and the Pacific, the grand idea of a new 'European Community' constructs another questionable historical myth (after the failure of the 'melting pot' integration in the USA) already subject to increasing conflicts over the definition of national or transnational 'insiders' and 'outsiders,' citizens, foreigners, immigrants, refugees, and minorities. Ironically, the problem of the definition of 'Europe' and of defining 'Europeans' as members of a certain community or as representatives of a shared culture arose at the very moment when the Quincentenary celebrations of the 'discovery' of the New World met resistance from Latin Americans, Native Americans, and Latinos who view the Columbus legacy rather differently. While I was living in Houston, Texas, my frequent visits to the Rio Grande/Río Bravo territories made me aware of border realities that were distinct from my European experience but set my own displacement and the question of border subjectivity into sharp relief. My own languages, and the postmodern corpus of Euro-American cultural theory, became inadequate.

I became familiar, however, with an independent movement in San Diego/Tijuana ('Border Arts Workshop/Taller de Arte Fronterizo') that had developed cross-cultural dialogues between artists, activists, and intellectuals from Mexico and the USA through critical writing, site-specific performances, media and public art projects with direct political action. After eight years of collaborative projects, Guillermo Gómez-Peña argues today, this cross-cultural dialogue had become increasingly appropriated and exploited by mainstream Anglo-American institutions, thus facing the prevailing mechanisms by which the dominant culture promotes the so-called North–South dialogue under its own legitimizing framework. This framework is an extension of the historical metropolitan–colonial paradigm, and the current scholarly and curatorial attention lavished upon multiculturalism produces the dangerous illusion that cultural differences are not only celebrated and appropriated as objects constructed within academic discourse but also negotiated and embraced in a struggle for economic and political equality. The current promotion of 'border art' and the rhetoric of multiculturalism create a paradoxical situation in which racial, ethnic, or cultural difference is something that is sought after and, frequently, celebrated on the stages and in the museums of the North. The seemingly inclusive postmodernist celebration of the simultaneous existence of diverse cultural productions and local vernaculars, our 'magicians of the earth,' is a dangerous illusion precisely because the current condition of world-culture industry and media communications has produced the effect of a narrowing and leveling of the distance between cultural formations. Not all voices are being equally heard, however, and not all the images that are produced speak about border cultures in a comprehensive and concrete way. Rather, the process of viewing images of sameness or difference has become increasingly self-conscious and anxious.

I sought to describe and criticize the conspicuous leveling effect of postmodern technological-promotional media in my earlier book, *Theater, Theory, Postmodernism* (1991), but my reflections on the transnational/global shift in the political economy of Euro-American capitalism focused on the metropolitan centers and on aesthetic production under a technological domination in which commercial mass media and the arts (high culture and the avant-garde) are aligned as 'information' or 'arts/entertainment' and thus, consequently, subject to the political and market manipulations of these categories of mediation. I tried to approach the limit or border of this ever-expanding technological aestheticization of the life-world and the social imaginary in the experience of the *dispossessed body*, in the performance of such dispossession. My references to a (potentially) revolutionary consciousness of the alienated body remained inconclusive, however, since the irreducible difference of real bodies, of real pain or real illness and death, tends to be edited out in the postmodernist production of aesthetic surfaces.

The border remains an infected wound on the body of the continent, its contradictions more painful than ever. The border as a region of political injustice and great human suffering still exists, even as border art has become a casualty of a dominant culture that continues to ransack ideas, images, spiritual strength and exotic lifestyles from without and its own Third World within.

(*Guillermo Gómez-Peña*[5])

I see my films as cutting across several boundaries – boundaries of fiction, documentary, as well as experimental films. Thereby, they question both their own interiority and their own exteriority to the categories. . . . I am mainly working with the look. How the West has been looking at other cultures, how these cultures look at themselves being looked at, and how my own story as onlooker-looked-at is enmeshed in such a reflection.

(*Trinh T. Minh-ha*[6])

Figure 3 East Berlin 1991. Occupied house.

Figure 4 Havana 1994. Destroyed hotel.

In thinking through my border experiences in Berlin, Eisenhüttenstadt, Ljubljana, and Havana, and on the German–Polish and the US–Mexican border, which evolved parallel to my documentary/community work on the AIDS crisis in Houston and Chicago, I want to address both the simultaneous existence and the non-synchronicity of different cultural performances, embodied practices, discourses, historical codes, images, memories, and modes of looking and consumption. My interest in performance and media, and their intersections with social movements and political activisms, is grounded in a practice whose epistemology is a bodily-sensory one. It is primarily kinetic, working through physical action and participation, moving through emotional and erotic relations, resonating with desire and reflexive awareness, dancing exercising movement consciousness, and inhabiting and exchanging energies.

I will continue to return to my body and other bodies and the limits of its/ their displacement, and especially to the distinctions in representation and perception that arise from the borders of gender and race as they are constructed in narrative configurations. My own slowly aging body, with its meandering queer consciousness, is written into my narrative. It is not easy to re-educate the body and live in this bewildering time of mourning and melancholia. My body is still negative, after all these tests. When do I stop counting the tests? How will I tell my story? How will the story be tested? What is the negotiation, the process of consent, between the rights of the narrated and the narrator? What complicity connects me to my collaborators, and how often have I been deluded by the sharing of power and the exercise of privilege? Was it enough to be critical of my own temporary status in the university or to undermine this status by shifting the work – and my emphasis here on the experience of collaborative performance rehearsals and site-specific cultural interventions – outside the legitimate sites of intellectual, scholarly inquiry? If I preferred to work outside, wasn't it time to leave the university altogether?

Before my departure for Houston in early 1997, I presented two programs at academic conferences: 'Ritual Decomposition' (Hispanic Theater Research Group, University of California-Irvine) and 'The Future of Utopia' (Performance Studies Conference, Northwestern University) – both intended as cross-cultural dialogues between artists who had had to leave their countries or whose countries had undergone radical political transformations. My films of Grupo Chaclacayo's work in exile provoked strong and empathetic reactions among the Irvine group, even though some of the bodily images were inexplicable and profoundly unsettling. The 'Utopia' roundtable, on the other hand, nearly fell apart. One of the guests I had invited, Magaly Muguercia from Cuba, was denied an entry visa by the US authorities in Havana. I left her empty chair on the stage in Northwestern's theater, and at some point during the symposium I played a few minutes of a conversation with Magaly videotaped during my previous visit to Havana. In the passage she speaks eloquently (in Spanish) about her theater workshops in the Centro Martin Luther King, a community center created to promote the improvement of the surrounding neighborhood and to contribute modestly to the participatory integration of all levels of society – a courageous

Figure 5 Imma Sarries-Zgonc dancing in *Lovers Fragments*, Chicago 1995.

grass-roots activism that faced an uncertain future. Sadly, the screening was interrupted by members of the audience who objected to having to listen to her voice in (untranslated) Spanish. A furious debate over the use of Spanish-only followed, insults and condescension were traded among the scholars, a young Latina rose and, visibly disgusted, left the room. Magaly's voice remained unheard.

I was dismayed, and in my frustration I imagined that both reactions, the need or desire to understand difference or to give it intelligible artistic and linguistic shape, were false and equally predictable, if we agree that translation is the forgetting of differences. Chaclacayo's physical work cannot be translated; Magaly's voice was not allowed to travel, her body remained absent, her image without mirror. Our meetings, in the future of utopia, are the diaphorous dances of separation, *entre-deux*, in which nothing can be resolved, least of all our terrifying and necessary illusion of dialogue. In performing on the edge of illusion and crossing borders, the body is a medium between different, and sometimes antagonistic, narratives of legitimation or resistance. If borders are regions of political injustice and violence, then the body subjected to and altered by violence also re-enacts other subjected bodies, or 'written bodies,' as Susan Leigh Foster calls them in her book on *Choreographing History*.[7] It re-enacts political discourse and, carrying its marks and images, even the movement of history itself. In this sense, the wounds of the border testify to the emergence of political meanings. The wounded body becomes a political subject that can act up to break the silence of a festering wound or the silencing that is imposed upon the carrier perceived as dangerous to the fictions of social order. I have more to say about the showing of wounds in the chapters on feminist and queer performance art in my companion book, *Media & Performance*. The showing as sharing can make the body a crucial political agent through which social transformation is effected while it is also the primary site for visualizing the conflicts of community. I tried to enact this showing of an unhealed wound in the opera-installation of *Parsifal* (1995) created by our company in collaboration with Peruvian and East German artists in the ravaged Festspielhaus of the former utopian arts colony at Hellerau. The transcontinental prologue to this experiment in a devastated former 'colony' was inscribed in Grupo Chaclacayo's decompositional practice, which forced them into exile.

The notions of community and exile, once experienced in the context of social and liberationist movements, now recall an important moment in contemporary local politics of educational and community-oriented coalitions against the devastating effects of the HIV/AIDS crisis. During the painful months of working, first in an AIDS support group, and then on a concert-exhibition (*AD MORTEM*) in Houston and subsequent documentary exhibitions on the AIDS crisis (Chicago and Atlanta), I learnt to understand a new meaning of 'border' in the complex experience of multiple and conflicting social identities and roles affected by the health crisis. The crisis cut across differences in class, race, gender, and sexuality while reinforcing inequities on all levels: within institutions (medical science, government), within and between local communities and service organizations, and within and between cultural productions (discourses of knowledge, mass media rhetorics) and the lived experience of the HIV epidemic.

While working in different urban environments and artistic/educational contexts I observed the limits as well as the potential of self-determining community practices and activist performances. In 1990 I began to network with local AIDS support groups and with media artists and activists in and beyond the alternative arts community. At the university level I tried to organize an international group of artists and researchers, creating workshops on the 'politics of intervention.' In these performance-oriented workshops we set out to explore the multiple levels of AIDS discourse in the social service, government, educational, and media representations of the disease and of the various meanings of HIV and AIDS in lived, bodily experience.

The objective of this work, which informs my writing on activism in *Media & Performance*, is to study the various interrelated levels at which the epidemic is experienced in multicultural society, and at which issues of government responsibility, ethics, sexuality, grass roots action, mainstream paranoia and homophobia, stigmatization of victims, increasing public control over definition and management of health concerns, community self-determination, etc. are negotiated. Our research involves pertinent questions of censorship and disinformation (border controls), of the production and movement of knowledge and information. Our focus on the *mediation* of such new knowledges and narratives of the body (including the staging and commodification of illness, healing, and the therapeutic body) has challenged us to produce our own 'counter-representations' (counter-memory) of the AIDS crisis as a cultural crisis: in writing, video, graphic works, performance, and other actions. Activist media production stands in an immediate relationship to the growing visibility of performance and music productions among black and Latino artists/ communities and gay, lesbian, bisexual, transgender and feminist artists/ communities. I wanted to include all the materials I had collected in the present book, but they exceeded the scope of this volume. Thus, my critical reflections on dance, visual art, video, media activism, and the new cyberspaces/virtual communities of the Net, appear in the companion book, *Media & Performance*.

At the heart of *Performance on the Edge*, however, lies the fundamental question of how we can reinvent conditions for intercultural creative practices that link politically engaged art, activism, and self-empowerment to urgent questions of the survival of our life-worlds and our bodies' integrities. The question also addresses the future of utopia, and some of my rehearsals with collaborators in Cuba (Magaly Muguercia, Víctor Varela), Slovenia (Marko Peljhan, Marko Košnik), and East Germany (Fantasielabor, Gruppe RU-IN) confirm my faith in the necessity and validity of utopian strategies. In the aftermath of the revolutions I addressed in the beginning, the question of how we cross borders and experience the intersections of cultures is crucial for a critical understanding of different historical developmentsof art and performance in cultures that may share the postmodern spaces of transnational media and markets but cannot be assimilated into an imaginary global village. Based on my experiences of the East–West and North–South borders, and of the shifting coalitions of individuals and groups within and between differently affected AIDS communities in Houston and Chicago (not to speak of the completely different situation in Cuba), I expect that national and local political conflicts over imaginary communities will have a powerful effect on artistic practices willing to participate socially, ecologically, and spiritually in contexts that cannot be subsumed into the postmodern aesthetics of replication, parody, or calculated indifference. The work I describe is committed to oppose and expose the cynicism of such indifference, and it is equally impatient with the rhetorical abstractions of academic gender-bending in the promotion of drag, parody, and deconstruction.

Social-political activism and art production take place outside the university, they have no-place, no particular place, inside the controlled environments of hierarchical power structures, disciplinary conventions and mechanisms of credibility/creditability, teacher–student models, and predominantly abstracting, rational discursive media (scholarly texts). While the struggles between disciplinarity and dissent are politically valuable and significant, the claiming of embodiment, radicality, and creative social action within postmodern ethnography, performance studies, and cultural studies often amount to sophisticated theory-parodies of artistic process. They mimic process by lodging bodies, kinaesthetic, tactile and social energies in the euphemistically politicized arena of language games, deconstruction's video arcade.

While meanings certainly are constructed discursively, and the process of making meaning is ongoing, they are not constructed only in language or within the practices of repetitive signifying. Performance or art cannot be reduced to the discursive space of language, nor is it subject to the same constraints of repetition. Performance, most obviously in the case of dance, is predicated on the limits or failures of language, even though it does not transcend, by its own volition, the context-bound, site-specific, and internal processes of its production. Deconstruction in First World academies has also tried to take care of the reputed essentialism of the category of art. At the 1995 Performance Studies conference at Northwestern University I was repeatedly jeered at for offering observations about specific differences in artistic practices and aesthetic strategies, as if I were needed to be perceived as defending the making of art against currently fashionable claims for a more radical 'performativity' (Judith Butler's term). Western high theory's parasitical relationship to 'art' tends to get entangled in its contradictions since it often doesn't acknowledge its own artistic pretensions in writing the body or rewriting gender, racial, colonial relations or choreographing history and cultural practices. Most recently, in performance studies, the theoretical attitude is one of blissful condescension toward art practitioners and art's historical locations and diverse compositional practices. When theory identifies itself as artistic, having abandoned a separate category of 'art,' it often tends to be uninteresting, intellectually arcane, inorganic/simulative, baroquely quotational, and invested in a political rhetoric of radical transgression that is blind to its own location of (re)production within the benevolent liberal academy. The politics of transgressive style in theory depends on the benevolence; it therefore tends to overlook that its radicality is produced on borrowed time and rarely translates into subversion of anything.

I don't think it's only a matter of methodology or of revising the linguistically and psychoanalytically derived rhetoric of performativity in the current theorizing of gender, sex, and 'bodies that matter.' What concerns me is the experiential and social-political side of real and symbolic differences that are taken to be discursively constructed and thus ought to be deconstructable, according to Butler's complementary constructivism that defines sex as a 'performatively enacted signification' which, separated from its 'naturalized interiority and surface, can occasion the parodic proliferation and subversive play of gendered meaning.'[8] The aesthetic promotion of parody fetishizes construction as subversive play but somehow seems to forget that the formation or constitution of sexual bodies and bodily boundaries is not only an effect of regulatory, discursive norms or of psychic identifications with which one can play around. What such accounts of inscription and subversive reinscription often leave out of the equation between psyche and material reality is the quite real economic and *physical* pressures bearing upon the weight of human bodies and their abilities to create a social space – inside and alongside capitalist relations of exploitation – in which to rehearse strategies of expressing, voicing, and asserting identity.

As economic inequality and social structures of discrimination continue to exist, the conflicts over imaginary identities and imaginary communities will produce competing narrative formations of the political subject and her/his body. The political formation of new identities will involve border transactions, restricted exchanges in the reciprocal constitution of otherness and community. Perhaps layered, cross-cultural identities will be comprehensible and performable only relationally and collaboratively. The continuity of collaborations is not entirely predictable, however, if at all. Even the 'Warrior for Gringostroika' would probably admit that. The border is the imaginary and material context within which the subjectivation of politicized bodies will emerge. Multiple self-identities will be written and performed as border crossings within and between imagined communities, as travels across the local/global spaces in which diverse histories, languages, memories, and traces continually intersect. Both literally and figuratively, we inhabit border cultures. As I write this down, I am of course aware that Latino and Chicano artists and activists have prepared the path for such a critical understanding of *la frontera* and of cultural hybridity. More importantly, they also help me to think through the necessary and ongoing redefinitions of concepts such as the politically corrected multiculturalism that is officially tendered. In my conversations with Coco Fusco and Guillermo Gómez-Peña we repeatedly debated the need to change strategies and invent new irritations to counter any rhetoric that seeks to belittle, assimilate, or control political art that can have different functions depending on linguistic, cultural, and economic context.

I want to approach such borders as specific sites of control and resistance, looking and being looked-at, reinvention and transformation. As in my documentary films and performance works, the writing of *Performance on the Edge* simply continues the rehearsals; it implies a double focus on the political and the artistic. My explorations of borders are based on processes in political cultures and in performance cultures, and my interest in specific and concretely experienceable sites at which meaning is produced is informed by performance as a movement of connections.

CONNECTING BODIES

In the early 1990s I developed a dance-theater workshop/studio which focusses entirely on physical-mental practice, concentration, self-awareness, rehearsal, performance, movement, and creativity. I explore methods of warming up and of breathing, of releasing tensions and building energies or flows of perceptions. I tell the participants that, naturally, the work involves the full body/mind, and all of our organic functions, anatomies, sensory perceptions, and fantasies. The workshop is not a technique class, but we work with 'techniques' all the time, exploring the discipline necessary to create or change our bodies and their languages with which we speak and move. We reflect on the group process and on the idea of collaborative learning/working. The participant is the teacher of his or her body/mind. And vice versa: the body minds us.

Born into a world that from the very beginning disturbs and limits our physical and mental development, we take our work as occasions to involve ourselves with our own bodies intensively, lovingly, in order to enable the broadening of perceptual capabilities and physical change. Making contact with a partner, moving together in the group, exploring the spiritual and energetic force of the circle and of the trust built through touch and sensory contact (not based exclusively on vision), we learn to challenge ourselves without competition. It is a matter of listening to other bodies that move us, and of noticing the boundaries that separate/connect us. The contact work is about the permeability of our weight. It heightens the sensibilities of the skin.

The workshop also provides an opportunity to examine the effects of various contrasting discourses and practices on our bodily experience and on the body's representations in contemporary live art, as well as in the recording technologies that dominate Western culture reproduction. The work therefore also involves a willingness to play with our own recorded images. We are always seeing things, but our fantasies are not hysterical. They drift along with the intensities of our bodies that desire to feel themselves again. The aim is to respond to a present and detectable desire for a move toward a 'new authenticity' that accepts notions of the body's essential experience and constitution as well as its fragmentary and constructed nature. The ideas informing this workshop, which I taught during cold Chicago winters and in more subtropical climates, are partly indebted to a workshop on the 'Connected Body' I attended at the School for New Dance Development in Amsterdam. It was inspiringly organized by Scott deLahunta and Ric Allsopp.[9] Deborah Hay and Eva Schmale, together with the other participants in our groups, taught me to reconsider my body and my movements with respect to a 'new authenticity' which has nothing to do with any claims to origins or essential, natural being. On the contrary, I understand this authenticity to be based on the perception of impermanence and change, of *discontinuity*, and it is creatively related to others and to attention for others. The body is a movement of boundaries. So is the camera as it moves in and out, exploring distances to the skin. In the interactive environments and invisible 'nervous systems' (sensors, motion detectors) we now use, this movement is further extended: the body moves and shapes sound, lights, image projections. It literally orchestrates the real space of diverse virtual compositions.

In this sense, the writings in this book treat performance, and the productions and collaborations of self and other in shifting, overlapping contexts, as a fundamental dimension of culture and its transformation. I will expand on this in Chapter 4 on the 'transcultural imaginary,' tracing the notion of transculturation back to Cuban anthropologist Fernando Ortiz. The Cuban context, in which part of my new work is being developed, is in fact crucial for a new understanding of cultural performance that I wish to describe here as a (Cuban) counterpoint to my earlier Eurocentric writings on postmodernism in the North. In the last chapter, I will try to move to another side of this fundamental dimension: the reconstructions of love and desire as I learnt to explore them in one of our productions, *Lovers Fragments*, a work that specifically addresses the discontinuity of sexual identities in our shifting, powerful erotic attraction to the precarious forgetting of boundaries, forgetting of selves, and losing of selves in dangerous pleasure. Emphasizing dis-continuity in the formation of the normalized pleasure/representation of sexuality, the performance of *Lovers Fragments* mobilizes the play of bodily pleasure, and the playing with our 'technologies of the self' (Foucault), away from accepted rituals of romantic or pornographic fantasies and closer toward a choreography of the abnormal, toward a potential excess of boundary-images that destabilize the restricted categories of art/ pornography and the psychoanalytic framework of the economy of the male gaze elaborated by feminist and Lacanian (film-) theory. Our performing our own pleasurable erotic movements and movement-narratives implicitly involves a new theory of production and spectatorship in performance that locates the 'object of the gaze' differently, not on the side of the spectator but in-between performers and their incorporation of mixed, heterogeneous genre/media frameworks.

The question of looking, which I take up in the beginning of the book in reference to the political complicity of the West's fetishistic disavowal of the destruction of Sarajevo ('Ulysses' Gaze'), will thus return at the end of my exploration of alienated, abject bodies, transformed into other questions and ideas about the functioning of fantasy and collaborative creation in fluid pro-cesses where the artwork (the satisfactory fantasy) belongs to no one to the extent that all power relationships inherent in a medium are decomposed and borders are liquid like rivers. An aesthetics of sexual plurality and gender blurring, out-side the narrower context of camp, is here adopted for a politics of pleasure and non-alienated marginality that critiques the dominant Western patriarchal and heterosexual hegemony. If such a performance eros contradicts both state and internalized censorship and the ideologies of social/national identification, it will also contribute to a more radical understanding of the (fascist, xenophobic, homophobic) paranoia about the 'theft of enjoyment' that plagues the guardians of public morality and the spectators of 'legitimized violence,' as Slavoy Žižek and Renata Salecl so poignantly suggested in their studies of the fantasmatic structure of power and the aggression perpetrated on Others' fantasies.[10]

Crossing between the political unconscious and the political conscious, the embodied actions and activisms of performers and cultural workers participate in an ongoing social process and in the production of knowledge about culture. As the boundaries between aesthetics and popular culture, art and everyday cultural commodity production or consumption blur, performance itself becomes a con-tested concept, a contested 'property.' It is being squatted by contemporary theorists and philosophers, and it is celebrated in queer parades and in our doing it together, not thinking about fucking up, not thinking about dying.

The blurring is necessary. Crossing the line and coming out and testing the limits of separation and rejection that are culturally reinforced yet always incompletely. If border relations are also property relations (whose border? whose bodyguards?), then my writing here will also emerge at the intersection of diverse genres and 'techniques of the body writing,' rehearsal methods, warm-up exer-cises, physical and video diaries, critical theories, re-viewing habits, dinner con-versations, memories, performance scripts, story-boards, bad dreams. How do I look? How do I re-view the looking? *Performance on the Edge* looks at the movement of fantasy. It collects ashes.

It thus re-enacts the contested borders of scholarship, ethnographic fieldwork, autobiography, fiction, and performance theory, enjoying – hypothetically – the fantasy of not belonging. There is nothing playful about it, although playing is taken for granted in the rehearsals. Full concentration is needed to play well. Above all, this book hopes to show that the politics of research and performance are existentially experienced, a searching for and writing about possible communities and shared borders.

1

AFTER THE REVOLUTION

(VIDEO DIARY)

San Ygnacio, 13 April 1990
THE RIVER PIERCE: SACRIFICE II

> Living on the 'northern'edge of the Rio Grande, on what officially is the edge of Latin America, has had immeasurable impact on my life and work. I have had a front row seat in the *ongoing* drama of two distinct cultures hemorrhaging into each other; the physical migration itself, the cultural nullity, the sociological angst and despair, and the legal miasma. The monstrous political *cynicism* has infected my soul/heart and probably my body.
>
> (Michael Tracy)

> Para mí, la frontera es como una franja, no necesariamente un comienzo. Yo prefiero el término castellano de franja fronteriza, franja del material. Algunas faldas tienen una franja. Es un dobladillo amplio, pero no es el final. Cubre y traslapa o se da la cara por ambas partes.
>
> (Norma Cantú[1])

Berlin, July–September 1990
BORDER-LAND

Documentary film, archaeology project, phase I.
Shooting on location in Berlin in the death zone/no man's
land of the former Wall on a 3-mile stretch from
Kreuzberg to the Invaliden-Friedhof, where the film
ends with an East German theater group performing
Hölderlin's *Hyperion* in the death zone.

(female voice-over, sound of hammering)

*that time you went back that last time to look
was the wall still there
where you hid as a child*

when was that

all gone all dust nothing stirring

that time you went back that last time to look
was the wall still there
where you hid as a child
pressed against the cold stone
eyes closed
forgetting it all
where you were

not looking
huddled against the stone
not a thought in your head
only get the hell out of it
and never come back

or was that another time
but that time away to hell
out of it and never come back

then suddenly this dust and these ruins
the whole place suddenly full of dust
when you opened your eyes
from floor to ceiling
nothing only dust and not a sound
the desecrated soil your native country too
eyes closed

huddled against the stone
trying to read those smiling screaming
hieroglyphics

Figure 6 *Border-Land*, 1990.

(male voice-over, close-up of face, Hölderlin text of
Hyperion, map of 'Topographie des Terrors')

when you receive this letter I shall have returned
and shall be writing from a great distance. After
leaving Berlin I feel even more deeply confounded
by what I saw than I had expected. I had come to
search for the spirit of the revolution that had taken place.

So I arrived among the Germans. I did not demand much,
and was prepared to find even less. I came here humbly
like homeless blind Oedipus to the gates of Athens,
where the sacred grove received him, and fair souls
came to greet him.

How different my experience.
I stand like an alien before my native country,

which lies about me like a vast graveyard.

The breach has occurred, and I am gazing
through the cracks and holes of this modern-day Pompeii,
trying to find the radically altered reality in the traces
of historical forms and in the skeleton remnants of an
unfinished present – the construction site of this new
Germany.

Close-up I am trying to decipher the physiognomy of the
not-yet-known. . . .

Yet I am trapped by the history of this Wall which
appears concretely in front of me as the mortification of
matter, congealed images and discarded chunks of another
reality that has survived in this city of walls and broken
monuments.

I am trapped in a transitory space, a captive both of my
memories and the physical transiency in front of my eyes,
with its displaced architectureand its riddles. . . .

Berlin: Pale Mother of Germany's self-divisions. . . .

Can a death zone be transformed into a liberty zone?
What is happening to the voluntary prisoners who
inhabited this city on either side of the imaginary line? . . .

As I walk along the no man's land, without the
protection of guardian angels, I feel a growing sense
of disorientation. Which side of the still remaining
wall fragments am I looking at? Where was the east,
where the west, where is the inside of the outside? . . .

THERE IS LIFE BEHIND THE WALL

DO OR DIE

These large remnants of the Wall will soon be
exhibited in museums all over the world. Smaller
pieces are sold to the tourists by Turkish and Arabic
peddlers who profit from the desire for nostalgic souvenirs.

Like the classical ruins in Rome and Athens, the ruins
of the Cold War and of ideological division are on
display. But the scenario is more ironic, since it is
immigrants and foreigners who are selling the German
past to foreigners.

The violence of history is not exposed in these commodities.
And yet, the abandoned urban zone of the death strip

is there for our seeing. . . .

Everything is eerily quiet.
Like an immense shipwreck, when the gales have been
hushed and the sailors have fled and the corpse of the
shattered fleet lies on the sandbank unrecognizable, so
lies the Berlin border before me, and the forsaken pillars
stand there like the bare tree-trunks of a wood that at
evening was still and green and, the same night, went up
in flames.

Can *this* be reconstructed?
What dreams are left after the revolution has been sold?

The sand is getting deeper here. I am wearing the wrong
shoes, and my camera feels heavier than usual. The zoom
lens enlarges the damaged reality before my eyes. I follow
the jagged strip of no man's land that seems to lead nowhere. . . .

I cannot find the Potsdamer Platz, the old center. . . .

Everything is eerily quiet.The dancing on the wall has stopped.
That was an ephemeral performance.
DEUTSCHLAND ERWACHE.

How can one join two countries together that live in
different time-zones?

Why have the squatters built this silver ship and placed
it in the middle of their camp on the no man's land?
Are these homeless urban squatters preparing a Trojan
Horse for their battle for freedom inside the border-land?

The Brandenburg Gate is hidden behind colossal scaffolding
constructed for the renovation of Germany's new collective
history. At the foot of the old monument: tourists and
sight-seers, and a few natives mingling uneasily with the
new homeless proletariat, the refugees and immigrants from
Eastern Europe and the Middle East who have come here to
find freedom. . . .

What is left of Potsdamer Platz is a sequence of pictures
from a doomed civilization forsaken by the gods.

Was this not like a battlefield on which hacked-off hands
and arms and every other member lay pell-mell, while the
life-blood flowed to vanish in the sand? Could one think
of a people more torn and at odds with themselves than
the Germans, barbarians from the remotest past?

Alas, alas for the stranger who journeys in love and
comes to Germany . . .

East Germany/Poland/CSSR, Summer 1991
ASYLUM

Documentary film, archaeology project, phase II. Return
to Berlin and the same locations as in 1990. Shooting the
disappearing Wall and central neighborhoods in East Berlin,
especially the former Jewish Scheunenviertel.
Interviews with East German citizens about their experience
of the social/political transformation. Shoot-on-location along
the East German–Polish border. First visit to Eisenhüttenstadt
and encounters with border police, immigration and refugee
organizations. Examination of asylum policies and political
reaction to the disintegration of Yugoslavia. Journey across Poland
toward Moscow, interrupted by the *putsch* in Moscow. The Soviet
Union collapses, communism in Eastern Europe seems to have
ended. The civil war in Yugoslavia breaks out. Returning via
Hungary to Prague. Shoot-on-location; performance script
development for 'Kafka's Odyssee.' The film is shown at the
'Festival of Nations' in Houston, under the title *After the Revolution.*

Chicago, September 1991–May 1992
ORPHEUS ~~AND~~ EURYDIKE

NOTES ON DESCENTS AND RETURNS

Keeping step with the story
I make my way into death

To speak with my voice
To dance with my body
I did not want anything more, anything different.

Only there, at the uttermost border of my life
Can I name it to myself

There is something of everyone in me

15 May 1992. One week before opening night, we haven't yet found an ending,
nor are we in agreement about the opening movement of the new opera. So we
keep retracing our steps, rehearsing again the pain of beginning and remembering. We called the opening movement 'Dismemberment' – no longer a reference
to Orpheus (who is torn apart by women at the end of the myth-narrative that
bears his name) but to women's recollection of their losses, their experience of
pain, their silences and disembodiments. The Orpheus myth is a disembodying
narrative. Since it also pretends to be about a couple and about desire (or is it a
story about looking and not listening?), it is an unavoidable dramatic plot that
happens to pervade western music and poetry and provide the foundation for the

beginning of opera. (*L'Euridice*, composed by Peri and Caccini in 1600, has not survived; Monteverdi's *Orfeo*, written for the Mantuan court during the Carnival season of 1607, is considered the first major work of continuous musical theater. Even better known today are Gluck's Italian [1762] and French [1774] versions of *Orfeo ed Euridice*, operas contemporaneous with Mozart's and the evolving German and Italian music tradition still dominant on today's opera stages.)

Orpheus doesn't die in Monteverdi's or Gluck's operas but is elevated to the gods. Descending from the classical myth that tells the story of Orpheus's loss and suffering, symbolically confirming the redemptive power of (his) music, our new production tries to offer a different look at the sexual fantasy of redemption through the eyes and ears of Eurydike, through the stories of women's experience as objects of male fantasies. And as subjects and actors in an ongoing social process in which they reinvent themselves and their social world. The underworld: a border territory.

Such a reinvention is a difficult process, as certain myths and certain realities tend to continue to exert their oppressive power in our culture, and perhaps it is trivial to invent a new opera (regardless of what one might think of the deadly conventions in the theaters, movies, and melodramas of our daily television). But working on a new opera, with our bodies, voices, and imaginations, is rather more challenging and complicated if such work is not only about myths and stories but also about our own histories (of the body) and the relations of power in which we produce and make ourselves heard or seen.

Our uncertainties, before showing the work to our audiences, are therefore quite understandable, since they are a part of a long process of composition that started in 1991 and traveled through the many stages of a collaboration between composers, dancers, musicians, performance artists, filmmakers, and designers. We wanted to make our descent a shared experience between people of different ages and cultural backgrounds and with different artistic sensibilities and insights into the performer's role in the choreographic/compositional process. Since the work is based not on a libretto or text but on our own resources and creativities, we need to trust our own bodies and voices and yet encourage each other to do things we wouldn't normally do. In this sense we understand Eurydike's descent less as a psychological or an emotional excavation of our unconscious than as *a journey through the body* and our embodied knowledge toward political questions about production, sexual desire, loss, death, survival.

Such questions have as much to do with the cultures and histories from which we descend, as they are intrinsically connected to an ongoing process of constructing our social realities, especially if we want to avoid the violent narcissism of the Orphic vision and the perhaps suicidal fatalism expressed in Cassandra's words quoted above (rewritten by Christa Wolf in her effort to invent a feminist poetics that could disturb 'compulsory readings' and compulsory heterosexual ways of looking).[2]

Who's looking? Who is looked at? How do I look? These are some of the questions we kept asking ourselves as we looked back to feminist film theories of the male gaze and the lesbian gaze and forward to the currently emerging critique of sexual politics in music; for example, in Catherine Clément's book *Opera, Or the Undoing of Women*, or Susan McClary's *Feminine Endings*, or Elizabeth Wood's 'Sapphonics: Desire in a Different Voice'.[3]

September 1991. Almost a year after the initial plans for a new opera were made in 1990, we meet for the first time to start a workshop phase entitled 'Male Fantasies' during which we explore the mythological couple Orpheus/Eurydike and its logic of female sacrifice (a sacrifice necessary for the production of art?). We discover the conditions of a familiar story: the representation of woman as fetishized object on her way down to marriage and abandonment, madness or murder at the ending of the traditional genres (opera, ballet), with woman as sexual object of male voyeuristic fantasies, musical narratives, and the relationship of production and visual consumption. Orpheus's desire is writ large, Eurydike's story silenced. In Monteverdi's opera, for example, she literally has no voice as if she were always already dead. In Wagner's *Parsifal*, the lone female voice (Kundry) is gotten rid of by the beginning of the third act; she is silenced and made invisible, as the hero and the brotherhood of the knights of the grail continue their search for purification and triumphant redemption.

At this early conceptual stage, we have to find a balance between our research and theoretical speculations on structure/narrative on the one hand, and our personal feelings and misgivings about 'the couple' (and the mythic tradition of opera) on the other. My own trauma of loss and separation, overshadowed at the time by the immediate impact of the AIDS crisis which was the focus of my work in 1989–90, motivated me to confront anxieties about death, dismemberment of the body, dissolution of identity, loss of control, loss of immunity. Orpheus's descent into the underworld is supposed to be a controlled enterprise, like a military action, a re-possession. It is a failure. We looked at such fantasies of control in the history of catastrophic failures of male aggression in this century, and in the social history of ordinary misogyny (reading, among others, Klaus Theweleit's *Male Fantasies*).[4]

Looking death (and the death of desire) in the face, how does one compose music or dance or art? Orpheus's blindness is a warning, and I want to confront my own blind spots by relinquishing the role of the director, the illusion of control. The group process develops its own dynamics, there is not just one story, but many stories and many cross-overs between stories. The borderlines break down. The women in the ensemble begin to rewrite the compositional process; questions of structure and form are constantly interrupted, no 'feminine endings' are in sight yet. It is clear that as long as 'Eurydike' is framed by male myth production, she is trapped, her only recourse is a kind of death, her going-under a coming-out, a becoming herself. We look at Mimi's questions in front of her mirror (in Sally Potter's film *Thriller*), looking back to *La Bohème*: 'I'm trying to remember, to understand. There were some bodies on the floor. One of them is mine. Did I die? Was I murdered? If so . . . who killed me and why?'

March 1992. Our large ensemble of twenty-one women and three men has come

Figure 7 Orpheus and Eurydike. 1992. Photo courtesy of Mary Hanlon.

together for the first time onstage. For three months we have worked with our bodies, and through our dis-memberings and re-memberings, in the dance studio, and the dancers have found languages of expression that can be shared. To bring the physical work in relationship to the musical and filmic composition is more challenging than we had even imagined, as our experimental process demands extreme flexibility on the part of all the practitioners. We improvise together, and quickly find out that one cannot easily improvise with so many different languages. Can one compose an opera that is sufficiently 'illogical' and non-linear to allow for the kind of polyvocal, polyphonic, or schizophonic vision that is emerging among us? At an earlier point, we knew that the work, given its concern with looking and listening, presents a unique opportunity to experiment with the aesthetic and technical processes of film/music performance, the visualization of music and of voice, the musical and electronic transformation of live dance, and the interface of pre-recorded and live, closed-circuit image/sound projection. Can the choreography of the dance and of the camera be developed concurrently? If Orpheus's fantasies of Eurydike are 'pre-recorded,' treating 'Eurydike' as an echo-effect of male desires (as in most conventional operas in our culture), can these fantasies be played back in counterpoint with an interrupted loop between live recording cameras and video projectors, with the women dancers gradually surpassing, stepping out of, separating from the screened images she (Orpheus) generated?

At the end of the workshop, we have no solutions but a better sense of what motivates us to continue. We have completed a seventy-minute version of the new opera, improvised upon our earlier rehearsals and descents. We now think of

Figure 8 Orpheus ~~and~~ Eurydike. 1992. Photo courtesy of Mary Hanlon.

the opening ritual as a remembering of the descent and as a *rebirth*. The main body of the work is dedicated to the stories and voices of Eurydike telling of other lives and other desires not connected to the myth's trajectory. The work has traveled a certain way, its spiral path headed in several directions at the same time, and this is important because we learn to discover our fragile sense of community, the differences among our languages, our shared commitments and also our painful memories that cannot be fully displaced. If the work is transformative and empowering, it is also always reminding us of the boundaries that exist and that we seek to cross as we look back to what must not be forgotten.

MAY 1992. COMPOSERS' NOTE

The chance to work in a new way creating a new definition of the concept of opera has been always stimulating and at times controversial. Each member of the ensemble and the three composers have been encouraged to be part of the creative process from the very beginning. One of the most exciting aspects of the *Orpheus ~~and~~ Eurydike* project has been the opportunity to work with composers from very different musical worlds. Gwynne Winsberg has composed, sung, and recorded music from the experimental rock music perspective. Tim Tobias is a jazz and film composer and is a skilled jazz keyboard improviser. Patricia Morehead has written many chamber music scores in the more traditional atonal style as well as several works that use extended instrumental techniques.

These three musics will come together in the new performance juxtaposed against one another, superimposed on each other, and even in the context of joint composition and collage techniques. The concept of collage is used, in a visual and musical sense, along with the superimposition of film and slide projections and dance choreographies created for this new opera. In this performance the classically trained musicians will improvise during the prologue which was created ahead of time by all three composers using predetermined musical materials as well as improvisational techniques. During the main performance there will be alterations and overlays between and among our compositions. All three composers are performing their musics both live and pre-recorded.

(Patricia Morehead)

June 1992. The breakdown of traditional musical structures and musical authorship/control corresponds to the filmic and choreographic exploration of the descent. Speech, voice, movement, and film images are created collectively by the ensemble, drawing from the rehearsal process of Tanztheater and pushing the boundaries of asynchrony even further. The conjunction of live performance and audio-visual technologies of projection allows unpredictable dislocations of sensory experience, especially since the parallel films, projected on the east and west sides of the stage, contain abstract and concrete real-time images that can be altered and converted through the mixing board, including the mixing of film music as an overscore to the live music. The film images refract the simultaneity and multivocality of the women's stories and remembrances. The challenge in this production lies not so much in the reformulation of opera; rather, as Henry Sayre pointed out at the symposium on 'Music and Sexual Politics' we organized after the premiere, at the heart of the descent lies the 'creative experience of a community of artists working across and through their emotional boundaries, across and through the limitations of their own training, and across and through the social realities that define them.' In my own reflection on the process of creating the opera, I feel the immediate and unavoidable link between this community process and the question raised by my return to the borders in my divided homeland. 'What remains?' Christa Wolf asked after the Wall had come down. Her question was ill-received on the other side of her home-land, but the future of a divided consciousness no doubt depends on asking the question and on working through the pathologies of recovering the correct distance to its projected selves.

East Germany/Poland, Summer 1992
ALIENNATION

Documentary film, archaeology project, phase III.
Return to Berlin and the same locations as in 1990–1.
Shooting the physical transformations of the border-land
in the new capital and the infrastructural accommodation
of the east. Extension of the theme 'Asylum' with strong
focus on the new militant neo-Nazi activities along the

German–Polish border and the public assimilation of
xenophobic attacks against foreigners and immigrants.
Shoot-on-location in Solingen, Hoyerswerda, Guben, and
Rostock, after violent attacks against refugee asylums and
homes of foreign residents. Interviews, gathering of information
about German aggression and the counter-politics on the left
and among anti-fascist groups. Return to Eisenhüttenstadt and
Frankfurt an der Oder, starting collaboration with local cultural workers.

Chicago, December 1992–April 1993
FROM THE BORDER

The performance, exhibition, and film festival created under the working-title
'From the Border' is based on the premise of cross-cultural collaboration in an
intermedia production process bringing together an international group of
thirty-five artists and students committed to exploring shared rehearsal and
compositional methods. We wanted to examine how cultural diversity affects,
and is in turn affected by, the institutional setting (the university theater/art
gallery) and the power relations that exist in structured, production-oriented
processes. How can performers and visual artists, trained in different aesthetic
and cultural traditions or speaking and working in different languages of art-
making, come together to develop a shared process?

> *Whether we choose to concentrate on another culture, or on our own cultural knowledge, our work will always be cross-cultural. It is bound to be so, not only because of personal backgrounds and historical actualities, but above all because of the heterogeneous reality we all live today. A reality, therefore, that is not a mere crossing from one borderline to another, or that is not merely double, but a reality that involves the crossing of an indeterminate number of borderlines.*
>
> (Trinh T. Minh-ha, *When the Moon Waxes Red*[5])
>
> *Border-crossing involves a process of decolonizing the mind and the body. It always reveals the ambivalence at the source of traditional narratives of the nation, of authority, of identity.*
>
> (Homi K. Bhabha, *Nation and Narration*[6])
>
> *Borders are set up to define the places that are safe and unsafe, to distinguish us from them. A border is a dividing line, a narrow strip along a steep edge. A border-land is a vague and undetermined place created by the emotional residue of an unnatural boundary. It is in a constant state of transition. The prohibited and forbidden are its inhabitants.*
>
> (Gloria Anzaldúa, *Borderland/La Frontera*[7])

1. THE POLITICS OF PRODUCTION

We are particularly interested in the traditional 'narrative' of production, the politics of locations, participatory processes in performance and audio-visual creation, and decentered pedagogies of production in educational institutions. 'Production' is understood here in its most complex sense; namely, combining the social, artistic, and technical processes of creation, within the specific conditions of the producing organization (e.g. university theater), with diverse aspects of the political economy of their mediation and reception. The concept of the 'border' is introduced to explain image-making and image exchanges in/between different constituencies and hybrid cultures. 'Border performance' addresses the issue of cultural identities by subverting the idea of an established/dominant cultural production mechanism or by exposing US mainstream cultural institutions as derivative (*una cultura derivada*) and indissolubly affiliated with those black, Latino, and Asian expressive cultures they seek to marginalize.

Our development and public presentation of a range of different performances and exhibitions allow cross-cultural dialogue about the intersections of cultural imagery and physical/material processes. The presentation also intends to address, in its configuration, the relationship between images/media and live performance in terms of the political issues raised by cross-cultural collaborative projects at the level of institutional settings and the existing power relations within First World economies of spectatorship, funding, promotion, and commodification. It also intends to demonstrate how the politics of participatory production translate into intersubjective relations within a group of professional artists, teachers, and students arriving from different backgrounds and with conflicting motivations, and how cross-cultural artistic work, as a performance process, can rehearse and create oppositional pedagogical spaces within hegemonic institutions by constantly – and unavoidably – unveiling the contradictions and repressive accommodations (in power and gender relations) in the productive process itself. The critical role of the *performance process* (as process) needs to be emphasized, since it is especially the physical contact improvisation that reveals our languages and points to the intersections of teaching, artistic creation, and translation.

2. UNSAFE PLACES

After we begin to work on our borders, we discover that there is no comfort in this process of mutual learning, of acknowledging our differences, and of recognizing our oversights and miscommunications. There is even less comfort in the fact that we manage, inside a predominantly white, elite institution of higher learning, to open up spaces for cross-cultural rehearsal and production. Space is limited from the beginning, and we are asked to adhere to the generally established production schedules within the university theater and under the directorship of its administration, design shop management, and bureaucratic budget logistics. The little border-land we create remains an uncertain yet passionately contested space of exploration in which we have to be alert to the implications of exclusion and inclusion, and to the long shadows of the power relations and surveillance mechanisms in the educational system. Only apparently removed from the marketplaces of multicultural art and entertainment, the university nevertheless participates in the same political economy of promoting diversity while maintaining inherited standards of aesthetic judgement and production procedure, specialization, and classifiable knowledge. *From the Border* is conceived as an interdisciplinary/intermedia work-process without a predetermining script, libretto, or design plan. Its process is deliberately open to improvisation and to the diversity of our cultural and aesthetic sensibilities, and from the beginning it is apparent that no singular or integrating rehearsal/compositional method is appropriate or available to us, since we want the work itself to evolve from the concatenation of different viewpoints on 'borders.'

It is not enough, however, to speak of cultural diversity in an ensemble of African-American, Asian-American, Latin American, Native American, and European/Anglo-American artists, as long as the power relations and the circumstances of aesthetic and technical choices are not examined. And as long as new ways of thinking and acting, speaking and keeping silent are not tested. The potential of testing them on the proscenium stage or in the art gallery is limited, especially if a joint event, as our production was planned to be, can have the effect of transforming unresolved ideological divisions and antagonisms into a packaged tour of the local color of gender, race, sexuality, ethnicity, region, nation, or class. How does one promote a cross-cultural performance event, both to the participants and to the potential audiences?

To cut across boundaries and borderlines is to live aloud the malaise of categories and labels. It is to resist simplistic attempts at classifying, to resist the comfort of belonging to a cultural or aesthetic genre, and of producing classifiable works.

(Trinh, *When the Moon Waxes Red*[8])

Since its inception, *From the Border* has remained full of paradoxes, since we could not resolve our differences of aesthetic approach to rehearsal, nor did we sufficiently resist the pressure/desire of working within a known bodily technique, although altering one's embodied techniques of movement/composition and expression raises another set of questions altogether. We decided that, instead of creating a single collaborative stage performance and a collective exhibition, we would rehearse in a parallel mode with regular interfaces producing five different performances and eight installations in a group exhibit. This process of separating and distributing the responsibilities among thirteen production units should not be considered a failure since it resulted from the process of negotiation we had started. As a process of inter-creation, it should not be romanticized either, since it incorporates many conflicts. At the same time, the fact that the process has been accomplished and carried over a period of five months cannot be underestimated, since there have been real obstacles and structural limitations ranging from practical concerns (insufficient budget, lack of transportation, lack of rehearsal space and time) to artistic disagreements about the integration of rehearsal methods, sensibilities, and levels of craft. Our parallel methods require a constant modification in consciousness, and a recognition of the central significance of gender relations at the heart of the whole process that questions the role of (single) directorship or authority, the nature of collaboration as such, and the unavoidable presence of master languages and technological codes (in the design and construction process).

> *Is it possible to create in sharing a productive space that belongs to no one, not even to those who create it?*
>
> (Trinh, *When the Moon Waxes Red*[9])

How are 'identities' in production, and in unsafe spaces, claimed? What is carried over in these relationships between women and men of different nationalities, racial and cultural backgrounds, life-stories, and political/aesthetic motivations? How improper is it to speak of collaboration and community when the aesthetic languages of choice vary and carry multiple meanings depending on the contexts and positions from which they are articulated and viewed? Did we make the proper choice in deciding not to create one shared production but thirteen different ones in two overdetermined sites? How has our emotional and physical process of working together (and together separately) transformed our fragile understanding of the degrees of cultural difference?

Who owns the privilege of describing the process and the works that have been created, changed, modified, subjected to internal group critique, changed and modified again, and then presented to the public, the all-owning spectatorship of the art patrons, subscribers, and specialized critics or academic evaluators? How do the different works, shown together, border on each other and on the expectations or viewing habits of a western (mostly suburban) audience? How does the proscenium alter and affect the different languages used in the works, or the differences in the dances, the voices, the silences, the color and lines that are not quite the same or similar (comparable) at all, the movements that combine gestures known and not known?

I raise these vexing questions here without wanting to provide my own subjective answers. While the questions address larger concerns that can be shared by the reader, I would indeed feel uncomfortable, in this particular case, if I drew conclusions from the work experience, because in our case the parallel productions created also a climate of (unacknowledged) competition over resources, times and spaces of rehearsal, and positioning in the public frame of the presentation. The constraints under which we worked are specific, although they resemble production constraints in the professional and alternative art-worlds. I think it is helpful, however, to be honest about the problems and contestations, which in my case also included critical objections raised by some participants over the use of video documentation/analysis of our own process. The objections arrived precisely because the question of who 'owned' the process could not be resolved, and I had too naively assumed, believing Trinh, that the shared creative rehearsal space is not owned by anyone in particular, but, if at all, by the group. Legally, of course, we found out that it is owned by the sponsoring producer, in this case the university.

One of the goals of the *Border* project was to create the conditions for a new dialogue, for an active learning environment in which we could explore and test intercultural strategies for performance and the respectful translation of knowledge from one context into another. Or, alternately, the subversive translation and collage of doubled, reframed and resituated contexts in our recuperation of memory, our ironic quotation of authentic experience, or our dialectical reversions of ideological narratives, seeking to locate the danger.

> Nuestro proyecto no concive las fronteras como limites físocos, sino como intersecciones vitales. Queremos examinar el potencial de los cruces culturales y de la "conciencia de frontera" en el marco artístico y en los distintos procesos en los que reinventamos nuestra historia.

When I wrote this passage in December 1992, our preparations for two workshops were under way (designed by Margaret Thompson Drewal and myself), intended to focus on the Columbus Quincentenary and on postcolonial writings, as well as on site-specific visits to museums and galleries to examine prevailing or emergent strategies for exhibiting cultures and the curatorial role of art and ethnological museums in maintaining distinctions of values.

Connecting this focus with our interest in intercultural performance, our project group made contact with Guillermo Gómez-Peña and Coco Fusco during their two-month residency in Chicago and their presentation of *The Year of the White Bear* (see Chapter 2), a multidisciplinary project consisting of an art/anthropology exhibition (Mexican Fine Arts Center Museum), a post-Columbian performance at the Museum of Natural History, a live radio performance (Randolph Street Gallery), a film presentation at Latino Chicago Repertory Theater, brochures, publications, and a radio workshop at Chicago Experimental Sound Studio. The radio project, in which I participated, brought together a group of Chicano and Anglo writers/multimedia artists committed to the production of a series of public service announcements addressing a range of public issues (AIDS, discrimination, xenophobia, education, and bilingualism).

Although our starting-point in the university was a different one, our relationship to *Year of the White Bear* has been affected by the conceptual and theatrical strategies behind such work, work that teaches us perhaps less about understanding the Other than about our own projections, prejudices, and illusions. During our rehearsals for *From the Border* we asked ourselves whether it is in fact possible to create a safe space of conceptual freedom, a space of a necessary illusion, in which our political, aesthetic, and spiritual concerns can intersect to produce a trance, a dialogical process. If there is a transformative effect, it perhaps cannot be 'displayed' in a show, a showing of the product. It may only be discovered in the intersubjective relations of the producers and the entranced process itself. The product most likely tends to obscure or hide the contest of production.

3. PERFORMANCE AS PROCESS

Since I cannot speak on behalf of the other members of the group about their experiences or from their viewpoints, I shall relate moments from the process that I find particularly significant. In an early workshop in January I showed a video collage of four films to our group, including segments from Julie Dash's feature film *Daughters of the Dust*, from a documentary film on Palestinian refugees (*Occupied Territories*), and from two of my own documentaries shot in San Ygnacio and Berlin, *Border Sacrifice* and *Border-Land*. I was also in contact with exiled Yugoslavian filmmaker Zoran Masirević, who had moved to Los Angeles and accepted our invitation to join our festival and screen his latest film, *Granica* ('The Border'). Although the films use different formal strategies ranging from epic narrative, drama, and *cinéma verité* to ritual performance and political documentary, their thematic concerns intersect through variously repeated images of migration and displacement, exile and homelessness, the denial and recuperation of history or collective memory, and the ritualization of crossing-over. A Palestinian man talks about being treated as a refugee in his own land, and of a trial in which an Israeli judge named him a *natash* (someone who walked away) without acknowledging that he was in fact driven from his village by the occupying army. An African-American sea island family, on the verge of departing for the mainland, recollects its history of enslavement during the ritual preparation of a migration into a different, unknown future. A group of Mexican and North American artists meets on the Rio Grande/Río Bravo to perform a ritual burning of a cross in the border river. An elderly East German couple explains the disappearance of a Jewish cemetery in their Berlin neighborhood. In Masirević's film, a family nearly disintegrates under the consecutive blows of tragic, senseless blood-shedding on the Yugoslav–Hungarian border. The strongest response in our ensemble came from Mariko Ventura; hearing the voice-over of the Unborn Child in Dash's film, she expressed the desire to build a sanctuary installation and to find a ritual process for the observance of her Jewish and Japanese ancestors. Her exhibition project was the first one to emerge. Entitled *My Story Began Before I Was Born*, Mariko's clay sculptures were envisioned as concrete and symbolic shapes/shapings of recollection. Memories of her childhood in Kyoto are retold inside the installation, and the sculptural shapes resonate as touchstones of a life-process marked by the losses incurred (symbolized in the ashes from her father's urn, associated with Hiroshima and the Holocaust).

Even more essential, however, is the process of firing the clayworks (in a kiln), letting the images and surfaces emerge from the pressure of hands and body, from the heat of fire. As Mariko explains it to us, the clay is used to form bridges between her inner and outer self: 'My childhood and my first impressions cannot help but flow forth in the language of clay.' Three months later, the ensemble

Figure 9 Mariko Ventura, installation, *From the Border*, 1993.

meets at the West Geneva Pottery Farm in Wisconsin to spend a weekend at the wheel and the kiln, observing the process of a medium and the shaping of a poetic dialogue between bodies and clay, between different hands and the same material, between the awareness of the eye and the malleability of form. Working together for hours near the blaze of the fire creates a heightened physical sensibility toward an organic process, and the shared experience also reflects back on the difficulties we sometimes have in finding a similarly organic process for the joint stage reheasals. During the weekend we complete an outdoor shoot with Imma Sarries-Zgonc for a film scene used in *AlienNation*, one of the Border performances that deals with transitional consciousness in a moment of historical transformation. Such transitions have to do with breaking away from fixed, static assumptions about identity. The heated revolutionary moment, captured in the breaking of the Wall, is burdened with a history of failures and a history of misconceptions about the fantasy of 'one people' or a closed harmonious totality.

Jennifer Marx brings her own 'wheel' with her to the farm, a turntable that rotates in the center of the performance-installation she is working on. Her idea is to theatricalize the relationship between center and periphery, between gendered spaces in western culture, arguing that in a society where women remain constantly at odds with occupied territories, they can only situate their social spaces precariously on the edge/in-between diverse systems of power and ownership. Such asymmetrical relations of power also lie at the heart of Ivor Miller's installation project, *The Invisible Island*, which uses slides, telephones, foodstuffs and text to present the US/Cuba embargo/Cold War border crisis – the suspended stalemate of a historical crisis that appears to be the dialectical opposite of the transformation in the two Germanies (ironically conjured up in *AlienNation*). Ivor had just returned from Cuba before joining our ensemble, and he expresses particular concern over the severe food restrictions faced by all Cubans partly as a result of the US embargo, at the very same time when US-led forces land in famine-struck Somalia to deliver humanitarian relief, in another mode of interventionist politics.

Ivor's bilingual installation also reflects a strong current in all the works prepared for *From the Border*, namely a tendency to shift in-between languages and contexts, and to invite the voices of others. Peruvian sculptor Kukuli Velarde joins the ensemble to present several of her current works-in-progress from the series *We, the Colonized Ones*, a project she began in 1990 and partly exhibited in *Remerica 1492/Amerika 1992* (Hunter College Art Galleries) and in *Uncommon Ground* (SUNY-New Paltz Art Gallery), two exhibits dedicated to the 'Other America.' Kukuli's clay sculptures symbolize emotional consequences of colonization, and she decides to perform her story inside the environment of her visual objects. They express the point of view of the defeated, of those who saw their cultures and societies disrupted by the imposition of another culture and religion. They also embody a communication between the American past and the American present, and between the Western and non-Western cultures that cohabit the continental drift. In the week before the opening, a terrible irony strikes home. One of her sculptural figures from the *We, the Colonized Ones* series arrives in a UPS shipment that was not sufficiently insured because of our low budget, and when we open the package the head of the sculpture is broken off. Kukuli decides to exhibit the broken body of the sculpture as it was delivered at its destination.

Mirtes Zwierzynski is another guest artist who joins our ensemble to work on a mixed-media project with which she plans to address the violence of displacement and the potential loss of voice that can follow the radical uprootings and dispersions of people driven away (like the *natash*), deported, incarcerated, or 'disappeared.' Mirtes tells us that she is precisely interested in the violence of, and resistance to, such 'disappearance' and the enactments of state terror (not only in Latin America and her country of origin that she left during the years of military dictatorship) that feed and reproduce fear and repression. Her installation, *Memory/Exile*, is aimed at the relocation and reappearance of individual and collective memory.

During these months we have many debates and arguments over the politics and ethics of resistance, especially as we begin to see the emerging points of departure in the performance projects directed by Avanthi, Marianne Kim, Anna Scott, and Jerry Curry. Perhaps the most critical and significant dimension of our project is the development of three new works by women of color, and thus the question of the framework overshadows more immediate concerns of the production. As stipulated by Avanthi, the question concerns the transport of self-identified marginalized productions by black, Asian-American and South-east Asian women performers to the center stage of a white institution, exposing them to the potentially homogenizing effects of the proscenium stage, the spectacle space where difference is either exoticized or made to disappear.

Figure 10 Marianne Kim performing in *From the Border*, 1993.

Choreographer Marianne Kim's new dance solo, *uh buh/to carry*, renders a highly personal story of crossing over from one world to another. Her minimalist, butoh-like movement captures the gestus of a contradictory experience: a woman's flight from the Korean War and the pain of arrival in exile. Though

Figure 11 Avanthi Meduri and Marianne Kim in *From the Border*, 1993.

trained in Western modern dance forms, Marianne works through the stylistic influences of Korean traditional dance and butoh in order to reach an expressive medium with which to explore the crisis of identity caused by war, loss, and displacement.

Anna Scott's *Ships and Whips: I Remember* is, according to her design sketches, a multi-media Afrological dance/memory piece developed in collaboration with actors Sheila Richardson and Daniele Gaither. It becomes quickly apparent in our early joint rehearsals that Anna, who has studied West African, Afro-Caribbean, and Afro-Brazilian dance techniques, can draw from the extraordinary range of movements in African and African-derived dance. But the focus of her piece has to do with the remembering of a particular historical passage, and with the impact of the Middle Passage on people of African descent and their lives in the diaspora of the 1990s. More specifically, Anna plans to take an irreverent look at the sexual stereotyping imposed on black skin and at sexualized performances ranging from the roles embodied by Josephine Baker to current representations of black women in rap music and music videos. For several months she has worked on interweaving dance and story-telling in a powerful visual and poetic choreography, choosing to concentrate her energies on the work inside her dance troupe. At one of the regular meetings with the full ensemble, she mentions something to me that Ntozake Shange had written:

'Dance is how we remember what cannot be said.' I remember another moment in Shange's choreopoem (*for colored girls who have considered suicide/when the rainbow is enuf*): 'i usedta live in the world . . . this must be the spook house/ another song with no singers/lyrics/no voices/& interrupted solos/unseen performances.' The challenge of *Ships and Whips* to all of us is to recognize the (in)visibility of black women/directors on white stages, and the particular ways in which the dance speaks, and the words and movements become whips. At the same time, the symbolic reference to a concrete history (the 'ships' of the Middle Passage) raises a specific cross-cultural challenge to the mechanisms through which gender and race relations determine our bias, and to the unspoken hierarchies that settle into theater and performance research that pretends to conduct research on a non-ideological or pre-expressive level.

It is symptomatic, for example, that some European experiments in 'theater anthropology' (in the work of Eugenio Barba and ISTA, but also in the multicultural productions of Peter Brook and Ariane Mnouchkine) continue to analyze and speak for other cultural performance traditions and techniques included and tried on in Western workshops, insofar as the Western fascination with the stylized formal techniques of Japanese and Asian Indian dance, in a postcolonial context that continues to produce notions of 'otherness' at all levels, exacerbates the historical appropriations of others (especially the 'Oriental' female) when it does not address the symbolic languages and frameworks within which it receives/assimilates other forms, gestures, movement-energies, and embodied narratives/content. The incorporation of other-cultural performance techniques, codes, and metaphors in mixed productions raises enormous problems for the dialectics of exchange promoted in Euro-American culture. We need to become much more critically aware of the exchanges, and the ground of exchanges, we produce, as well as of the context-changes we are engaged in as we produce (showcase?) theater and dance forms of intermixed cultures for Western institutions of learning or consumption, as we include performers of different backgrounds in our theater work, and study how other aesthetic and spiritual languages operate in their cultures or choose to interact with our own.

Jerry Curry's performance of *The Art of the 'Q'* could be said to enact a kind of mythic allegory of such transactions, of the engineering of cultural death and the birth of new culture, modeled upon the pattern of the presumed asymmetries in East/South-West power relations or upon the historical narrative of Columbus's 'discovery.' Through poetic movement, symbol, and sound, Jerry's story creates an imaginary people called the Qualiawebe who meet an enterprising group of explorers. As the explorers re-enact the colonial impulse to render the unknown exotic and then seek to manage the fantasy, the performance begins to offer an ironic parable of ordering, manufacture, and classification of the fantasy scenario. The implications of the allegory for our own production are manifold, but the issue of the manipulation and transformation of cultural identities or fantasy projections has primarily revolved around the role of the male directors or producers within our ensemble. The focus of the critique was necessary and inevitable, and it moved into the center of our attention at an early January workshop during which Avanthi presented her own work-in-progress, a *bharatha natyam* dance-drama titled *Matsya* ('The Fish') – an acute postcolonial dramatization of the gender and race relations between margins and center. In this early workshop we realized that our main *Border* theme had less to do with issues of authenticity, cultural tradition, or the hoped-for equality of cross-cultural dialogue than with the reversal of spectatorship from the center to the margin.

If Avanthi were to restore and examine the sacred narrative of the 'Das Avatharam' (the ten incarnations of the Hindu god Vishnu) on the Western proscenium stage, thus re-performing an explicitly Asian Indian national dance-tradition in order to grapple with the silencing of her female body and voice, then the context created by the work might be undermined in advance by the presence of the larger Euro-American framework of avant-garde production and my own presence as a white male director/performer in a production shown side by side with *Matsya*. I was aware of the danger and of the contradictory implications of my own privilege (as teacher and as director/performer in *AlienNation*). In the spirit of collaboration with which we had set out to test our borders, we deferred the issue, even as it became increasingly apparent that the issue of gender and power relations cannot be deferred. My collaborators in *AlienNation*, Catalan dancer Imma Sarries-Zgonc and Anglo-American painter Tara Peters, agreed to perform in *Matsya*, while we also continued to rehearse our dance on the failure of the newly reunited German couple. In my performance I play a bureaucrat who is ordered to carry out a task I do not understand (adopted from Heiner Müller's surreal sketch 'Man in the Elevator'), and I mix my parody of the functionary as innocent 'angel of history' with filmic references to the fall of the Berlin Wall, the East German revolution, and the benevolent, white, voyeuristic angels in Wim Wenders's *Wings of Desire*. Influenced by discussions with Avanthi, I try to draw attention in my angel-dance to the unacknowledged whiteness of the European avant-garde and its modernist conception of a universalist history of revolution. The male European role in 'defining' history, no longer in center stage, is reframed and distorted in our performance by the two parallel, emergent female narratives danced by Imma and Tara.

In the larger political context of inclusion/exclusion and discrimination, aesthetic performances of self-marginalization or self-reflexive expression of alienation (cf. the European avant-garde from itself and from its history) have their limits, of course, as long as they block a real transformation of the conditions and relations of power in the production apparatus itself. Avanthi's *Matsya*, especially in its relation to the other works under construction and through the prolonged negotiations with design shops and production staff over the precise scenography of the dance, has become the catalyst in our understanding of borders and difference. Any critical evaluation of the learning process in our ensemble will be indebted to her insistence on addressing the production's unresolved gender and neocolonial relations. We are almost at the point where the works are shown to the public for the first time, and the history of our project reflects both the pitfalls of mistranslation and the potential of open confrontation, the moments

Figure 12 Imma Sarries-Zgonc and Johannes Birringer in *From the Border*, 1993.

when silences are broken and emotional conflicts and different positions are acknowledged.

The silences and the breaking-points constitute the most important aspects of the transitions and border crossings within and between each of the works prepared for *From the Border*. Probably to an extent not desirable or achievable in professional or commercial productions, the artistic process has been subjected to an ongoing political interrogation, and each artist willingly subjected her/his work to a group critique. The evolution of Avanthi's *Matsya*, with its focus on the displaced female body and its postcolonial performance as both a reproduction and a subversion of metaphors of the nation-state, constitutes the most critical mass in the overall production's compositional process. *Matsya* dramatizes the Indian classical dancer's inability to identify, name, and interrogate the spectatorial gaze which appropriates female subjectivity and endows it with an ideal name (*bharatha natyam*: the 'dance of India') that cannot speak to the concerns of the physical, gendered body. In this dance-theater work Avanthi uses the myths of origin, the stories of the ten incarnations that the god Vishnu assumes to destroy evil and re-establish peace and goodwill on earth – the order of time and memory. In one section of the stage she introduces the incarnations through embodied dance, voice, and her vision, while in another part of the dance each is re-created through a male persona, her internal 'other.' The juxta-positions of the dances-in-the-dance explore the splitting of the right from the left hand, the self from the other, woman from man, spectator from performer, native language from English language.[10]

Matsya attempts to suture this splitting and in the process exposes the use and misuse of idealized notions of Woman, Tradition, God – discourses that the nation-state uses for strategic nation-building processes and patriarchal ideolo-gies or fantasies of national identification. But in *Matsya* Avanthi urges us to consider the woman, her body, her voice, in the moment of her own cultural production. She ends by asking us to consider the consequences of woman's abdication from the nation-state, her arrival on the international margins, in the situation of bilingualism and multiculturalism and what all of this might mean both to the international audience and to Indian nation-state nationalism.

These are large and complex questions about fantasy structures and their dislocations, and they cannot be answered by a single production, even though they aim at fundamental problems of contemporary constitutions of identity, especially if we follow Renata Salecl's suggestion that late capitalism must be seen as an epoch in which the traditional fixity of ideological positions, such as fixed sexual roles or patriarchal authority or nationalist identification, has come to hinder the expansion of consumer society (cf. *The Spoils of Freedom*). In this sense, it is not possible either to assume that the audience attending our produc-tion will be prepared for or sympathetic to a viewing of a sacred narrative of origins (*Das Avatharam*) – as it crosses from the mythical world-view to the critical dance interpretation of the woman performer – within the secular con-texts of the proscenium (at Northwestern University) and of the other perform-ances created on and for the proscenium. The intervention of women's voices is crucial for our production of spaces of difference in the proscenium world of spectacle, because it is precisely their voices, hitherto often prohibited, erased, or spoken for, that will call on our blind spots and on our aggressive defenses with which we tend to redraw the borders in our cultures.

If education is part of cultural politics, as is the art of image-making, symbolic-textual expression, movement and performance, then our practices, including the discovery of blind spots, have a significant impact on expressions and group experiences constitutive of our social imaginations. Framing or nam-ing the arena of possible or (un)desirable performances, our rehearsals help to shape cultural politics that inform concepts of knowledge, learning, process, production value, significance, and desire. The production of new work material-izes through the questions that are asked. The presentation/distribution of *From the Border* to the public is a trans-action; the articulation of differences produces a (new) space that is subject to ideologies of authentication and evaluation. The translation of process into public dialogue confronts the boundaries of spectatorship and the conventional exchanges of values, meanings, and priorities. The main question, therefore, is how the differences in and between the performances unsettle the shared context in which they are viewed or into which they are subsumed. The politics of production must ultimately shift attention to the specific locations and occasions in which the work can engage and transform culture-specific practices of consumption. Cross-cultural collaboration challenges us to rethink the whole process of production; it also challenges us to reconsider its relation to audiences in mainstream and alternative venues, to audiences whose process of reception is equally complex, non-homogenous, and informed by often contradictory memories, imaginations, and experiences.

Germany/Slovenia, July–September 1993
THE POLITICS OF PRODUCTION

Documentary film, archaeology project, phase IV.
Return to Berlin and the same locations on the Polish
border as in 1991–2. Shoot-on-location in the steel plant
in Eisenhüttenstadt and the salt mines in Bischofferode,
meeting with hunger strikers, documenting rising
unemployment and East German infrastructural
transformations. Interfaces with cultural workers, activists,
artists, and students in Eisenhüttenstadt, and with the
Slovene theater group Project ATOL in Ljubljana.

Havana, December 1993
THE POLITICS OF PRODUCTION

International Congress of the Union of Democratic
Communication, School of Film & TV, San
Antonio, Cuba. Shoot-on-location in Havana and
interface with filmmakers and cultural workers at
Casa de las Américas.

New York City/Sarajevo, Spring 1994
WITNESSES OF EXISTENCE

A fragile cease-fire has momentarily brought relief to war-torn Sarajevo, although the war against Bosnia does not seem to be over yet. The 'cease-fire' barely helps us to understand, momentarily, the extended time of inhuman atrocity and violence visited upon a city and its population, under siege for more than twenty-two months. The news media reported the violence, death, and destruction, as well as the endless diplomatic negotiations and conversations that took place elsewhere, among the Western nations united in their indecision and apparent helplessness. While the destruction, the rapes, and the 'ethnic cleansings' took their course, while a city's multicultural and cosmopolitan way of life was humiliated and shredded by cannons and machine-guns, our observations fell silent since we did not seem to know how to speak to this violation of human existence.

As with other genocides that haunt our twentieth century, we will have to learn to listen to the witnesses and survivors of this horror, and such a confrontation with testimony will not come easily. There is nothing reassuring in what I have to report, and I may not have the words to express the visual and emotional 'evidence' of destruction that was brought to us by the emissaries from Sarajevo. Except that this mission is an extraordinary statement of a creative human spirit that reconstructs its will to survival from within the ruins of reason and the annihilation of being.

Witnesses of Existence could be called a work-in-progress. The artists and members of the Obala Cultural Center in Sarajevo had worked hard toward the opening of the reconstructed Sutjeska Cinema, which they had redesigned as a theater-gallery. Shortly before the festive opening, the war began in April 1992, and the building was one of the first that was destroyed by shells. In an act of extraordinary defiance, Zoran Bogdanović, Sanjin Jukić, Edo Numankadić, Nusret Pasić, Tanja and Stjepan Ros, Mustafa Skopljak, and Petar Waldegg joined Obala director Mirsad Purivatra in an exhibition project that was staged in the ruined building as a 'permanent' installation (October 1992 through April 1993). In the immediate proximity of death and destruction, these artists built a series of exhibitions, accompanied by intermittent performances, video screenings, musical concerts and poetry readings, which gave testimony to the spiritual act of resistance while quite literally transforming still available materials (bricks, broken glass, burnt logs, sand, ashes, paper, found objects) into 'portraits' of an existence under extreme pressure. When word got out that this exhibition was being upheld under siege, an invitation was issued from the Venice Biennial in the summer of 1993; yet because of the blockade, neither the artists nor the work obtained UN permission to travel. The artists continued to develop their work, and some documentation (provided by video artists of the SaGA collective) reached the outside world, together with Ademir Kenović's harrowing film collage, *Sarajevo Ground Zero*, (available on video through Globalvision, New York). After months of insistent planning and hard negotiations, Martin Kunz was finally able to bring the artists together with their work to his 'Kunsthalle' in New York's East Village – ironically a building which is itself under reconstruction after being partly destroyed by fire last year.

Witnesses of Existence was open to the public for six weeks in the spring of 1994, occupying the dark, bare, skin-and-bones structure of the gutted brick building on East 5th Street. The arrival of the Sarajevan artists coincided with a massive Open Forum, 'Sarajevo New York: The City under Siege,' organized by the Cooper Union in downtown New York. Panel discussions, slide lectures, film screenings, and 'speak outs' brought together a huge international audience willing to learn more about the political and cultural implications of the war against Bosnia. The quiet presence of the traumatized artists from Sarajevo created a very visceral, and perhaps even unacknowledged, counterpoint to the relentless, bustling energy of the conference organizers, speakers, and representatives of the more than thirty humanitarian relief organizations and solidarity committees that had sponsored this call to action. The provocative agenda of this public forum included a critical analysis of the struggle for Sarajevo's survival with respect to the larger, and thus *shared*, struggle against the degradation and destruction of the very idea of the culturally diverse, multiethnic and multi-national city at the end of the century. Sarajevo stood as the symbol of resistance against all barbarisms that would seek to destroy the possibility of such cultural existence of diversity and equality.

At the end of a long day of debates, the young Sarajevan filmmaker Srdan Vuletić showed a ten-minute video, *I Burnt Legs*, which depicts his job, namely taking amputated limbs from the hospital to the place where they are cremated. As he reflects on the weight of the bags he carries, he is seen standing in front of what once was Sarajevo's central park, now empty except for a few left-over stumps of former oak trees. Speaking hurriedly into the camera, Vuletić explains: 'This park really suits me. I like much more these stumps than trees. Its empti-ness matches some inner emptiness of mine.' There was a long silence after the screening of the film.

When I met the artists during a reception at the Kunsthalle on the following day, I realized that the work they had brought to the USA will have to cross this incredible abyss of silence that separates us from a knowledge of this particular horror, and from the unthinkable recognition that the people in Sarajevo have been forced to accept the war as a 'normal' condition of existence now. Vuletić admitted that his feelings have changed, and that he finds it increasingly difficult to accept such a normalcy. The reduction of human existence to pure survival, and thus to an acceptance of war as a normal condition, comes at a price that is too heavy. In fact, the exhibition of *Witnesses of Existence* is not merely an existen-tial outcry. Bogdanović's installation *Memory of People*, Numankadić's *War Trails*, or Jukić's sardonic *Sarajevo Likes America and America Likes Sarajevo* convey more than remembrances of violence; they are ethical acts of intervention into a monstrous scenario which they interpret creatively and consciously. They build meaningful compositions of the human spirit and intelligence in midst of the war's insanity. Thus they become also witnesses of our indifference; their irony and resiliency shame us. Their work also proves that it is neither impossible nor frivolous to make art in the time of war; perhaps making art in such a time is as necessary as finding food and shelter and healing the wounded. Within extreme circumstances, each creative act is as vulnerable as the flesh of the human body, since the very idea of aesthetic distance has collapsed. *Witnesses of Existence* exhibits work that was held hostage by war yet became a symbolic site of 'reconstruction.' The architects Tanja and Stjepan Ros designed the exhibition for the destroyed Obala Gallery by treating the ruin as a 'new cathedral of the spirit,' while they also noted that this ruin had become a place of rest for those passing through it, using it as a short-cut and a passage safer than the open streets.

This reality of destruction of course cannot be 're-created' in the New York

Kunsthalle, and to do so would be absurd and misleading, since the suffering and pain experienced by the Bosnians cannot be adequately shared through representation. This is the fallacy of the media's instantaneous coverage of war elsewhere: such coverage cannot but blend into the stream of images of violence we are programmed to forget. While Bogdanović's *Memory of People*, a long, narrow band of photo-portraits culled from the obituary pages of the (still existing) Sarajevo newspaper *Oslobodenje*, invites us to remember the growing number of the dead, Jukić's installations challenge the media's insidious spectacularization of violence in a different, and highly poignant, way. In *Sarajevo Ghetto Spectacle* he puts neon letters of the word 'SARAJEVO' on the wall, quoting the Hollywood hills logo and simultaneously reminding us of the grand parallel event of the Olympic Games in 1984 (Sarajevo and Los Angeles), that moment when the eyes of the world were directed at the beautifully and glamorously organized winter games in the Bosnian capital. On top of the logo Jukić projects video images from the war zone, ten years later. A small written commentary accompanied the original installation:

> The opening day of the exhibition was a paradigm of a ghetto spectacle. Everything that originally inspired this display was present. All the primary signs were repeated: the shelling, destruction, killing, wounding. Then again it all ran on television. And there were secondary signs: notorious problems with UNHCR, the hopes and glances of citizens of Sarajevo aimed toward the USA; the indifference and incompetence of Europe, the establishment of the war crimes court, etc. The Sarajevo ghetto spectacle daily reaches the world mega-stage which has already been full and brimming with other and different spectacles. That is why I think that art has to play its remarkable promotion role. The fight continues. We will be the winners.

In his other installation, *Sarajevo likes America and America likes Sarajevo*, Jukić's cynical humor goes even further, as he puns on the title of Joseph Beuys's first action-exhibition in the USA (*I Like America and America Likes Me*, performed in 1974) and constructs a 'likeness' between the two worlds, once again posting the maps (of the USA and of the Olympic Mountains above Sarajevo) on the brick wall, with a dinner table for two beneath. The meal: 'American-way-of-life' Coca-Cola cans and Marlboro packs (both empty) next to empty Turkish coffee-cups on an old, hand-carved wooden table. Perhaps we remember that Coca-Cola once was the main sponsor of the Sarajevo Winter Olympic Games, but that was in another world.

Numankadić also registers the changes that have interrupted his artistic work-life. On an easel he places some of his pre-war color paintings, small studies of minute changes in the emotions of color and light. In front of the absurd-looking easel we see the painter's work-table, now covered with the scattered utensils of everyday survival: penicillin, a bottle of water, an oil lamp, a piece of old bread, papers, a few books, one Duracell battery.

Nusret Pasić, whose *Witnesses of Existence* installation gave the exhibition its

Figure 13 Sanjin Jukić, installation, *Witnesses of Existence.*

overall title, has hung tall, narrow linen strips from the ceiling, each depicting a very elongated, thin human figure whose head seems to float upward toward the sky. Down below lies the rubble of destruction – broken glass, shrapnels, burnt logs, ash and soot. Yet these thin suspended shapes have a strange, almost magic power. They rise upward like totem poles that command our respect. Right behind this installation is a second one, *Martyrs*, depicting an altar-like table on which bricks are placed. Stepping closer, one sees tiny wooden, snake-like figures nailed onto the red bricks, strangely contorted limbs that seem to be choreo-graphed into the hieroglyphic language of a *danse macabre*. The young graphic artist Petar Waldegg has built a triangular staircase out of bricks; it is an open form, tantalizingly hinting at the spiritual task of reconstruction that will begin with the collection of energy or hope needed for such a difficult ascent. Finally, upon entering the space one must pass by the grave-like earthen mounds built by sculptor Mustafa Skopljak. These earthworks are surrounded by glass pyramid sculptures that look like trees, a surreal forest of memories now symbolically contained in the tiny burning lamps. What we cannot see are the painted wooden portraits, faces of the dead, which Skopljak buried in the earth and only opens up to our momentary gaze during a ritual performance.

Even if I were able to describe the installations in words, such words would only insufficiently capture the power that emanated from the exhibition as a whole, in the presence of these Sarajevans who had come, for a few weeks, to visit us before going back a ghostly city whose future has been severely mutilated. They all know, however, that they must go back so that the city can also reconstruct its imagination for a possible future, built on the refusal to give up, or to give over one's spirit to the corrosive impact of the destruction of elementary rights. I have never felt so strongly what it might mean to consider creativity an elementary right. If we accept Jukić's ironic gesture (*America Likes Sarajevo*) as an invitation, which it is, we will have to think about our own choices, our own appeasement politics or accommodation to fascist aggression.

Germany/USA/Cuba, March–May 1994
ALIENNATION and EWIGE SEELEN–EWIGES LAND

Performances presented at 'Border-Land'/'Grenz-Land'
Festival in Eisenhüttenstadt and Frankfurt. **Border-Land**
travels to West Germany. **AlienNation** is presented at
Cleveland Performance Art Festival 'Outside the Frame.'
Participation in the CONJUNTO 1994 at the Casa de las
Américas, and presentation of **Border-Land** in a workshop
on 'Medios mezclados – Culturas híbridas.'

Chicago, June 1994
CULTURE UNDER SIEGE

A tribute to Bosnia, Beacon Street Gallery. Public forum
with video presentations and discussions on the war against
Bosnia and on women refugees, organized in collaboration

with Katarina Vidović (Zagreb) and the Balkan Women's Empowerment Project.

Germany/Holland/Slovenia, June–September 1994
CLOSED SPACES

Documentary film, archaeology project, phase V. Return to Berlin and the Polish border, shooting on the same locations as in 1992–3. Interface with cultural workers and artists in Dresden, and filmic preparation of a new site-specific project in Eisenhüttenstadt.

Amsterdam, Summer 1994
THE CONNECTED BODY/RECONSTRUCTIONS

International dance workshop at the School for New Dance Development. Film lecture on bodies, locations, reconstructions of destroyed buildings and memory.

Ljubljana, September 1994
PRIHODNOST FIZICNEGA GLEDALISCA IN SODOBNEGA PLESA

(The future of physical theater/dance)
Workshop at Mladinsko Theater and interface with Project ATOL and Marko Košnik's Egon March Institute (a radio program). Shoot-on-location and interview with SaGA video collective from Sarajevo during the open forum 'Sarajevo in Ljubljana.'

Hellerau, September–October 1994
FEST III: KUNST UND GEWALT

Performance festival organized by Europäische Werkstatt für Kunst und Kultur, Hellerau-Dresden. Interface with Peruvian Grupo Chaclacayo.

Havana, December 1994
TEATRO Y INTERCULTURALIDAD

Participation in international workshop of Centro Nacional de Investigación, Havana, and performance of **AlienNation** at Gran Teatro de Habana.

Irvine, February 1995
BORDER MEDIA

Video demonstration for the Organized Research Group on Hispanic Theater Conference, University of California-Irvine.

New York, March 1995
STATE DOUBLES: THEATER STATES AND OTHER DOUBLES

East–West Dialogue/Open Forum at New York University,
First Performance Studies Conference. In collaboration with
Goran Dordević, Elena Siemens, Eda Čufer, Marko Peljhan, and
Ivor Miller.

Cleveland/Chicago, January–June 1995
LOVERS FRAGMENTS (ACTs I, II, III)

Production development and premiere at Cleveland
Performance Art Festival and Barber Theater,
Northwestern Theater Center. (See Chapter 6.)

London/Montréal, April–May 1995
THE OBSCENE/OFF-SCREEN BODY: LOVERS FRAGMENTS

Film installation/Performance of fragments of the new
production at 'Border Tensions' dance conference,
University of Surrey (London), and FIRT Theater Congress
in Montréal, Canada.

Helsinki, May 1995
MOVEMENT/CAMERA/GENDER

Dance-film workshop, conducted collaboratively
with local artists at Helsinki Act Festival, Finland.

Eisenhüttenstadt, August 1995
VERSCHLOSSENE RÄUME/CLOSED SPACES

Urban action/performance workshop and creation of
'Fantasielabor' ensemble. Shoot on several locations
with focus on abandoned sites of cultural production
(during socialism). Occupation of former cultural center,
squatting performance, manifesto for new independent
production center. Collaboration with local artists, media,
and neighborhoods.

Festpielhaus Hellerau, Dresden, August–September 1995
PARSIFAL: IRRITATIONS – MYTHOS – UTOPIA

Parsifal, an experimental opera-installation, is a work in progress developed in a
sequence of different performance concepts, each one with a particular focus and
artistic design. It is inspired by a year-long collaboration with the Peruvian
Grupo Chaclacayo after their initial exhibition of *Parsifal Prolog* at the1994
'Kunst und Gewalt' Festival staged in the partly destroyed Hellerau art colony in
Dresden, East Germany. Grupo Chaclacayo decided not to participate in the
ongoing performance project, and subsequently members of AlienNation Co.

extended the project development in collaboration with the Dresden-based Gruppe RU-IN.

The new opera is created in the crumbling architecture of the old Festspiel-haus Hellerau in Dresden where a group of artists and social reformers founded a utopian art colony in 1911, dedicated to free dance, music-theater, visual arts, and the integration of arts and crafts workshops in a 'garden town' designed after a philosophy of alternative, ecological, and communitarian living. Abandoned shortly after the First World War, the site was later occupied by the Nazis and then by the Soviet Army at the end of the Second World War.

Parsifal is designed as a site-specific acoustic installation and architectural choreography in fourteen different rooms of the east wing of the dilapidated Festspiel-Theater complex. The opening prologue is created as a dance solo (cho-reographed by Imma Sarries-Zgonc) in front of the Festspielhaus façade modi-fied with video stills created by Jo Siamon Salich, and performed to a sonic transformation of Wagner's *Parsifal* overture (created by Salich). Members of AlienNation Co. and RU-IN jointly create the acoustic and visual installation and the cycle of fourteen performance actions which is also transmitted via surveillance cameras from the fourteen rooms of the east wing into the centrally located foyer of the decaying auditorium. The main auditorium itself remains empty, closed and inaccessible, although the audience can look into it from two upper-floor windows.

The focus of the installation-performance is the slow and deliberate fragmen-tation of the Wagnerian myth of the grail/redemption in the modified archi-tectural ruins of an abandoned German utopia. While working in the collective

Figure 14 Parsifal rehearsal, Hellerau, 1995.

process, each of the performing artists individually acts out her/his associations with the contaminated site and the terminal condition of a dead myth and its psychopathology. As a result, many of the simultaneous actions will appear accidental or circumstantial, completely severed from any allegiance to Wagner's score and libretto. No music from the opera will be heard inside. All acoustic and electric sounds audible in the installation are produced by the performers and the building. The only clearly marked interactions between performers happen during the three physical alterations of the temporary interior design (suspended iron grids normally used for construction-work) in the largest of the fourteen rooms. Otherwise, the individual actions follow their own logic of 'reconstruction' – some of which are based on acoustic samplings of the ruin, others on biographical stories and symptoms of the body, and others again on 'leitmotifs' that explore the dangerous implications of dissonant resemblances with the racial ideology of blood sacrifice and purification that underlies Wagner's mysterious communion (identification with the father) among the knighthood of the grail. The installation-performance thus touches intimately on the concrete resonances of the ruined site: the perversion of utopian aspirations is everywhere visible, and Wagner's final opera is remembered as a failure precisely of its will to metaphysical and total power (the totality of the *Gesamtkunstwerk*), a lingering trauma of the epiphany of necessary bloodshed, the castrations and exclusions that consecrate the rites of purification.

Act II will be created on-site in Alamar, Cuba, in a film collaboration with the group La Jaula Abierta. The leitmotifs of this production will be based on the poem 'La lógica que se cumple' by Manuel Avila, a member of the group. This phase of the production will relocate the Christian mythology of our theme into an Afro-Cuban context and into a confrontation with the revolutionary experience of the people of a former colony. It will be the second stage in the decomposition of a European myth and its racist ideology, and its emotional content will focus on an exploration of the significance of utopian ideas at the end of the century and in midst of the most disillusioned and precarious period of the Cuban revolution.

Parsifal represents a process of cross-cultural, site-specific research that has organically evolved for members of AlienNation Co. in their collaborations with other artists over the last few years. In cooperation with the East German performance artists of RU-IN, we continue to explore extensions of the *Parsifal* material and questions it raises about contemporary media and sensibilities that replace opera and theater and the traditional frames of visual art alike. Over the past several years, we have explored the connections between live performance and cinematic/video space-time, testing processes of composition that combine dance-theater choreography with video choreography, acoustic and electronic music, poetry and the visual arts. Experimenting with both site-specific and cross-cultural performance materials, the company's collaborations have been particularly concerned with physical-emotional experience (in the body), the ideology of visual objects/images, and the continuing evolution of an analog video memory that is now also being transfered to CD-ROM formatted memory and digital reprocecessing. Grupo Chaclacayo's participation in the *Parsifal* opera project has been vital and dynamic, even as a synthesis of our diverse approaches to the broken building as a schizophonic/sonic environment could not be achieved. The Peruvian group, concerned about the integrity of its visual aesthetic *vis-à-vis* our projected editing, mixing, and erasing of spatial and acoustic images, could not reconcile the issue of control and compromise and decided to withdraw from the performance. To our great disappointment, the site-specific story of our transcultural *Parsifal* production resulted in a partial failure of reconciliation, even as we were able to agree upon the existence of polarizing interpretations of meaning and value in our diverse approaches to the circular ruins of the myth we had set out to dismantle.

Chicago/Havana, December 1995
LOVERS FRAGMENTS: ACT IV

Performance at Blue Rider Theater Festival and completion of a dance-film version presented at the Casa de las Américas, and later at theDanceScreen Festival in Lyon, France. Workshop and shoot-on-location in Cuba, developing **La lógica que se cumple** in collaboration with La Jaula Abierta.

Chicago, March 1996
THE FUTURE OF UTOPIA

East–West Dialogue/Open Forum and film-performances presented at the II Performance Studies Conference, Northwestern University. In collaboration with Magaly Muguercia, Sergei Bugaev Afrika, Marko Peljhan, Ute Ritschel, and Jo Siamon Salich.

Amsterdam, June 1996
CONNECTING BODIES

Dance Symposium and 'Bodies of Influence' workshop at the School for New Dance Development in Holland. Video documentation of new digital choreographies.

Chichester, July 1996
LBLM

Performance/Digital Art workshop with independent artists created for the 'Split Screen' Festival, Chichester, England.

Dresden, August 1996
LOVERS FRAGMENTS

Workshop on 'Körper und Sexualität,' presented at the Deutsche Hygiene Museum Dresden. Performance

installation of a new version of *Lovers Fragments* at the
museum in collaboration with Gruppe RU-IN.

Berlin, September 1996
BEWEGUNGEN IN DER MITTE DER DRITTEN STADT (ORT 1).

In this dance film I try to create an eccentric perspective on contemporary Berlin
and the largest European construction site in its central area (Potsdamer Platz) by
following the journey of two dancers to their performance on the rooftop of the
only remaining historical building in midst an almost grotesquely futuristic
excavation of the ground that once was the no-man's land of the Berlin Wall,
separating the East from the West. The site is now reconstructed into the most
grandiose mega-architectural shopping/office and entertainment center for
Germany's new capital. The film is a poetic meditation on the movement of time
and the disappearance of historical ground and memory. The dancers' bodies
connect us to the loss that is prefigured in the film's ironic treatment of the
architects' simulation models of the new 'virtual city.' I see this project as the last
stage of the video archaeology I started in 1990.

In a collaboration between the Berlin-based dance company RUBATO (Jutta
Hell, Dieter Baumann) and Imma Sarries-Zgonc (AlienNation Co.), the concept
and choreography for the dance performance on the rooftop of the old Weinhaus
Huth at the Potsdamer Platz in Berlin was developed during the summer of
1996, and the new work, *Ort 1*, was first performed under the direction of Jutta
Hell on the weekend of 14–15 September 1996. I met the dancers during their
rehearsals in August, and began filming on location after discovering the various
vast and interconnected construction sites on and around the Potsdamer Platz in
the center of Berlin. The location directly intersects with the territories I filmed
in the months and early years following the fall of the Berlin Wall in 1989 and
the process of German reunification. *Border-Land* remains as a series of
unfinished and unfinishable films (1990–5) that have traveled widely to other
contexts of performance/production. I decided to discontinue the archaeological
project in 1995 when it became too difficult to find a coherent narrative form for
the confusing political, social, and economic disturbances created by the German
reunification.

The dance project, *Ort 1*, with its particular concentration on one concrete
historical location, the only remaining house on the Potsdamer Platz that was not
destroyed by the war or the subsequent division of Berlin (the Potsdamer Platz
had been an empty no man's land on the death-strip for more than thirty years),
offered a unique opportunity in 1996 to return to the locations where the first
phase of *Border-Land* was filmed after the revolution. No traces of the Wall, still
quite apparent in the early summer of 1990, are left now, and in 1996 the central
areas of Berlin, and especially the former no man's land, have become highly
prized arenas of venture capitalism and transnational investments into the construction of a new composite office, shopping and entertainment mega-mall
adjacent to the newly constructed government administration buildings that will
host the political leadership in Germany's new capital.

The dance takes place at sunset on the rooftop of the old building standing in the midst of an immense construction site which has been hailed and promoted as Europe's largest, controlled by the most advanced state-of-the-art, high-tech logistical operations and computer/communications management. On the east side of the building, across from the excavation site, stands a raised platform/ information center which displays the various computer simulation models of the futuristic architecture designed for the new Sony and Daimler Benz 'city center.' The sky and the landscape of the construction site are dominated by a vast sea of cranes, machines, and tools. The film *bewegungen in der mitte der dritten stadt* takes a close look at the movement of the cranes and the symbolic significance of the futuristic late capitalist building and investment politics, while following the missing traces of the border (the Wall) and the missing connections between the history of a living, organic city and the simulation of the new 'virtual Berlin' at the end of the century.

This film, therefore, is not a documentary dance film as such but a conceptual exploration of the dancers' bodily movements, gestures, their listening, and their careful tracing of sensory experience and memory, within a space that is being radically gutted of its grown and sedimented history and its connection with the heterogeneous urban population and the memory of inhabitants. The future center will in fact not be an urban center for any local communities and their social and cultural resonances but a homogenously controlled and fully designed artificial environment, irrespective of the geographical and historical urban context, whose dominant logistical and topological model is the disembodied network of electronic interfaces and consumption environments that mask physical realities. The term 'third city' (*dritte Stadt*) refers to this modeling of new virtual-urban space in which the older associations (in the historically grown city and the modern industrial city) between physical and architectural space and experience are shattered. One of the implications of this future design is the question of how human bodies – specifically situated human bodies in their lived experience – are superimposed and hybridized with a hyperreal information environment.

The film *bewegungen in der mitte der dritten stadt* thus poetically grounds its dance movement *vis-à-vis* the simulation of urban 'centers' in the new mega-architecture that erases history and displaces grown, organic urban life. The whole future city is already on display in the red plastic information box, while everything around is dug up and under. But Rubato's dance performance specifically

Figure 15 *bewegungen in der mitte der dritten stadt (Ort 1),* Berlin 1996.

raises the question of the body's memory of *place*, surrounded and converted by the techno-tools of futurevision, which SONY likes to link, symptomatically, to its new Berlin IMAX theater: nineteen movie auditoria in an artificially land-scaped total environment, with hotels, casinos, restaurants, shops, and offices. The totally 'controlled' environment implicates further questions about trans-national Japanese and American compact-design ideologies that re-create nature (artificial lakes, artificial ski-slopes, artificial trees and everything else that can be commodified) on a large scale within urban space. Today these total designs are imagined in reference to advances in 'cyborg' designs (humanoid, prosthetic, electronic enhancements) for the new 'transhuman beings' of the next century.

Ort 1 is a still point in the vortex of high-tech construction. The foundation of the old building (completed before the First World War) now rests in a pool of green water that is welling up from the ground of the construction site. The dancers listen to the wind and the sounds of the cranes at work, and their body movements invite us to make connections to the place and the repressed history both of the promise and vitality of Potsdamer Platz in the 1920s and the dis-placements and destructions caused by Hitler's war that continue to haunt the phantasmagoric core of the inner city.

Havana, December 1996
LA LÓGICA QUE SE CUMPLE

World premiere of collaborative film at 18th International
Festival of New Latin American Cinema. Subsequently
invited to the Chicago Latino Film Festival in the spring of 1997.

Houston, February–April 1997
ARTISTS IN TRANCE

Art/ethnography project created by Transart Foundation
and Rice Anthropology Department/Rice Media Center,
directed by Abdel Hernández. Uncompleted documentary
performance-film capturing the interactions between Latin
American artists and local scholars and audiences.

Atlanta/Cleveland, April–May 1997
BEFORE NIGHT FALLS

Performance-installation presented at 3rd Performance Studies
Conference in Atlanta and at Cleveland Performance Art Festival.

Dresden, July 1997
LOVERS FRAGMENTS/BEFORE NIGHT FALLS

Performance-installations at Dresden Castle, the
Hygiene Museum Dresden, and the Baroque Gardens
Grossedlitz, Germany, in collaboration with RU-IN.

Dresden, August 1997
LBLM

Performance/technology workshop, Projekttheater Dresden, in collaboration with Medienwerkstatt Dresden and RU-IN.

Internet, October 1997
MEMBRANES

Participation in *Globalbodies*, international online teleconference with mirror sites in Germany, USA, Mexico, Argentina, and New Zealand.

Houston, October 1997
SKYBOOKS

Documentary film on documenta X and Makrolab, presented at Sewall Art Gallery. [See Chapter 3.]

Barcelona, January 1998
MEDIA I ACCIÓ

Public workshop and video/CD-ROM exhibition, Mediateca, Fundació la Caixa.

Houston, February 1998
BETWEEN THE PLACES

Dance-film environment presented at Diverse Works.

Houston, February–March 1998
PARACHUTE

Site-specific performance and installation cycle, in collaboration with Sandra Organ Dance Company and singer/composer Lourdes Pérez, prepared for FotoFest '98.

Houston, May 1998
NORTH BY SOUTH

Dance-film concert, Diverse Works.

England, July 1998
MACHINES AND MIGRATORY BODIES

Performance & technology workshop at Chichester Institute, presenting five interactive installations.

Figure 16 North by South, 1998.

Houston, October 1998
EAST BY WEST

Digital dance/music concert at Winter Street Art Center
in collaboration with Houston FotoFest's
mixed media exhibition 'Blurred Boundaries.'

Internet, November 1998
PARACHUTE ONLINE

Webcast performance, based on the Parachute project
and published on AlienNation Co's website:
http://www.ruf.rice.edu/~orpheus/

Houston, December 1998
MIGBOT

Film-performance and sculptural installations in four
spaces at Winter Street Art Center. This architectural project
initiates a new work cycle, the MIRAK project, exploring
inner and outer space, navigation, and the concept of 'slow space.'
The first phase is focused on the VESPUCCI film, the science-fictional
scenario of the reconstructed memoir of Russian cosmonaut Vespucci
who drifts out of orbit in an abandoned spaceship. The completed
opera, MIRAK, is projected to be AlienNation Co.'s last work of the
decade.

Figure 17 Angeles Romero performing in *Vespucci Project*, 1999.

Houston/Phoenix, January–March 1999
SLOW SPACE

Workshop in performance technologies and interactive designs.
Elements from the workshop are also presented at IDAT 99,
the international dance and technology congress held at
Arziona State University.

Houston, March 1999
LITANY FOR A DEAD EARTH

Collaborative performance-exhibition presenting new
photographs and digital prints by Hans Staartjes and
AlienNation Co.'s sculptures and Vespucci film in a live
mix concert with DJs Fluxx and Solar Plexus.

ULYSSES' GAZE

> The world needs cinema now more than ever. It may be the last
> important form of resistance to the deteriorating world in which
> we live.
> In dealing with borders, boundaries, the mixing of languages, and
> cultures today, I am trying to seek a new humanism, a new way.
> (Theo Angelopoulos[11])

If our bodies are intimately connected with, and constituted by, our rememberings, then the places of remembering and the movements of recuperation form
the intersection, the cross-roads of what I have here called 'border performance.'
The eccentric movements I have traveled and described sketch a personal journey
and a cycle of encounters and collaborations, without harboring any religious
faith in a return to the *Heimat*. The intimacy I remember is not with the land or
with (my) native consciousness but with a conflicted consciousness of the
instability of distance (self-distancing), the ill-affordable irony of displacement,
and the necessary connective power of identification with others who share the
navigation of complex existences. Existence is exile, and the darkly ironic language of the Internet now recycles our cultural metaphors: search-engine, navigation, explorer. Yet if the movement of the twentieth century is a hugely tragic
shipwreck, as Greek filmmaker Angelopoulos implies in his epic film *Ulysses'
Gaze* (1995), then it is all the more important to revisit certain myths and fantasy
identifications in order to examine how they change or can be changed. Slavenka
Drakulić calls her book *How We Survived Communism and Even Laughed*,
although the political and economic realities for women in post-communist
countries have not inspired much comfort. Gloria Anzaldúa stubbornly writes
inspirational poetry about the borderlands and urges us to think about becoming, not possessing: 'To survive the Borderlands/you must live *sin fronteras*/be a
cross-roads.'[12] Trinh Minh-ha, whom I quoted above, speaks about the question
of looking/traveling: depending on who is looking, the eccentric or exotic is the
other, or it is me.

In dance and video production rehearsals with others, we become acquainted
with the difficulties of equal exchange and of changing one's position and not
desiring to be confirmed. What I have learnt from my collaborations is the
difficult truth that one's loves or identifications are not confirmed, and subjectivity becomes fluid, unsettled, unsettling. I see no historically justifiable reason
to romanticize the fluidity of a 'traveling theory' (Edward Said) of exiled and
shipwrecked persons, yet the existential journey each of us makes inevitably faces
many moments in which we notice how badly cracked the mirror is, and how
strongly our performance depends on others or, rather, begins with the other. In
that sense, changing places or thinking through moving helps our bodies to
remember anew and to mark a new past. The production experiences or navigations I have related here are based on face-to-face encounters, and on the
unpredictable vagaries of the borderland-video archaeology I began in 1990
under the distant impact of a revolution whose deteriorating fantasy I came to
locate in myself and, beyond the pathetic (erotic) relation to my self, in the
genuine otherness of the experiences my collaborators witnessed.

The testimony of others implies an ethical challenge that is not reducible to
imaginary identifications or the dream of a common language or a homecoming.
The dream of the daughters of dust is a departure. Consequently, I'm not sure
where Angelopoulos seeks the ethics of a 'new humanism,' if his central metaphor in the film is the shipwrecked male Homeric protagonist, identified as A.,
in search of the lost 'gaze' (the first films made by the Manakis brothers, the

originators of Balkan cinema), which he finally, after a long journey through war-torn and bleak landscapes of Eastern Europe, locates in besieged Sarajevo. Sarajevo is not Ithaca, or it is a different Ithaca that resembles Hiroshima, Dresden, Havana, or Chaclacayo. The film's composition itself is hauntingly beautiful and evocative, traversing a huge minefield of historical, cultural, social, political, and personal resonances up to the last few moments when A.'s Jewish Bosnian friends are killed in the fog by unseen sniper fire. I cannot forget a long scene in the middle of the film journey, when we see a giant, disassembled statue of Lenin floating on a barge up the Danube River toward some scrap yard in Germany. Along the riverbanks, thousands of peasants stand motionless and watch the strange apparition pass by. When A. locates the lost film-reels in the bombed-out Sarajevo film archive and finally gets them developed, they are grey and blurred like the fog that settles on the city.

This 'homecoming' to the first Balkan film is a perversely beautiful and bitter parable of the blindness of a 'look' that seeks to find an answer to the self in the re-enactment of a mythic journey back to itself. All the loved ones are dead, and no Penelope and no guardian angel with wings of desire appear to provide transcendence. If the old myths have become corrupted and offer no redemption, the archaeology of fantasy becomes aware of its limits. What we share, *sin fronteras* or at the cross-roads, are failures of fantasy and limits that may bind us together in and for another search, another departure, dancing with the wind on rooftops of soon-to-be-forgotten buildings.

2

DIALOGUES AND BORDER CROSSINGS

Border media/border performance: In introducing these terms and the conversations that follow, I need to backtrack for a few moments and convey my understanding of performance as cross-cultural mediation. Throughout the 1980s, many artists working on the margins of US mainstream culture began to experiment with the interrelations of performance and audio-visual media or computer/video technology in order to explore popular and dissident image-making processes as a political/aesthetic tool. More interested in popular culture, and the ways technological media infiltrate communications structures, than in formal aesthetics, such work often grappled with the mass media or featured

Figure 18 Berlin, November 1989. Videostill from *Border-Land*, 1990.

issues generally suppressed or distorted by mainstream media. Gradually, video installations and multi-media work dealing with the AIDS crisis, sexuality, gender, race, and the politics of multiculturalism entered the museums and galleries that had previously excluded time-based art as low culture or as simply unmanageable and uncollectable. As Néstor García Canclini points out in his book *Culturas híbridas: Estrategias para entrar y salir de la modernidad*, the contemporary blurring of genres and the collapse of paradigmatic modernist configurations in the West – high, popular, and mass culture – come hardly as a surprise to artists in Latin America, for example, who had always been aware that their heterogeneous societies are the results of cultural crossings and hybridizations.[1]

The issue of hybridization has become more intensified, globally, as governments, museums, and universities no longer control the institutionalization of defined cultural spaces or historical perceptions of symbolic meanings and forms. Parallel to the emergence of hybrid and interactive media in the 1980s, new collaborative and community-directed practices of public art, activism, and self-representation have begun to create expanding networks of alternative, socially and politically engaged media production and distribution. Good examples of this expansion in the USA are the growing visibility of independent videos that address specific community needs and interests (e.g. gay and lesbian experience; identity politics; women's health concerns and AIDS education; environmental issues), and the formation of media arts collectives that nurture progressive cultural dialogue between diverse communities or implement media literacy outreach programs in the schools. The activist dimensions of this work are explicit. In the workshops I have attended there was considerably less emphasis given to aesthetic or technical concerns than to videography as a tool for self-reflection, social analysis, and the political articulation of cultural identities. During the 1994 'Women in the Director's Chair' International Film/Video Festival, the thirteenth of its kind in Chicago, much attention was given to the inauguration of *Espacios Nuevos/Nuevos Encuentros*, a new program of Latina cinema and video which expands the already existing women's production programs, prison projects, traveling exhibits, youth outreach, and community collaboration projects, all of which are designed to initiate cross-cultural dialogue and to share resources.

Production workshops are performative encounters. One cannot use media, shoot and edit footage, or manipulate visual languages without exploring power relationships and the conditions of production. In my experience, video and computerized editing technologies have not so much changed the modes of production in the arts as they have foregrounded the reorganization of visual cultures and complicated the processes of interaction. To initiate cross-cultural production means to acknowledge the precarious gender and race relations that need to be negotiated in the process of finding a structure for the mediation of different languages, experiences, and sensibilities. The image/sound technology itself, highly fluid and capable of infinite reprocessing and reconversion of recorded or generated signals, affords the producers an immediate experience of the constructibility of imagery and image relations, and of decision-making and selection processes. Participatory video production, therefore, is an organizational process that moves the creative operations across social relationships. As in performance, it rehearses interdependence.

The performative reinvention/production of identities of difference – from the minority perspective – is now the focus of progressive multicultural and postcolonial theory. In the Chicago festival, the Latina video program featured new work under the title *Identidades*, a reference to the compulsive identity politics that characterizes much contemporary work in North America. And when Homi Bhabha, in *The Location of Culture* (1994), speaks of 'border lives' as 'the art of the present,' he appeals to one of the most popular metaphors in current debates on border culture, decolonization, migration, and hybrid identities. He in fact echoes Gloria Anzaldúa's poetics of an existential border subjectivity, which she had described, in *Borderlands/La frontera* (1987), as the *nepantla* state of being – of being *dis-oriented* in space and in-between time-frames.[3] Anzaldúa's writings, of course, dramatize a 'coming out,' a mythopoeic and highly politicized exclamation against sexual and racial prohibition and oppression, which seeks to transform polarities and their built-in violence. Disorientation thus gains a new meaning; it performs a dissonant movement across imposed hierarchies.

It is in this sense that I understand the meaning of *border performance* as a material practice and lived experience, embodying a shared commitment to cultural production as a mode of intervention into specific local contexts or institutional sites. Addressing the confluences of cultures, the migration and crossing-over of ideas and images between different cultures that arise from specific historical experiences, such border art acts upon our understanding of territories and separations. Collaborative work rehearses dis-orientation: it evolves from encounters and experiences of diverse local infrastructures, common and dissimilar ground shared by people of different cultural backgrounds and border knowledges, and from the creative and expressive methods, practices, and perceptions exchanged.

The exchanges I present here are a series of conversations with artists in different locations: Chicago, Eisenhüttenstadt, Ljubljana, Sarajevo, and Havana. They took place during production workshops. The dissonant movement described in my itinerary, departing from Chicago, my intermittent home base, toward working in East Germany, Slovenia, and Cuba, in fact follows a simple course of action and interaction, based on performance projects and workshop encounters I have participated in since 1991. They have generated a growing network of communication between us. The conversations recorded here mostly happened spontaneously and were not planned as interviews but evolved from the urgency of our collaborations or the pressing need to reflect on the processes that had been set in motion and, simultaneously, were overshadowed by particular local crises and concerns. The contexts of these concerns differ, and the position from which Ademir Kenović speaks (war-torn Sarajevo) is even more precarious than the existential and economic crisis in Havana described by Teresa

Cárdenas, Felipe Oliva, Magaly Muguercia, and Víctor Varela. But their experiences help to throw into sharp relief the dramatic transitional crises of consciousness in Slovenia and East Germany, two regions that have enjoyed a brief and exhilarating moment of liberation and independence. In the aftermath, the struggle for reintegration, and for the survival or the invention of alternative/independent processes of art-making, has only just begun, and what may seem possible in Ljubljana is already threatened with collapse in Eisenhüttenstadt.

I will introduce our exchanges by addressing the relations between artists, alternative performance media, and the 'state,' using the comments made by Guillermo Gómez-Peña and Coco Fusco during our meeting in Chicago as a way of framing the 'myth' of the border or the margin, negotiating processes of redefinition (borderization), and repositioning 'independence' *vis-à-vis* residual, collapsing or emerging state power. In the late capitalist context of the US, the state has a much more marginal influence on the ongoing trans- and multiculturalization of the North, while in the former communist East the question of the survival or growth of a multinational, pluralist culture can no longer be asked without reference to neo-nationalism, the destruction of Sarajevo and dismemberment of Bosnia, the brutal campaign of 'ethnic cleansing' in Kosovo. The attack against a multiethnic state of Bosnia symbolizes the destruction of the very concepts of heterogeneity, multiple repertoires, and border crossings that are at stake in our exchanges here. Sarajevo, therefore, has become a shattered mirror for all our high-minded assumptions about civil society and postmodern syncretism.

1. FRONTERAS: FROM THE LOCAL TO THE TRANSLOCAL

Reality in Tijuana looks and feels like a cyberpunk film
directed by José Martí and Ted Turner on acid.
(Guillermo Gómez-Peña)

Chicago, January 1993

In their 1992–3 touring exhibition/performance *The Year of the White Bear/The New World (B)Order*, Guillermo Gómez-Peña and Coco Fusco created a savage anthropological fantasia of 'discovering' North America at a moment when the official culture celebrated Columbus. Gómez-Peña, born and raised in Mexico City, came to the USA in 1978. Since then, he has been working in performance, radio art, book art, bilingual poetry, journalism, and installation art. He was a founding member of the Taller de Arte Fronterizó Border Arts Workshop [TAF] and editor of an experimental arts magazine, *La Linea Quebrada*. Fusco is a Cuban-born, New York City-based writer, curator and media artist who has published widely and curated several touring media and visual arts exhibitions. For several years since 1989 she has worked collaboratively with Gómez-Peña, performing and touring throughout the US, Canada, and Europe. Her video *The Couple in the Cage: A Guatinaui Odyssey* was released in late 1993, and two years later she produced another video, *PochoNovela*, and started to perform with Chicano artist Nao Bustamante. When I met the performers in Chicago, they explained that they wanted to bring back the ghosts of colonial history and *exchange* the imperial gaze, looking at the North to explain/interpret Western ethnocentrism to itself.

BIRRINGER: Your work, and what I know from the history of the Border Arts Workshop, has been an inspiration for many of us, and what you're trying to do here in the community and in collaboration with several Chicago arts organizations needs to be understood in light of the earlier work at the border. Tell me more about the project and where you're moving in your work.

FUSCO: There are different components. *The Year of the White Bear* is an inter-disciplinary arts project that involves an exhibition, two performances, one of us in the cage as the 'undiscovered Amerindians,' which we're going to do at the Field Museum here and which we've already done at the Smithsonian (Washington), the Walker Sculpture Garden (Minneapolis), the Plaza de Colon (Madrid), and at Covent Garden (London). The other performance is a language-based multilingual performance we're going to do at Randolph Street Gallery. We've also produced an experimental radio piece *Radio Pirata/Colon Go Home* which is the soundtrack for the exhibit here, and it's also being broadcast on NPR [National Public Radio]. And the idea was to take apart the myths around this so-called discovery through all these different kinds of strategies. The exhibition combines popular cultural junk and material culture and pre-Columbian arti-facts and velvet paintings and other paintings that we commissioned for the show, and a multi-image installation. It's a mixed-media environment that deals with the history of the representation of the discovery, but also parodies the way a lot of European and American museums create these global culture shows. And we're doing a kind of parody on a small scale, complete with pseudo-ethnographic dioramas, simulated Mayan temples, and fake collectors' items. The whole thing.

BIRRINGER: And the choice of the museum [the Mexican Fine Arts Center is located in the Pilsen barrio]? You wanted it to be in the Mexican-American community?

FUSCO: Most of the work we do is highly specific. I think that perhaps one of the political powers of *performance*, defined as a social experiment, is precisely its possibility of working with context, and therefore developing these other layers of political meaning, so the work we do inside of museums very much comments on the history of representation of other cultures and notions of the primitive, otherness, etc. The work we do in the streets is very much meant to activate historically or politically sensitive *sites* and to establish historical connections between intercultural practices that have been formed, the European and North American mentality about the Other and contemporary political incidents. We're also very much interested, along the same lines of using performance as a social experiment, in just pushing the boundaries of performance and venturing into other territories: ethnography, social science, education, political activism, media.

We work a lot with the methodology of recyclement. We recycle images, texts, actions, vignettes, recycle and reformat them and recontextualize them into multiple mediums and so on. What you are going to be seeing, in many ways presented as a visual art exhibit, are also the archaeological residues of performance pieces, you know; so many of these pieces are in fact a kind of residue of an experimental archaeology and also of a performance journey that we have undertaken in these past two years across cities, countries, and sites that are charged with historical meaning.

You will also see that some of the symbols that exist in our visual art exhibit are symbols that we utilize in our site-specific performances or in our radio work. We're constantly looking for ways to reformat our ideas, for different strategies of communication, performance as social communication. I think that also another important aspect of our work is this whole notion that the 'West' tends to have a very historicist and aesthetic notion of the Other, and we are interested in unthawing the notions of the Other, picking the Other out of these historicist ice cubes and bringing the notion of the Other back into the present so we are no longer seen as passive historicist images existing outside of history, outside of society, outside of the present, outside of the borders of the US, but as contemporary citizens in this time and place. As people that can exercise their political will.

BIRRINGER: How long have you worked together? In the 1980s, in Tijuana, you were working alone and in collectives, Guillermo?

GÓMEZ-PEÑA: I think that the Chicano border artists and the Mexican border artists were working in a process of redefining US–Mexico relations, and were in many ways putting a kind of mirror right on the border line with its back to the South. Through our art we were shifting the notion of center and margins, and creating a space for the South becoming the speaking subject and the USA becoming the object of analysis, adoration, criticism, etc. While this was happening on the West Coast, a similar project was taking place on the East Coast by artists of color, and I think that Coco was very much part of this other parallel project in which she was performing a similar function in terms of analyzing critically the relationships between the USA and the Caribbean. And so while we were working with this other cultural axis, you know, the Mexico/Aztlán/California axis, she was working in this Caribbean East Coast axis, and at one point we started a kind of comparative dialogue. And out of this dialogue emerged *Norte/Sur*, the first project we did together in San Francisco, which was our attempt to start comparing notes between the East Coast/Caribbean experience and the West Coast Chicano experience.

Then the next step was to begin integrating organically our findings, our theories, our strategies, and so on. I think another reason why we both worked together was that we felt very strongly that the Latino community had to enter into a new stage, you know, and I just want to try to explain what I mean. In the 1960s, a lot of the work produced by Latinos in the USA intended to explain ourselves to ourselves, and then later on we entered into a different stage in which we were trying to explain the Other to ourselves, or the dominant culture to ourselves. Why are we *jodidos*, why are we fucked over, you know? Then we entered into a different stage in which we were trying to explain ourselves to others and that is pretty much what the whole multicultural movement was about, you know what I mean? Here we are, deal with us. Attempting to create a kind of epistemology through our art of who we are, you know?

In the past couple of years, and precisely because of the whole Columbus issue or counter-quincentennial efforts, we have entered into a new stage, which is that of explaining *the Other to the Other*, explaining the dominant culture to the dominant culture, you know. In other words, the philosophical premise of the work we've been doing is . . . it's a kind of historical, political, and cultural contingency. *Este*, what if the continent turned upside down, what if the North was the South, what if Spanish was English, what if pre-Columbian America had discovered Europe, you know? What if Mexican-Chicano-Latino art were the dominant discourse, so to speak? In other words, to place ourselves in a mythical center, to deconstruct the border that the US media paints as a war zone, to push the dominant culture to the margins, to anthropologize the North, so to speak, and this perhaps has been the philosophical premise behind most of our recent projects.

You will see it in the exhibit. We turn the colonizer into the colonized, and vice versa, so, for example, instead of an excavational site of indigenous people, you have an excavational site of tourists from Wisconsin. You see? Instead of showing the collection of a collector, we show the collector's room itself, the actual room of the collector, and so on, and also in the case of the cage piece the two undiscovered Amerindians, who are meant to be passive recipients of the northern gaze, suddenly become the observers. And we turn the gaze 360 degrees and become the anthropologists creating experimental anthropology from our fictional center. Am I being clear?

BIRRINGER: Yes. Let's review the history. The concept of 'border art' goes back to the Taller de Arte Fronterizo/Border Arts Workshop founded in 1985 by you and several other Latino artists. Emerging from within the Chicano cultural movement, it started out as a specific local and community-based practice of intervention, acting directly upon the Mexican–US border in the Tijuana–San Diego region. Grounded in the immediate world of the border as a politically charged site, the group work developed tactical, performance-derived theatrical actions staged directly on the border, as well as 'broadcasts' (telephone, fax, radio, mailworks) and, in 1989, the two-month *Border Axis* project which created a temporary 'internet' between twelve cities in the US, Mexico, and Canada. In your 1986 report, 'Border Culture: A Process of Negotiation Toward Utopia,' you began to describe your understanding of the border region as an 'intellectual laboratory' for experimentation, a new practice of cultural theory 'capable of understanding

our incredible circumstances,' and the building of an artistic and activist infrastructure through TAF. The early performances and radio works dealt with an
infinite number of contrasts and shocks on the Tijuana–San Diego border. In
contrast to conceptions of the border as the limits of two countries, TAF
envisioned a more unified border – the common ground shared by North America and Latin America, not a dividing line of threatening otherness. Politically,
the work needed to address the asymmetries in the North/South dialogue,
illuminating the difference between tourist and undocumented worker, the different implications of border-crossing for a person of color coming from the
South, and an Anglo-American coming from the North.

Now you suggest that the relations can be shifted and are shifting: the emerging border culture conveys a tendency toward the 'borderization' of the North
American hemisphere. The artistic challenge is to construct 'alternative realities'
through cross-collaboration and international dialogue. Your current translocal
work no longer resides, so to speak, on the literal border, yes?

GÓMEZ-PEÑA: I think that the strategies we use are completely syncretic. We
borrow from all kinds of traditions to create these composite strategies, because
precisely the kind of art that we want to make is a kind of cross-over art, not just
informed by one tradition and not only made for one community, but taking place in the interstices of more than one community and attempting to
describe more than one cultural reality. I think that in many ways we see each
other very much as children of multiple communities or citizens of multiple
communities.

Now, we are continuously redefining our strategies year after year. What
worked for a performance workshop three years ago is no longer viable. The case
of the Border Arts Workshop is a good one, it developed a very effective set of
ideas to broadcast our view of the border into the two countries. Our work
became so popular we were appearing in airline magazines, *People Magazine*, and
television shows that were being made about us, even Taco Bell wanted to do
series of food commercials using murals of border artists, and Macy's had a
border fashion shop, etc. So that's when you decide that it's time to shift your
strategies, and you are constantly rescuing your work from the hands of commodity culture. Sometimes we are successful. I think that one of the reasons why
artists nowadays have more possibilities to do that than, say, ten years ago is
because nowadays we have grown very smart about the notion of multicontextu-
ality. We know that before we only had two options, so to speak. We could be the
insiders or the outsiders, and now I think we know that we can be both. We can
be insiders and outsiders. Half of our body can be in and half of our body can be
out.

FUSCO: This is the problem that I had with a lot of the theorization of border
culture, with the inability that so many theorists have had to distinguish between
one kind of borrowing and another. The border is one element of the dynamic,
then there's the political dimension of the border that puts some people on the
disadvantaged side and other people on the advantaged side, and the fact of the

matter is that European and American culture would not exist now had it not absorbed, appropriated, and otherwise borrowed from non-Western cultures throughout its history of existence, starting with the Greeks. So to talk about it as something postmodern, a new recognition of the non-West, to me is totally absurd. What I find problematic are these strains of poststructuralist interpretation that choose to negate the difference between a Mexican artist in Tijuana who's putting Mickey Mouse in a painting and trying to talk about cultural politics using an American icon, and an American artist on the San Diego side who's paying Mexicans in Tijuana $2 an hour to paint his paintings of the Virgin de Guadalupe, or whatever he's doing. I mean I do think there are power differences that still exist which the proximity offered by border cultures is not going to eliminate altogether because we're not all equal, and not all forms of borrowing are exactly the same. I mean, that's often disappointing to people. There's all kinds of crazy theorizing going on right now, taking cross-dressing as a motif to an extreme that I think just denies certain political realities. As much as I'm interested in the concept of transvestism and understand how it's very much a part of our era, I also understand that there are still real women who live as women, and have a different kind of existence than a man who dresses like a woman, and also that the economic conditions that most transvestites live in are terrible. So that to champion it as this kind of model of liberation, it's like, well, liberation for who, really? What are we talking about? And I think that the same thing goes for the border.

GÓMEZ-PEÑA: But, for example, to put it in a very graphic way, I think the question of free trade comes to mind; it's inevitable at this point, it would be naive to oppose it, it's part of the future, of this part of the world, and theoretically it sounds right, theoretically it could benefit all sides. But still, we cannot help but to think out loud, given the endemic inequalities and the different negotiating powers that the treaty partners have, Mexico, Canada, and the US Can we think that the three are going to benefit equally? Think of the Statue of Liberty and the Virgin of Guadalupe, what is going to be their relationship? Is the Statue of Liberty going to devour the Virgin of Guadalupe, or are they just going to dance a *cumbia* together, you know what I mean? I think that precisely because of this lack of symmetry endemic to the relationship between North and South, English and Spanish, dominant culture and minority culture, Mexico and the US, the question of appropriation has a very different connotation.

FUSCO: And there's the classic fallacy of the avant-garde always to assume that because the change takes place at the level of the imaginary, that it somehow or other effects a political transformation at the same time, and I just do not agree with that, philosophically or theoretically or even in terms of my sense of social experience . . . I see there is always some kind of gap there.

GÓMEZ-PEÑA: There are different kinds of transvestism too, some are extremely liberating and other ones are bizarre. I am talking now about cultural transvestism, you know, we all are cultural transvestites in different degrees. I think that cultural transvestism is very much part of contemporary performance media; however, there are certain problematic forms. I think a lot of North American sympathizers with Latin American causes often think that by impersonating people from other cultures they can avoid the responsibility of accepting the historical implications.

FUSCO: A good friend of ours, Celeste Olalquiaga, has argued that American culture only has one way of assimilating otherness and that is through commodification and consumerism, and this tendency, which already existed before multiculturalism, laid a kind of framework for how multiculturalism could become a commodity. For a lot of people, crossing the border means going to eat Mexican food, you know? Or going to a show, it's these things that you can buy, objects that you can own, and thereby somehow or other assimilate the culture. I'm not so sure whether this commodification isn't just a kind of fetishistic process that enables them to disavow the existence of radical otherness in their midst, that it's this kind of protective mechanism of primary assimilation, and then a secondary one that's never really attained. And I think that that's where we are.

BIRRINGER: Transforming the North is a difficult task. You are relocating your practices, contesting in particular the myth that artists of color are only meant to speak for or from within their own 'ethnic communities.' On the contrary, in your travelling solo performances, pirate radio projects and collaborative productions you've donned the role of the *trickster* by promulgating a new international activism *ex centris*, acting as a cross-cultural 'diplomat,' 'nomadic chronicler' or 'coyote' (smuggler of ideas) promoting the so-called 'free art agreement' (*el tratado de libre cultura*) – your version of NAFTA – which focuses strongly on cross-contextual alliances. Is the trickster a transvestite, a parody of the diplomat?

FUSCO: I think it's a sign of the times that we would have to make a choice to work in a parodic form as opposed to a more direct form. There are kinds of social and aesthetic critiques that you can make using humor and irony at this particular time that you can't really get away with saying directly. We come out of, you know, five years of multicultural political wars and are both fatigued with being in this battleground all the time.

GÓMEZ-PEÑA: It's a political strategy, knowing how to subvert an established model, knowing the model, knowing the language of that model, taking it to an illogical extreme, then subverting it through humor.

FUSCO: But in the case of the cage performance I also think that part of the strength of it is in the live encounter. For me it was very important that we were doing a site-specific performance outside of the context of a theatre. There was something about being unannounced, not being presented as artists. Just being out there. It enabled us to enter into direct interaction with audiences about very sensitive issues. You can't do this in conventional settings or conventional media. People are very guarded and very defensive about their feelings about racism . . .

no one's going to show it to you unless you catch them off guard. So I'm very happy about that, having moved in that direction. We might present it in Germany next year.

GÓMEZ-PEÑA: We'll try to link it to the immigrant question.

BIRRINGER: The foreigners in a cage? That will be *unheimlich* to the Germans.

2. PERFORMING POSTCOLONIAL HISTORY

Inside the academy, the debates on postcolonial cultural studies, the diaspora, multiculturalism, identity politics, and on African, Asian, Latin/Latino, and black American perspectives on the production of culture, have grown increasingly visible. Several international journals, such as *Transition*, *Public Culture*, *New Formations*, *Social Text*, *Feminist Studies*, *Trans* or *Third Text*, have vigorously contributed to the debates by offering political and artistic challenges to First World perspectives while also dramatizing or questioning the role of 'public intellectuals' and their relations to various ill-defined public spheres. The struggle in the streets, in urban communities and labor markets, has been rather more messy than in the universities and museums, and recent anti-immigration legislation and the steady dismantling of the social welfare system under a democratic presidency don't bode well for the future of multicultural identity-creation. Black and Latino voices play a crucial role in the production of cultural discourses in the US context, and this is without doubt significant, since it has already been recognized by the current majority in the US Congress, and by the Republican Party's 'Contract with America,' whose ideological and legislative agenda recycles the 1950s Cold War paranoia about Unamerican Activities, except that its reactionary discourse about race and social difference is much broader and much more desperate in trying to define national values, as you can see in its xenophobic and discriminatory rhetoric, its anti-immigration, anti-welfare, anti-choice politics, its homophobia, and its fear of artists, writers, and NEA/NEH-funded projects that have been accused (during Congressional hearings) of corrupting mainstream American standards and of blaspheming the values of Western civilization.

If we find ourselves in opposition to this rhetoric, we will share an interest in performance, media, and popular culture, and in the politicization of art, as processes that allow us to experience and visualize the construction of our social identities. Institutions and circuits of knowledge (schools, museums, etc.), like the popular culture industry, reproduce our mythic arena, our theater of disciplines, popular desires and fantasies, 'where we discover and play with the identifications of ourselves, where we are imagined, where we are represented.'[1] This is the arena in which the borderlines are reconfigured, and the ideologies of inside/outside, of belonging and not-belonging, can be reconceptualized. Appreciating the historical and conceptual differences in the understanding of the term 'performance' or 'media', and without ignoring the painfully (necessarily?) elaborate 'negotiations' of difference described in Diana Taylor and Juan Villegas's prologue and epilogue to their new book (*Negotiating Performance: Gender, Sexuality, and Theatricality in Latin/o America*), I add the following brief observations about production, performance media, and self-representation of Cuban and Latino artists, in order to contextualize my conversation with Coco and Guillermo and the stakes claimed in their theatricalization of institutional and public space. These stakes also involve our understanding of public spheres and our existing or non-existing organic relationships to what we call 'local communities.'[2]

One of the terms I overheard in the academy was 'reverse ethnography,' coined by an Anglo postmodern anthropologist (James Clifford, *The Predicament of Culture*), quickly recycled by First World ethnographic fieldworkers who began to write about the 'repatriation' of anthropology as cultural critique of Western institutions (cf. George Marcus and Michael Fischer, *Anthropology as Cultural Critique*) and to practice 'self-ethnography,' almost as if to make themselves 'culturally visible' again, as Renato Rosaldo suggests in *Culture and Truth*. The self-ethnographers imitate the obsessive sado-masochism in some recent performance art while defending their positions of power against the growing impact of black nationalism and the reframing of cultural analysis by African, African-American (mediated by British Black Studies), East-Asian and Latino/Chicano discourses on conjunctural postcolonial experience between cultures and borders. When Homi Bhabha, Abdul JanMohamed, Manthia Diawara, Henry Giroux, and many others now speak of border crossings, double consciousness, and reversible techniques, they are also echoing a radical performance poetics that has been known in Chicano borderlands for years, especially since the site-specific interventions of the Taller de Arte Fronterizo/Border Arts Workshop and Gloria Anzaldúa's or Emily Hicks's writings.

If I understand Guillermo correctly, references to the border may now have kitsch value; they are part of the 'cannibal's system' of reverse colonization, as Celeste Olalquiaga would argue when she observes the vast Latin American immigration to US urban centers that has forced 'a redefinition of traditional cultural boundaries, one that both shapes and is shaped by the circulation of images.'[3]

La otra orilla

If you look at the images in the cannibal's system, however, they may strike you as having different resonances depending on how close they are to an existential or merely rhetorical knowledge of borders, blockades, censorships, and repressions. On the rhetorical side, one may find the debates in Canada about the imaginary Québécois 'border' and its relation to Anglophone Canada and the USA quite illuminating, as they imply anxieties about the desired nation-state and demarcations of difference that link the image-making for an imagined community to the postcolonial and anti-imperialist struggle in Latin America. But the stakes in countries such as Cuba, Nicaragua, Peru, or Guatemala are vastly different since the coherence of local and national consciousness is subjected both to internal oppression and outside pressures.

In recent Havana Biennials, film festivals, and theater meetings I noticed that these pressures are both acknowledged and obscured by the official curatorship of events. In private conversations, a fearful anxiety over the present conditions in Cuba, mixed with a stubborn pride in the paradoxes of the revolution, is readily communicated, but in the larger public art events I feel an overwhelming frustration at the limitations placed upon open cultural exchanges by official policies in Havana and in the US. These limitations severely curtail the vitally necessary dialogue between Cubans on the island, Cubans in exile, anti-Castro *fanáticos* and leftist *cubanólogos* in the USA. In her 'Miranda's Diary,' Coco has written extensively and heartbreakingly about the strained, damaged, broken yet never-ending real and imaginary dialogues between Cuban exiles and nationals, while Gerardo Mosquera and Luis Camnitzer have pointed out that the most vibrant generation of Cuban visual artists, emerging during the 1981 'Volumen I' exhibition, is now almost entirely in exile, scattered over the face of the earth. Younger Cuban artists remaining on the island have started to invent their own local and transnational references to the existential political experience of economic scarcity and a stonewalling insulation that imposes a paradoxical blockade of the imagination in the very time of global intercultural relations. Whether sarcastically or opportunistically, several local artists featured in the 1994 Biennial courted controversy and censorship by looking outward and adapting the themes of tourism, export, and Western patronage or media hype for their work. Such irony speaks to an incontrovertible reality during a period of miserable scarcity since the economic collapse in 1991, which is also a period of the Castro government's desperate negotiations with foreign investors from Europe, Mexico, and Canada. The painting series by Eduardo Ponjuán and René Francisco entitled *Dream, Art, and Market* gleefully conjures up their future success in foreign art markets, while the prints by Abel Barroso depict dollar bills raining from the sky as a young prostitute awaits her tourist customers (titled *Carpeta de grabados para resistir y vencer*). With devastating irony, Barroso's prints comment not only on the prostitution of revolutionary independence to the highest bidder, but also on the local 'hustling for dollars,' as Coco describes it in her uncompromising feminist critique of the newly emerging (self-)exploitation of women *jineteras* in the sex tourism that is reintroduced through visits of foreign capitalists, tempting young women and men to ease some of their hardship and to gain access to leisure and pleasure affordable in dollars.

Even more fantastic are the narrative pieces by Fernando Rodríguez -ten painted wood reliefs with varying titles – which show a couple (Fidel Castro and the Virgin of Charity, Cuba's patron saint) getting married and going off on a pleasurable shopping spree in the Crafts Palace. Unthinkably, the latter piece, *Comprando artesania*, was actually hung in the Crafts Palace itself. The images of the impending conversion of the national economy are shadowed by the even more persistent motif of the *balsas*, the floating rafts or boats that have carried so many Cubans away from the island toward *La otra orilla*, as a special theme exhibition at the 1994 Biennial was unexpectedly called. The concept behind 'The Other Shore' was to invite foreign artists to address in their work the impact of migrations and the diaspora on cultural transformation. US Cuban artists from the other shore were not invited, yet several local artists, including Tania Bruguera, Sandra Ramos, Rolando Rojas, Ricardo Brey, and Kcho, created lyrical and surreal works that captured fantasies of emigration or dramatized the lament over the dead *balseros* who never made it to the other side and who were declared *gusanos* or traitors to the Revolution.

In Marianela Boán's choreography for *Antigona*, danced by her group Danza Abierta, the law of the state is an empty, dark stage on which patriarchal author- ity and the political morality of the Revolution no longer appear. Antigona is alone with her naked, dead brother. Boán calls her dance work 'contaminated,' referring to the very real limits and obstacles that are imposed upon her creativ- ity. Even though she speaks about the disastrous economic conditions in Cuba, and the complete sense of isolation and uncertainty she experiences under these conditions of scarcity, her dance quietly improvises with the dancing bodies' obdurate strength of survival and ethical self-assurance. In her solo *Fast Food*, she also displays the kind of grotesque humor and morbid irony that you will find among artists in Sarajevo who experienced a similar sense of isolation in their city under siege. Images from the other side of the border don't travel very well, in this case, since they are too closely and authentically connected to the brute facts of survival. When Boán and her group was granted a visa to travel to the International Theater Festival at Hamburg's Kampnagel Factory in 1994, her performances were reviewed in the German press as suffering from a lack of sophistication and formal brilliance.

However, we need to recognize that Boán and other contemporary visual artists in Cuba are very self-confidently producing 'contaminated art' in the sense that they understand their work as closely linked to their contextual reality, the political mechanisms of overdetermination, and to direct social response as well as to a 'new' eclecticism that self-consciously draws on Cuba's racial and cultural hybridity and its very old habits of assimilating cultural practices and images. This 'contamination,' positively expressed, has always existed. Cuban critic and writer Antonio Benítez-Rojo, who now lives on the other shore, has spoken of 'The Repeating Island' and speculated on the Caribbean generative syncretisms, in all their apparent 'disorder', in terms of chaos-theory. In the present post- colonial moment, Cuba's artists are aware of the precarious (im)balance they inhabit between existential, personal dilemmas they willingly depict in searing and critical ways (including a range of satirical dimensions such as in Tonel's ambivalent installations that mock the US blockade and the Cuban self- blockade), and the attractiveness that their art now holds, willingly or unwill- ingly, for the global capitalist circuit and the art-tourists/collectors who come to Havana during the Biennial. In previous years, the Biennials were staged as fiercely independent laboratories of Latin American and peripheral art resisting the hegemonic First World art market. Paradoxically, it is in spite of, or because of, the blockade that the Havana Biennial has now reached the point of entry into an unavoidable globalization and delocalization of art: any transcultural reformulation of visual thinking will irreversibly process the migrations, passages, and interchanges of image ideas. A whole generation of Cuban artists has already lived abroad and revisited the island, and Ponjuán and Francisco's ironic *Sueño, Arte y Mercado* performs a cruel joke both on the economic realities of dependence and on the predictability of the market's interest in 'ethnic' or 'exotic' Latin art (in art that is yet more affordable?). The irony here, of course, lies in the simple fact that many Latin American artworks 'identify' themselves through their complex and sophisticated postmodern collage techniques and transcultural/pop-cultural quotations, as in the case of Pedro Alvarez's triptych *El fin de la historia* for the Biennial, which incorporates the newly arrived 'United Colors of Benetton' billboards (near the Havana airport) into his paintings of urban landscapes. Columbian artist Nadin Ospina, who exhibited in the section *Apropriaciones y entrecruzamientos*, had built identical-looking ceramic and stone versions of little toy figures (most notably the Simpson family), arranged as if the US pop-culture icons were in fact descendants of pre-Columbian mass-production. He refered to this astonishing 'repatriation' as his 'neo-pre-Columbian' series, entitling it *Los criticos del High Tech*.

Figure 19 The Year of the White Bear. Guillermo Gómez-Peña and Coco Fusco. Field Museum, Chicago. 1993. Photo courtesy of Encarnación Teruel.

reconverting history

Guillermo and Coco's *The Year of the White Bear/The New World (B)Order*
creates a similarly savage 'post-Columbian' fantasy during the postcolonial
moment of the Columbus Quincentenary celebrations in the USA. The perverse,
politically incorrect remembering of colonial history by official culture was of
course greeted by protests from the Latino community activists, and Guillermo
suggests that such blind monumentalizing of history flies in the face of a quotid-
ian reality in the US borderlands which 'looks and feels like a cyberpunk film
directed by José Martí and Ted Turner on acid.' The same ironic and humorous
punk-high-tech attitude runs through Guillermo and Coco's ghosting of the
'discovery' in their exhibitions and performances that, like vampires from the
mythic past, exchange looks with the imperial gaze, sucking blood from the neck
of the North and explaining/interpreting Western ethnocentrism to itself.

The *White Bear* project was turned into an elaborate participatory community
event involving a range of local minority arts organizations and volunteer workers, and also including a local radio production workshop in which I participated. In the Mexican Fine Arts Center Museum they constructed a fictionalized
collection of artifacts mimicking Western scientific display of the 'exotic,' except
that all the artifacts were either inauthentic or mass-cultural hybrids and
'reconversions' (e.g. Mexican 'socialist-realist' velvet paintings of Madonna or
kitsch murals or Mickey Mouse sculptures). During their site-specific installation
at the Museum of Natural History, Guillermo and Coco exhibited themselves as
'Two Undiscovered Amerindians' on display in a gold cage, performing 'aboriginal' postmodern everyday life-styles, complete with body-building, laptop
computer and video equipment, surrounded by confused and wide-eyed
museum visitors who had arrived unawares. Many of them thought the couple
was 'real' and behaved as if the exhibition of aboriginal peoples in cages was not
inappropriate in a Museum of Natural History. Many did think it was
inappropriate to 'abuse' their faith in the authority of the museum.[4]

The New World (B)Order was performed some weeks later as a live radio show
in an alternative gallery (Randolph Street), introducing a futurist parody of free
trade agreements in a transcontinental America turned upside-down conceptually, where whites were a minority migrating around and across various syncretic
postnational cultures, looking for work. Using the vibrantly irreverent, sarcastic
humor of *rasquachismo*, Guillermo wore grotesque wrestling masks, wigs, uni-
forms, and kitsch paraphernalia while haranguing his audience in various
double-speaks (Spanish, English, Nahuatl, French, and their hybrid versions),
playing with conventional stereotypes, and inventing bizarrely intertwined cultural bastardizations in several mediums. Coco, her face painted green, spoke in
the controlled voice of a TV anchor woman, while in front of the audience,
centre-stage, hung a dead chicken, upside-down – a complex and disturbing
metaphor of the *pollo*.

No nation, community or individual can claim racial, sexual or aesthetic
purity. In the new society of Gringostroika, the great fiction of a

state-sponsored order has evaporated. We are held together by imaginary networks. The new transcontinental youths are global culture cyborgs. Their objective is to avoid Reality # 1, a euphemism for what used to be called 'social reality.' Entranced by their virtual reality games, they have gained experiential immunity.

The performance turns into an increasingly surreal prophecy, evoking the dystopian Reality #2 of an official global transculture that cuts close to the bone of our contemporary interracial warfares, economic crises, ecological disasters, and hypertechnological support systems. The kids are watching the virtual reality TV marketed by this transculture, and are likely subscribers to *Mondo 2000* and *Future Sex*. Guillermo's and Coco's relentless conceptual mapping of future-past cultural topographies is dangerously ambivalent, since it allows us to enjoy a horrific vision of our social agency in which we are joined in fear. But not all of us are crossing borders from the same sides of fear, nor do 'we' enjoy the same experiential immunity. Who is this 'we' that is held together by imaginary networks, and how different are the projections of our imaginary territories, lands, nationhoods, citizenships, cultures?

At the same time, Guillermo suggests that the relations can be shifted and are shifting: the emerging border culture conveys a tendency toward the 'borderization' of the North American hemisphere. The artistic challenge, he believes, is to construct 'alternative realities' through cross-collaboration and international dialogue. In fact, the *Border Axis* project, which took place one step removed from the border in northern California (Capp Street Project, San Francisco), already points into the direction of Guillermo's current translocal work that no longer resides, so to speak, on the literal border. The initial Taller de Arte Fronterizo group broke up in 1989 and later reconstituted itself with new members. In 1993, a mixed-media exhibition, *La frontera/The Border*, was co-curated by the Museum of Contemporary Art (San Diego) and the Centro Cultural de la Raza (Tijuana) and dedicated to the border arts movement. The curators, in fact, admit that there had been major controversies over the gradual appropriation and cooptation of 'border art' by the mainstream Anglo art world. Guillermo, for example, refused to participate in this institutional project, which is partly a paradoxical maneuver on his part, since he has accepted sponsorship from other major Western institutions in the USA and Europe. And yet, questions of control and participation are vital if alternative 'border performances' are to avoid being subsumed and managed within the safe parameters of the art world.

Guillermo's response was to relocate his collaborative media practices and his outreach, contesting in particular the myth that artists of color are only meant to speak for or from within their own 'ethnic communities.' On the contrary, in his travelling solo performances, pirate radio projects, and collaborative productions he has donned the role of the trickster by promulgating a new international activism *ex centris*, acting as a cross-cultural 'diplomat,' 'nomadic chronicler,' or 'coyote' (smuggler of ideas) promoting the so-called 'free art agreement' (*el tratado de libre cultura*) – his version of NAFTA – which focuses strongly on

Figure 20 The New World (B)Order. Guillermo Gómez-Peña and Coco Fusco. Randolph Street Gallery, Chicago, 1993. Photo courtesy of Peter Taub.

cross-contextual alliances and inter-community projects. More recently he has performed in *The Shame-Man, El Mexi-Cant & El Cyber-Vato Come to Chicago in Search of their Lost Selves (or The Identity Tour)*, together with James Luna and Roberto Sifuentes, in *Borderama* and *The Temple of Confession* (with Sifuentes), and in *Mexarcane International: Ethnic Talent for Export* (with Coco Fusco). The *Mexarcane International* performance-installation takes the cage piece one step further, playing quite directly into the commercial public space (Dufferin Mall, Toronto) of an ongoing commodification of postcolonial 'exotica.' Coco's consumer-interviews, conducted as (a parody of) market research into specific consumer desires for exotic entertainment (provided by Guillermo), conflate the shopping centre with the 'advertisement' of ethnicity as human service provider, pushing the ironies to their extreme edge.

'We are held together by imaginary networks . . .'? In light of the international range of performance opportunities and interventions these artists have been able to afford, it remains vital to understand the principle of 'conversion' that is applied in such unaffiliated performance art that draws on local knowledge and the concrete experience of the North–South border while at the same time reapplying street-wise Chicano sensibilities and creativities mixed with avant-garde, experimental strategies to Euro-American high culture and corporate settings. This interplay or borderization deals with localized problems by returning, in a manner of 'free trade,' a performed action about a social or political issue to different cross-national contexts. Such trading implies, as a matter of fact, the knowledge that local affairs (e.g. California's Proposition 187) have international ramifications and that, in turn, global economic and ecological processes, human rights, women's and gay/lesbian emancipation, racial relations and cultural dislocations, cannot be grasped at their level of global interdependence without awareness of local political organization. I conclude by drawing attention to a local concern of building real networks and meeting grounds in a daily struggle linking schools, families, workplaces, leisure time, neighborhoods and streets in the culture of the barrio. For most of the Latino youth in Chicago's barrios, Guillermo's and Coco's international trickster diplomacy may not be an option, but that doesn't mean the young activists are not equally sensitive to and knowledgeable of the needs to construct viable communal identities that also address the demand for cultural and national citizenship.

I know several community-based projects being created in Chicago that are committed to rebuilding the fragmented social fabric on a grass-roots level, and in doing so they raise the very question of what constitutes 'community' or collaboration in multicultural neighborhoods or in a Latino barrio such as Pilsen, for example, where the Mexican Fine Arts Center Museum may be centrally located but not perceived to be a cultural center for the working-class residents or youth. There are independent groups of artists and cultural workers, however; for example, 'Ojos del Pueblo' (Pilsen), 'Inside Art' (Rogers Park), 'Around the Coyote' (Wicker Park), Beacon Street Theatre or Teen Street Theatre, whose creative activities are all neighborhood-based and instrumental in linking expressive culture (arts, crafts, music, media, communications) with social services and education (especially for children and young people in the barrios). With its emphasis on *human services* and on organic processes of art-making, self-realization, and practical self-organization, such work connects urban youth culture with issues of health, employment, and education, with the concerns of the elderly, the handicapped, and the poor. And in fostering teamwork and the spirit of cross-cultural cooperation, the actions of these groups help to create the very sense of community identity they need in order to survive and develop resistances to systems of domination based on class, race, or ethnicity including the heterosexual matrix within which differences are generally represented.

On 1 January 1995, I took part in a solidarity performance by 'Ojos del Pueblo' – an evening of food-sharing, music, poetry, dance, agit-prop, and discussion dedicated to the anniversary of the 1994 uprising of the Chiapas movement in South Mexico. In creating this solidarity event, staged in a converted space of an empty building in the middle of their neighborhood, the young Latino high-school students/artists linked the highly visible 'Zapatista' mural they had painted on one of the street walls to the poetry and music they wrote for an emotional evening of sharing their independent voices with the other *pueblo*, the independence movement of Chiapas. There were a number of posters, signs, and photos drawing attention to the Frente Zapatista and their particular demands articulated from a specific regional, ethnic base, yet I was not surprised to see posters that also called for opposition to the Californian Proposition 187 and the increasingly undemocratic, racist discrimination of Mexican migrant workers. The connections between the Chiapas uprising, the labor relations and anti-immigration policies in California, and the struggle for self-expression among Chicano youth in Chicago were emphasized throughout the evening.

The most important aspect of the event, attended by more than 250 young and old people, was the process of preparing it and making it happen, of taking the initiative to clean up a decaying house and create a temporary 'center' in which they could communicate their own struggle and its relationship to the larger political or global powers of domination. Most of these youth, when they listen to their own punk-rock bands, will not need a postcolonial theory of reverse ethnography, yet their process of self-management in the creation of their own space may already be a historical process on which your and my reflections could be based. Such reflections would not necessarily shift away from the representational strategies of theater or performance/art, but they would place less emphasis on the organization of meaning in artworks as such and, rather, seek to learn from *community organizing* just how contaminated the dance of resistance already is. It means learning to link the local minority experience (based on migration and marginalization, racial discrimination and socioeconomic disadvantage) to contemporary neo-(post-)colonial situations in other (real and imaginary) homelands, such as to the duplicitous role that political and military authorities in Mexico played in negotiating/denying justice to the indigenous peoples who have created the very culture that is officially sold to world-wide consumption (cf. the *Mexico: Splendor of Thirty Centuries* exhibition that traveled to the Metropolitan Museum of Art in New York).

If the performance figure of the trickster can be applied to this experience of the micro-borderlands of our cities, it will have to engage multiple differences and identities in the political process of building *space for coalition*. I agree with Guillermo Gómez-Peña that cross-collaboration (on the local level) and international dialogue are absolutely vital steps toward a broadly based movement for justice, based on an understanding that borders are generally ignored by those (i.e. transnational corporations) who can afford to do so to their own advantage founded upon neo-colonial exploitation of alienated local or migrant workforces in the urban and off-shore *maquiladoras*.[5] In order to be able to build an alternative reality, or to resist the self-prostitution implied by familiar ideological mechanisms of *sueño, arte y mercado*, the trickster cannot of course rely on ironic quotations and appropriations alone; s/he also needs to work through the costs of hybridity and ex-centricity because they reproduce marginalization. Many of us will be paying the costs of the New World Order, and most cannot easily choose, alter, or abandon expressive identities when the terms of obtaining or maintaining citizenship rights are themselves under pressure. Our mutual identifications, with each other and with the cause of justice and the rights to free expression and citizenship, will depend to a large extent on our desire to negotiate with the ever-evolving boundaries of ethnicity and nationality, and to insist on the democratic articulation of coexisting differences. In the following section, I will continue to explore the complex demands of non-confrontational coexistence in times like ours when cultural and national identifications cannot even rely on a shared language, and when 'citizenship' may indeed move toward local and regional levels, heightening the challenge of self-management and local responsibility that I observed in the example of Ojos del Pueblo.

3. GRENZLAND

jegliches hat seine Zeit

jegliches hat seine Zeit

jegliches hat seine Zeit

jegliches hat seine Zeit

Anderland ist verloren gegangen

(*Ewige Seelen–Ewiges Land*, 1994)

Figure 21 Ewige Seelen Ewiges Land. Grenzland Ensemble. Choreographed by Imma Sarries-Zgonc. Eisenhüttenstadt, 1994.

Eisenhüttenstadt, August 1993–March 1994

Near the German–Polish border, an industrial town awaits its future. Eisen-hüttenstadt, one of the model workers' cities designed by the German Democratic Republic's Communist Party central planners, has been looking for an investor to take over EKO STAHL, the local steel plant – and main employer – that was largely shut down after the revolution in 1989. Built in the 1950s but never fully completed to process steel through all the production cycles, the steel mill in Eisenhüttenstadt (the name means 'Ironworks City' in German) had been a symbol of all the hopes for communist East Germany's industrial growth, and it gradually became one of the largest industries (together with brown coal and chemical plants) exporting and trading successfully in the Eastern bloc markets. When the plant and the surrounding city were built in 1953, their design had futurist dimensions, almost as if a new socialist-industrial culture could be created *ex nihilo*. Architecturally, the plant is the center of life; its immense production facilities stretch along the Oder river (the border), and all the streets, like arteries, lead to them, especially the main Lenin Allee that links the factory to the City Hall. Initially, the city was named Stalinstadt, and early propaganda pamphlets refer to it as the place where 'the future bids you good morning.' Residential housing for the workers projects a collectivist dream based on a social realism that had in fact elevated classical architecture as the true form of its social ideal. Identical high-rise buildings, rising like proletarian palaces with neo-classical columns in the front and spacious children's playgrounds in the inner courtyards, form a web of symmetrical order. The predominant color in the city is a slightly faded gray, and many of the buildings now look dilapidated. The popular ballroom-pub 'Der Aktivist' is boarded up and looks like a ruin from a forgotten time. The streets are eerily quiet in the evenings. On the corner of Karl-Marx Allee there is a brand new ARAL gas station, where you can now buy West German beer and American pop music. By 1992, most of the old street names honoring Marxism-Leninism have been changed into more innocent ones, sometimes with minimal effort (Lenin Allee now is Linden Allee).

Dana's father, Harald Selle, is a retired electrician and one of the three local amateur dance teachers. Together with Hanna Dreessen and Dieter Jahnke, he teaches dance-gymnastics, beginner-level ballet, folk and a little jazz dance to young children in primary school, while his colleagues direct the older high-school students who participate in two local amateur dance groups, 'Oderland-reigen' and 'Fire & Flame.' After I had returned to Eisenhüttenstadt in the summer of 1993 to continue working on my documentary film about Germany's internal and external borders, Dana introduced me to her father who then helped me to get permission to film inside the steel plant.

To my surprise, the local Cultural Center had formed a project-group named after my documentary, *Border-Land*, and was planning an international theatre/dance festival in 1994 to draw attention to Eisenhüttenstadt's location on the border. According to the plans that were developed and debated over many months, the festival was to bring together amateur dance groups from the Oder region, from Poland and Hungary, and from sister cities in France and West Germany. Dana had joined the 'Border-Land' project and was rehearsing with Imma Sarries-Zgonc, a Catalan choreographer/dancer and collaborator in my cross-cultural ensemble in Chicago. Earlier in 1993, we had created a new sur-realist performance/film (*AlienNation*) which explores the tragicomedy of the German unification. With some trepidation, the festival had invited us to bring the piece to Eisenhüttenstadt and to develop some interactive workshops.

'You need to see the plant from the inside,' Dana suggests. 'All our parents used to work there. Perhaps it will be a museum one day.' She laughs, but it is not a happy laughter, and her father's expression betrays the sense of bitter resigna-tion that weighs down many of the workers here. The revolutionary moments of 1989, and the social movements that carried the protests and demonstrations up to the night of the opening of the Wall, seem forgotten or evoke bitter and embarrassed memories. Harald offers to show me around the plant, where he worked from 1968 to 1990, the year he was laid off. 'At least I can continue to work in my hobby,' he tells me without any sign of pride or relief. For twenty years he had been teaching dance to children, pointing out that the collectivist, state-owned steel plant had organized all the cultural and leisure activities in town. 'Since 1954 we've had workers' ensembles in amateur dance and theatre, in cabaret, film, and popular music, and the plant also supported all the sports clubs. Some of them are dissolved now, others try to continue independently.'

We are driving through the plant, and Harald shows me the gymnastics and dance studios, which are located to the side of the huge steel mill. 'The central planners made a mistake, though; they never completed the hot-rolling mill, the crucial intermediary stage between making steel slabs and cold-rolling the finished product. So we always had to send the slabs to Russia before finishing the final stages of production here. By the time we were ready to build our own, in 1985, we had run out of hard currency to buy the parts. Another costly problem is transportation; the Oder river is not navigable for heavy boatloads of steel, coal or ore, and the bridge connecting us to Poland was destroyed in the last war.'

The nearest crossing to Poland is in Frankfurt an der Oder, where a major East–West highway connects Berlin to Warsaw, and further to Belarus and the Ukraine. The border-crossing is so heavily used that sometimes trucks are backed up for many miles on the German side. Border guards all along the river watch out for illegal immigrants and seek to stop the flow of refugees that has poured into Germany over the past few years. The bridge that crosses the river has become the heavily guarded eye of a needle. It also serves as the logo for the newly founded Europa University which is located directly on the banks of the river. The logo shows a bridge that is still under construction and almost connects the two sides. During the foundational ceremonies in 1991, the president of the state of Brandenburg announced that the university would contribute to the future realization of European integration and economic and cultural progress, and thus to the removal of borders. His euphemisms proved to be just that. The borders are heavily guarded despite the ongoing negotiations about the Maastricht Treaty and the European Community.

The irony of the official cultural politics does not escape the workers in Eisenhüttenstadt. While the university has launched its first two cross-cultural Schools of Economics and Law (with a predominantly West German, British, and American faculty, and only a few Polish scholars), economic and cultural progress has been brought to a near standstill in the steel town. After Germany's rapid unification in 1990, the re-elected West German government set up the Treuhand agency to overhaul and sell off East Germany's mostly state-owned economy, restructuring and privatizing more than 10,000 enterprises, liquidating thousands of companies and closing plants. EKO STAHL was considered a hopeless case, making poor-quality products and huge losses at a time when Europe was already producing too much steel.

'They kept 2,000 of the original 13,000 jobs, and then proceeded to tell us they were actually trying to save the plant and find a new private investor, paying large subsidies to EKO to cover operating losses,' Harald explains as we walk through the cold-rolling facility among mountains of steel slabs. Those workers who kept their jobs have been anxiously waiting for this investor, and after several years of abortive or collapsed deals, after more unkept promises, they have grown cynical. 'They slashed the workforce to less than one-sixth of its former size; the compulsory retirement age was cut to fifty-four, and our city will become dysfunctional if the plant has no future. We all have emotional ties to it, and what are we to do with the new shopping malls and car dealerships if we have no jobs or can't support our schools, hospitals, and cultural programs?'

When Dana introduced me to the other young dancers, we didn't talk much in the beginning but started to work physically together. We danced. Later on, Imma Sarries-Zgonc sketched out the concept of bringing the dancers from the two separate groups together and developing a professional working method (modern dance and Tanztheater) toward the creation of a new work for the festival. She invited them to participate in a creative process that would be as much about them as it would be about exploring new performance possibilities and collaborative working methods.

I spoke with Dana and the other dancers at several occasions during the following year, and I also offered to make a music-video for one of the young local punk bands, Projekt Vier. The young people know each other from school; they rehearse in different places, the dancers on the factory site, the band in a small cellar room in the Cultural Center, where they were allowed to keep their music equipment and play after having been kicked out of three previous locations. This is their fourth attempt, explaining the choice of the band's name. They tell me that there are very few places for youth culture; they are under age for the bars and the new commercial disco, 'East Side.' The Cultural Center itself caters more for children (musical education, arts and crafts workshops, puppet theater, etc.) and adults (exhibitions, occasional readings and lectures, etc.). The local Stadttheater was closed in 1990; it now functions as a movie house showing second-rate commercial films or musicals. If they go to a rock concert in Frankfurt, they have to watch out not to get entangled in the drug scene or in fights with the neo-Nazi skin-heads. Attila Rhenau, the sixteen-year-old band leader and song writer, is eager to talk about the problems he sees, while Dana, who has recently turned eighteen, seems overwhelmed by uncertainty. But she is also proud of the work that was created for the festival. The premiere had become a watershed moment in her life.

DANA SELLE: First we didn't know what to think of the whole idea, it was like a culture shock, to work every day for weeks, to write notes about our theme, 'the border,' to bring personal memories to rehearsal, to develop them into our own stories that could be danced. We had never worked this way, and we also weren't used to work with the dancers from the other group. Both groups had their own repertoire of folk dances and short 'modern' pieces which we repeated year after year. We had never worked with anybody except our teachers. It was scary.

RHENAU: We started out in 1992, as a school band, but we wanted to do our own thing and tried to find spaces outside the school. It's really hard to work here in Eisenhüttenstadt, most people look at us with suspicion, and so we get kicked out. We don't have a place to perform, but we don't want to hang out on the streets like so many of the young people here. Our lead guitar player, Peter, got beaten up a lot by the skins, because he doesn't believe in their Nazi slogans and their violent attitudes.

BIRRINGER: Violent toward what?

RHENAU: Just violent. They would attack foreigners, but also us, and the trouble is we all know them, we used to go to the same places. But I don't believe it makes sense to shout nationalist phrases and so on, and then destroy your own state.

BIRRINGER: What do you mean by 'destroying your own state'?

RHENAU: Their actions create a bad impression of Germany, it doesn't help us in our situation here. This town, for example, is growing more and more desolate. It's really *öde*, completely *öde* ['barren,' 'desolate']. Sometimes I feel I live in a ghost town, like those towns where they shoot American westerns. But I am writing songs against this feeling of desolation. One is called 'Hey, what's wrong?', it's in English, and it deals with our destruction of the environment and the new materialistic greed.

SELLE: Something has gone wrong in the past few years. We never had time to learn about the new Germany, all the new values and mechanisms of the free market. They have transformed everything, we were never asked, but we had to reconstruct our daily lives and deal with the fact that the Wessis [new slang word for West Germans] managed the whole restructuring process, and everything here began to look really bad, antiquated. We felt like second-class, like the poor cousins from the countryside. And now, with all the troubles at EKO, we have 28 per cent unemployment here. What can you do when you are unemployed? How much energy do you have to be creative?

BIRRINGER: I noticed the high unemployment, the general depression, and a growing sense of resentment that occupies the minds of many citizens here in the East who a few years ago rushed to vote for the quick reunification of the two Germanies. After having seen your performance at the festival, *Ewige Seelen – Ewiges Land*, I am profoundly impressed by your willingness to explore the emotional cost of a memory that has to be suppressed or revised now, under the new conditions. Your performance was not about the current aggressivity, or xenophobia, or nostalgia about the old socialist days, or the growing intensity of resentment between East and West Germans, but rather about a very ambiguous experience of loss. While you show a certain loss of national identity, you also emphasize the time it takes to acknowledge that the former socialist experience of solidarity was perhaps an illusion, yes?

SELLE: I can't explain it very well in words. In our dance we tried to show images

of certain rituals, or habits and qualities, which were positive, which gave security. We could feel safe because the state took care of everything, work, wages,
education, health care, leisure activities, and so on. The whole range of collectivist achievements, the simplified life, including the restrictions, we were used to it,
and there was no lack of freedom, except perhaps as far as traveling to the West
was concerned. Well, so we traveled to the East. Now all this is changed, and we
need to learn the new values of free market society, of mass culture. We can
travel, whatever. Everybody here feels that solidarity has been evacuated, people
must compete to survive. You have to look after yourself, the state only tells you
lies, and in our city many bureaucrats from the former Communist Party are still
in power, again. They haven't changed actually.

RHENAU: Among our friends in the punk scene, we are also against the state,
because people feel there's no future here, our town has been written off. I'm
writing a series of love songs that deal with this problem, how to love someone in
this chaos.

SELLE: Something continues, however, and in our dance we tried to repeat these
scenes of aggression, violence, shame, and impotence. These feelings existed in
the former country, and much of the solidarity was enforced, and led to some
very warped perceptions of who we were. I think I am learning to see the
problem of how to express this individually, how to come to terms with my own
fears and desires. I don't know yet what I will do, but I want to continue to
dance, to learn more about international dance ideas, about how others work and
express their feelings.

BIRRINGER: The 'border' in your performance seemed to be a psychic one, and
you say that individual creativity or a critical spirit were not encouraged. How do
you relate to the actual border, say, with Poland?

SELLE: I don't know much about Poland. Officially we were brother countries
under socialism, and in school we learnt Russian. But people here despise the
Poles, we have little contact, and now we have enough problems with the
refugees and immigrants that roam the city.

BIRRINGER: But the refugees are kept behind security fences in the asylum.

SELLE: Yes, but we ourselves feel like strangers in this new capitalist country, and
when you see the aggression of the neo-Nazis, I think it unfortunately expresses
their sense of frustration or even despair in a future that holds few promises for
us. Most of my girlfriends are leaving our town, looking for jobs in the West.
Some want to emigrate, to England, or France.

RHENAU: Many of the guys in the band want to go to the army or air force, when
we are eighteen. That's the only safe job, and you can train there. I want to be a
pilot; our bass player wants to study industrial design, all of us will leave this town.

BIRRINGER: Let's return to the question of the 'foreigners.' In the last three years,
we have witnessed hundreds, even thousands of racist, xenophobic, and

anti-semitic attacks in this country. In 1992–3 we saw the ugly racist violence in Hoyerswerda and Rostock, and I was actually in Eisenhüttenstadt when the asylum here was fire-bombed last year. It angered me a lot because I had spoken with a whole group of Bulgarian and Rumanian immigrants at the asylum, one afternoon; I saw their children play. They told me that *they* were afraid of walking into town, and they were scared of being deported home. Many of them belong to ethnic minorities persecuted in their own homelands. They've come to a democratic country to be fire-bombed? Why is there no solidarity? On the other hand, I should mention that I saw the 1992 exhibition of Jewish art and the Israeli orchestra in Frankfurt (the first event of its kind since the 1920s), and attended the German-Polish Music Summerfest organized by two radio stations on either side of the border, and the international public forums *Nachdenken über Europa* ['Reflecting on Europe'] at the Frankfurt concert hall. These are specific cultural efforts to bridge the walls of resentment; have you been involved in such projects?

RHENAU: Yes, we talk about these issues, at the one club for young people that exists here, Club Marchwitza, and this is where the left punk scene meets, and we have guest bands from abroad. The skinheads come to the concerts too. But the neighbors complain about the noise, and the city wants to close it.

BIRRINGER: The left punks? What is 'left'?

RHENAU: I can't explain that. You can tell from the way people dress and behave. It's clear in Germany.

BIRRINGER: I didn't think it was. The Social Democratic Party supported the new asylum legislation which dismantled the former liberal law.

RHENAU: Perhaps it has to do with the fact that our friendly relations to Poland or Russia were ordered by the state. We dreaded these official orders, I never understood them. But I understand that people here, without jobs, are angry and worried about social services being cut, and about being, well, relegated.

SELLE: I think all of these questions came up in our rehearsals with Imma. The idea of a border culture or multiculturalism was new to us, we didn't know what a united Europe could mean. When the Polish or Hungarian dance groups come to our festivals, we don't really interact with them; the dancers from Zielona Gora present folklore, and I don't think you can exchange ideas with folklore. In the socialist era we were not encouraged to think about change, real change, or even novelties. The school dances were to please the parents and our audience. You noticed the bizarre responses you received to *AlienNation*, the average audience here does not know how to read multimedia performances, or does not want to be provoked by 'foreigners.' I am learning to believe that I must go away in order to look at our work in a new way, in a critical way, and to find out who I am. When we finished our performance project, we all felt empty, lost, because we knew we had to continue, without Imma, to push these issues of our identity, our potential identity.

Our contact with the dancers has not ended. We continue to return to Eisenhüt-tenstadt, and later in the summer of 1994 we meet again at Club Marchwitza, during the night when the punk rockers meet to listen to a music group. It's an Irish band playing country-rock, and we sit outdoors and talk about music and the future. About half of the students who graduated from high school have already looked for jobs in West Germany. Dana and her closest dancer friend, Udo, have been admitted to a dance school in Belgium; Inga wants to live in London and proudly displays a John Lennon T-shirt and a hippy look that mixes strangely with the pierced and tattooed punk style of the others. All of them seem to be testing the disapproval of their parents and the proletarian com-munity values of Eisenhüttenstadt, ready to drop out. Yet they keep coming back to meet the friends in the ghost town.

Since I was interested in exploring the role that dance or music plays in the shifting of projected borders for the teenage East Germans, I also want to relay the reflections and comments made by Imma, since she experienced the chal-lenge of collaboration with these young artists at the very moment when the system in which they grew up was fully discredited. All authority had become suspect even though the authoritarian patterns of behavior continued to linger on underneath the veneer of substituted economic and ideological values. Since dance deals precisely with 'techniques of the body,' as Marcel Mauss and Michel Foucault suggested in their study of habitual and disciplined bodies, I wanted to ask Imma how her young collaborators processed the present social upheavals in their town, how they reinscribed their memories and fantasies, and whether she considers dance a medium that can negotiate shifting identities within a radically restructured social terrain where German or European 'unity' is continuously refracted.

BIRRINGER: You started to teach classes to all the age-groups?

SARRIES-ZGONC: I taught the little ones just wanting to see how their training evolved from early on. Each dance group has three groups; the youngest one from seven to twelve, then from thirteen to sixteen and the oldest one from sixteen and up. In the latter group the oldest one is now thirty-two years old and the youngest one was fourteen. There had been always a lot of competition between both dance groups, so I wanted to break that border between Fire & Flame and Oderland in the very first place. I was interested in how open people would be to what I was going to bring to them, and also how much they would be willing to participate and interact with me.

BIRRINGER: What kind of role did you see yourself in?

SARRIES-ZGONC: It was strange but very exciting, because I always had in the back of my mind the possibility of making a piece with them, and that put me in the position of a choreographer. Teaching them was also new for me because before that I had always taught either professional dancers or beginners, so people would be completely open to what I was teaching either for the need of fresh air or for the hunger to learn what they didn't know at all. But in this case I knew they had some background in classical dance and jazz training; I noticed right away that the training they had wasn't very good, and that is always problematic because it's difficult to face that what you have been taught isn't quite right, it's difficult to accept it and to change it in your body and in your mind. I also was nervous because I knew people in the East perhaps would see me as this Western worker coming to impose something, knowing better, instead of collaborating with them. Also the fact that I am very young, given that their teachers are much older than me.

BIRRINGER: At what point was the vision for the festival developed?

SARRIES-ZGONC: The organizers wanted to risk something new. Talking with the dancers and the friends I was starting to make, and getting to know more about the city, the living situation, I realized there were so many tensions and problems that I suggested making a piece about themselves. There was a lot to be explored, historical factors, and then to try to relate them to the memories of the dancers and their families, and the present situation, the moment they are living in. It so happened that during the first week I had to teach both groups separately because they had their own teaching times which couldn't be changed for logistical reasons, and then in the weekend I had to try to get them to work together. Right away I saw they divided the space in these two groups, so I forced them to work together by starting with a choreographic workshop in couples and groups. I had to invent strategies so that they wouldn't be going back to their old friends. It was the only way to break that wall down. So we started working with some ideas I thought could motivate them, and indeed after that weekend many people were very thrilled and enthusiastic, it also helped the communication level between groups, something was starting to happen between people.

I noticed, nevertheless, that many people were very negative and skeptical toward the work I was offering, toward my teaching and my way of approaching them. I tried to be very friendly, and I tried to let them see that all these new things I brought with me weren't that overwhelming. I told them to ask me whenever something was not clear. Some people couldn't take the new material (for example, they would reject the yoga classes feeling ridiculous or ashamed), and much less the discipline I was asking for in order to keep the creative mood open. So, a lot of people didn't come any more, they didn't want to face either me or the new challenge. At the beginning there were forty or so, and at the end of the two weeks I had some sixteen people working with me. When we announced the new production, it gave those who were left an extra motivation, beside the physical work, and they worked very hard during the following weeks of the workshop.

BIRRINGER: How did you, at that point, understand dance as communication?

SARRIES-ZGONC: I think already in my own school I was always nervous about having chosen classical ballet, I had my doubts about its place in the world and in my life, it bored me, so there was something at the communication level not quite working for me. So, whenever I had to create a piece in school for the composition classes I tried to do something original in the sense that people would be pulled by the performer and would have to think about it, questioning the expression, what the dance would mean to them. My vision of theater, dance and performance media was very narrow in a school where we received very little or no information about performance groups and movements. Research at that level was not encouraged, it would distract our minds from the everyday school routine. Later, I left for foreign dance companies in Belgium and Luxemburg, because the dance situation in Spain was pretty poor, and I started working professionally in companies where I realized that contemporary and new dance were communicating something else to me as performer and to the audience . . . something close to the modern mind, instead of looking at a fairy-tale. But eventually, I was tired of being told by others how to move. I even considered giving up dancing and going into Political Science, but then I came to Chicago to create *AlienNation*. The cross-cultural work we were doing and my interest in politics let me see that I could direct my work toward society, acting as a social worker using my dance skills to communicate. I am still completely committed to production on stage.

BIRRINGER: How do you experience cross-cultural productions? What was your perception of the socioeconomic situation in Eisenhüttenstadt?

SARRIES-ZGONC: Having worked in the USA was of great impact. I had a very narrow vision of this land from TV and newspapers. For me it was very strong to see all the diverse cultures, communities, sensibilities. Working with the diversity of cultures in the ensemble was eye-opening. I learnt how difficult dialogue can be, how we misunderstand. Avanthi [an Indian dancer in our ensemble] used to say: 'We don't speak the same language.' Nevertheless, we practiced tolerance, dancing as a kind of listening to the various points of view exchanged.

When I came to Eisenhüttenstadt, I had been in East Germany just once before, to Leipzig in 1991, and I remember feeling very sad, everything was grey, like in black-and-white TV. There were people in the street selling all sorts of things because they had no money to pay the rent for a shop. So I noticed the same grey buildings I remembered from Leipzig, and all those new cars and big shops with the same brands and products you can find anywhere in Germany. When I started meeting people I realized they were very different from people in other cities, they were very distant and reserved toward me, with a kind of softness that made me very nervous. It wasn't anything against me, it's a general attitude. There is a sense of guilt, an induced need to look up to authority, call it teachers, grown-up people . . . Maybe this attitude of fear had nothing to do with me but with the fact I was coming from the West. So they would observe before they would talk. I had to be careful, but I decided the only way to handle those attitudes was being with them as a colleague, especially since some of them were much older than me. So I tried to be like one of them, only with a bit more dance experience, being open knowing that they had experienced things I didn't because they had lived political situations and changes that I hadn't lived.

When we discussed how to do a new work about them, their history, memories, and hopes, they realized it depended on their creativity, their will to be ready and active, to allow themselves to talk about things that were not spoken, that were being forgotten, things that were hidden and avoided. I asked them to reflect on how the situation had changed after the fall of the Wall, after they were forced to become Western; how their lives, their daily practice changed; what did border, freedom, 'fatherland' mean to them. Had there been changes in the human relationships within their own community.

Most of them, they didn't like to become 'Wessis,' they still call themselves 'Ossis,' using these strangely infantilized words; but they never identify themselves with the other Eastern European countries or with the transformations those countries suffered and are suffering. They just refer to other Eastern European countries as places where they used to spend their holidays. For example, for them Poland is just the country where they can purchase cheaper items such as cigarettes, but they don't really like Polish people; although some Polish groups were invited to the festival, I noticed there is a guarded attitude toward them, and certainly they don't feel identified with them at all. Also during the festival I didn't have the feeling there was a strong will to use dance as a medium to create any kind of link with the Polish groups, I didn't see them do any step forward toward this *Folklore-Tanz-Verbindung* ['folk-dance-connection': the festival motto].

That has a strong relation with the difficulties I had to face during the process: artistically I sensed they wanted to know some other kind of dance they were eager to learn, but I think they were not very clear why they wanted to take part in a project which had as a subject this '*Verbindung.*' You cannot create 'connected bodies' without an organic process based on mutual interest, on a shared goal.

I felt very often some rejection, some resistance. They didn't want to answer questions; it was even more difficult to get them to comment on each other's answers. At some point of the process, after a two-week break, they realized they had missed these discussions and exchanges of experiences. It started when Jana, sixteen years old, expressed her shame to say she was German. So, I found out they were not happy with the present; now they had access to things they never dreamt of, but they resented the actual human behavior which the capitalist competition had brought with it.

BIRRINGER: Did the work develop through these psychological issues?

SARRIES-ZGONC: I thought this kind of psychological work and analysis would not be something to give shape to the piece but something for the training of the dancers, because we needed strong personality and will-power, strong enough to live the work onstage and not just do it, but putting it into their own skin to try to communicate it to the people they live with and work with. I needed them to get into a new mode of thinking about their own situation and experiences,

Figure 22 AlienNation, Choreographed by Johannes Birringer, Imma Sarries-Zgonc and Tara Peters. Eisenhüttenstad, 1994.

which would affect their body language and attitude, in order to communicate that onstage, in order to live it.

BIRRINGER: Why did you call the dance *Ewige Seelen–Ewiges Land*?

SARRIES-ZGONC: I brought them some texts to read; the first one was a beautiful book written by Egon Schiele, *Ich, Ewiges Kind*, it was the easiest one for them to start introducing the reflection on text to the dance work. It's part of Schiele's diary in prison, where he explores his soul and feelings, how life evolves in different moments. I used the word '*ewig*' ['eternal'] because I simply liked how it sounds. Then it made me think how people are never the same but nevertheless are because each of us belongs to a certain community, has a certain history. Countries are also changing, but history and certain struggles keep coming back. Countries also shift their political position on a 'land' that stays the same hosting different people, different languages and traditions, different problems and always new conflicts and wars.

BIRRINGER: But they no longer live in the same country.

SARRIES-ZGONC: The superstructure has changed, but they live still on the same land. One could argue whether it is still the same land after the political, economical, and monetary system has changed, after everything has changed. But for some people this is their land, they have an attachment to it even though the situation might be different, they feel they belong there because they have raised their families there, they have always been there and it has become a very important part of their lives.

BIRRINGER: The city was founded in 1953, workers came there to work, now the industry is in limbo. How deep is the historical memory?

SARRIES-ZGONC: In the work we talk about history, and of course about German history, for they are German and have trouble acknowledging it. This affects their future.

BIRRINGER: They seem afraid of the future?

SARRIES-ZGONC: There has to be place for hope, especially for young people. They have some strong bonds to the city in the same way they have links to things in socialism because it is part of their childhood memories, something that psychologically is very important for human beings.

BIRRINGER: I worry about eternities. How does one remember a totalitarian system?

SARRIES-ZGONC: Right now, the new freedom they didn't have before feels like a great amount of pressure. There is a certain nostalgia, a melancholic feeling toward the time without pressure: food they used to eat, furniture and cars they had, how difficult it was to get certain things, etc. There is always this kitsch nostalgia underneath.

BIRRINGER: Did the group achieve a consciousness of change, of the knowledge that the past is a foreign country?

SARRIES-ZGONC: They danced their point of view, their emotions, we didn't try to deconstruct them. I think they are still in a very young state of mind, and that shows in their political activities as well as in their cultural and artistic activities. I couldn't change their points of view of West and East, it is a paradox; like the dialectics of love and self-hatred. They feel feminized, rejected, exotic, shamed. The subject of national unity is taboo. So we tried to approach it through the idea, the memory, of perhaps the false consciousness of solidarity. But there are other examples. There are many women in the city who live alone with their children after having left their husbands; they raise the families on their own with a lot of strength to motivate this young generation to keep going.

BIRRINGER: What about the political conflicts in the city? For example, the refugee asylum and the neo-Nazis?

SARRIES-ZGONC: I never heard about the asylum until August 1994, when the project was over; nobody wanted to talk about it, they are hiding it; it might be an added thing to be ashamed of. They do talk about neo-Nazis, but more out of a private fear, not because they take a stand opposing racism or fascism.

BIRRINGER: This worries me, also in terms of the response to your work and to *AlienNation*.

SARRIES-ZGONC: Yes, *Ewige Seelen–Ewiges Land* was welcomed because people recognized their own dancers onstage, surprised to see them dancing like that. But there was not enough effort for some further development of the work, utilizing the public responses, the letters to the newspaper, etc. The older teachers have a very conservative, fearful mind about everything they consider new and provocative. *AlienNation* sparked weeks and weeks of controversy because they recognized something, the unification as surreal farce, but thought we had no right to use all those images and provoke these associations, since we don't belong there. On the other hand, the young dancers looked at the piece with a lot of respect, with open eyes, asking about every little detail. It reminded them of something they didn't want to think about. It's the same old story as always; people try to forget, to hide everything they feel uncomfortable with, it has been happening always in history and it keeps following the same patterns.

BIRRINGER: Our intervention as cultural workers: if we cannot help opening things up, making things fluid, exchanging and inciting ideas for the next step, does the production aesthetic fail? Are we learning to understand that the continuous work process, as organic process, is more important than any final performance or media event? That working with our resistances is more important, in fact *is* the performance? I think we have achieved something if we get to raise an issue addressing it with honesty. Cross-cultural work is an exploration of the geographies of emotion and, therefore, one must consider dropping the academic and social/market pressures to 'show off' and come to another level of exploration, of research and challenge, shifting our cultural practice into a social context of collaboration focused entirely on the human relationships which can be built across differences. It is the option of cross-cultural border work based on research, not on aesthetic product, dropping the hunger for power that so many artists have, and which is so dangerous and self-deluding. Or are we deluding ourselves when we believe in collective process?

The idea of collaboration is more interesting and complex than a 'border artwork.' With product many times we have to cover things over; cover political, spiritual, psychological, human dilemmas which too often are not being addressed fully and with consequence. I guess I am not so interested in the aesthetics of production, its 'entertainment value,' but more in a method of collaborative rehearsal, shifting from performance art to performance art methodology. How do you think about dance as an activist medium?

SARRIES-ZGONC: Yes, of course collaboration is one of the main goals, but it is very difficult to get to a certain complicity, reached at a personal level to be in an ideal creative mood and atmosphere. How would one use this complicity to direct a process involving new visions, shareable interests? You remember how difficult it was in Ljubljana where some people felt obliged to participate because of the artistic community pressures. In collaborative process one should, very carefully, take some specific responsibility, avoiding falling into a power position, learning to share, to listen to what might be the basis for a productive and real activist exchange. Another important responsibility to take is the commitment to a certain intimacy in the work which will reassure sincere honesty with yourself and with the group, getting ready to grasp some very personal levels and to lose the privacy that we granted ourselves. On the other hand I think one can be also activist showing the work onstage, because we want to challenge others not in the group we might be working with, addressing other 'privacies.'

BIRRINGER: If a medium carries something from one place to the other, what is your philosophy of medium? What are you mediating?

SARRIES-ZGONC: So far in my work I have been trying to communicate, to the people I have worked with, some motivation for whatever issues came up, and I try to apply it to *movement*. That motivation is a means to provide hope and strength, emotions very much needed especially between the young generations just starting to build their lives on their own. To get to it, I have tried to convey self-respect and respect to the others and to life, as well as self-discipline, an ethical discipline of life, a commitment to it with all its responsibilities and tolerances to allow ourselves to be receptive and to keep an open mind in our reactions and expression.

To go over the border and communicate things between and through people, we can refer to body-language, movement-language, since movement creativity always produces a meaningful relationship between bodies and subjectivities, between individuality and sociality. In that sense, dance always creates new relationships in space-time. Such creativity, if it's explored organically, motivates a care of self and other that supports people and communities through the irrational moments and the dangerous situations they are forced to live in.

BIRRINGER: I agree with you, and believe you've pointed to something very important in our physical relationship to the dancers here in Eisenhüttenstadt; a caring and continuing dialogue between us will need to address the changing sense of not-belonging, no-longer-belonging to the place in which they have lived, taking movement positively as a point of departure and not just as a way of remembering what might be lost. It is perhaps necessary to become an outsider to understand better the bodily signs of melancholia or of change in the everyday life as well as in the impositions of the new 'outside' (Western) culture. The responses from the young people seem contradictory because they welcome the new possibilities that move them, while they are not really sure what to fight against, as Attila admits when he says he's against right-wing violence and against the state, although he never explains what this 'state' is or means to him. Perhaps this idea of belonging to a state is always predicated on very shaky assumptions; I think your performance was so moving to the audience precisely because it made them feel that the culture of the 'land' is not eternal at all but, especially now that the authoritarian state has imploded, always subject to change and to a becoming-other. The problem is whether and how we care to admit our desire to remove fixed or authorized images of local identities.

4. TRANSCENTRALA

[Sarajevo in Ljubljana]

> The Western media thought they had come across some kind of primitive, barbaric Balkan ritual when our troubles started in ex-Yugoslavia. Their first reaction was an ironic, mocking attitude at these primitive Balkan peoples stuck in their atavistic nation-state myths and ethnic conflicts. Now it's becoming clearer and clearer: we in the Balkans are the future.
>
> (Slavoy Žižek)

Ljubljana, August 1993–September 1994

Thinking of my experience in Slovenia during 1993–4, a lot of previous assumptions about border crossing and solidarity become untenable, even if I were able to explain the different historical contexts, political realities, or the synchronous if asymmetrical relations between East and West. Since I cannot fully explain the difficulties I sensed in the physical workshops and encounters with artists in Ljubljana, any language or rationalizing semantic scheme with which to grasp the displacements of warfare becomes a trap. Another unsettling trap is the issue of (solidarity as) voyeurism which is implicit in the Bosnian perspective on the West addressed throughout my conversations with Sarajevan filmmaker Ademir Kenović. But this perspective, and a critique of the voyeurism of multiculturalism, may help to undermine the deep inner media processes that have positioned us, in the West, into a mindless tolerance of our own illusions about basic civil and legal relationships in the world.

Postmodern theory may rhetorically celebrate multiculturalism, yet it often fails to reflect critically on the aesthetics of 'hybridity' and 'appropriation' which it promotes as a global concept. It is a concept that remains enmeshed in the gaze of the West, and it often is fundamentally hypocritical. In reality, it is true that the recent history of performance or visual/video art has overlapped precisely with the increasingly globalizing technology of the electronic media and the promotional industries' commodification of all spheres of culture and of all images of the body. But the 'scene of the body' is not 'empty,' as Jean Baudrillard would have us believe. Rather, such cynical affirmations of the end of the Real fail to account for the battlefields and border-lands in which some bodies, and not others, are made to process very contradictory and very hurtful information. Following a certain male trajectory of avant-garde thought in the West, and echoing Paul Virilio's technological 'aesthetics of disappearance,' Baudrillard declares that the 'ecstatic destiny' of acceleration has taken place: 'Today art no longer creates anything but the magic of its disappearance.' Referring to the Gulf War, he claims that this war could not have happened except as a 'hyperreal scenario' where truth is defined solely in rhetorical terms. Filmmaker and television producer Kenović is speaking from the trauma of a very real terror experienced in the war in his country when he refers, ironically, to the 'normal daily life under siege.' Kenović's realism and Baudrillard's anti-realism meet in the ghostly space where today's (im)morality and politics of representation are contested under the mounting pressure of social, economic and military/peace-keeping crises.

After talking to Slavoy Žižek in Ljubljana about the 'future' of the Balkans vis-à-vis the 'outside' world and its fantasy-projections, I ask myself whether my thinking about identity politics and the performing body is overdetermined by Western postmodernism, and whether my assumptions about 'de-centered,' post-Yugoslavian identities in the transitional space of new national formations across the former Eastern bloc anticipate their reception as 'postmodern'? Hoping to avoid any facile translations of post-communist experience – in the case of Eastern European artists thinking about their own conditions of production – into Western discursive constructs, I will nevertheless propose that cross-references to the failed project of modernity in the East *and* the West share a powerful dialectical tension. Moreover, this dialectic is now overshadowed by the resurgence of ultranationalism, fascism, and ethnic separatism contesting the ground of the collapsed central authority in communist culture. My dialogue with Slovene artists concerns the redefinition of their positions, not only *vis-à-vis* the 'unofficial' culture of the Slovene spring (1980s) that devolved within the now transformed horizons of East and South Central Europe in the uncertain period of its transition to democratic capitalism, but also in regard to the highly speculative address to the future which their art undertook, thus prefiguring unavoidable dislocations in the Slovene social and ideological context.

In their 1993 video *Transcentrala*, Marina Gržinič and Aina Šmid capture this address to the future in a very powerful way. All the interviews with Slovene artists-on-video (members of the Neue Slowenische Kunst collective) are slightly out of sound-synchronization, as the camera pans continuously and restlessly across artworks, the artists' bodies, interior spaces (apartments, studios), walls, and a map of Central Europe. At one point we see a glimpse of 'Moscow' on the map, then a spinning black cross that grows larger and traverses the frame before dissolving in a face that is superimposed over the flickering geographical representation of 'Slovenia' [independent since 1991]. The unidentified artist to whom the face belongs speaks of a 'perpetuum mobile' that is now being built, a 'moving bridge' whose central part, the Transcentral, is a 'cross rotating around three axes.'

> Geographically speaking,
> we represented the last province of the totalitarian system in the 1980s,
> regarded from the point of Moscow.
> The position of the cross
> between the East and the West
> proved advantageous for us.
> In the '80s, the idea of ideology in art was very actual.
> Compared with the West, we had a personal experience of this.
> We enjoyed the privilege of being born here.
> Our eclecticism originated from our place of birth. . . .
>
> We represent a kind of reaction to nationalism -
> the most significant result and symptom of the 1990s:
> war, nationalism, and the establishing of the new state.
> As a collective of artists, we started thinking about the idea of state as a form,
> which is on the way to get rid of the ideologically colored 1980s.
> (*Transcentrala*, video transcript)

All the artists' statements on the video are uttered in English, in a tone that is probing and ironic but also sincere and passionate. Most remarkable, however, is the camera movement, and the time movement, so to speak: out of focus and out of sync, the temporal sequence of visual and sound images takes on the character of a broken continuum which, although continually rotating and always in motion, stands in a dissociated relationship to itself and to the evolving portrait of a future project. It is the time-image in the video itself which is crucial. It does not have an outside, nor does it tell a story. Rather, it creates layer upon fractured layer of an incomplete meditation on space, time, subjectivity, and the conceptual extension of their relations into another form.

prayer machines

I begin to look for manifestations of this other form. While staying in Ljubljana I meet with theater director Dragan Živadinov who is in his mid-thirties and a member of NSK (Neue Slowenische Kunst). We are on the tenth floor of an office building he shares with the theater magazine *Maska*, and he explains his visionary designs for the architectonics of the new *Noordung* space machine he plans to build inside another building. The *Noordung* project refers to Herman Potočnik Noordung (1892–1929), a Slovene scientist and the first person to deal with the problems of space travel. Potočnik's research was published in German under the title *Das Problem der Befahrung des Weltraums: der Raketenmotor* (1929). Two of Dragan's previous ballet-theatre productions (performed by his group 'Cosmokinetic Cabinet') were already dedicated to this research: *Kapital*, in 1991, and *Molitveni stroj Noordung* ('Noordung Prayer Machine') in 1993. I know films of *Kapital* and witness the restaging of *Noordung* in August 1994, and also talk with Dragan while attending his rehearsals. He speaks in a mixed English/Slovene to me, and I am transcribing his aphoristic comments.

He tells me that his productions explore a kind of metaphysics of traveling through space, built on an iconography indebted to science fiction as well as to the original avant-garde, futurist conceptions of the temporal extension and trans-evaluation of spatial art. In fact, one could consider *Noordung* the Slovene version/revision of the pre-revolutionary futurist opera *Pobeda nad solntsem* ('Victory over the Sun'), created in 1913 by Aleksei Kruchenykh, Mikhail Matiushin, and Kazimir Malevich. Dragan's visual choreography, especially in the use of figurines or marionette-like astronauts who represent the 'future-countrymen' and women who must learn to build the new satellite *they will become*, reinvents not only the *de facto* revolutionary non-objective designs Malevich created for the futurist opera (designs to which Malevich attributed the origins of his Suprematist paintings), but also the transrational thought (*zaum*) that is needed to inspire belief in a constructible future *after* the burn-out of revolutionary horizons. I always have the impression that Dragan is speaking in *zaum* language, which of course could also be a conscious posture of mythification.

Noordung experiments with the transcendent idea of the human 'satellite' floating in space-time. Dragan argues that 'the concept of the "prayer machine" invokes a metaphysics of communality, or a theology, that points to the para-doxical intersections of materiality (machine) and spirituality (cosmic faith).' The most extraordinary construction of this paradox involves the actual place-ment of the audience into separate little cubicles *underneath* the staging area; the heads of the collective, separated audience are on ground level, so to speak, able to look up into the space of the theatrical action. The actor-astronauts perform above the audience's normal horizontal/perspectival vision, and judging from the exact geometric, grid-like configuration of the audience capsules, one can think of the actors as moving *beyond* the collectivized order which is physically con-strained, bound by a certain enforced gravity. The 'new realism' of this construct-ivist space hints at a non-perspectival, higher theater that must be intuited; it is no doubt ironic that Dragan names his *Noordung* project after a Slovene space engineer whose utopian visions remained unfulfilled. In its double allusion to the Russian avant-garde's revolutionary constructivism and to the monumental Soviet failure to create a 'scientific socialism' through social engineering, *Noor-dung* positions itself outside Soviet reality, retracing a suppressed Slovene 'scien-tific memory' grounded in a movement toward metaphysical horizons. Dragan's theater work, so to speak, is space research, and his architectural visions are perhaps based on a fundamental desire to change perception-experience, interrogating the implications of the difference between optical and topical/bodily looking for his theory of relativity. Given the Slovene theater's peripheral relation to Russia or the West, it is in fact most significant that Dragan's *zaum* has a method, and it is one he practices in his rehearsals. Instead of dismantling the bankrupt belief in a transcendent utopia, he is retracing the steps of a futurist art that is now, at the dystopian moment of socialism's collapse within a European civilization littered with destroyed metaphors, a vehicle for a prospective *reconstruction of another world* – not, I emphasize, a return to an imaginary or mythic Slovene center or national consciousness. The *Noordung* ballet is a highly abstract montage of image/movement/sound-spaces floating above the topical viewers stuck in the wooden capsules but able to follow the outer spaces with their eyes.

Figure 23 Molitveni stroj Noordung (Noordung Prayer Machine), directed by Dragan Živadinov and performed by the Cosmokinetic Cabinet. Hamburg, 1994.

This is also my understanding of Dragan's new architectural drawings and models which remind me of the compositional forms of Malevich's *Planits* and *Architektons*. All of his rehearsal concepts are based on the notion of anti-gravity. His future anti-gravity theater implies a kind of altered state, a mental space traveling that shifts theatrical perception of the real to a different, planetary level. The audience in this theater would become a 'space shuttle,' so to speak. While I am trying to follow his flight of the imagination, he suddenly interrupts himself and makes a gesture toward the window. I look out and see a placid Slovene

Figure 24 Molitveni stroj Noordung (Noordung Prayer Machine), directed by Dragan
Živadinov and performed by the Cosmokinetic Cabinet. Hamburg, 1994.

summer sky over a peaceful city. 'A radical evil has appeared in the south,' he says
without finishing his sentence. I knew he had pointed toward Sarajevo and the
genocide that is happening in the midst of Central Europe.

ghetto media

I cannot forget this gesture. What is happening in our culture remains inscribed
in the denial of its belief. This is our chaos of coherence, the terror of our own
pogroms, expulsions, and denials, the deep crisis of our internalized rationale.
Why is the unthinkably strange scene so real, as if it were almost believable (it
must be real since it's obviously on television), as if our fantasies were fatally
attracted to an other side in us which we would prefer to be outside? Our
apparent incapacity to confront fascism is as disastrous as it is symptomatic;
Western European disdain of ethnic strife, racism, and fascism concentrates on
the East where the Serbian fascist violence of 'ethnic cleansings' is perceived as
the tragic recurrence of ancient Balkan conflicts. The Bosnians in besieged Sarajevo and other destroyed towns, now referred to as 'Muslims,' have become total
aliens to Europe. But the horror of the war against the Bosnian state also lies in
the appeasement policies of the West. The latter's unwillingness to confront
fascism, xenophobia, and racism in its foreign policy reflects back on its own
history and politics, and the scenario is nowhere more explicit than in united
Germany which continues not to recognize fascism, xenophobia, and racism as
internal. As Tomaž Mastnak points out in his 'Journal of the Plague Years,'

fascism may have been defeated militarily in the last world war, but the West 'never deconstructed and destroyed it symbolically and politically.'

In the following dialogues with Sarajevan filmmaker Ademir Kenović, and Slovene video and theater artists Marina Gržinić, Eda Čufer, and Marko Peljhan, we will discuss the idea of 'translocality' in relation to the new nationalisms and structural transformations in Central/Eastern Europe. I will propose the notion of 'post-alternative' or 'post-utopian' art, describing the transitional stage in which the Slovene dissident, collectivist performance/media groups now find themselves, after Slovenia's post-communist independence. These artists had developed their own infrastructural organization (social activities, alternative venues such as ŠKUC Gallery, Disco FV or Glej Theater, Radio Študent; video and design studios, print media and fanzines; specific tactics of presentation and distribution; documentation of their programmatic conceptual interventions into the public relations of art and politics, and of the cultural actions that galvanized in the 1980s underground, especially around the performances and exhibitions of the anonymous collective NSK). They had also developed their own conceptual vision of a 'parallel state' (NSK declared their theater, film, design and visual art production a 'State Organization' in 1986), and they now find themselves caught between international capitalism (replacing the former totalitarian system) and conflicted versions of a new local nationalism that are promoted by the various political parties and factions.

During the conversations, Eda explains the new process they want to explore, namely the creation of a 'state in time,' an anonymous transnational collective organism. Marina's conceptual video, *Transcentrala*, already articulates this suprematist state, and NSK's first 'embassy' action was staged on the Red Square in Moscow in 1992. It consisted of rolling out a huge black cloth in the shape of a cross. Simultaneously, the *Moscow Embassy Project* unfolded as a conceptual seminar on international relations: 'How the East Sees the East.' NSK now issues passports for voluntary citizens of the new 'state in time:'

THE NSK STATE IN TIME IS AN ABSTRACT ORGANISM,
A SUPREMATIST BODY, INSTALLED IN A REAL SOCIAL
AND POLITICAL SPACE AS A SCULPTURE
COMPRISING THE CONCRETE BODY
WARMTH, SPIRIT AND WORK
OF ITS MEMBERS.

NSK CONFERS THE
STATUS OF A STATE NOT
TO TERRITORY BUT TO MIND
WHOSE BORDERS ARE IN A STATE OF FLUX,
IN ACCORDANCE WITH THE MOVEMENTS AND
CHANGES OF ITS SYMBOLIC AND PHYSICAL COLLECTIVE
BODY.

One of the NSK designers brings me my new passport, and I am witness to a ceremony at KUD gallery during which Kenović and his colleagues from the SaGA film group receive honorary diplomatic passports. The Sarajevans had been able to leave their city and pass the UN security borders to attend the *Sarajevo in Ljubljana* project of performances, exhibitions, and screenings. For one week, the project displays testimony and artistic work from the survivors of the ghetto, as Kenovic calls the Bosnian capital.

BIRRINGER: Marina, you organized the project and simultaneously apologized for this 'attempt at a presentation' of cultural resistance to the war in Sarajevo? Why?

GRŽINIČ: The unbelievable artistic production and reflection that have persevered and survived in Sarajevo take place in a ruined city where the war is still going on. We were not sure whether the artists could or would leave to come here; perhaps only the videos or photographs, hastily patched together and sent here, would be on display and the project attended by the audience only. From our external, and almost touristically voyeuristic, point of view, it's difficult to understand the closed Sarajevo environment, how it functions, how events take place, how they are coded and presented, how the presenters have managed to survive. Our invitation to them is a kind of gesture, a civilizational gesture toward them, but also a 'pose' of (self-)presentation. In a cynical way, we might say that now, as we have entered Europe, we must make this civil self-presentation as a matter of fact, of coding the political, civil, legal, and social Slovene environment and ourselves.

BIRRINGER: Earlier you spoke of voyeurism and 'squatting.' I've noticed the new squatters' movement here in Ljubljana (the occupation of Metelkova, a former Yugoslav army facility, by young artists and punks), but your reference is probably to the positions we occupy *vis-à-vis* an event, an action, a war elsewhere?

GRŽINIČ: Yes, our project of presenting these films/videos and photographs associates us with the war in Bosnia, in the way in which European peace organizations, or even the UN peace-keeping troupes, can be said to be squatters, although we are only in the vicinity of documents, images, and confessions. These recorded narratives or images and electronic processes reveal that something is taking place, but they free us from the physical effort of traveling to that place, and so we become squatters of television.

BIRRINGER: We don't have to act?

GRŽINIČ: It spares us a great deal, yes, the information of war crimes is simultaneously broadcast and *tolerated*. The psychological position of the voyeur is privileged. So I think the war in Bosnia questions all our basic civil and legal relationships in the world we inhabit. The information, the pictures, become a war by other means.

BIRRINGER: Ademir, your film *MGM Sarajevo* ('Man, God the Monster') is shown here; I recognized some scenes from videos that were smuggled out of

Sarajevo last year. Perhaps you explain briefly, is it a recollage of film material that was already available, or is it a new collaboration?

KENOVIĆ: It's a mixture of all you mentioned. Our SaGA collective had almost forty short documentaries, about 300 hours of materials, documents that we had shot during all this period of the siege of Sarajevo. Now we fused these three projects, which are forty-five minutes long each, into *MGM*. One part is called 'Confessions of a Monster,' an interview with a war criminal who was captured in Sarajevo [this is the part Kenović directed together with Ismet Arnautalić];

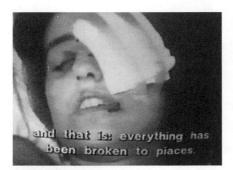 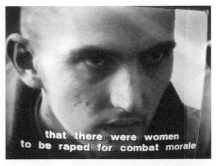

Figure 25 Video stills from *MGM Sarajevo* (Man, God, the Monster), 1993–94.

then we had 'Director's Diary,' made by our friend Mirza Idrizović, a filmmaker with thirty-five years of experience, who worked on this every week for one year, shooting his life in Sarajevo. The third part is 'Godot/Sarajevo.' Pjer Žalica, our friend from Zagreb, made this film about the making of a theater production in Sarajevo, *Waiting for Godot*, which was directed by Susan Sontag. So last winter I had the idea to put the three films together, and to add some more material, and recreate it in absolutely new way, making a kind of semi-feature/document[ary]. We added some 30 or 35 per cent of new material, we re-edited the concept, making it like a feature; we re-transferred it to 35mm, added music, effects and all the things a film assumes, and then we finished it the day before the opening of the Cannes film festival. We worked on it for some time in Berlin, Pjer helped to edit it, we also got help from Mexican filmmaker/editor Dana Rotberg. Then we melted it into this form, which is neither a document, nor an essay, nor a feature, nor a horror, nor a science fiction film, but maybe it has all of these dimensions in itself.

BIRRINGER: Can you describe the history of SaGA? Was this video/film collective created after the war broke out or did it exist before?

KENOVIĆ: We had this small production company from the beginning of the 1980s. Ismet and I were producing different short forms, apart from our jobs. I was working in TV, then in film features, and I was an academy professor, but this company we had all the time. The word SaGA means 'Sarajevo Group of Authors.' When the war broke out, Izmet and I were just in pre-production for two features, ready to start shooting, but the war stopped us, and so we put all our energy in gathering people, a big group of thirty to forty people able to survive, and then we established day-by-day shooting, which was my idea of making a document from a ghetto; then we gathered more filmmakers, film students, artists, writers, poets, musicians, computer engineers, and other people who were just amateurs wanting to work. So we just established ourselves trying to work under these circumstances, most often without electricity, without anything. We had to use electric generators, and we worked with candles.

BIRRINGER: SaGA under siege: how can one make film production under war conditions? Were you able to obtain tapes or cameras, how did you improvise under these horrifying conditions?

KENOVIĆ: Well, we did, being filmmakers, meaning that you are often very close to war conditions, you are used to improvise. In the actual war it's of course much more difficult, but it gave us more strength, more energy, more vitality, you just do it, no matter how, because you see the use of it. We had some tapes, we had some cameras, some generators, small, modest, but we didn't consider the technical quality the most important part of our task, because there is a *document*, made under these circumstances, and that's it. We improvised, making this wild form of existence, using all possible ways, and we had our friends, journalists, who came to give us tapes. We also broke some generators, so we went to the shelters that people had, filling up batteries where people had electricity or generators, we were trying anything we could to preserve this production. It often felt insane, you know, to preserve something which is not preservable, but now we are very happy, we were always conscious of the importance of the work. I was always saying, if they had had a film crew in the Warsaw ghetto, we would probably have a better knowledge about what happened. We didn't want to wait another fifty years to get a Sarajevo version of *Schindler's List*. We made a *Schindler's List* live in Sarajevo.

BIRRINGER: Before the war and Bosnia's independence you worked primarily in television or feature film; but did there also exist an alternative or independent video movement? And after the collapse of communist Yugoslavia and the outbreak of war, did your understanding of media change? Do you see video production now as a form of spiritual or cultural activism, of gathering witnesses, testimony, or is it mainly a communication/broadcast device, or is it still a kind of artform, or a pure survival mechanism? How do you see the role of media as it changed in your life-experience?

KENOVIĆ: You almost said it better than I would be able to elaborate: all of these dimensions are part of our points of view concerning what we do. I'll tell you this: I'm like a transmedia person or artist – although I don't believe in the term 'artist,' it's for others to say, it's just a word, words are nothing now, anyway. First I worked in the university, I graduated from the Academy of Literature, then I graduated from the Academy of Theater in 1976, then I went to school in the USA to study film, then I applied to TV and worked in TV for fifteen years, and I had my studio in order to work on my video, and then I made my two features on 35mm [*Kuduž*, based on a script by Abdulah Sidran, was completed in 1989, and *Ovo Malo Duše* was made in 1991].

I always had this mixture of interests in media I approached; I made all kinds of programs for TV, from classical music, which I loved, to programs for children, then of course documentaries, shows, cabaret, features, TV dramas, and so on. It is one way of expressing myself in our media, including working in the theater or the visual arts. For example, I had my first video exhibition here in Ljubljana, in 1983, eleven years ago, in Cankarjev Dom. Many of us had these multiple interests, which we were building up into something that I assumed had a strong attraction to everyone who is interested in visual culture.

I don't consider these new video works artistic achievements; we were forced to make these documents, because we had to fight media in the world that were in a horrible and shameful way supporting the general political line in the world, which was, again, in a most shameful way, supporting the fascist regime in Belgrade, supported by all these governments, in Russia, Greece, Germany, etc. French and English media, and most of the big news agencies, like Reuter, were establishing those words and representations which created a misconception about our situation. For example: 'civil war.' There is no civil war in Bosnia, there is no civil war in ex-Yugoslavia at all, it was always just war against civilians. There are no three sides in this conflict, as they are calling it, because there is no conflict. There is a siege, and there are two sides; there is one totalitarian-minded, extreme-nationalist side, supported by all the leading world politicians, and on the other side there are people. It was always like that, and in Bosnia and Sarajevo you cannot make these insanely constructed borders and divisions, it's like drawing borders through bedrooms. It's something that is absurd, it's something that is sick, that is insane, something we had to fight against.

Of course, not being politicians, we can say this very easily, very openly. And of course not being politicians, we were not doing it by political means of media, but we were doing something which we thought is much stronger, more important: we were showing the normal human life of people in Sarajevo, and how the normal human beings are seeing and feeling what's happening around them. Maybe one or two examples won't amount to something very interesting, but if you have hundreds, if you have dozens of different themes, realms, and experiences, it's different. We were sending our crews out to many different locations, also outside of Sarajevo, to see how the situation is over there, we were communicating with all the people appearing in our vicinity, and now we are crossing the world up and down, trying to communicate this idea of a just normal human approach to things. It's very simple: killers are killing people, and robbers are trying to rob territories. What the big world media were making, we were trying to oppose with different instruments. For example, I used to tell this story about a bank robbery in a Chinatown neighborhood, say in New York or London; when the robbery is over, you see police coming and saying, 'Freeze,' and nobody freezes, and then they say, well, anybody hungry? And then they start feeding the people, and then journalists arrive, and they say, well, this is a Chinese quarter, it's probably an Italian mafia gang that attacked them, and the bank is Jewish, so we have these three civil sides in conflict, because they are from this town: this is a Jewish–Chinese–Italian civil clash. And that's how they started treating the Bosnian horror. People have to understand this, because Sarajevo is close to everyone very soon, if they make Sarajevo the paradigm of how the events are being mediated.

So, our counter-documentary form is one way of doing it, and the artistic and survival dimensions are absolutely a part of it, material survival, it's also psychological survival, because you get so many horrible shocks that if you are not doing something which seems meaningful in that situation, then you go crazy. At the same time it's obvious that all our experience showed the extreme expansion of our abilities of human emotion and sense; our minds are unpredictable, the limits are absolutely beyond possible comprehension.

BIRRINGER: Last night at ŠKUC Gallery, in the video/visual art exhibition, I saw a scene in the video *A Street under Siege*. A woman says: 'I hope that something like this horror will never happen again, and I will teach my children about this.' And then she says: 'But this "never again" – we already said that after the Holocaust, after Nazi Germany, and now it's repeating itself.' You mentioned the Warsaw Ghetto earlier. Now we do have your documents, the reportage from Sarajevo; you created all these images of being attacked, a life under siege, and you say: it was our way of reporting differently. Marina argues that this difference is in fact consumed by the society of the spectacle. Do you think there is a possibility of creating alternative video images that will not only be shown around the world [in Chicago I saw *Sarajevo Ground Zero*, an earlier video-documentary compilation distributed by SaGA via New York] but can have a different effect? You know the world is watching, either TV news (CNN, etc.) from the global media, or they see small local stations, or the footage produced by you. Alternative production hasn't achieved any change in the political realm: is video not strong enough to affect political decisions?

KENOVIĆ: The world-mind is controlled by media, and media is controlled by political leaders or major political-economic interest groups, so the world in fact didn't see alternative pictures. The world saw maybe one to a thousand everyday informations, which are informations of the established media; but the effect of our alternative production of something absolutely, unpredictably vital and strong, all of a sudden, could be amazing: it could wake up a lot of people's consciousnesses in the world, I mean, making them have to realize how danger-ous and incompetent politicians are, not just dangerous for Sarajevo, but for the world. The world is approaching an inevitable catastrophe, because these polit-ical world leaders, while they are not in favor of killing, they just have the wrong, preconceived notions of what should be done. They are making a mistake, it's a dangerous play with fire. I'm aware that the democratic instruments are some-times holding somebody's hands very tightly, but what we are doing should provide another viewpoint. It's not all journalists who are to blame, it's mainly a question of editorial politics. Sometimes it's because they follow what global political strategists are thinking. We are warning the global audience by getting our information out. It has to be done.

It's not that we are not strong, or that video images are not strong; they don't have any power if they're not used by stronger media who are willing to use the footage to shift global points of view. I think the shift of global points of view has to happen, that's why we are offering our point of view, not that we have any utopian idea that they will change the world by itself. That's not going to happen, the whole structure of the world media has to be changed, little by little, by unpredictable pushes like what we're doing here.

BIRRINGER: Can we reflect on the fact that you are in Ljubljana, during this week-long event, and you are traveling to other cities? Marina argued that war-fare taking place simultaneously in our televised environments produces the end of real, social solidarity. Consider our proximity to the attack on Bosnia, here in Ljubljana, so physically close yet so infinitely removed. We cannot tolerate that we tolerate what we see. I remember seeing a short excerpt from 'Confessions of a Monster,' in Chicago; I also saw *Mizaldo*, a quite extraordinarily cynical, hard-hitting film directed by Benjamin Filipović and Semezdin Mehmedinović. I was very disturbed by both films, because one portrayed a kind of absolute horror, the blank, emotionless face of a soldier who describes how he killed and raped; the other seemed structured as a clear parody of Western commercial advertising (the ruins of Sarajevo as exotic backdrop for Marlboro Man and French *haute couture*) suffused with an unbearable ironic sensibility addressing human survival. I did not know what to do, except showing these videos to others, and volunteering to travel to Sarajevo to help with further exchanges of information and video materials. Now you are screening the films in Ljubljana: what is the kind of audience you seek to address? Do you think you can mobilize people, or actually alter people's habits of viewing, or are we already living in such an overdetermined media information environment and hyperreal/virtual world, where even this film, directly from the battlefield, will not alter people's actions?

KENOVIĆ: I don't think that one showing, or one day of watching something, will do anything. Last year in Los Angeles I took these tapes and showed them the first time. It was like, how do you say, a fission, an explosion which multiplies by very high numbers, more and more people wanting to see it. Now we have shown them in over 200 places in the world, in Canada, the US, the whole of Europe, Mexico, and now we are going further, we are making a global outreach. First of course we are informing the people from the media, hoping to get their attention, making them willing to grasp what we showed; it's not up to us, we have no power to immediately address the big world media. But the pressure on the French media, for example, by showing our films there on many occasions, became a part of this mosaic which turned the French media, which first supported the international mainstream diplomacy, around toward their current, quite critical positions. It works little by little, moving the general audience feelings into the direction where they have a chance to recognize the danger for general humanity. I don't have illusions, and don't assume people are inevitably good and want to do good; I know that people act in their own interests, especially now in this very uncertain time, subjected to these big tectonic political global changes. But anyway, little by little we can move in this persistent way all those who want to look at some other point of view, and this may affect global public opinions. It's not a fast process. I don't believe anything will change overnight. But we had one showing, and after a year we had over 200 showings; then you enter a larger space, as the videos also get distributed, passed on and on, and slowly you can shift consciousness little by little.

Of course, this is an optimistic point of view. I also have a pessimistic one: if this is not understood, then there is no hope for the world. I may seem too dramatic, having walked out from an extreme tragedy, but we in Sarajevo and in Bosnia don't care any more, we just had our third world war; we just want to say that it's very close, it's just next to you, you may not expect it. It's like death, it always happens to someone else, not you, until it comes to you.

BIRRINGER: You mentioned the future of a time after the war, after the conflict. Sometimes I speak with friends in the alternative community about the need for *reconstruction* in our work. How do we reconstruct what has been devastated? Pjer told me that you are planning to work on a new fiction feature. Do you see your continuing imaginative-creative work as a form of social reconstruction?

KENOVIĆ: I need to correct you, first of all: there is no conflict in Sarajevo. It's a concentration camp. In a conflict you need to have sides, but we are in prison. Yes, of course I assume that our work, little by little, can contribute to the possibility of reconstructing normal life. We are hoping to make a feature, in 35mm, with a film crew, about the people living in a war situation, but this time with actors. I know it's a little too close yet, shooting the volcano from the middle of the volcano, but we did have this experience already, with our documentary approach, and so now we thought that we should try to radiate something else, it's difficult to explain, but it's something only a feature film could radiate. At the same time, it provokes people to think at least it's not impossible that this place could survive.

rehearsing the future

BIRRINGER: Let me ask you, Marko, how you see the work of some of the younger generation artists here in Ljubljana who emerged in the 1990s after Slovene independence, after the alternative social and counter-cultural movements of the 1980s had lost their role of fomenting and promoting the separation of civil society from the state/power. The political scene is now dominated by the national-cultural conservatives who occupy the discourse of ideology and reconstruct the state institutions along the lines of Western capitalist democracy. Are there post-alternative or new independent artistic projects, for example, vis-à-vis the 'moral majority' of the nationalist bloc? Can the collectivity of the NSK movement and its radical conceptualism of a 'transnational state' be sustained under capitalism and the new legality of all art?

PELJHAN: Our dilemma is not a war or the denial that there is a war. There plainly is chaos right now in our transitional culture, and we have to compete for scarce resources because our infrastructure doesn't really exist any more. You mentioned the squatters at Metelkova, it's a good example. The civil society initiative, the 'Network for Metelkova Street,' has not really succeeded in turning the facility into a center for alternative culture, there are too many struggles and incompatible ambitions, and the cultural administrators in the city don't support independent artists. Under the new market conditions, we are forced to re-evaluate our positions, not toward only the state and the political colonization of social life, but also toward the market and the assumptions that govern 'public culture' within the European context. I don't want to talk about struggling for survival. But I feel that our dream of creating an autonomous, parallel civil culture will be difficult to realize.

ČUFER: When I was involved in NSK during the 1980s, I freely accepted the conceptual proposition of anonymous collectivity which was our working philosophy. Today I have to reflect on my decision to subject my individuality to the manifesto and its total concept of a 'theater state.' We are in a confusing moment of transition, when all of our alternative, autonomous cultural arrangements are sliding back into the private sphere or are coopted by the official cultural institutions. Our work on ATOL is a response to this uncertainty; Marko wanted to explore a new theatrical form or experimental activity with which to question the rhythms of the individual within this emerging social field.

BIRRINGER: Marko, can you describe the experiment?

PELJHAN: I am observing this social field, and at the same time I am being observed. We are creating our own system, a kind of utopian environment, for the exploration of our inner rhythms, and our system or transmitting space is functioning also as a method. I am interested in finding new objective conditions for establishing individuality; I am not interested in the shallow individualism of Western democracy, but in the 'individualism' of the East. I will give you the manifesto I published for our project:

Project ATOL manifesto

IN SEARCH FOR A NEW CONDITION

The 'end' of this century is the era of the erosion of utopias, constituted in its beginning. The revolutionary strategies have failed, new social organisms, orders, have not been successfully implemented or developed. Physical imperial powers have transformed themselves into intangible, invisible forces that control and dominate the social, spiritual and economic fields. The FRAGMENTATION of large dimensions is still going on. We, Europe, the World, are living the dawn of utopia which has been substituted with the experience of the white noise of communication. The insight into future is lost in the channels of the eternal present.

The decision to use art in the present state is not an efficient solution to the problem described above. Every human being as individual has less and less possibilities to become a 'creator' or somebody who has influence on a 'new social organism.' EGORHYTHMS I, II, III, IV, the one that will follow, and the rhythmical-scenic structure ATOL are an 'evolutionary ec(g)o-system,' a small scale closed environment which presupposes that in spite of the politically forced unimportance of the individual in the present social system (be it democratic or totalitarian), the only force that can overcome the present is the wisdom which is withdrawn in SILENCE. The thoughts, images and emotions of which we think are useless for the world as it is, because there is no one who could listen, think of them or watch them.

These glimpses of oppressed wisdom, whether they belong to a well-situated individual in the West or to a physically endangered individual on the battlefields and concentration camps of the East, are the real power to produce NEW EVOLUTIONARY STRATEGIES. The ongoing political, social, economic and spiritual division that is spreading throughout Europe and farther is going to result in the complete isolation of the constituent parts of the planetary macro-systems. The closed environments will have to develop new strategies of survival in order to re-establish the lost and disappearing channels of communication. Only freed and creative individuals can produce new objective conditions for a small leap into the future of human relationships. The shaping of history has yet to be defined by a NEW HUMAN BEING capable of walking on the edge of globally controlled communication, without losing its integrity, that is: the possibility of BECOMING, not just BEING.

(Marko Peljhan, June 1993)

BIRRINGER: One might see this model for a new evolutionary organism or performance *ecology*, directed against/developed within the space of transnational technocratic capitalism and its militarized communication-control system, as a kind of survival research. What is the role of the 'actor' in this laboratory?

PELJHAN: We are avoiding theater, avoiding choreography, avoiding repetition. We are interested in a thinking actor who is learning how to behave in the environment we construct, learning to find unrealized potential.

rituals/reconstructions

Near the end of my stay in Ljubljana, I participate in a workshop on 'the future of physical theater.' For several days we try, unsuccessfully, to find a shared language in which to address the schizophrenia Eda had conjured when she spoke about the contradiction of needing to find a 'closed environment in an open society ruled by a new mental violence.' I am asked to address contemporary modes of physical theater, and I proceed to invite the participants to a dance-theatre rehearsal and some exercises in bodily awareness. I create a structured improvisation, but there is reluctance on part of the Slovene directors and theorists to join the dancers and actors, and a rift opens up between the older and younger workshop participants which is exacerbated when Dragan intervenes to postulate the history of a Slovene avant-garde committed to abstraction and not to a recovery of 'real' bodies or body-centered movement. The language of the workshop shifts to Slovene, translation begins to falter, and the younger dancers who would prefer to experiment with movement turn silent and a little resentful. Composer Marko Košnik tries to defuse the tension by offering a long philosophical rumination on the isolation between bodies and language. His comments seem to imply a critique of intellectual overcompensation; he knows that we talk too much when we don't trust the body, and when the environment is too violent to allow respect for the body's time, the time of learning.

The ATOL environment indicates such a search for a 'cultural asylum,' as

Marina calls it, and I need to remind myself constantly that some of the terms my colleagues use are coded differently and stand in a deeply ironic relationship to the experienced totalitarianism under communism. ATOL itself 'repeats' a total system, and like Dragan's space-craft it designs a post-utopian zone for an ecology of the mind which operates on the margins of states and technological controls, within and without, always in relationship to the screens of power yet unlearning the ideologies of domination in the daily practice of consciousness. The emotional power of the ATOL performance, which I saw in 1993, rests in the uncertainty and irony of this post-utopian process. The 'rhythmical-scenic structure' has complex sound/vocal/musical and visual textures but no narrative or linear dramatic action in any conventional sense. As a 'collective' inhabiting an ecosystem shared with plants, fish, bees, organic and inorganic matter, video screens, laptop computers, musical instruments, and two huge *vetars* (propellers that look like radar systems), the individual actors – Peljhan, Bojan Ažman, Tanja Kustrin, Nataša Matjašec, Anja Medved, Gregor-Tao Vrhoveć-Samboleć – do not interact but each separately lives her/his inner rhythms: thinking, sleeping, reflecting, watching. Being watched by the audience. The central video screen, on which satellite pictures of the earth appeared, at times seemed to become a radar or air-traffic control screen and a global broadcasting device blindly transmitting messages, images, colors, codes, including one small photograph from the war in Bosnia.

Figure 26 Egorhythm II, directed by Marko Peljhan for Project ATOL. Moderna galerija, Ljubljana, 1992. Photo courtesy of the artist.

Figure 27 Egorhythm I, directed by Marko Peljhan for Project ATOL. Moderna galerija, Ljubljana, 1992. Photo courtesy of the artist.

Project ATOL suggests that the individual's creative survival strategies would have to emerge as a result of this condition of extreme alienation, plugged in yet isolated, unable to create an autonomous zone (social/artistic) yet expanding her/his emotional, cognitive, and spiritual experience toward the rebuilding of new exchanges. But what would these communications look like? This ATOL system displays a future of 'physical theater' or body work that abandons most conventions of theatrical communication, but perhaps it is not completely different from the dance process I described in East Germany. What is shown here is an analytic experiment with the actors' biorhythms, thoughts, inner emotions, dreams. As spectators we are made aware that our position as voyeurs is conditional; we are also under surveillance, invited to monitor a heterogeneous organism and the rhythms of living species, existence: of bodies contained within technological organicity yet resistant to their own exteriorization of mind. Whenever the actors downlink to us (via amplified speaker systems), we overhear their reflections and the stories they create for themselves to understand the body's invasion by the big Other. At one point, Peljhan picks up a large sheet of glass and shatters it on the ground, shouting his refusal to 'become an object of recombinations and interfaces.' Peljhan's refusal to accept this occupation of the human body indicates a refusal to escape from the political question of how our 'objective conditions' are shaped, and how we avoid becoming absorbed into the fascism of the New World Order.

(Afterthought: like the shattered glass strewn over the ground of existence, aesthetic consciousness is composed of so many fragments of historical revolutions that have been defeated. To practice such a consciousness is to realize the collective parameters of our nightmares. The Slovene artists seem to reinvent a futurism and constructivism on their own terms, conscious of the trauma of the avant-garde's historical assimilation into state power. Their rehearsals thus function as exorcisms.)

When I talk to Marko after the screening of *MGM*, I notice how disturbed he is by the apathy among the Ljubljana audience and the absence of many of the local artists, and how difficult it is for both of us to speak about the future. The cohesiveness and collective purpose of the 1980s alternative-culture movement have disintegrated; the state's independence and the ongoing privatization of the economy have created an ideological vacuum for the young artists who have to struggle for survival in a new competitive climate. Independent and informal theater or dance groups complain about the lack of appropriate spaces and funding or, worse, about the growing isolation. In particular, many of the promising young choreographers (Mateja Bučar, Matjaž Farić, Natasa Kos, Ižtok Kovač, Sinja Ožbolt, Matjaž Pograjc, Tanja Zgonc), whose efforts to establish a contemporary dance-theater in Slovenia are not acknowledged by the conservative Cultural Ministry, are thrown back to themselves and are groping for new directions and a distinctive style of their own. Their often instinctive withdrawal into a crudely physical, hyperenergetic, and self-abandoning emotional realism betrays a lack of trust in, or a disavowal of, the patient process needed to reconstitute a new subjectivity under changed cultural/political conditions. The young punk artists who squat on Metelkova Street perhaps capture the mood of the day when they hold their first summer festival in the partly destroyed, decaying buildings and give it the theme: 'The Bitter Fruits of Civil Society.'

Marko meanwhile has started work on a new project, LADOMIR FAKTURA, a further development of his search for a new, integral individuality that extends the conceptual futurism of his anti-theater. In the projected stages of the LADOMIR process he intends to invent and test ritual procedures (he also calls them 'rehearsals') for the construction of *insulated environments* in which, over time, a science of the individual can be engineered that connects sensory, psychic, material, and spiritual evolutions independent from 'the actual entropic social conditions.' *MICROLAB – The First Surface*, completed in 1994, presents an extraordinary, digitally generated (re)invention of Kandinsky's 1928 cycle of abstract visual compositions inspired by Mussorgsky's *Pictures at an Exhibition*. The real-time computer film investigates the relation between form and time, conjuring an evolving and increasingly complex flow of abstract shapes and geometries that gradually gain the shifting outlines and transparent volumes of a city architecture built of colored modules. Kandinsky's lines and planes gain a new futuristic form in the digital architecture of communication bits generated by algorithms. After this conceptual exploration of digital time/processing, Marko tested himself, in the second 'surface' entitled *WE WERE EXPECTING YOU!*, as an individual sleeper, during a twelve-hour action performance staged in a bed, connected via short-wave radio to various radio stations all over the world. The research motif in this phase, based on the futurist poet Khlebnikov's utopian vision of scientific/artistic radio communion with the world, is the relationship between the individual human being and macro-natural systems (e.g. weather, electromagnetic waves). The transmissions that happen during his sleep are recorded and can be monitored by the audience that happens to observe the individual in his habitat. The last word I heard, over email, was that he is now moving forward, little by little, toward the third and fourth 'MAKROLAB' and 'contact' surfaces. The latter will experiment with a complex constructivist scenography (in real time-space) juxtaposed with several parallel live transmissions of randomly (illegally) captured satellite feeds. The 'contact' explored is that between scenic-rhythmical structures on the human level and technological communications (intelligent machines, news satellites, military machines) on the logistical macro-level of satellites, Internet, ISDN lines, radio and cable systems. In Marko's conception of the possibility/reality of civil war, it becomes necessary for the artist to gather information on the technological media systems proficiently used by the military-industrial complex. Artists, he suggests, can gather information that enables citizens of 'civil society' to develop their own systems and applications of virtual reality. Only if we are able to analyze information systems through our physical experience of technological reality, will we be able to locate creative modes and structures of *civil defense* for ourselves.

5. BLOQUEO/RESISTENCIA

Havana, May 1994/December 1994/December 1995

I now turn to another contested site where the fluidity of the border and border media has been subjected to the pressures of containment, isolation, and the brute outside force of anti-communist ideology. My conversations with Cuban film and theater artists address the disastrous effects of the US blockade on the local economy and their struggle for survival in a collapsing infrastructure. When I first arrived in Cuba, the situation was very critical; the country seemed to be in midst of a free fall, and economic output had dropped 40 per cent between 1989 and 1993. The Castro government had to announce a 'special period' and introduce severe rationing of food and energy supplies when Cuba's economy suffocated after the disintegration of the Eastern bloc and the subsequent loss of trading partners and Soviet subsidies. However, during my workshops in Havana I have also learnt to recognize the spiritual strength of resistance that the *bloqueo* has fomented among the people on this island, this atoll (cf. Chapter 5). In the following, we debate the extraordinary Cuban talent for improvisation, the function of new and old media, the continuing vitality of Cuban film, theater, and music, and the new queer visibility. [I had wanted to intercut these discussions among artists with comments by a *santero* suggesting that Cuban *Santería* (and the music it influences) is now the most vital border medium. Unfortunately, the *santero* didn't grant permission to reproduce our conversation.]

I met my discussion partners by accident. I emphasize this because I trust the spontaneity of our interactions. Felipe Oliva was playing the violin at a ceremony for Santa Bárbara/Changó that I attended, and Teresa Cárdenas was dancing for hours at the ceremony before I happened to cross her field of energy. The first meeting with actor Jorge Perugorría took place in a dark theater; he happened to sit behind me at a performance, but somehow I knew instantly that I recognized him. Teresa and I had already been discussing his role in *Fresa y chocolate* at length before the chance encounter happened. The work of Víctor Varela's Teatro del Obstáculo I had first seen in performance, and later I was invited to meet the actors at their rehearsal space.

Generally, my visits to Cuba also include a more official side of workshop encounters; for example, at the Casa de las Américas or the Centro Nacional de Investigación de las Artes Escenicas, both of which are official government-sponsored cultural institutions. My disregard of US foreign policy legislation (the prohibition against 'dealing with the enemy') is welcomed there; for a while now we have been trying to develop an open exchange of ideas and working methods that also seeks to minimize our vulnerability to internal and external politics. There are other vulnerabilities, on my part, that have more to do with the emotional economy of crossing (and having the privilege of choice) the border to Cuba. Perhaps I am exorcizing my own traumas of having failed to understand how my generation in Germany accommodated the Cold War divisions.

The crossings that became central to our discussions are cultural, economic, and sexual, intersecting in the convoluted ideological environment of *nation* and *revolution*. Already during my first visit to Havana in 1993, everyone was talking about the most important film that had come out in recent years to surprise Cuban audiences with its unexpectedly revealing, even riveting treatment of the oppression and the exclusion of homosexuals from the Revolution. *Fresa y chocolate* ('Strawberry and Chocolate'), the new film by Tomás Gutiérrez Alea and Juan Carlos Tabío, was screened for the participants of the CONJUNTO theater workshop at the Casa de las Américas in May 1994. Teresa, a black Cuban dancer and poet from Matanzas, is not a member of UNEAC (Union of Cuban Writers and Artists) and thus officially not allowed to attend the workshop, but she accompanies me upon my request. She is kind enough to translate some of the film's dialogue and musical references, and throughout my stay in Cuba she playfully acts as a kind of spiritual adviser inviting me into the rich world of the religious and cultural practice of *Santería* that would otherwise have remained obscure to me.

I ask myself how she looks at *Fresa y chocolate* and the moving and tragically unresolvable love-affair between a gay man and a straight young communist activist (David), and how she evaluates this story about Cuba's national, revolutionary, and socialist past at a moment when the film is unavoidably perceived to dramatize present implications: Diego (Jorge Perugorría) is an openly gay artist and intellectual who loves his culture but is no longer willing to accept the contradictions of a revolution that had identified homosexuals as 'undesirable.' His desire and affection for David (Vladimir Cruz) become the vehicle of the film's warm, subtle, and unaggressive examination of Cuba's sexual politics, interweaving several related themes (black market transactions, revolutionary surveillance or vigilance, spiritualism, the freedom of artists *vis à vis* dogmatism and censorship) that highlight Diego's charisma and maturity in such a way that his melancholic passion for Cuban literature, music, and architecture becomes the symbolic ground on which the film makes its plea for tolerance emotionally gripping. In fact, a tender friendship between Diego and David evolves because the older gay man has so much to teach (while officially being denied the right to work as a teacher); he becomes a mentor for the younger, idealistic *compañero* who had never heard the voice of Maria Callas, the poetry of José Lezama Lima or the older Cuban music of Ignacio Cervantes and Ernesto Leguona. The film very poignantly chooses allusions to the forbidden literature of gay writers and the pre-revolutionary piano music of Cervantes (especially a pair of dance melodies called 'Goodbye to Cuba' and 'Lost Illusions') as leitmotifs for its portrayal of political discrimination, thus raising the question of how Cuba's revolution can sustain itself if it suppresses its full potential and denounces difference. The music prefigures Diego's departure at the end; he leaves the country because he can't bear his internal exile.

Teresa and Jorge point out that the film is set in the late 1970s, just before the Mariel Boatlift in 1980 during which many gays and disaffected Cubans left the island, but they suggest that the film's enormous popularity might be based on its emotional appeal for reconciliation, not only between Cuban revolutionary machismo and homosexuality, between revolutionary governance and political or artistic dissidence, but also between the island nation and the exile Cuban communities. (The issue of the Cuban diaspora is thorny since Cuban exile communities in the USA and elsewhere include militant anti-Castro organizations, wealthy conservatives and disaffected working-class Marxists, destitute families who fled on rafts and intellectuals teaching in universities, as well as diverse human rights and cultural groups advocating dialogue and negotiation with the Castro regime.) Teresa interprets the film's continuous references to literature, music, art, and religion as a strategy of cultural inclusion intended to bridge the chasms that have opened up in the social and political reality of the current economic crisis. Although she refuses to speak about the blockade and its debilitating effect on Cuba's effort to start economic reforms in 1992, it is apparent that the current austerity – the scarcity of food, medication, electricity, gas, social services, jobs and transportation – weighs heavily on her. It is hard to maintain one's dignity and confidence to live, she tells me, and the government's recent measures to introduce property ownership and legalize small businesses, artisans, and farmers' markets, and the dollar exchange have done little good to people like herself who are unemployed and have no access to dollars. On the contrary, the government's encouragement of foreign investment and tourism to bring in hard currency has led to resentment among many Cubans who fear that the dual peso/dollar economy creates social division and stimulates the resurgence of prostitution (or *jineterismo*, a new Cuban expression that describes the freely chosen exchange of sexual favors for access to economic goods) that was supposed to have been eradicated since the revolution. *Fresa y chocolate* portrays the existence of the black market (and, by implication, prostitution) as a necessity for survival, and perhaps the film hits home emotionally because it shows the 'lost illusions' of revolutionary ethos unflinchingly. There are a number of scenes full of bitter sadness and sardonic humor, involving Diego's neighbor Nancy (Mirta Ibarra) who works as the revolutionary 'neighborhood watch' but participates in black market dollar trading and is so frustrated sexually that she is prone to suicide.

I notice Teresa is not laughing during these scenes, even though the actress is very popular in Cuba after already starring in her role as a suicidal woman on the verge of a nervous breakdown in a previous film comedy, Gerardo Chijona's *Adorables mentiras* ('Adorable Lies,' 1991). What keeps Nancy alive in *Fresa y chocolate* is her friendship for Diego, her growing sexual attraction to David, and her faith in the *orichas*, the deities of the popular Afro-Cuban religion. The film suggests that many people's religious practice, their ongoing dialogue with the *orichas*, is a vital source of spiritual strength in times of existential crisis when the official Marxist dogma of atheism has lost all credibility. The governing Communist Party in fact abandoned the official doctrine in 1991 and declared all religions acceptable, probably because it knew that the African and Christian religious cultures in Cuba, connected to popular traditions and especially to dance, music, food, healing and other spiritual ceremonies, had always sustained themselves throughout the revolutionary era and were empowering media of resistance.

Unlike Jorge, Teresa does not talk about the revolution in our conversations. The film is perhaps too painful in its depiction of Diego's choice to go into exile despite his love for David and the country. It makes us both uncomfortable to realize how powerfully it forces the Cuban audience to confront its national self-consciousness, and its *resistencia* on behalf of the psychological and emotional identification with the popular revolution. I understand Teresa's conflicted silence to mean that the revolution is no longer popular and defensible, although most Cubans on the island are aware that it has provided free education, the best free health care system in Latin America, a high degree of social and racial equality, and a strong sense of national pride and self-determination. The majority of Cubans are black; they have benefited from the revolution and cannot imagine going back to US-supported dictatorships and the economic dependency before 1959. The change that everyone expects has to come from within, but it is not at all clear how the current reforms can grow as long as the US-imposed *bloqueo* continues to divide the nation. The most recent US foreign policy measures (the 1992 Torricelli law; the new so-called Cuba Libertad Act) stiffen and internationalize the economic, trade, and financial embargo against Cuba, and poor black Cubans like Teresa and her family are most directly suffering from the entrapment.

What keeps Teresa alive and resilient, what enables her to keep dreaming and writing down her dreams in her poetry? After the screening Teresa invites me to come to a rehearsal of Felipe's theater group, La Jaula Abierta. Unsupported by

Figure 28 Grupo La Jaula Abierta in rehearsal. Alamar 1994.

anything except their own creative energy and strength of will, this small group meets in the town of Alamar, 35 miles east of Havana. We take one of the few buses that are still running, then walk for a while and arrive at a flat concrete building in the middle of the bleak workers' town. It is the community center, Galeria Fayad Jamís, where the group is allowed to rehearse, and Teresa slips into the role of her monologue, *Me voy a buscar un Pepe*, which could mean 'I'm looking for work,' or, more precisely, 'I'm looking to catch a trick.' Felipe wrote this piece, exploring the moral dilemma of prostitution at a critical moment of 'political regression,' as he calls it, referring to the Cuban advances to lure tourist capital to the island.

Monologue performances are very popular here, and Oliva's prose has an emotional and poetic texture that is quite challenging; his stories *Me voy a buscar un Pepe* and *La reencarnación de Mateo el Reprimido* ask for the embodiment of split personae and different presentational styles by the same actor. After observing the rehearsal, we sit down and discuss different methods of performance, but our thoughts are stuck with the material. Teresa admits she is haunted by the liberating experience of performing this role, since she no longer wants to remain trapped in being type-cast as a *folklorico* dancer. The subject of the performance itself pushes her close to the edge of an emotional crisis, since she is very poor and knows the hunger caused by deprivation. She recently left her mother's house because there was no food and she didn't want to burden her family. She currently lives in Felipe's small two-room apartment.

CÁRDENAS: This performance means a lot to me. My health is not good at the moment, I have been vomiting for days. I stay alone at the house, there is no work, and Felipe is out playing the violin. I try to cook a meal when he comes home, but we have only rice, and how much can you do with rice? The electricity is out all the time, but I can hear the neighbor's loud radio. I know the songs. I am sad because I feel ugly inside, I don't know. I want to write my poetry but there is no paper. We are so dependent on gifts, on what friends give us. We live from gifts. So I am very excited about doing this monologue, I want to show it to people, because it deals with real situations, with sexual trouble, with our desires and our pride. I also need to keep working, it's so important, because I am beginning to lose my body.

BIRRINGER: Your poems seem full of childhood memories, or perhaps they are dreams expressed in the language of childhood memories?

CÁRDENAS: Yes, these are my dreams of flying and traveling, and they are also dreams addressed to the *orichas*, especially to Yemayá who is my *santo*. The poem I gave you is addressed to Yemayá, the goddess of water and life. Now I'm trying to write projects for kids, and I also want to learn French for myself. I'm doing a project on love which I can't tell you about. Did I tell you that last week we saw Charlie Chaplin's *Gold Rush* at a friend's house? My friend is also stealing movies from satellite, it's very easy, and so we can watch American movies, and I can practice my English. I want you to bring me magazines from the US, I need to read. I saw the magazine with black photo models you showed me, I didn't realize that this existed in the US, that black women feel proud to be black. Here it is not so. Did I tell you my dream from last night? I dreamt I lived in a house with a bathroom. A bathroom just for me.

BIRRINGER: Could you join a dance company or work with an independent dance group?

CÁRDENAS: It's difficult for black dancers to find work except in folkloric dance, and I don't want to do folkoric dance for tourists. Apart from that I dance all the time, because it's part of my culture and my music.

BIRRINGER: Felipe, I'm interested in your experience with the communication spaces in Cuba. For example, I was puzzled when I saw no announcement of our performance of *AlienNation* at the Gran Teatro last week, and knowing that there are practically no daily papers except the limited edition of the state newspaper, *Granma*, I wonder how the news about events or cultural activities travel amongst the population. And since there are very few advertising billboards (except those that carry revolutionary slogans and song titles), magazines or journals, I wonder how you think about image transmission or visual culture? And since you work with actors, you will also know about the situation of film and television in Cuba's current 'special period,' and about the subjects that are broadcast in this moment.

OLIVA: Do you like me to comment on the public culture or my own experience?

BIRRINGER: Well, you could tell us first about your work, your artistic backgrounds and your understanding of 'media' in Cuba, how you use them.

OLIVA: I am a *creador*, an artist who writes different kinds of literature: fairy-tales, poetry, novels, theater, children's and youth literature, and I have also written for radio and television. I am also a musician; my training, since my childhood, has been linked to art and culture. I have received different kinds of influences in my training, and I am a kind of '*sui generis*' Cuban.

BIRRINGER: You mean 'autodidact' . . .?

OLIVA: [laughs] No. I had an academic education, but since my childhood, when I was still at school, I envisioned myself writing and making theater. I also liked films a lot. That is to say, all kinds of artistic and cultural manifestations came to me and have made me someone, let's say, with a certain complex training. In Cuba, there are artists and creators who are dedicated only to one branch, like literature or music; in my case, I have been quite permeable. I have been into all this since I was a little child. It also interested me always to direct actors, as well as work with dancers and visual artists. It gives me a broader vision of reality, of our Cuban culture.

My experience comes from very different fields; even as a musician my first training and job was in a symphony orchestra, in classical music, but then I wanted to integrate myself more into what we understand as popular culture, and I began playing in dance orchestras, in places where there would be a lot of people. This has influenced me artistically, also intellectually. I feel I write with a popular consciousness. I also believe that this process, also living through the revolutionary process in our country, has given me a vision of reality that you might call 'marvelous' . . . you know what I mean. I think Cuba is a magic country, full of surprises every day. Miracles. I try to pour this surreality of ours into my work and my writing.

BIRRINGER: How 'marvelous' is the reality at the moment? I ask myself how people live or imagine reality when it is so overwhelmingly marked and overshadowed by scarcity, the continual food and medical shortages, the blackouts, the uncertainty about imminent economic and social collapse, the looming exodus, and the family divisions that have torn the nation into two sides with practically no bridge in-between.

OLIVA: For those of us who have been linked to the creation process in this country, it is interesting to see the process in this moment we are living, to see the various different shapes that we artists use to project ourselves. Today, there are a lot of people writing, there is a lot of literature, a lot of theater, a lot of ideas, but not all of it gets to the public, because of our great economical difficulties which we all know. Much interesting work cannot get published or put on a stage. The same happens with music; at present, there is a readjustment of our identity as people, and there is a tendency to go back to our cultural roots in all the various fields, especially in folk and popular music. To me this is fascinating because I think it is a very vast field from where work of great transcending force could emerge, works which distil the great amalgam of cultures we have.

In my case, as *mestizo*, I have been receiving this culture-mixture since I was born. At this point I feel that in my writing and in my theater everything is being connected, in this *mestizo* culture, and I bring these connections to my vision. I work with my theater group, La Jaula Abierta ('The Open Cage'), and I want to produce different manifestations in which there is a presence of dance-theatre and folklore, not the aboriginal folklore, but the mixed folklore, let's say, one in which folklore is intermixed with contemporary dance, visual elements with music, and in which the identity of Cubans (*nuestro hombre cubano*) today can emerge with all its contradictions, hopes and despairs, and all the accumulation of experiences we are facing now. We are trying to create performances which can deal fundamentally with our cultural mixture, thus bringing onstage our Afro-Cuban culture as it mixes with contemporary, new theater.

BIRRINGER: Choreographer Marianela Boán (Danza Abierta) says she is doing 'contaminated theater,' and I wonder whether she is refering to the difficult conditions of dance production during the economic crisis or whether she means a 'new' eclecticism that self-consciously draws on Cuba's racial and cultural hybridity in the danced expression, on its ability to assimilate cultures. But you are arguing that this eclecticism is not new, that it has always existed, perhaps in the sense in which Cuban critic and writer Antonio Benítez-Rojo has spoken of 'The Repeating Island' and used the metaphor of chaos-theory to speculate on the apparent 'disorder' of the Caribbean generative syncretisms.

[While I speak, I am aware that Felipe knows of course how many of Cuba's poets, writers, visual artists and musicians have left to live and work abroad, and he probably knows that Benítez-Rojo teaches in the USA. His own brother and mother have left for the USA and live in Miami (in 'Little Havana'), but his sister continues to work in Havana as an operetta singer, and we have dinner at her house one night. I have rarely spent a night witnessing more miracles of food preparation with practically no food, and yet we eat and drink and listen to the old records (Cuban music of the 1940s), and to newer ones which feature Susy Oliva in her many performances. I watch the old turntable as it comes alive, perched on top of the grand piano in the center of the living room, with the neighbors dropping in, the young daughter returning home with her boyfriend (she studies acting and English), and our host radiating the energy of someone who loves to entertain large audiences. Felipe affectionately explains the popular music to us, introduces the songs, gives background information about the singers, musicians, conductors, as if they all belonged to the family. In the course of this evening we decide to work together on a joint video production, bringing members of La Jaula Abierta and AlienNation together for a process of script development and rehearsal.]

OLIVA: At present in Cuba, there are a lot of groups trying to do very interesting things, we call them 'projects.' For example, there are different dance-theatre groups approaching, in very diverse ways, our reality. Given the great difficulties publishing books, if there is something necessary in our culture, it is theater that reaches out, giving performances in different spaces, in the streets, a kind of theater where the people will see themselves represented, where they can participate, a *theatre of communication*. A theater still authored and rehearsed, but involving the people through their collective experience, and their existential questions as individuals.

BIRRINGER: What is more important or popular now, the theater or the cinema?

OLIVA: As a popular medium, the cinema has been more important, and even more so television. Television is the main mass media, not only in Havana, but also in other towns or the countryside. There is a TV in every house, and people consume a lot of TV, because they have difficulties finding or keeping work, there are transportation problems, and so they can't travel or go out and thus spend a lot of time enjoying the soap operas, the musicals, the salsa . . . although it is not the best programming. However, it is not below the quality level of other Latin American countries, on the contrary. But you can tell that people would like or prefer to go and see live performance, because there is a massive attendance at the popular theater festivals. Yet tickets are much easier to obtain for the cinema [they generally cost 1 Cuban peso], and so people like to go to the movies.

BIRRINGER: What are the production processes and availabilities for film and video? Are they limited to ICAIC [the Cuban Institute of Cinematographic Art and Industry], the university, the television station or the International School of Film and Television? Can people produce video when there is such a lack of technical resources due to the current economic crisis?

OLIVA: In fact there is always someone who tries it, there are always little groups trying to make films or amateur videos, but yes, the camera might be missing, the tape is missing . . . there are very real material difficulties. As I told you, I write literature and theater pieces, but my imagination is often very cinematic, and so I write filmscripts without being able to film.

BIRRINGER: What is the relation between *Afro-Cubanidad* and the music? And then I am interested in the relationship between the music in the religious ceremonies, such as the one where I met you [dedicated to Santa Bárbara/ Changó], and the representations of Afro-Cuban culture in television or radio. What are the differences between religious practice and the institutionalized/ official media? Why has the government lately relaxed its prohibition of religious ceremonies and allowed *Santería* to be practiced openly? Is religious practice understood as an escape or safety valve from the existential economic and political problems, or is it perhaps even used and instrumentalized as a distraction from the stakes of a democratic political future or the changes in the economic system that would become necessary? Or has the Afro-Cuban religious practice, as long as it had to remain unofficial or camouflaged, served as a refuge for popular expression, spiritual or even political 'organization'?

OLIVA: We should philosophize about this . . . At this point there is a great religious effervescence in a very large portion of the population. There are so many economic and political problems which have not been solved, and yes, people seek refuge in God, the saints, the *orichas* – now we are getting into the issue of our syncretisms – in hopes of help and consolation. What people want most is health, and feeling good with oneself, and after that the rest is going to be solved step by step. I think religion always carries within itself a certain evasion or escape, not only in the Cuban case, but for any human being. For us religion is something ancestral; we had it here for ever, whether it came from Africa or Spain. Many people are religious but they wouldn't profess it for social or circumstantial reasons. Nowadays it's no longer problematic; there is a great extroversion of anything having to do with religion, and it also has entered TV, the books, the cinema, and the music, maybe even too much. It tends to commercialize what the Afro-Cuban religion is in reality. It is not a state policy, but many people started to profess openly when they realized that religion was compromised by Marxist philosophy and historical materialism. Today people can belong to the Communist Party and have religious beliefs. It's a very interesting cultural phenomenon.

Here in Cuba, we live with the gods, with people, with the *orichas*, and in our Afro-Cuban religious understanding we have hopes and aspirations, and we have imperfections like them. This is for us something we've got in our blood, we assume it without difficulty. To bring all this to the literature and the theater needs a transformation with a certain cultural and artistic vision, which is what I am developing right now. If I approach a religious subject, I don't do it to escape or to worship, but as a part of our existential complexity, and taking this as my basis, I don't criticize only the *orichas* but also aspects which appear in the Bible. Currently I'm using passages from the Bible and I translate them into our terms; I'm mixing a lot of what has influenced me since childhood. For example, in a play I can put together a dialogue between Ochún (which would be the Virgin of Charity) and Judas Iscariot. This kind of projection makes the audience for which I write receive it with the appreciation that is based in our identity, our reasoning, and our surrealism. I think that if there is any surrealist country in this world it must be Cuba. And at the same time I ask myself how Cubans can step outside of the problems we are having. How can we move forward?

BIRRINGER: What is your understanding of media? In the USA we don't tend to include theater or music in the general concepts of media culture or media communications. How strongly do mass media here in Cuba influence perceptions of reality or history?

OLIVA: I never asked myself this question. Years ago I was reading in a school from a book of mine that had won the children's literature award, and a nine-year-old girl asked me since when I had written for children, and I realized I had written for children since my own childhood, already in primary school I started writing stories and filmscripts, without any kind of orientation, without advice, just as a means of communication. Later I wrote also for youth and adult audiences, and sometimes I would be inventing a 'Hollywood' theme [a melodrama] without knowing anything about Hollywood. The cinema has always been very popular in Cuba, but now it is slowly being replaced by TV because of the problems we are facing. The films are no longer attractive enough for the people's tastes that are shaped by television.

BIRRINGER: Would you argue that Brazilian or Mexican imported soap operas influence Cuban theater production?

OLIVA: Not in the drama, but perhaps it's true for the lighter genres, comedy and humoristic theater where they are caricatured. People here love Brazilian soap opera, and when the Brazilian directors come here to our film festivals, they say they've learnt it from us. Years ago, Cuba was one of the main popular soap opera producers; this had its start in the radio, since Cuban radio always had very high technical standards of production, and everybody listened to the radio. At night, when there are no blackouts, people turn on the TV, and that leaves only certain audiences for the live theater, students, people whose work is connected to culture and art, and those interested in particular subjects, whether marginal, religious or folkloric. In fact, I know a lot of people who only go to the theater because it deals with marginalized or crucial existential themes, and that may explain the popularity of Alberto Pedro's *Manteca*, for example, or the attractiveness of *El Público* to gay audiences. Ballet performances are also always sold out; everybody goes there for different reasons, I don't know how to explain it, whether it's the high quality of the Cuban ballet, or the good publicity, or the pride in seeing such good work created under extremely difficult conditions. The people in Cuba have such a good cultural education that anyone can make a critique of a performance and talk about it without having to be an intellectual. I like this about our culture, and I try to write with the diversity of tastes in mind, trusting the people and their understanding of art.

Cuban artists of the young generation articulate *resistencia* in their own creation of alternative spaces, performance projects, and ironically provocative refractions of scarcity. It is expressed in the spiritual will that propels the creative determination of Felipe's actors who rehearse for five hours in a dark building without electricity or running water. The only props they have for *La reencarnación de Mateo el Reprimido* are a few pieces of wood simulating a construction site, and a sign that reads *Paraiso en Reparación*. Another form of 'reconstruction' is becoming visible in cultural efforts to address the suppression of homosexuality in Cuba, and thus also the relations of sexual education, machismo, women's equality, and AIDS prevention. There are clear indications that this new openness, galvanized in the discussions over *Fresa y chocolate*, is officially supported by the programming of literary and theatrical events – at the Casa de las Américas and other institutions – which address the memory and consequences of suppression and censorship. I also heard rumors that the Cuban Catholic Church is planning a National Ecclesiastical Meeting to formulate its future role in supporting efforts toward democratization and mediating between the government and sectors of civil society. The Church also supports the so-called Concilio Cubano, a new umbrella group intended to unite dissidents and human rights advocates in Cuba. In the Pogolotti neighborhood in Havana another new community initiative has gotten underway. Magaly Muguercia, a theater researcher who has dedicated much of her work to the exploration of utopianism in Cuban performance, tells me that she now works for the Centro Memorial Dr. Martin Luther King and its outreach programs. The Centro, directed by Raúl Suárez Ramos, also publishes a new journal of social theology called *Caminos*. Magaly describes the new initiative as community work or *educación popular* committed to the improvement of participatory integration of all levels of society. Puzzled by the group's name and reference to the black civil rights movement in the US, I ask Magaly whether the Centro Martin Luther King attempts to solicit international solidarity. She explains that 'the Centro is an institution derived from Christian inspiration, but it is in fact macro-ecumenical. Besides the fact that the founding nucleus is Baptist, a branch of Protestantism, it seeks to incorporate all the various religious practices in Cuba, Christian and non-Christian, because in Cuba we have many African religions that are not Christian although at times heavily mixed up with Christian ideas. The Centro is also interested in integrating believers and non-believers and in creating exchanges among them. At this point, it primarily seeks dialogue and integration here in our country and on the concrete local level, with the single purpose of serving to create a more just society. All of the work has an explicit socialist philosophy, but it carries a strong, conscious awareness of the need to discover new paths for promoting popular participation and the people's self-transformation.'

I respect her cautious answer since it is obvious that such new initiatives are monitored by the government, and so far Castro has refused, for example, any public dialogue with the Concilio Cubano, which doesn't bode well for the future of the Communist Party's democratic imagination. The fundamental challenge, however, is precisely what Magaly refers to as the people's self-determining and participatory transformation. It is the people who need to claim the freedom to design a new model of social justice in light of the specific circumstances that prevent a national dialogue – and a dialogue that crosses the borders of isolation from the North.

The more I listen to my Cuban friends the more I sense their desire to speak openly and uproot the inhibitions of self-censorship that sometimes make them cautious. I meet a young painter at Galeria Habana who tells me that artists have started to become more active in circulating their ideas and launching their own independent publications. In November 1993 visual artist Tania Bruguera and several others published the first issue of a newsletter called *Memoría de la post-guerra*, and in the same year the Pablo Milanés Foundation (supported by Cuba's famous singer/composer) started a new cultural journal, *Proposiciones*. As both publications claim freedom of expression for themselves, they will be crucial in testing the viability of the new opening toward dialogue that was also advocated, in a passionate critical-utopian spirit, by the two special issues – *Puentes a Cuba/ Bridges to Cuba* – of *Michigan Quarterly Review* edited by US-Cuban anthropologist Ruth Behar. The independent efforts of the youngest generation of artists to articulate themselves outside of bureaucratic paternalism or the confines of UNEAC and ISA (Instituto Superior de Arte) are especially noteworthy since the extraordinary strength and cohesiveness of the controversial plastic arts of the 1980s, which had created such an important collective cultural dynamic since the 1981 'Volumen I' exhibition (described extensively by Gerardo Mosquera and Luis Camnitzer), have been drained by the departure from Cuba of most of the painters, sculptors, and photographers who had focused on critical issues of social and national identity in their work. Since many of these artists recently emigrated or work abroad in the hope of living off sales of their work and participating in the international art market, their absence has cut short the teaching and mutual dialogue among the younger generations of cultural producers. Progressive musicians such as Carlos Varela and most performers that I met have decided not to leave Cuba but to experiment with the spiritual renewal of a cultural 'aesthetic' of survival. Tania Bruguera, for example, has been trying to reconstruct the late Ana Mendieta's body-art for several years, seeking to perform it by rediscovering the ritual dimension of Mendieta's erotic spiritualism.

It is the Cuban sensibility of improvisation with fragmentary information, need, and scarcity that I find most immediately significant with respect to our questions about *border media*. For example, two of Varela's most notorious songs ('Guillermo Tell' and 'Robinson') mix rock with Cuban percussive rhythms and make eclectic reference to European literary or mythical allegories that gain a specific political meaning in the Cuban context when they are received in cathartic moments of reflection on Cuba's isolation and the young generation's oedipal struggle with the patriarchs of the revolution. The song 'Guillermo Tell,' released in 1989 just after the fall of the Berlin Wall, became so popular that Varela's generation (those born in the 1970s) began to call itself 'the children of Wilhelm Tell.' When fourteen young Cuban artists were shown in the group show *No Man is an Island* (in Finland's Pori Art Museum, 1990), Mosquera titled his review 'The 14 Sons of William Tell' and sought to clarify the misleading application of the term 'postmodernist appropriation' to contemporary Cuban artists. He persuasively argues that Cuban eclecticism is not derivative or equivalent to First World postmodern pastiche but dependent on an ethical impulse to make sense of deprivation and isolation by drawing on a variety of languages and 'replacements.' Tania Bruguera expresses this ethos in terms of a wider concern among her generation to challenge political commonplaces and revolutionary slogans as well as the negative, dogmatic anti-imperialism that would denounce colonizing influences. For her, using foreign information is morally justified if such 'technical information' is made socially useful within the broader concern of Cuban art to integrate different positions and, above all, renew faith in a cultural autonomy that doesn't succumb to nihilism, alienation, or superficial asthetic cynicism. A cultural *aesthetic of survival*, according to

Uruguayan artist Luis Camnitzer, is not postmodern but closer to the utopian spirit of the revolutionary 1960s in Cuba; the 'eclecticism of survival' of the 1990s, however, is a kind of 'nationalization' of various devices and scarce resources driven by despair and vitally committed to regenerating cultural identity.

The search for an integrality of forms that interconnects artistic languages with political and ethical concerns clearly exceeds the boundaries of the purely aesthetic. Most artists define their work in existential terms; Carlos points out that all he wants to do is 'write songs that reflect how my generation of Cubans lives: our dreams and fears, our likes and dislikes, and what it means to be living in Cuba at this moment.' He then refers to the Cubans inside and outside, claiming that he wants his songs to be like 'scissors that cut the strings that have made us puppets for so many years, inside Cuba and out. I believe that all of us Cubans have the right to defend each other and work with each other, everywhere.'

With his potent theatrical metaphor in mind, I turn to Teatro del Obstáculo and my encounter with actors who have dedicated their lives to the long-term process of reconstruction. It's a rainy Thursday afternoon in Havana, and Imma Sarries-Zgonc and I arrive a little early at the house where Víctor Varela's group works to prepare its next performance. When I knock on the door, there's no answer, but we can hear a faint sound of music. The group's rehearsal must still be on, and since daylight is precious to them, we decide to wait until they are ready to see us. We are both quite exhausted, after the bus trip from Alamar and a week of hard work on a video project we started with Teresa and Felipe, but we feel exhilarated and full of anticipation. Varela (not related to Carlos) did not want us to see his rehearsal but agreed to a meeting. The house is located on the corner of Ayestarán and 20 de Mayo, directly overlooking the immense Plaza de la Revolución. In the distance I can see the statue of José Martí. The Plaza is empty, and in its emptiness it appears like a vast gray island made of concrete. It's a ghostly landscape, and I walk to the bench where I remember sitting fifteen months ago after the performance of Varela's *Segismundo ex marqués*. It was the first time I saw the work of this young independent theater collective, and it had been a disconcerting and profoundly moving experience which left me stranded. I had witnessed a most unusual theater work in which barely a word was spoken and the impact on the viewer was almost entirely visceral. The movement language the group used was unknown to me, and I could not place it among all the other Cuban performances I had seen. I had also heard the comments of the Cuban theater critics and writers; many of them spoke with great respect and admiration of the young director's work, but very few seemed willing or comfortable at explaining to me what they had seen. I sensed that they perhaps wanted to partake a little bit in the mystery surrounding Teatro Obstáculo, as it was mentioned to me that the work of the group for a long time could be seen only in their house, which seats only eight people, and when they produced a new work once a year, there were always long waiting lists. One friend told me he had to wait five months until he could finally see the work. As I reflect on this, I begin to wonder whether such a strategy of restricted access has any larger implications, in the political context of Cuba's critical condition of extreme scarcity. Or was the withholding of broad general access a philosophical decision connected to the 'private' nature of this independent work? I walk back over to the house where the group now works; it's not a theater either but a chapel-like building that in the nineteenth century belonged to a Freemasons Lodge, one of several secret societies that played a role in Cuba's cultural life and political struggle for abolition and independence (religious secret societies exist till this day). A plaque on the wall next to the entrance door says *Logia Masónica 'Hijos de la Patria'* ('Children of the Fatherland').

The door suddenly opens and Víctor welcomes us warmly, inviting us in. There is a small hallway that opens into a round space which is used for rehearsals and performances. A few wooden benches form a half-circle, and on the left side near the two big windows is a small area for meditation. There is no furniture, except a carpet and a tiny wooden box, with a book and candle on it. Víctor notices the expression on my face, and he smiles: 'That is our library and reading room. We have only one book at the moment.' Then he offers China tea. The other group members approach us quietly, and I can see that their bodies and minds are still captivated by the rehearsal. We introduce each other and decide to sit down on a bench overlooking the inner space and some constructed objects or kinetic sculptures. Víctor comes back with small, elegant porcelain teacups. He is a charismatic, beautiful young man with fine, sensual features and long, dark hair. I notice the softness of his voice. Intuitively I can sense in him a peculiar mixture of intellectual authority, discipline, and a quiet sincerity that has no need for conspicuous behavior. He acts not as the director but more as an interpreter of the group's work, patiently listening to my tentative questions, and gradually we all get caught up in the intensity of the conversation. I feel it is important to the group members to take time; they want to share their philosophical work principles, they even demonstrate a scene for us.

BIRRINGER: Are we looking at the space for your new work, *El arca* ('The Ark') – When is the first performance?

VARELA: In January 1996. We already showed it in two performances at a theater festival in Italy, but it's not finished yet, because we had worked on it only for a month when we got invited to participate in this dramaturgy festival which we didn't want to miss. We made a first version in a relatively short time, and now we are changing a lot. The event took place in Torino, and our script was even translated into English. I can give you a copy. I'm very sorry that I was unable to come to the Casa de las Américas and see your work last week [*Lovers Fragments*], but we had too much work. Here you see our working team where everybody does everything; we're hammering away and constructing the space and all sorts of things. What happened is that in the beginning, after just a month of work, we were not happy with the way the performance went because most of the plasticity and space had been worked on at the periphery; the inside space work had been missing. So we create new elements for the inside space.

BIRRINGER: Before starting to talk about *El arca*, could you introduce the group and describe the beginnings of Teatro Obstáculo?

VARELA: The group started in 1985, when all the Cuban theater was linked to the institutions, and the Grupo de Teatro Obstáculo has the honor of being the first group in the off-culture. We decided to work in the living room of my house where we had 4 square meters per actor, and we performed for eight people at a time. For four years we made theater paying it out of our own pockets without getting any money for it. Many people were watching closely to see what was going to happen with us, and when they saw it worked, a lot of independent groups started up. Then we had problems at the house with the police because some neighbors complained about the noise, and we were left hanging in the air. The Cultural Ministry tried to look for a solution, and they gave us place which until recently was the studio of a puppet-maker.

Everything you see here now has been constructed by us, we brought in the iron rails and other materials to hang some lights, but we don't have much, well, you know how the situation in Cuba is, we have few resources. Look at this, it's an old lighting board some people in Paris gave us, because for quite some time we did not have electrical light. In any case, we wanted this theater to exist, regardless of whether we have economic help or not. We don't believe in lamenting about the lack of resources. I also think it's a problem that exists all over the world as well; one has to invent with one's imagination.

SARRIES-ZGONC: Since when have you been working in this house?

VARELA: Since 1989. But let me introduce the other members who founded the group nine, almost ten years ago: Barbara Maria Barrientos and Alexis Gonzáles de Villegas are founding members without whom the investigation would not have been possible. They have incorporated in their bodies and psyches the entire process since we started out up until now that we know a little more. Then there is Noemí Gregorio Bonet, who joined us two years ago, and another new member, Mara de la Fuente. Coming into a group like this is not easy; in the beginning, when we did not know where the group was going, it was easier to determine who really believed in the process of investigation. We have always believed that theater creation must be a vehicle to acquire a knowledge of life, to acquire a new level of being. It is not about doing performances, or to become famous, although we like to have audiences come to see us, but it is not the goal. When the group started actors like Barbara or Alexis were very organic for they came in without having any advantage at all: nobody knew me as a director, nobody knew us, and anything could happen. But six or seven years later we were facing danger because we already had a name and a reputation. In fact many actors came to the group wanting to accept the concept of working a lot with us to get the technique, the physical control, to learn the secrets of our theater, well, but they actually came to us because of the fame of the group, which allowed us to travel to other countries, and they wanted to use it as a bridge. Very few actors, however, succeeded in adapting themselves to a group like this. Noemí and Mara are two actresses who from the beginning connected with the group's ideas and were not concerned about other things. And finally, Harold Glez works with us on stage machinery and lighting, and Fresia Castello is the group's producer.

BIRRINGER: I remember a text you included in the program for *Segismundo ex marqués*, it was a kind of manifesto of the Teatro del Obstáculo. Did it express your group philosophy?

VARELA: At the beginning we made theater without resources, working on a naked floor in a very reduced space with very little ventilation, and creating work nobody was asking for. What saved us during all this time was the postulate of turning the obstacles into creation. Every time a problem came up that almost led to a collapse, we would say: why don't we turn it into creation? And that is how our 'philosophy of the obstacle' developed. It was an evolution; when we realized the importance of obstacles for our creation, we started consciously to produce our own obstacles, and the so-called '*estética de la dificultad*' emerged. It's now our working philosophy. For example, *Segismundo ex marqués*, the performance you saw, was conceived to be played at night, with lighting, but at the time the blackouts in Havana happened almost daily. The day we were going to show the piece to a group of invited people we had a blackout half-way through the performance. Everything went dark. So we decided to do it at three in the afternoon, during natural light, the way you saw it, which is actually more interesting than the original way. So this obstacle led to a creative change, and you have to work this way, otherwise the problems crush you. You also find invented obstacles in *Segismundo ex marqués*; for example, we used no set in that performance, whereas in *Opera ciega* ['Blind Opera'] we had a lot of objects and scenography, and each time we start out from a new obstacle. Our first performance, *La cuarta pared* ['The Fourth Wall'], had no text, and so when we started *Opera ciega* our obstacle became working with language because the actors had gotten used to performing without text and felt very comfortable although they had not said a single word in the theater. After *Opera ciega*, in which the actors supported themselves with the objects, the set, the lighting, and the soundtrack, we decided to drop all objects and technical support in *Segismundo ex marqués*. Our new work, *El arca*, is perhaps the most difficult of all. Perhaps I say this because we are still working on it now. The other pieces were also complex. But in the new work the obstacle is how to get the group's wisdom to be popular, since we felt that the elaboration of our special technique in *Segismundo* was quite elitist, to which perhaps only a small and sensible minority audience had access. How can we put our technique in the service of something more popular? That is the question we try to answer without falling into vanities, vulgarities, or bad taste. The obstacle is the premise before each performance process, depending on what was left out or unexplored in the previous work.

As to our working process: we work through organized improvisation. Improvisation without structure is a chaos, and afterwards one does not know which

Figure 29 Cuarta pared II, directed by Víctor Varela and performed by Teatro del Obstáculo. Havana. 1990. Photo courtesy of Teatro del Obstáculo.

Figure 30 Opera ciega, directed by Víctor Varela and performed by Teatro del Obstáculo. Havana. 1991. Photo courtesy of Teatro del Obstáculo.

material to use. So I give the actors a subject of investigation; for example, I tell Barbara to work with the idea of elevating herself above the Ark level and to build a chain of physical actions. We work almost always with physical actions that engage the whole body, which gives us the result of something very close to dance. It is something very much incorporated, involving our whole body in the sequence of actions.

We have our own training called *el árbol del pan* ['the tree of bread'], divided in three parts. The first one is the physical training called *el cuerpo suspendido* ['the suspended body'] which came out of the obstacle of having to work on the floor; very physical work on a hard floor is not good for the bones, but we did not have a mattress or boards, and so we had to create a mattress with our own body. The only way to do that was to suspend the movement, learning to work with the weight in such a way that the body would not be mistreated. The second part is the vocal training called *el ojo que escucha* ['the listening eye'], where the voice directs the audience's eyes. You saw that in *Segismundo*: there is no space but a voice treatment very similar to what is called tessitura, which resembles religious singing; for example, in Gregorian chants. So there is no space, but the voice creates a space giving you the feeling of being in a sacred place.

The last part of *el árbol del pan* is the integrating work of voice and movement, integrating each actor's structure as well. In this training the basic principles are already known to the actors, so when we improvise we can rely on the work we have done already. The training is developed into training for technique, structure, and organicity. All of it comes from having taken part in different trainings and realizing that most of them are very technical. You can train a lot but if you only stay with the technique, you cannot make good use of it afterwards. In other words, there is a technical part which contains all the secret laws an actor should know, in our case this means working with weight, balance, shifting, etc. The actor has to learn to be well structured on stage. This does not mean we are against other improvisational methods, but the actor must master all that he or she does in space and time to be able to repeat it, to achieve a stable level of quality which will remain even if sometimes the inspiration is not fully working. It is something that the Grotowski actor Ryszard Cieslak used to say; for him the shape was like a glass with a candle, and when he was inspired the candle lit up, and when he was not inspired the candle wouldn't burn but he still had the glass.

Finally, the organicity is something that cannot be conducted and belongs to each actor's irrationality and to her or his levels of sensitivity, but in a way it's connected to the meaning of what she or he is doing. If the actor is conscious of what she does on stage, if he knows everything he is doing, then the actor can stimulate sensitive and emotional reactions from his or her body-mind. Everything is very much linked to the process. The process is about learning to learn. One of the dangers now is that we already mastered the technique, we are forgetting a little our beginnings, the times when we had no technique but worked more with the heart. Now we are trying to come back to the beginning, forgetting a little the technique to strengthen the performance energy.

BIRRINGER: Is the 'aesthetic of difficulty' based on your personal vision or the result of a collective process?

VARELA: It is a mixture of both. On the one hand I had the need, as the group's guide, to reflect on what we were doing, because almost always the creative process was produced by inspiration, especially in the beginning. Furthermore, I have choreographic impulses in me that are very strong. At the beginning it happened to me a bit like to Martha Graham who brought her body-logic into the dance. For example, in *La cuarta pared* the actors immersed themselves fully into the work and the different forms I gave them; I asked them to fill them with very strong temperatures. But afterwards I started to reflect on my own logic so that I could give the actors all the tools I knew, and they would be imaginative in their own ways. I also realized I was deconstructing movement behaviors a lot; my imaginative inspiration relies on that. The actors learnt this, and they understand deconstruction and practice it now, and so our process is a shared process.

BIRRINGER: Didn't you also work with Marianela Boán? How much are you or the actors interested in contemporary dance? From the point of view of your own autonomous group method, how is your work related to Cuban theater and dance, and to international dance forms?

BARRIENTOS: Before I answer your question, I would like to explain how I got into the group with Víctor, and how I understand the 'aesthetic of difficulty.' I was – and I say was because I had to change – a very emotive actress. I did not give a lot of importance to technique, and that was a big problem I had with Víctor. For me emotions were much more important than technique. When we worked together I soon realized that I could not do many things, because the work was not only about emotions. I needed the training to get that technique, the possibility to work with my whole body and not alone with the heart. At that time Víctor was not only doing theater, but he was also choreographing with Marianela, and I found it very stimulating. I saw many of his choreographies, and when I left the theater I wanted to dance, but I felt I could be a dancer in the theater. In a way, *Segismundo* was the greatest performance the group has ever done, because it involved all of our senses, our entirety, and at the same time the training was immensely pleasurable. To me *Segismundo* is a dance-theatre piece; it made me work very hard on body techniques, on the voice, on emotion, everything. I think an actor has to be very physically prepared, just like a dancer. Víctor works with us at all those levels, with the bodily rigor of a dancer.

BIRRINGER: Do you practice every day?

GONZÁLES: Yes, every day. Generally we have trained in stages, developing the group method, but once we enter the creation process we concentrate on that. At the same time we always continue our daily exercises, and we create specific exercises that relate to the scenes we are working on, and vice versa.

BARRIENTOS: The training is done in special sequences. For a while Víctor taught us *el árbol del pan*, and we investigated it and found that it was a very complete and good training for us, and so we continued it for a long time. Then Víctor was invited to Brazil to give a workshop, and we stayed here and continued the training. When he came back we stopped and began rehearsing a new performance Víctor had written. During the process we began to train ourselves for something we did not know, something we were getting to know through the creation.

VARELA: The only training we do systematically every day is cleaning the space inside and outside. We always do that.

BIRRINGER: How was the experience of integration for the new members?

BONET: Since I came to the group I got three trainings, and now I am working on *el árbol del pan*. I had to learn a lot after having been away from the group for a while, and immediately we faced a new creation process. The process was very violent for me, because I never studied theatre: this is my first school. What I did was looking at everything I saw, trying to imitate every good thing I saw and could do, and then I began to ask questions about the technique, I started explaining it to myself, talking to the others, and then I started discovering. I am at a stage now where I discover those secrets little by little, the secrets which are already the truth of the group. It is deeply satisfying to do technical things with actors who have so much experience. They are my guides, and I have to be very awake to learn all the information.

BIRRINGER: How do you start the creation process? With an image, an idea, a physical difficulty, a text? How does the process evolve?

VARELA: I always write a text before starting. I tried to do it without a text, it does not work for me. I hope it will some day because I am getting bored with writing, it's a very lonely act. It depresses me very much. But the text is like the foundation for a building. In *La cuarta pared* the space is a theater, because there is a group of characters from a libretto rejected by the author. The author has to tear it and throw it into the garbage. The characters have to find their scenes in the garbage. The situation is different from Pirandello's, because they cannot look for an author, they have to find their own scenes and make their lives on their own. That was the setting of the space. During the creation process we still had this text, and it had a lot of words in it, and some textual passages were very long and full of images. It ended up being an obstacle to the creation, and so one day I literally tore it up and threw it away. The actors were astonished and didn't know what to do, and so I suggested to them that the loss of the text had affected their vocal cords, and we started to work on a performance which became completely extra-verbal.

Opera ciega has a text as well. It happens inside the head. *Segismundo* takes place in an indeterminate space; there are no stage directions. In the beginning it says: ' *I ching den ching*' ('From my spirit to your spirit'). It is a form of Tao, namely the empty space following Tao's postulate that the usefulness of everything is in the emptiness. Every character is a sign. So I consider Segismundo to be Yin, I am Yang, and Natse Nagai is Tao. Although the space was undefined, the signs defined it. *El arca* is an ark composed of three blackboards, so there is always a defined space, but we are now transforming it, and it's difficult to explain because it's a plastic process. This comes from my first motivation, which is painting. What happened to me was that I went to art school and theater school at the same time, and all of a sudden I realized theater interested me much more. I said to myself I like theater more because in theater I can paint in time.

So in fact my starting-point is visual art, and through visual art I learn to do my own theater. For example, something prevails in this space which is very geometric, in the combinations between wood and cardboard, as if they were natural elements but a little artificial. It's a strange process, one starts seeing shapes and begins to guess what is needed. What is important to me is the idea of scenography-as-actor, namely a set that changes and moves. I never like watching a performance in which the set does not transform itself into many things. All these objects here are made to change.

[Víctor and Alexis get up and walk into the space, demonstrating some of the shape-changing objects, pointing to some of elements that attain different meanings and associations in the course of the performance. All of the blackboards have cut-out parts, invisible doors, or seem suspended in such a way that they can turn and alter their configuration.]

SARRIES-ZGONC: Do you have this scenographic creation process already in your mind when you write the text or is it something you create together? Do you imagine the characters? Or do you let the actors choose and develop their own personae?

VARELA: The text proposes perhaps 30 per cent of the changes, but we really find out only during the rehearsals and transformations. For example, these objects I just showed you were not in the text. But I always impose the characters on the actors. That is because I write thinking of them. I have to write characters that are not like anything the actors have done already. I also do it thinking of the actor's level of experience. The most difficult roles are given to specific actors. I tried it once in the other way, but it did not work. I was reading about Ariane Mnouchkine and her way of telling the actors to pick the character they wanted and to defend it, and the one who did the best version was keeping the role. But this is also a very long process; it doesn't fit with the rhythm in our group. But one important dramaturgical decision in Teatro Obstáculo is that all characters are equally strong; there are no supporting roles.

BIRRINGER: What is your understanding of independent theater or, more precisely, I want to ask Fresia how it is possible to produce this kind of work in Cuba at this moment? How much are people interested in it? What is the relationship between this work and the popular Cuban theatre? Do you consider your group to be marginal, or does the work reflect a new and significant evolution of a young, independent theater movement in Cuba?

CASTELLO: Well, production is very difficult, but there are some resources. I think this work is integrated into other tendencies, but it's a rather different theater, and it is important.

VARELA: We are just making our programs for the new work. Fresia, tell us about the problems. [She shows me a beautiful hand-designed program book which is several pages long.]

CASTELLO: There is no place where we could get the designs photographed and printed.

VARELA: We will have a set of four performances, and we want to make posters, flyers, and programs. This is the rough draft. Normally in Cuba you only get a little slip of paper with the names of the actors. We wanted to make something more ambitious, including explanations of all our performances with photos and pictures of the characters. Fresia met a friend at the Polygraphic Center who told her she would make them for us for free, but she obviously thought we'd only have a little slip of paper. First we were all very happy that she offered her help, but today we found out that our plan is too complicated. We would have to pay for the printing. The problem is that it has to be paid in dollars.

BARRIENTOS: It is a mess. If you go to a corporation and pay in dollars, they make it on the spot, and with good quality, but we would have to pay in dollars, and it's too expensive. If instead of earning 148 pesos I earned $148, I would contribute to it, but it's impossible.

BIRRINGER: How many productions do you create in a year?

VARELA: One. We have to share time between the creation, the investigation process, the training, and the theoretical-practical conferences we hold to disassemble the performance and tell people about the technique. It is important to carry on all of these processes simultaneously. We are investigators, not a group to produce a lot of performances.

BIRRINGER: Magaly Muguercia told me that she considers your theater a kind of utopian project. We talked at length about utopian thinking in Cuba, and I wonder how you feel about this subject. Magaly spoke about the necessary social process of transforming reality. How do you see your group in relation to such social process?

VARELA: Well, I am going to start with the most powerful utopia. I believe absolutely that everyone has to work on his or her own level. Each one of us has an eco-system inside and has to work with it. In this way one can reach a certain level and this will attract a certain level of life. We are all attractors. Life is not something apart from us. One often hears people complain, life is of no use, or life treats me badly, but the truth is you are the one who is not well, and that is why you attract that kind of life. That is to say: everyone has to start by himself or herself. I don't believe in geographic determinism. I believe there are contexts where situations are more difficult because there are economic deprivations, and especially information deprivations. This has been discussed very well in G. I. Gurdjieff's philosophy. He is a Russian writer and connected to Sufi philosophy, and he started to write about this practice of knowledge in the 1950s. It was called 'the fourth path.' It influenced my own utopian thinking for our group, like the warrior's utopia in Castañeda's writing. We have a passion for utopian ideas. We cannot stand the postmodern and nihilist tedium in the West. When I say to myself, there is nothing I can do, then I will die.

Furthermore, I had the opportunity to travel, to get to know the world; for example, the Japanese society which is superindustrialized, and there you find very high levels of violent alienation. There are problems everywhere in the world, and everyone complains. Everyone thinks these are political problems that need to be asserted in political ways. I prefer a world where we think of these issues as creative problems, in the way in which Joseph Beuys proposed that all human beings are artists. It would be a world in which everyone is responsible for creating their own inner eco-system. This is my greatest utopia, and I think the actors here share this belief. [Víctor acknowledges that Beuys's actions inspired *El arca*, and he specifically mentions Beuys's 1974 action *I Like America and America Likes Me* at New York's René Block Gallery, during which he lived for three days and nights locked into a room with a coyote.] All of this is demonstrated in the theatrical work, how the actors develop technically and intellectually. The other day Barbara surprised me in a radio interview, declaring that the work with me had helped her to live and to love. She didn't mention theater at all.

On the other hand, to act means to fight against the fragmentation which we are living. We live in a fragmented world where there is usually separation in the relation between body and mind and language. I think a movement structure is a thinking structure; it is like an indirect exercise to experience unity through theater. So even if it is not done consciously, developing as an actor one develops oneself as a person as well. We have also access to materials which give us very useful advice. For example, the other day we were reading Zen philosophy, and a passage said: in the measure in which a man becomes more powerful in know-ledge he should soften his heart and be more humble. I think everyone in our group reflected on this and considered it very important.

We have produced an important change in Cuba when you think of it in social or cultural terms, because we were the first group to start the off-culture, and the first group to be accepted without having an official diploma from an art school. They have now given us a space, and since they had to do it they invented a law through which anyone who wants to associate themselves and create a theater group or a cultural project can do it if they have a project proposal. In other words, Teatro Obstáculo produced that change in the institution. The question of utopia starts with yourself concentrating on what you must do. I don't believe much in going outside carrying placards and organizing public demonstrations. One has to do things well, and this will serve as a motivation to the audiences who will see the work. For example, with this new idea we had about the intimate program books: if we succeed in publishing them, other theater groups will perhaps also spend more time and concentration to create better informa-tion. In Cuba we have a serious problem; many people protect themselves by pointing to the lack of resources. They abandon their initiative, and so you find a lot of dirt in the streets which has nothing to do with the richness or poverty of the state. It depends on people cleaning up. I think our behavior can stimulate other people to understand this. This is more or less how utopia can manifest itself.

I think about revolutions and repetitions. And about paradoxes. The country is outside, and this is our country, Víctor suggested, and what he means has something to do with the Cuban idea of *resistencia* that raises an internalized pride of national independence to an ethical level at which the future of being Cuban is creatively defended. Víctor's work with his group identifies itself with a metaphysics of becoming/transformation that, he claims, is already ahead of the state which has fallen into an ideological vacuum after the delegitimation of world communism, pathetically clinging to worn-out slogans (*socialismo o muerte*). Is Víctor's independent theater collective in the old Freemasons Lodge an artistic model of evolution comparable to Marko Peljhan's ATOL? Can the 'Ark' become a popular model of collaboration that stops the desperate flights of rafts to the other side of the Florida Straits?

I don't think one can easily reconcile the notion of *resistencia*, understood as the struggle for the survival of the Cuban nation, with the bitter fact of the exodus of the rafters that has been politically manipulated by Castro, the right-wing Miami Cubans, and US foreign policy. The exodus is a form of defiance against Cuban socialism that reflects the emigrants' despair about the conditions on the island. But a growing number of Cubans protest the conditions in other ways, realizing that the nationalist movement of the revolution is no longer sustained by the bloc politics of the Cold War but subject to world market dynamics. Domestic private economic activity, capital investment, and expanded trade will become as necessary as participatory democratic processes, and what Magaly described as the new *educación popular* depends to a large extent on the openly creative collaborations I witnessed in the cultural sector. In my talks with Jorge he relives the time of preparation for the difficult role of Diego which, he believes, changed his life and opened his eyes. 'Perhaps this crisis is good for us, we need to come to terms with ourselves. I'm an actor, I like to experiment and experience everything, and I've been privileged to have this happen to me. I also work in a group called Caribbean Theater in which we do primarily Afro-Cuban performances. You can come to the rehearsals, and you'll notice the Caribbean influence, and how the work interconnects rhythm and dance, music and poetry and spiritual expression.'

I ask him how he would describe the faith of the younger artists who are creating such exciting work under these difficult conditions. 'People don't have many resources,' he admits. 'For example, there are a lot of young people interested in videos but there are no resources and facilities. The resources that do exist are controlled by the state or by the film and television school, as well as by ICAIC. The Cuban theater cannot escape the crisis that the country is undergoing. But you can see it's a theater done *as if* there were resources. It's more from the personal efforts of the creative people than anything else. I believe the essence of theater is the creative energy that lies in it and flows from it.'

And then his eyes light up: 'I'm interested in working because I'm an actor, and I can work anywhere, but the more difficult the situation in my country gets, the more important it is for me to work here and live here among the Cubans, trying to improve our situation to the extent I can.' There is nothing more to say, I can only embrace him. I remember Ademir's insistence on small steps that might provoke change. Little by little.

3

MAKROLAB: A HETEROTOPIA

Somewhere at the southern end of the 'Parcours' – the itinerary of exhibition sites composed by artistic director Catherine David for documenta X (dX) at Kassel, Germany – one found a strange sculpture on the banks of the Fulda river. Rising from the grass with its slanted staircase and closed doors, the white structure, titled 'Transportable Subway-Entrance,' had been created by Martin Kippenberger before his recent death. It is the last one completed in a series of imaginary subway entrances, exits and ventilation systems (*Metro-Net*) envisioned to form an imaginary network around the world. Others stand in Canada and on a Greek island, the next one was planned for Africa, and in Kippenberger's sarcastic vision they figured as a parody of global transportation networks. They can continue to be built even after his death, and we also have access to his provocative prototypes via the Internet where they have been scanned into sites. In fact, the entire dX could be visited in the World Wide Web during its 100 days and, like Kippenberger's fantasy subway-system, this important art event became part of a virtual network.

The focus of this chapter is another prototype, Project Atol's MAKROLAB, which assumed a unique position in the spectrum of displays at dX by remaining virtually invisible and thus performing an even more poignant subversion of the material strategies of exhibition. Rather than parodying global networks or creating an aesthetic version of them, MAKROLAB's scientific investigation of globalization took on a concrete political dimension that most of the other works at dX lacked entirely. I will try to sketch this dimension after some initial remarks about the subtext of the 1997 documenta.

Much critical attention was given to dX for its relentless examination of the museum, the place of contemporary art and curatorship, and art's dialectical relations with cultural markets and the remains of a modernist aesthetic. According to the logic of David's itinerary, art is situated in relation to its historically grown, postwar urban contexts. Architectural representations were given considerable space, similar to her selections of documentary photography, *arte povera*, and the politicized conceptual art of the 1960s and early 1970s (shown in special sections David called 'Retrosperspectives'). The polemical works of institutional critique by Hans Haacke, Gordon Matta-Clark, or Marcel Broodthaers were prominently displayed, along with the relics of urban actions by Brazilian artists Hélio Oiticica and Lygia Clark whose work has rarely ever been shown or discussed in Europe. Particularly poignant was David's rude expulsion of painting and abstraction. Most of her selections emphasized the critical dimension of art practices that create analytical distancing effects or engage in social-cultural performances.

The itinerary thus introduced the historical trajectory of a radical questioning of the categories of 'fine art' that laid the ground for today's debates over the ruins of the museum and the role of 'public space' and transculturation in civil society. It also moved more decidedly into a new direction with the staging of the open forum '100 Days – 100 Guests' and the manifestations of new multimedia, Internet and CD-ROM-based art (e.g. in the temporary construction of the 'Hybrid WorksSpace' media lab). The live webcasts of the speakers' forum and the presence of electronic art with its many user surfaces implied, however, that the conventional exhibition of fine art and sculpture, and its embedding in urban locations, will become redundant, if we indeed witness, as David argued, the final dissolution of the museum and of public space into the fully mediated 'society of the spectacle.'

The art exhibitions at dX, therefore, could be considered the pretext for a dramaturgy of ideological reflection, analysis, and the recuperation of a radical left politics which linked the speakers' forum and the voluminous 'Book' (the extraordinary 830–page theory-guide entitled *Politics-Poetics*, consisting of a montage of essays, interviews, and literary texts interspersed with documentary and artistic materials) to critical art practices focused on the critique of institutions and on social content and political discourse. Not surprisingly, the documentary function of art and the conceptual interventions of performance and process-oriented art practice were foregrounded, and the historical 'archive' of photographic realism received significant attention in light of the preponderance of electronic technologies in today's expansive global context of capitalism. Disappointingly, even as dX extended invitations to architects, filmmakers, and young artists working in time-based media and digital art, the dialog about current conceptual reformulations of artistic strategies remained largely theoretical. All too often controversial issues debated on the discursive platform – urbanization, territory, postcolonial identities, new forms of citizenship, the national social state and its disappearance, racism, the globalization of markets, poetics and politics – were poorly refracted by the surrounding installations or artworks. Most of the media installations I looked at didn't contribute much to the political discourse about our changing cultural and economic conditions in the world. Moreover, the work of web artists and activists (such as Antoni Muntadas' project 'On Translation') was disappointingly installed *in situ* on CD-ROMs without direct access to the Net. Thus dX raised the prospect of new online navigations, links/hypertext parameters and interactive electronic art without following them through or intervening into the infrastructures of telecommunications transmission.

2. PARAMETERS OF TRANSMISSION

It is late at night, and I am on top of a hill 15 miles away from the documenta. My laptop sits next to several other Internet, radio, video, and satellite transmission machines in a futuristic-looking research lab designed by Slovene artist Marko Peljhan and his team. From afar MAKROLAB looks like a UFO that has landed on the edge of the Lutterberg forest. Once I am able to locate its geographical position and the dirt roads leading to it, I recognize the functionalist design I had seen in the computer sketches on Peljhan's website. Erected on metallic stilts, the tent-like body of the ship houses two parts, one for sleeping, living and personal hygiene, the other for technological and scientific research.

After emerging from the local context of the collective avant-garde movement NSK (Neue Slowenische Kunst) in Ljubljana, Peljhan quickly found his own voice in a series of unusual theater projects he has directed for his group Projekt ATOL and staged in Slovenia and Eastern and Northern Europe since 1992. When I first saw the ATOL performances, they were accompanied by manifestos defining the work as long-term research into evolutionary utopian conditions. The twenty-eight-year-old artist, who developed an early passion for short-wave radio and technoscientific scenographies, harbors a vivid interest in the futurist visions of the Russian poet Velimir Khlebnikov (1885–1922). His own performances, installations, films, lectures, and constructions are neither fantastical nor limited to familiar conceptions of 'theater.'

If one were to speak of 'stage directions,' then, such an approach would be too

Figure 31 MAKROLAB, on location, Lutterberg near Kassel, summer 1997.

metaphorical to grasp the concrete operational framework of MAKROLAB. The team consists of nine persons, including the technical designers. During my first visit to Lutterberg after the completion of the lab construction, three are still there (Peljhan, Luka Frelih, and Brian Springer, a collaborator from the USA). MAKROLAB is the fourth phase in a work cycle named LADOMIR FAKTURA in reference to Khlebnikov's futurist poem 'Ladomir' written at the beginning of the century. In the poem Khlebnikov describes a universal landscape of the future arising through wars and the destruction of the old world and the synthesis of the new. Imagined as a kind of synaesthesia of abstract scientific and tactile, sensorial processes, the Khlebnikovian 'science of the individual' is a training stage for sensory connections to the environment. According to the poet, wireless transmissions and communications play an important role in the exploration of new concepts of time and space on our planet. The individual needs to study the experience in new time-space and reflect scientifically on changing constellations of harmony (*lad*) and peace (*mir*).

Khlebnikov's projection of the future, at the end of a century of failed utopias and broken revolutionary dreams, may appear pathetic, yet Peljhan assures me that he finds the poetry of the projection inspiring, and above all he is concerned with creating a method and technique (*faktura*) for individual, autonomous human beings. The performance dimension of the lab, then, requires learning the techniques of building isolated/insulated environments as a survival experiment in a narrow, concentrated workspace which at the same time functions as an independent communications organism designed to receive and transmit information.

Figure 32 Marko Peljhan and Brian Springer at work in MAKROLAB, 1997.

The lab is envisioned as an autonomous modular communications and living environment, powered by sustainable sources of energy (solar and wind power) and designed for a long existence in isolation. It is placed outside of the documenta and its Parcours; though invisible to the artworld, it remains linked to the world via hypermodern satellite, radio and computer technologies which form the operational base for its 'research and experience goal,' a combination of various 'scientific and technological logistics systems.' Set up on a hill Peljhan chose from his maps of the area, MAKROLAB has its antennae and satellite dishes directed toward the equator, and it has become a familiar sight to the nearby farmers and golf players who think of it as a weather station. None of them associates the lab with an artwork, and the steady stream of documenta visitors won't even know of its existence unless they pause to examine the informational archive at the small console in documenta-Halle. There one can find valuable insights into the construction, concept, background, financing, objectives, methods, and collaborative nature of Peljhan's project – gathered on microfilm and also accessible through the ML website. Included in this rich archive are sensitive materials (e.g. the document 'Command, Communications and Control in Eastern Europe') that examine military and logistical strategy in the post-communist East; others yield translations of Khlebnikov's theory of time and the 'skybooks.'

As an artistic 'installation,' the experimental arrangement is provocative: the ATOL team has secluded itself, and there is no work of art exhibited. If the visitor looks at the console, she or he won't actually see anything. It is a small, black metallic user platform, equipped with the microfilm device, two small video monitors for the microwave link to MAKROLAB and the Internet, and a radio telephone. One can establish communications with the crew via radio or email if one takes the time to read the instruction manual. Small metallic plates explain in a dozen languages the project's objectives which operate entirely on the level of mediation.

The console offers information and a place to work, a unspecific site with the potential to function as an intercom link to the people in the lab. Only very few documenta visitors seem to take up the offer. I observe that after initial curiosity, many leave quickly or click impatiently at the mouse for a while. Two days after the opening, someone breaks the glass of the microfilm device; one of the metallic plates disappears, and Peljhan tells me that he is dismayed by the apparent aggression triggered by the console. 'I thought to create a tool that people who want to know more about the project could use. It turns out to be a tool that many people who don't speak English cannot use and a tool that is not set into the right context. It is still an exhibition, people look at it. They assume that the gaze will provide something to them, an experience, a feeling, a thought. But the console is of course a completely functional element, a definite tool.' I wonder why someone would steal the metallic plate. The guards have now applied wires to keep the plates in place. A man sits in one of the comfortable chairs and holds his baby daughter who plays delightedly with the microfilms. To her the technoid surface of the console doesn't hold a negative appeal or create discomfort and disrespect. Moreover, the console is not a machine but a cyborg, a transmitter, a modem: on the monitors one can clearly see a video live feed of two people at work in the lab, somewhere else. A second camera shows the lab from the outside, the wind moving gently across the cornfield.

For Peljhan, working in an insulated/isolated environment is a progressive activity in time: the process of adaptation is a rehearsal and memorization of creative spiritual, social, and ecological relations to the universe. In another sense, the rehearsal in isolation is contradictory, since MAKROLAB is both an observatory that is scanning an emergent political economy of global transactions, and is itself not private or unmonitored since it operates within the frequencies of telecommunications. It also cannot avoid being checked out by friends, documenta staff, and those whose stubborn curiosity drives them out to the hill. When I ask Peljhan why he allows occasional visitors (like myself) to intrude into the lab, he explains that the documenta context makes it necessary to allow limited contact in order to facilitate feedback between console and lab. The funniest incident is reported in the ML bulletin 014:

> On Saturday the most amazing event and visit Makrolab has seen up to now – 60 children from the summer camp Elke and her friends are organizing. We had to pretend we were extraterrestrials that have just landed on Lutterberg, donned the funny white radiation protection suites that Luka left. It's all on camera for the documentary, the kids seemed to enjoy it, we felt stupid but it was fun. Played some interesting modulations for them and measured them. Quite a surreal scene . . .
>
> Today the last of the Makrolab news radio bulletins for hr2 was finished. We used intercepted communications and Khlebnikov's texts.

The time of a new 'synthesis,' Peljhan implies, has already begun with the implementation of vast global telecommunications networks and knowledge-based information industries. The open windows of analog communications media like short-wave radio are closing rapidly. As they are supplanted by the growing spread of digitized data transmission, 'this is a unique opportunity', Peljhan argues, 'to have one last glimpse at the curve of the analog spectrum before it closes for ever. A complete set of new knowledge is needed.' For the exploration of evolutionary social conditions in a world of increasingly complex intelligence systems, the individual needs to make appropriate physical, psychic, and material preparations for survival in post-territorial and perhaps ungovernable information societies. In the sense in which Peljhan understands the MAKROLAB process, ATOL's experimental research is not contingent upon the documenta or the art market. The exhibition merely offered an occasion to initialize the laboratory construction in the documenta framework of 'manifestations' and, in a way, simulate the construction of the module as a performance. Reminiscent of the Russian constructivist avant-garde, ATOL understands its working and learning process to take place in real time and concrete living-circumstances, enabling the creative communication of individual forces to converge into a scientific/psychic entity. In calling MAKROLAB an 'autonomous communications and living environment' that is designed to be self-sufficient, Peljhan sees isolation/insulation as a 'vehicle to achieve independence from, and reflection of, the actual entropic social conditions.' The lab thus constructs and monitors its own micro-social events in the communications module while testing the tools to monitor and observe the flow of data in the electro-magnetic spectrum.

This construction of the process is remarkable both for its consequences and its tactical subtlety, since Peljhan's declaration of LADOMIR FAKTURA as an artistic strategy meant that he had to invest considerable energy into its production and promotion as an independent work, especially as he sought to remain unaffiliated and to survive in the fledgling alternative scene in Ljubljana without signing on to private or industrial sponsorship. If one looks at the technical design of the module, it becomes clear that MAKROLAB has the contours of a scientific research lab, allowing the artists access to a wide spectrum of short-wave, L-Band and mobile radio frequencies, teleprinter and satellite telephone systems (INMARSAT), Internet and satellite video transmissions. They can communicate with radio amateurs around the world, but if their monitoring and decoding equipment gives them access to the electro-magnetic spectrum of transnational audio and data traffic, it means they can approximate the kind of surveillance and 'intelligence gathering' ordinarily reserved to the military, the state, and large private corporations or media conglomerates.

MAKROLAB thus harbors an emancipatory dimension that touches upon the electronic frontier as a new social space. Exploring autonomy and free access, the lab stakes its claim in the future of a decentralized Internet and open, uncontrolled user interfaces allowing the sharing of information. Peljhan's team has no illusions about the privileged institutional, governmental and corporate interests competing for the reconfiguration of telecommunications infrastructures and staking their claims for relentless commodification, universal or restricted access, encryption and censorship. Launching an artistic process that yields knowledge and insight into the evolution of the electronic 'public sphere,' MAKROLAB intervenes into the radio and telecommunications circuits to test the conditions under which transmission technologies operate and the relations among communicating individuals can be empowered. Intervention, concretely, means *observation* and communication, but it can also mean interception, reproduction, recombination. In monitoring radio and satellite links, Peljhan's team moves on the borders of legality and the power lines that exist among the regulatory regimes of various public and private data transmission networks. The question who controls which telecommunications services and transmissions within the global information-processing suggests a political minefield, and it is obvious that there will be countless disadvantaged users or off-line citizens in the world without access to the network infrastructures of the so-called 'cyber-community.'

The self-organization of the MAKROLAB-team presents an effort to develop an empirical and operational training in the use of scientific/technological tools, knowledge and systems, but with the intention of projecting them into the social domain of art. The 'system of art,' Peljhan contends, is used to transcribe invisible and micro-environmental activities, to render and document found data which can be sensed in the abstract areas of the electro-magnetic spectrum only via suitable interfaces and specialized knowledge. At the same time, the electro-magnetic spectrum is of course part of the global social-political space.

On its autonomous platform, MAKROLAB declares itself an observatory that uses suitable tools to monitor or 'sense' the spectrum. It can therefore gather information about valuable data concerning security, the environment, weather, health, economic and financial transactions, political conflicts, and scientific research. In doing the kind of observation and analysis generally conducted by institutional, private and state monopolies, MAKROLAB takes on a counter-position, a heterotopic praxis of 'information-gathering' that extracts valuable data from supraindividual, corporate and transterritorial infrastructural networks, making them available and also demonstrating how they can be shared. Brian Springer joined the team because of his concerns about 'deregulation' and the 'free market' of public transmissions. In his recent film *Spin* (1995), a montage of pirated satellite feeds (appropriated during commercial breaks or just before a television interview or teleconference), he created an extraordinary deconstruction of the routine manipulation of broadcast news and the collusion between US politicians and the media. Springer poses the question of legality differently. 'Anyone with a home satellite dish, which is 4 million, can receive these unencrypted feeds,' he argues, 'and the issue here is: what is a public broadcast and what is a common carrier. A broadcast is something that goes out to a mass public. A common carrier is something like a letter. For example, one could find Philip Morris Television Network doing, every now and then, a corporate teleconference which, from their lawyers' point of view, is a private transmission. My point of view is that it is public since it is not scrambled. What happens if a letter is broadcast across a whole continent, when it is not encrypted? Many contradictions arise over what is public and what is private. The satellite's broad beam pushes these contradictions to the surface.'

Springer's background is in independent video production. Watching him work in the lab day and night with complicated decoding equipment makes me realize to what extent older avant-garde production techniques (cut-up, collage, the readymade, situationist *dérive*, etc.) have been replaced by recombinant methods and transcriptions in the digital era of programming. Springer and Peljhan work at the interfaces of old and new media and technologies, but their operational reference points are no longer art but political economies and new semi-public spheres, no longer museums but NGOs and 'tactical media' networks such as *nettime*. Tinkering with the toolbox of net technologies and opening alternative channels of interaction and exchange (the 'gift economy' of net activists), such tactical initiatives imply economic analysis of corporate logistics on one hand, and new forms of self-organization, group-ware channeling, and non-profit models of decentralized public-access connectivity on the other. At the bottom level, for many of us who work as freelance artists, lies the issue of economic survival outside the offices of corporate states. With a bemused smile, Springer tells me that his work-in-progress is 'self-deregulation.'

Information infrastructures and interoperable networks exist in a highly contested arena of private interests and governmental claims, especially since politically the global information infrastructures cannot be governed. There are too many different national regulatory and operational practices, currencies, and stages of telecommunications development in the world today. The stunning success of the Internet as a decentralized communication system is a case in point, since its operation as a horizontal network disrupts familiar ideological conceptions of political authority, state security, data protection, and regulatory jurisdiction. Ironically, the origins of the Internet derive from the US Defense Department's Cold War strategy of decentralized computer networks (ARPANET), whereas recent attempts to impose restrictions to open communication and free content have been met with the counter-cultural resistance of programmers and hackers. The digital technology of instantaneous transmission and duplication operates in the borderlands of dissemination, surveillance, encryption and hacking, and the MAKROLAB teams knows it moves in-between the protected and unprotected areas of the spectrum interactivities. It behaves as a para-site. This is where communication starts to get interesting, Peljhan believes, and where 'the medium does what it does best, which is communicate. And where culture does what it does worst, which is communicate. We are investigating if the collision of these best and worst characteristics creates an interesting stage for intervening in the transnational flow of information.'

The 'art' of monitoring the information flow, with independent status and limited resources, is a long-term project which also requires mobility and the continuous accumulation of experience in the exchange and interpretation of data. Peljhan plans the successive transplantation of the module to Canada, Japan, Italy, England, and the Negev Desert, accepting invitations from other alternative artists or organizations. He had already been invited to present film lectures on MAKROLAB at the South Africa Biennial and the 'Code Red' conference in Australia, and in 1999 was to set up the lab on an island near Venice. Peljhan also attended the 1997 HIP (Hacking in Progress) meeting in Holland and exchanged information on decompression and decoding techniques that are shared in the underground. While computer users generally work out of their homes, the lab's position is transient. Its trajectory in time is in itself modular, and in this sense MAKROLAB does not position itself *vis-à-vis* geographically defined, juridical, or disciplinary territories, as much as it transcends common aesthetic categories of art. Its performance of a 'weather station' is a brilliant parody of the now dysfunctional 'panopticon' structure of immanent regulatory systems based on state authority or management control.

This counter-position *vis-à-vis* the power regimes of states and corporate industries articulates a 'heterotopia' – an incongruous 'site' in which 'all the other real sites that can be found within the culture, are simultaneously represented, contested, and inverted.'[1] This symbolic play of reverberation operates above all in transitory, temporal registers (like communication flows) and yet constitutes a break 'with traditional time' through its discontinuous structuring of openings and closings. Although the documenta-'book' quotes Foucault's description of heterotopias as 'deviations' and 'non-places of power,' its spatial analogies are mostly drawn from the discourses of decolonization, urbanism, and architecture (cf. Rem Koolhaas' project *New Urbanism: Pearl River Delta*). Peljhan's ATOL pursues a different interplay, one that is not between the spatialization of capital and the surveillance systems of the state, but is between the non-transparent movement-time and organization of communications infrastructures. MAKROLAB resembles a spaceship, a search engine that orbits around the spectrum of public and private data networks and telematic nervous systems, fishing and analysing signals, mapping voices, intercepting transmissions. The scenography is a covert theater of operations, mimicking Foucault's archeological approach to public facilities (network architectures) while upholding a strict regimen of self-observation inside the module, concerning climatic condition, diet, body weight, hygienic and medical data, energy supply, effectivity of communication tools, etc. In the regular ML bulletins published on the website, the crew members primarily report their technical maintenance operations, the evolving situation in their habitat, the physical encounters with visitors and their various communication interfaces; for example, with radio stations in Belarus and Estonia, with an anthropologist from Sudan, a biogas company in Denmark, and the cosmonauts from the Russian space station MIR. The first phase of the project during dX is designed to generate data and thought, creating a domain of memory for the reflection period. The analysis of life-in-the-module, and of exchanges and the decoded transmissions intercepted from the INMARSAT, is a work-in-progress. The MAKROLAB crew tends to simulate a certain secrecy when I ask about the content of intercepted messages. Not disclosing all of their observations is an aesthetic strategy. Peljhan argues that 'almost nothing is hidden to the view, except of course what we purposely hide from it, and thus we use the same mechanisms used by the systems we are countering in this mission.'

In the defense of decentralized networks, the appropriation of the means of production is vital for online participation in the new formations of political arenas. These arenas nowadays are constructed through electronically mediated communications – public speech and participation no longer characterize late capitalist, translocal spaces of communication without bodies. What the entrances in Kippenberger's virtual metro net merely parody is radically demanded by Peljhan's tactical logistics: MAKROLAB becomes a mobile space station on our planet of networks. It directs its antennae and satellite dishes at the increasingly virtual democratic 'communities' of civil society and tests the new human-machine assemblages that operate in transnational communications networks no longer based on identifiable public goods. Increasingly, the shared experience in contemporary civil society is one of disaffiliation. Entrances to effective sociopolitical orders, like cultural identification and the historical solidarity between citizenship and nationality, begin to disappear as the older national topographies dissolve. It is conceivable that soon we won't speak of nation-states any more but of interconnected infrastructures.

The MAKROLAB crew performs a symbolic analysis of intelligent systems, but according to Foucault's metaphor of the heterotopic ship, it has built a floating piece of space, a 'place without a place that exists by itself, closed in on itself and at the same time given over to the infinity of the sea.' Peljhan and his collaborators are aware of the climate of risk in which they maneuver their counter-surveillance strategies, and the artistic challenge is to make this risk experienceable in the social and existential construction of their atoll.

4

THE TRANSCULTURAL IMAGINARY

OR

STANDING WITH THE NATIVES

Dissonance is transformative. After describing Project ATOL's micro-environmental analysis of the relations of counter-surveillance and transnational communications, I now wish to pursue the open-ended process of local–global relations that I hinted at in my account of the Ojos del Pueblo project in Chicago. The most provocative experience in this local grass-roots project remains the active search for transcending the limitations of site-specific action directed at the ethos of solidarity of a community. There are always obstacles that may prevent our sight from traversing the boundaries of the local, especially if a local infrastructure and meeting-places for creative interactions are not to be taken for granted. Shortly after the solidarity performance in early 1995, Ojos del Pueblo lost access to the building they had just renovated, and a new process had to get under way. With the help of José David, a Cuban poet, activist, and builder, a new house was found and rented in Pilsen, and everybody got involved in the work that was needed to fix it up and turn it into a performance/gallery and meeting-place. The new 'Casa de Arte y Cultura' was opened in late 1995, with art exhibitions, films, concerts, and poetry readings, and with a celebration of the spirit of stubborn resolution. Our actions on behalf of the reopening of an *independent* cultural center may have motivated local actors to build participatory performances capable of expressing needs and political demands, but such repeated temporary efforts will need to sustain themselves in a growing volunteer network and a continuing strategy to redefine the local and translocal parameters of cultural production, especially in light of the fact that there are such scarce financial resources. In our vision, an alternative cultural community center, a 'house' or 'home' for expressive art and life, can be a catalyst for dialogue and change, if indeed the participants seek to extend their immediate emotional attachment to the site itself and perceive it not as a building or an end in itself but a meeting-ground.

In my chapter on 'virtual communities' in *Media & Performance*, I describe a similar site-specific action, originating in the squatting of an abandoned, decaying building in Eisenhüttenstadt during the summer of 1995. Over a period of several weeks, more than thirty high-school students, artists and workers joined together to form a 'Fantasy Laboratory' in order to gather insider information and ideas before launching a series of performance actions that culminated in the occupation of the abandoned site which city authorities considered valuable real estate but were unable to sell to investors. We performed our investment quite literally, taking over and cleaning up the outside of the building before staging its take-over as a symbolic, creative act to which citizens were invited. Subsequently, the negotiations with neighbors and city authorities became part of the artistic process of claiming the right to produce culture and to fill 'vacancies' that had opened up after the enormous economic and political transformation in the former socialist country.

What we need to construct is a dynamic vision of such *gathering-places* that can generate art and social advocacy, cultural education and progressive debate on a range of political issues that transcend the local economy. The latter, in any case, is subject to larger national and international processes of economic trans-formation that may change 'culture' the way we knew it (for example, the heavily state-subsidized high culture in Germany), and that will affect the localization of global forces in many different ways. This complex web of local and global relations, and the translocal imaginary that is produced under the impact of migration and the formation of global markets, is the subject of the present chapter.

My reflections are based on an event called 'Meeting Grounds', a weekend symposium/exhibition that took place at the Chicago Cultural Center in November 1993. In the current context of international debates on cultural and 'post'-colonial relations between nations, the presentation of the topics in 'Meet-ing Grounds' created a timely and important dialogue, especially so since it occurred at a moment when the controversial debates over multiculturalism (the culture wars) in the USA seemed to have reached a low point. As a public gathering in the well-known and widely accessible downtown Chicago Cultural Center, the symposium not only promised a cross-cultural encounter via lectures, open discussions, and video screenings, but in fact offered a rich menu of thoughts and stimuli that ultimately problematized, in a very productive way, the whole question of what constitutes a meeting-ground – in terms of location, discourses, media, and subject-matter. The choice of participants – artists, anthropologists, historians, sociologists, and traders – was perhaps the most significant and successful aspect of this extremely well-organized symposium. It was staged as a open ground, a experiment in dialogue, neither academic nor specialized, and it did not restrict itself to verbal address and critical discourse alone but included vital and necessary time for audience responses and discus-sions, for social interaction during the receptions, and for participation in the opening of James Luna's new installation project, *New Basket Designs: No Directions Known*, at Randolph Street Gallery. Organizer Robert Peters, a Chicago-based artist known for his politically provocative work, demonstrated his extraordinary capability of bringing together a truly diverse group of theorists and practitioners from different cultural backgrounds and locations of work, willing to share with each other their very distinct professional and artistic commitments. Peters also encouraged the interplay of different presentational styles (verbal and visual media, performances) and acted throughout as a congenial, unobtrusive, and supportive moderator.

In fact, what I enjoyed most during the entire weekend was the spirit of this convergence of ideas and practices; it was an honest gathering of people who may be working in different fields and countries but who share a commitment to the exchange of ideas and to the respect for others. I have rarely attended a symposium that breathed such an air of solidarity and constructive debate, and together with Guillermo Gómez-Peña and Coco Fusco's *Year of the White Bear* project earlier in 1993, 'Meeting Grounds' was the most important cultural event in Chicago during that year, as far as I am concerned. When I received the invitation in the mail, I noticed that Peters had planned the event as a continuation of 'Naming Others: Manufacturing Yourself,' an earlier public telephone project he had created inviting callers to respond to how they understood societal definitions of race, sexuality, and ethnicity. In his invitation to the symposium, Peters suggests:

> In today's shrinking world we are witness to an acceleration of unlikely and often unwanted cultural contacts. In this time of rapid developments in communications and transportation, every gesture, landscape, cultural practice and artifact becomes visible and thus available for potential absorption, annihilation, exploitation or explanation. In this world the Sony Walkman has transformed taking a stroll into a profit-providing activity and the unknown is tamed by transforming it into recognizable wholes and media fictions, as in the promotional promise of ". . . graded levels of adventure from easy guided walks to Outward Bound style hikes that make you feel like the real Indiana Jones" advertised by an Ecuadoran Amazon hotel. How do representations in this world, increasingly articulated in economic and material terms, take shape? How do these media fictions and fanciful idealizations intersect with local interests and realities? How and where are these representations contested and negotiated? What and who determine which parts of a cultural landscape to market and which parts to ignore, to hide?[1]

I can hardly claim that I was prepared for the rich continuum of interfaces that opened up so many perspectives – sociopolitical, economic, cultural – on the critical question of how cultural practices intersect, learn from, dominate, appropriate from, manipulate, and exchange with each other. What is significant about 'Meeting Grounds' is its unusually strong focus on the (political) economy of cultural exchange, of trade, and of contact. The role of artists and intellectuals as 'traders' or 'mediators' deserves special attention, and I will try to comment on some of the most important issues raised. I will structure them into twenty-four templates.

1

> In some way or another one can protect oneself
> from evil spirits by portraying them.
>
> (Michael Taussig[2])

I arrived late to the first session of the symposium on 12 November 1993, because on that morning I had arranged to make a field trip with my performance art students from the North Shore to the Museum of Science and Industry on the far South Side of Chicago. I was to wait for them in the 'communications' display room so that we could make a foray into the VR work station. Virtual Reality, cyberspace, and the *Mondo 2000* world of limitlessly accessible information flows are much on the minds of my young students who admire hackers and take the economy of electronic information for granted on a continuum of educational and class privilege, as they endow it with a sense of radical democracy, namely a technocratic vision of worlds (possessed, processed) without borders, internetted and merged by communications.

The trouble was that I waited in vain. My students, I found out later, got lost during the train ride from Evanston to the deep South Side, and then they got scared by the unfamiliar urban terrain and returned home. So much for traveling across urban territories in our Western metropolitan centers.

I reached the Chicago Cultural Center half-way through Robert Peters's introduction, a subdued and highly self-reflexive travel report on his visits to Bali which almost immediately proposed to problematize the role of the documentarian (i.e. his own photos representing 'Balinese culture') *as* tourist, or as an observer expected by the modern Balinese tourist industry to bring dollars in exchange for photographic access to indigenous subjects. By way of his introduction, representing himself as a traveler and an outsider/tourist, he set up an important issue of the conference agenda, namely how different perspectives on such cultural encounters could be brought into play, and how the cultural management and marketing of one's own culture for the 'Other' can be conceptualized in the current context of global relations/global tourism. As a self-critique from the position of the dominant Western metropolitan discourse, such an approach to the self-as-other struck an immediate chord with the large and very diverse audience, many of whom had probably come to the United States as immigrants or had descended from immigrant families or the enslaved Africans brought by force to the New World.

2

Peters ended speaking while an image was projected on the screen showing him standing there, next to a Balinese man/friend/host holding a portrait, both posing for the camera. A snapshot for the family album? A photo of the ethnographer standing next to the local informant? Two friends on holiday in Bali? All of Peters's slides rather look like snapshots, as if made (deliberately?) by an unprofessional photographer, not by an experienced ethnographer or journalist.

Peters reminded us of the dilemma or fortuitous paradox created by the demands of the tourist economy, especially as it generates the imperative to construct 'authentic' indigenous local cultures for display and for tourist consumption, as if only the sought-for 'authenticity' held real value for the paying customer. Meeting these demands implies the local production and staging of 'authenticity' for the other, thus perverting what postmodern ethnographers and cultural critics have insistently reminded us of, namely the constant flux and development of living and dynamic cultures that cannot be grasped by the fixing 'shot' that claims an authenticity similar to the preserved cultural artifacts in museums. Encapsulated in the staging of the photo is one aspect of the performance of culture outside of the museum; in the context of mass tourism over the past four or five decades, the tourist is brought to the local culture and presented with certain displays (e.g. folkloric festivals and fairs, dances, artifacts, buildings, local cuisine, etc.) that promise an encounter with local traditions and the authentic life-world of the site. The illusion of cultural transparency in such staged encounters has been deconstructed in many recent accounts by ethnographers who have explored the complexity of such simulations of 'authenticity' as well as the misunderstandings that result from the photographic representations of indigenous people, performances, or objects. The roles of the tourist, journalist, collector, ethnographer, etc., are different, and their modes of encounter may involve a range of genres, but what they share is the fundamentally disorienting mimetic relationship between the voyeur-observer and the observed-performer. This relationship is also part of an information economy which encompasses several narratives of cross-cultural contact and presumably unequal relations of power, although the latter cannot be subsumed under the terms of simplistic dichotomies between First World and Third World or tribal culture, between modern and traditional culture, or between Western technologies (such as photography, media) and indigenous or aboriginal modes of exchange.

Peters's photograph holds a peculiar irony insofar as it presents a portrait of an encounter which depicts within itself a second portrait, namely the self-portrait held up by the Balinese man, a prior portrait or sample from his family album. The photograph doesn't tell us whether this double scene was arranged by Peters or whether his Balinese partner always (or in this particular case) prefers to be photographed with his photograph. Almost too self-consciously, Peters's staged photo-scene also alludes to the time-honored anecdotes about 'native' fears of photography's power to steal the spirit or aura of the local culture exposed to the intrusive gaze of the outsider. The gaze of the camera is like the panoptic gaze of power, but in Peters's photo-scene this power is both reversed, rendered insubstantial, and reinforced by the obvious constructedness or artificiality of the portrait. The genre that is quoted, the tourist-collector standing in his paternalistic pose next to the smiling native, has a long, violent, and exploitative history built into the ironies of the quotation, and Peters frankly admitted his discomfort with it, urging us to pay closer attention to the reciprocal relations in such scenes.

3

What struck me was that he did not quite address the management of the scene from the other side, namely the Balinese man's self-address to the camera and his display of the tourist. An exchange economy had been created, and the Balinese man had engaged Peters into his playing with portraiture/photography with a strategy of reference that is not easily interpretable to the viewer. If he were showing off his portrait or family snapshot in the photograph, the viewer would need to know a great deal more about the context and the meanings of such showing off in order to transcribe the scene and what is happening here.

Peters's travel diary sounded a note of pessimism, and with this pessimism he initiated the questions that were to resonate through the symposium. What happens in the contact between cultures or between distinct traditions within a culture? How do representations of cultural practices and artifacts, increasingly articulated in economic and material terms, take shape? How do ethnographic or media 'fictions' and fanciful idealizations (including the implicitly traumatic fantasy of multiculturalism) intersect with local interests and realities?

4

Through the critical lens of the political economy of tourist industries (following in the footsteps of First World chronologies of 'discovery,' conquest, colonialism, slave trade, imperialism, and transnational banking systems/International Monetary Fund/GATT), Peters thus introduced at first the notion of 'traveling to' the other. I take it the issue of 'representation' is a logical corollary, currently understood among Western anthropologists as a challenge to experimental cross-cultural writing, epistemological critique, repatriation of ethnography ('traveling back home') as cultural critique, parallel writings, dialogue, etc. This involves 'us' – as consumers – and 'our' reception of ethnography. If we invoke the term 'consumption,' we could also refer to ethnographic representation as *spectacle*, given the logic of commodification and fetishization that generally rules the importation or staging of the other.

5

Among artists and critics of institutions (in the current playing field of multi-culturalist activism, alternative media, queer activism, and 'post'-colonial studies), this reflexive mode of conceptualism has of course addressed the very role that museums and institutions of higher learning have acted out in the 'tourist trade.' The issue of collecting and displaying was picked up very forcefully by James Luna later that day when he performed his own interpretation of being fixed into a stereotype, and also by David Avalos, one of the founders of the Taller de Arte Fronterizo on the southern Californian border with Mexico, who expressed his interventionist ideas about the economic function of dominant cultural interests in his examples drawn from the urban tourist industry in San Diego and from museums and grant-giving institutions in the US.

6

It follows, then, that one might want to ask what the location of the *Meeting Grounds* symposium means in terms of its own process of negotiation between cultures or cultural practitioners. James Luna was the only one who mentioned, in his own dryly ironic and subdued way, the 'usual discomfort' he feels when asked to perform in major Anglo-American bastions of culture, statues of Abraham Lincoln looming over him. Critiques of the white supremacist display management of native and tribal cultures have now been written (Gerald Vizenor's *CrossBloods* is one of most trenchant depictions of what he calls 'new tribal scenes'), but we are still surrounded by the same museums of natural history, the same ethnographic and science museums with their 'histories' of the progression of mankind. Chicago, the site of the grandiose 1893 World Exposition celebrating the technological progress of mankind, has its own infamous history of displaying the uncivilized natives.

Luna's lecture-performance was a wonderful, sly deconstruction of the Western narrative, and the main strategy of his work, forcefully demonstrated that same night at the opening of his performance/installation *New Basket Designs: No Directions Known*, seems to lie in the ironic re-representation of stereotypical ethnic notions and images (a Native American version of the improvisational, vernacular tactic of 'signifyin(g)' Henry Louis Gates described in *The Signifying Monkey*). Luna, reminding us of the fact that he unfortunately cannot comply with the white man's assumptions that the 'Indians' are either dead or resurrected only as mythic figures of the paternalistic white imagination (in the style of *Dances with Wolves*), interrupted himself during his talk, quietly got up and acted out a brief museum diorama: he put a feather into his hair, climbed a chair, and stood motionless as a living statue for a while, a mock totem pole looking into the Chicago Cultural Center, at a left angle from the colossal marble statue of Abe Lincoln.

7

The limits of stereotype? For artists this question has become excruciatingly complex, involving the whole politics of production, distribution, and the reconceptualization of the 'prisons of image,' the function of mediation in the mass media, the role of images and narratives in cultural engineering, and the issue of who has the power to control meanings or facilitate alternative perspectives and interpretations.

8

The contestation of stereotypes and cultural prejudices takes place in processes that have been dramatized; for example, in the 1992–3 'Culture-in-Action' public art projects, curated by Mary Jane Jacob for Sculpture Chicago. These projects, carried out by artists' teams working with local communities, directly addressed the issue of empowerment by shifting the work outside primarily aesthetic frames and into community-based processes of interaction revolving around civil rights and needs, identities within cultural diversity, political activism, and the social dynamics of people's lives in urban neighborhoods. Such long-term processes involve everyday experiences and specific contestatory practices within living cultural communities whose members may not share the same religion, class perspectives, or politics. Dynamic interactions therefore inevitably involve conflicts, negotiations, and diverse articulations that are 'full of inherent contradictions,' as Ahmad Sadri pointed out in his presentation. Sadri, a sociologist and anthropologist who had just returned to the USA after teaching in his native Iran, did not claim to speak from an Iranian or Islamic point of view. Rather, he introduced himself as someone preoccupied with the pragmatic problems of cultural epistemology:

> My interests in the area of intercultural understanding bifurcate into two distinct branches: the practical and the theoretical. I have attempted to understand my own life as a set of cultural cross-currents. My grand project involves translating, synthesizing, and recovering the Western democratic tradition for Iran. I call this 'reinventing the wheel.' This is not a fool's errand but often a necessity when intercultural collective learning occurs. Cultural transplantations usually do not take. Ways must be found to deal with different body politics and cultural immune systems. The wheel may have to be reinvented rather than imported.
>
> In my theoretical concerns I aim to advance beyond the current intercultural nihilism and develop a theory as well as define the contours of the practice of intercultural understanding without evoking the discredited language of nineteenth-century philosophical anthropology of modernism that remained ignorant of its rootedness in time and space. Secondly I address the question of agency. Here I argue for the necessity and importance of intellectuals and artists who straddle cultural fences and yes, the responsibility to ameliorate an increasingly volatile environment that seems to at once shrink and retain its tribal conviction about the people around the bend of the river and beyond the hill, i.e. the 'other.'

9

I was initially a little impatient with Sadri for dwelling so much on Western, Eurocentric 'paradigms' and conceptions of grasping global politics or international relations, since his expressed concern is to provide an understanding of Islamic fundamentalism, coupled with his effort to reintroduce democratic traditions into the Iranian culture of 'postrevivalism.' I assume he wanted to tell us that we – here in the West – cannot step back from our preconceptions about Islam without understanding the formation of Western paradigms of conceptualization. After some reflection, I began to find it necessary that Sadri went through the trouble of criticizing what he considers outworn conceptual apparatuses for political and social analysis, even though his proposed 'recovery' and synthesis of Western democratic principles in the Iranian context would seem to be contradictory, on the surface.

His main point is worth spelling out: in all cultures, Sadri argues, there is change and a constant response behavior to inherent (internal, and of course also external) pressures and conflicts. The diffusion of cultural practices is not something natural, but deliberate and selective, and this involves the kinds of imports/exports, plagiarisms, appropriations and re-inventions a culture carries out. Implying his concern over what the West perceives stereotypically as a threatening Islamic fundamentalism (linked in the US fantasy scenario to terrorism and bombs), he indicates that all the time there are also agents of re-invention at work, i.e. artists and intellectuals who are engaged in a reverse cultural engineering.

One of the problems here is the misleading notion of a singular culture, in the first place, which may extend to the false dichotomy between the West and Iran. In my history lessons, back in Germany, the assumption of a single, homogenous culture was never questioned. Having been brought up in the post-Enlightenment philosophical tradition of rationalist thought mainly structured around Hegelian and Kantian notions of 'universals' whose logic and ethic of natural and civil rights, freedom, and (aesthetic) judgement were based in the cultural and political formation of the modern European nation-state, I had come to infer, however, that the progress of Western civilization linked with modern science and industrialization (along with colonialism, slave-trading, racism, fascist genocide) was based on entirely paradoxical, bankrupt moral premises. If there ever was a Kantian or Marxist revolutionary fantasy of the essential totality of mankind, its logic of historical progress perpetrated a continual repression or destruction of those who stood in the way of Reason. Modern science and the technical organization of capitalist-industrial production successfully implemented 'rationalized' social conditions of existence based on the exploitation of labor. Freedom, justice, and equality remained abstract idealizations overshadowed by obedience to necessity, as Kant had already admitted. We are still waiting for what Marx considered the scientifically and objectively predictable collapse of capitalism and the end of our obedience.

The dialectic of enlightenment, in other words, contains its own colonialist and totalitarian structures, its own 'outside' or 'other' that it would ideologically impute onto the uncivilized and barbarian tribes, or onto unruly labor forces that needed to be held in check. Perversely, the ideology of liberal democracy pretended to be grounded in a shared cultural tradition, but its imagined European community itself ought to be seen as perennially contradictory and self-divided: the diverse European cultures (not to speak of the United States and its constitutional foundation) have always competed with and fought against each other, and they have always had their marginalized, oppressed, and stigmatized others within. The migrations, wartime displacements, religious pogroms, occupations, annexations, economic and cultural imperialisms, and the catastrophe of the Holocaust are therefore structurally linked to the double processes of colonization and decolonization, and the West as the self-anointed normative civilization has always relied on its colonies for self-definition, as Edward Said has demonstrated in *Orientalism* and *Culture and Imperialism*.

Third World writers and artists have indeed made major contributions to the critique of the Enlightenment, and Sadri's practical caveat to many of us in the West also suggests that we tend to universalize 'our' counter-enlightenment (in the critical tradition of, say, Nietzsche, Benjamin, Adorno/Horkheimer, Derrida, Foucault, etc.) without taking enough notice of Palestinian, Iranian, Latin American, Caribbean, Indian or African writers. Writers in Latin America, for example, have produced their own succinct theories of 'transculturation' (Fernando Ortiz), cultural creolization or syncretism, miscegenation, unequal development, and (neo-)colonial dependence, and filmmakers of the revolutionary 'Third Cinema' movement incorporated the political radicalism of the writings of Frantz Fanon, Edouard Glissant, Aimé Césaire, Che Guevara, Gilberto Freyre and others in their telling of their own histories. Developing their own narratives and epic, documentary or avant-garde techniques of montage, filmmakers such as Tomás Gutiérrez Alea (Cuba), Glauber Rocha (Brazil), Fernando Solanas and Octavio Getino (Argentina) were of course aware that they were mixing Third World politics and First World models of cinematic or theatrical representation (Eisenstein, Brecht, Resnais, Buñuel, Godard, etc.), but their transformational efforts were explicitly linked to particular political struggles, as in the case of Solanas/Getino's *La hora de los hornos* (1968) which aligns itself with the left-Peronist movement. The film also cross-references the inspirational Cuban revolution and, in a segment entitled 'Models,' quotes directly from Fanon's concluding statement in *The Wretched of the Earth*: 'Let us not pay tribute to Europe by creating states, institutions and societies in its mould. Humanity expects more from us than this caricatured and generally obscene imitation.'

Such films and writings reflect on the unavoidably mixed sites of political struggle and cultural influences, and on complex processes of redefinition taking place within the imaginary geographies of the former colonies in the Americas, Africa, and Asia. These processes don't share the same temporalities and cannot be synchronized with Western notions of History. The redefinitions of cultural and regional heterogeneity under the ambiguous ideological imperatives of national liberation, nation-building, unification or separation have generated their own painfully conflicted self-contradictions that surface, for example, in the embattled relationships between various kinds of nationalist integration based on modernization and authoritarian/patriarchal social restructuring of 'national culture,' and other modes of recuperation of an elusive 'traditional culture' often dependent on the actual suppression of marginalized indigenous or rural traditions. The scene of imitation/recuperation is ob-scene.

10

Reverse cultural engineering: In my mind I try to grasp these processes of liberation and recuperation, thinking both of the notion of 'repatriation' (how would

Sadri reintroduce democratic and non-hierarchical mediations of participatory culture into the Iranian political economy under the current conditions of post-revivalism?) and of 'reverse contact' (Taussig), this strange, perhaps magical circulation of mimesis and (un)recuperable alterity, this reproduction and reconstruction of the 'nation' or of culture, when the economies of othering are exchanged. Taussig's descriptions of sympathetic magic are always also reminders of the political violence associated with the contests of legitimating processes. Contests of legitimation and self-constitution act out the fantasies of engineering that are the agents of an allegedly unifying totality (nation, class, race, culture) which always seems to fail the engineers and their particular version of the symbolic order. According to Sadri's argument, the logic of the productive tension between desire for change and the actual or imagined symbolic order reinvents itself continuously. The prohibitions of patriarchal, religious Islamic fundamentalism must generate their transgressions, their *Satanic Verses*.

11

I would have liked to hear more about the actual practices of such agents of transgression or cultural change within Iran, but Sadri did not give, or did not want to give, specific names or examples. Immediately following him, a provocative presentation on agents of cultural process was made by Sharon Stephens in her very concrete and detailed description of the Sami people's struggle for recognition of the various ways in which their businesses, their survival, their lives and cultural existence had been threatened by the radiation fall-out after Chernobyl. Her analysis, from the point of view of a child health researcher and field worker, was fully embedded in the particular regional scenario of the Scandinavian Sami communities fighting for an immediate understanding of, and response to, a health and environmental crisis, which meant fighting against the so-called risk or fall-out management by government and 'outside experts.' Most significantly, Stephens could draw a vivid portrait of how such an ecological crisis, once the Sami took their self-representation into their own hands politically, implies diverse Sami strategies of ethnic/cultural self-dramatization of their identity as an indigenous community *vis-à-vis* majority culture.

12

Stephens thus opened a highly complex set of issues concerning ethnic identity within both a local political struggle and a larger international spectrum of social movements (environmental, civil rights, human rights, land rights, equally involving diverse aspects of gender and community politics) and inter-European governmental policy-making as well as domestic/foreign policy relations to the media coverage of nuclear accidents. These issues of *identity construction* were taken up again, in a dialectical echo, by Lisa Brook later that day, when she spoke eloquently about the historical invention of race as a political category, and about modern race consciousness in different cultural contexts. Brook pointed out that her research on comparative race identities among African-Americans and Afro-Cubans shows that there are significant, historically explicable differences in the consciousness of being black among people of African descent in the USA and in Cuba or Brazil. Her discussion of black identity stimulated a heated discussion among the audience after she reminded us of the thin line, often blurred, that runs between a conservative black essentialist nationalism (in the USA) and a critical cultural politics that contests the notion of race identity by inquiring how blackness is socially constructed, and what meanings are circulated among black artists, communities, and popular culture audiences.

Brook's presentation, 'On Being Black in the Diaspora: Reflections of Race and Other In-and-Out-of-Body Experiences,' embraced both an experiential and a historicizing approach to different ideologies of racial awareness. Perceiving black identity to be a state of mind mixed up with a 'body of culture' or cultural traits that can have radically different meanings in different contexts, Brook sought to distinguish 'multiple identities' aligned with race, class, gender, ethnicity, and nation:

> The historical development of, and interaction between, these multiple identities of class, race, nation, and culture seems to underline differences in black racial consciousness. An examination of the particular experiences of slavery and racism, of the conceptualization of nation and citizenship, reveals the distinctive creation and calling up of these separate alignments. There have been numerous works that have compared North American and Latin American slave and racial systems, but very few have actually addressed black identity, and what it means to be black in Cuba or in the United States . . .

After explaining how the struggle for abolition and national independence coincided in nineteenth-century Cuba, Brook argued that the historical stage of national class-consciousness, so to speak, was shared by white, mulatto, and black actors who – in the formation of a multicultural or transcultural understanding of *cubanidad* or *cubanía* – acknowledged and even celebrated racial diversity (cf. José Martí's popularization of *mestizaje* or racial mixing as the unifying signifier of national cultural identity; we should also remember that the transmigrations to Cuba included an enormous range of peoples, not just from Spain and Africa, but also from the Mediterranean, France, Britain, and China). Even though there were racial tensions throughout the three wars of independence, the commitment to the abolition of slavery shaped a strong ideological congruity between fighting for equality for nonwhites and against colonialism. On the other hand, the US history of slavery as an 'inclusive racial system' never allowed for the emergence of a mulatto social category, and the formation of the nation came into being almost a hundred years before slavery was abolished, casting African-American identity as distant and distinct from the broader American one (initially based in propertied while males). Whiteness and citizenship thus 'became juxtaposed to non-citizenship and blackness or Indianness,' and this juxtaposition, Brook maintained, has undergirded all struggles for black equality, to the point where today many whites see black achievement as an attack on their rights and seek to roll back the gains of the civil rights movement and affirmative action. African-Americans, therefore, 'marginalized from the nation as a whole, have fused their national inclinations with their racial identity, so that unlike other ethnicities in the US, very few African-Americans define themselves solely as Americans.' Brook then addressed the conflicting articulations of this fantasy of nation:

> This sense of national longing is what has led to so many redefinitions of our people, and it has also led to narrow racial constructions of so-called black nationalisms, and tremendous debates among intellectuals in the black community, historically, as to whether black Americans can be defined as a separate nation or not.

Given a range of black political attitudes, from Afrocentrism, protests and racial confrontation, to middle-class conservativism and Jesse Jackson's integrationist rainbow coalition, Brook would probably insist that nationalist separatism and cultural assimilation are not opposite extremes but expressions of the same continuum of longing for self-determining participation in the national public culture. In her discussion of distinct forms and traditions of black popular culture and everyday living, she emphasized the ever-changing renewal of the African elements of African-American culture, including the fabrication of Afrikanist styles of clothing or festivities that bear only a fictive relationship to imagined African origins. 'Our ancestors brought with them a rich tradition of numerous cultures; it was through food, religions, games, dress, music, dance, performance, and world-views that they were able to survive. Yet the culture that we know today is not the sole result of tradition: culture is always being constructed and reconstructed in the present, in an effort to make sense of a complex world.' The image she used was that of a circle with shifting boundaries:

> Thus the historical trajectories and multiple identities realize themselves in culture as overlapping circles of consciousness; they form to make one big circle of ever-changing boundaries that can be called black culture on the one hand, and Afro-Cuban culture on the other. Popular culture in the US and in Cuba has been an arena where domination has always been seriously contested; Anglo-American and Hispanic-American institutions have never been able to wipe out Africanisms in both cultures, because there has always been a conscious and natural resistance to cultural domination. Natural resistance emerges as people mediate, somewhat unconsciously, new realities through time-tested social, physical, and psychological patterns. In more conscious efforts to assert themselves, blacks have left their imprint on the white man's institutions, as we have seen in the arts, music, popular culture, and sports. This cultural contest has succeeded and failed to varying degrees.

In Cuba, on the other hand, Brook observed a much more fluid intermixture of cultures, deeply infusing Cuban society as a whole with Africanisms, since a strident conjuncture between race, class, and national consciousness had emerged during the twentieth century, especially after the 1898 US military intervention and economic control of Cuban affairs (by 1927, US-owned sugar mills accounted for more than 80 per cent of Cuban sugar production) throughout the first half of the century and the repressive Batista regime, until it was finally called up during the 1959 revolution and its pervasive social transformations.

The weakest side of Brook's argument is her missing class analysis which leads her to elevate Cuban *mestizaje* or Afro-Cuban culture into a more promising and successful counter-narrative to political and economic domination (within Cuba's earlier sugar plantation system and the nineteenth-century history of brutalizations under foreign influences and power relations, which of course continue right through the current US imposed economic/political blockade), compared to the violent racial divisiveness in the USA. Undoubtedly, the crucial role of Afro-Cubans in the plantation economy and the growing significance of African religions and values in Cuban culture (where Catholicism played a much weaker role than in the rest of Latin America) have influenced white Hispanic values much more strongly, but if we look closely at Cuban poetry, fiction, political writing, and art we might also infer that the outpouring of *poesía negra/mulata* by Nicolás Guillén, Emilio Ballagas, Ramón Guiaro, or Luis Palés Matos, as well as the novels of Alejo Carpentier and the ethnographies of Fernando Ortiz, represented the discursive formation of a nationalist cultural *ideology* – a space that all Cubans, regardless of color and class, would ideally inhabit on equal terms. The revolution sought to complete this political fiction by sanctioning *cubanidad* as the melding of Spanish, creole, and African elements into one social fabric. The discursive and ideological formation did not necessarily acknowledge actual social relations expressed in popular Afro-Cuban music, dance, and religious practices (*Santería, Palo Monte, Abakuá, Espiritismo*), and until the early 1990s these rituals and religions had to be practiced in secret. As with any other fantasy of national unity, this ideological construction, almost entirely articulated by male writers, legitimated a particular kind of paternalistic, collectivist, and transculturated state which, nonetheless, continued to silence or exclude women, especially non-white women, and homosexuals from the bonding ritual.

It surprised me that Brook never entered into the critique of the gender and sexual politics within the Cuban nationalist paradigm. She neither attempted to address the paradoxical projections of homoerotic *machismo* posturing across racial lines, which symptomatically reproduces well-worn feminized racial stereotypes of 'black rhythms' and the eroticized *mulata*; nor did she acknowledge that many Cuban artists and writers have recently argued that it is meaningless to speak of a separate black history or 'Afro-Cuban' culture since the African heritage in Cuba is so central that there is no Cuban music, dance, or cuisine that is not syncretized or creolized African-Hispanic.[3]

Is the lack of a discourse on 'black identity' in Cuba a reflection of ideologically suppressed racial consciousness, or is Brook trying to graft a North American politics of identity onto the comparative frame of her cross-cultural study of multiple identities in the diaspora? The unexamined application of the notion of 'diaspora' to the Cuban culture is also problematic, since it would have to separate out the African dimension of syncretized *cubanidad*. While it might be challenging to extend Ortiz's concept of 'transculturation,' and the complex issue of *syncretic performance* in the colony/postcolony, to Cuban politics and ideology, we may first have to define the terminology, methodology, and epistemology of this notion of performance before applying it cross-culturally to the question of how racial identities are socially constructed. What I learnt from our conversations at *Meeting Grounds* was the tremendous gap that exists between our well-intentioned contact improvisation, in the span of a short weekend, and the difficulty of actually approximating a mutual understanding of the methods that inform our interpretation of purportedly related phenomena, and thus of exchanging our practices of 'transculturating transculturation.'[4]

1 3

The concept of 'transculturation' was developed by Fernando Ortiz in the 1940s in one of his most important historical and sociological ethnographies on Cuban life and culture, *Cuban Counterpoint: Tobacco and Sugar*, and it has had a wide influence on Latin American and Caribbean political theories of cultural contact within the histories of colonial domination. Ortiz's notion of 'transculturation,' therefore, is both site-specific and influential, having recently been adopted or imitated, in a sense, by First World theorists of acculturation and intercultural performance, although there are of course many other theories of intercultural, cross-cultural, and multicultural performance or hybridity afloat in contemporary studies of local–global relations. The terrain of these theory debates is so crowded that it is impossible for me to address it here in any comprehensive way. My questions are guided by the conversations we had during our trading at *Meeting Grounds*, thus highlighting the particular predicaments we faced in our site, Chicago, and in the necessarily limited 'counterpoints' we could explore. For Ortiz, a transcultural process is like a 'call and response,' a transformative local process in which different cultural practices cooperate to bring about a new reality ('neoculturation') which 'necessarily involves the loss or uprooting of a previous culture, which could be defined as disculturation.' This aspect of Ortiz's theory has often been overlooked, and I mention it here because he describes the long and often painful process of economic, political, social, religious, and cultural transformations in Cuban history as one that is 'intense, complex, unbroken' and, consequently, suggests not so much the synthesis of one with the other (African/Hispanic) as rather the originality of 'new cultural phenomena.' Emphasizing the vitality and creativity of the transcultural process, Ortiz explicitly develops a counter-hegemonic theory that does not define itself only in an oppositional relation to First World colonizers but emphasizes the liberating force of the Cuban cultural and emotional patriotism.[5]

Methodologically, we can distinguish several levels of a transcultural process that involves cultural collisions or negotiations. First, Ortiz's study of transculturation is a comprehensive socio-economic one that seeks to explore the overall social and political transformations that affect a society and engender collective and individual identities within culture. If we think of Brook's image of the overlapping circles, we can include here the formation of physical and symbolic patterns, customs, discourses, and beliefs that are transmitted and developed as cultural knowledge and as attitudes toward life. As the culture continues to change through the imposition or adaptation of other influences, it transforms these influences to produce 'local knowledge' (Clifford Geertz). Second, transculturation implies complex ideological and political operations, as we have seen above, which make strategic use of cultural iconographies and symbols to articulate national integrity and independence or to obfuscate actual social problems and inequalities. Third, it is on the level of ideological and political repositioning of collective cultural identities that we can examine the particular role of literature, science, art, and media in the construction of a nationalist or 'official' discourse that often seeks to dominate or superimpose itself on the various discursive spaces of popular culture or the working class or rural populations on the periphery of the political and economic centers. The urban centers, at the same time, have historically been more directly exposed to transformative influences of foreign cultures and the cross-over dynamics of global trade. On the other hand, the dynamics of urban culture are intertwined with the various processes of popular cultural syncretisms and the resonances of the economic migrations from the rural to the urban areas.

Globalization and transnational economies today are understood to be processes of continuous border crossings that generate increasingly contradictory spaces of differentiation, which complicate or disperse cohesive ideologies of national or local knowledge, and here the situation of Cuba, cut-off and isolated by the blockade, is asymptomatic. But even on this small island there are different discursive spaces of cultural identification; for example; in the way in which the citizens of Santiago de Cuba position themselves *vis-à-vis* Havana. I suggested to Lisa Brook that she might find a considerably different, self-conscious articulation of 'indigenous' or local Afro-Cuban knowledge in Santiago's popular cultures and religions, and when I spoke with black Cuban anthropologist Inés María Martiatú during my last visit on the island, she affirmed that in the paradoxical Caribbean experience

> ethnic and cultural majorities have been excluded and dominated by ethnic and cultural minorities identified since colonial times with so-called European, Western or Universal Cultures of which they consider themselves heirs, rejecting the indigenous or African cultures which constitute the ethnic majority. This inverted order has its historical and class explanation, and it echoes the dialectic of *dominant and dominated cultures* in which a dominant minority controls a subjugated majority. In many cases, this minority is as mixed racially as the majority and shares the same

concept of nationality and even ethnicity though in its alienation it does not want to take on so-called popular culture as part of its class identity. The members want to deny it, they try to strengthen the concept of cultural values which they consider the only possible and desirable ones. Of course, there is contest over what defines popular culture, and throughout history we see circumstances in which positions are relocated, shifted. Fashion, necessity or snobbery drive the dominant culture to assume aspects in its discourse that are taken from abroad, with a paternalistic attitude toward folklore, in its desire for the exotic or the recognition of Third World art values which have become important since the last century. So we have a paradox, because at first, the most important characteristics of national art emerged from the talent and sensitivity of artists who expressed the essence of so-called popular culture, presenting it in valid ways or using techniques of the dominant culture but without diminishing it and showing it as an expression of a Caribbean synthesis.[6]

Martiatú raises a very important point, namely the ideological process of internal appropriation or attempted 'disculturation' of cultural, ritual, and religious practices deemed indigenous or authentic by the popular sector but considered residual 'folklore' by the educated metropolitan bourgeoisie. Ortiz himself, in his early study of *Los negros brujos: Hampa afrocubana* (1906), had refered to the black proletariat as the 'underworld.' By the 1930s – for example, in Carpentier's Afro-Cuban novel *¡Ecue Yamba-O!* (1933) – African spiritualism within Cuban culture was celebrated for its redemptive power, whereas the revolutionary leadership after 1959, especially under the influence of its Marxist-Communist policies, sought to diminish and delegitimize the same spiritualism once again. Martiatú suggests that from her point of view

we have to understand that the point is not to deny the legitimacy of a culture in which we have been educated and which enriches us. There is no pure culture, not for our mestizo people. The question is to see the unequal relationship of certain cultural values which are intentionally distorted. The situation is now changing. Folklore or popular culture play a new role, as the strength of religious and secular manifestations, which were considered plain folklore, has been gaining recognition (without a surname). Every day there are more artists, mostly in music, dance and theater, who show an evolution without borders that vindicates an art contemporary in itself because of its place in time, and which could not be linked to the chronotopes of the dominant culture in the Western centers nor seen as derivative any more. Many of them, in the case of the Caribbean and Cuba, are practitioners of the magic-religious systems or come from communities permeated by these manifestations. They had access to the formation and information that specialized higher education provides and had participated in the international centers. They are not artists going to the *sources* to quote them, or passive beings waiting for someone to discover them. They are making their own works and feel that their religions and influences are as contemporary as the artistic method. Then, there is a continuity among them which takes us away from the concepts of folklore, traditional culture, etc., reducing the distance between so-called *popular culture* and so-called *high culture*. In some cases it disappears. An important factor in this process is the social change and the interrelation between different ideas as expressed, for example, in our current conversation, or in music or dances so important and common among us. This is the case for many artists, those who play ritual, pop, jazz, and symphonic music, or the dancers, actors and singers of folklore groups such as the Conjunto Folklorico Nacional, the Cutumba, and the Cabildo Teatral of Santiago de Cuba, who in ritual centers as well as in the theater, articulate many aspects and needs of spiritual, social and professional life. We reject the concept of folklore as an abusive generalization which includes different forms as diverse as *Santería* (religion), the *punto guajiro* (a kind of country music), culinary habits, superstitions, crafts, etc.

The most important methodological distinction introduced here is the emphasis given to *unequal relations* between cultural values and expressions (re)produced within a transcultural process, and this political dimension of the power relations between cultural practices needs to be examined rigorously if we want to address cross-cultural exchanges between First, Second, Third, and Fourth World economies or compare cultural productions in different contexts. Perhaps not surprisingly, given the status of 'post'-colonial theory as a cultural theory in the metropolitan academic debates among First and Third World intellectuals (has it been noticed that representatives from former communist or non-aligned countries are seldom invited to participate?), it is precisely the inattentiveness to political and historical differentiation between particular modes of social formations and racialized class forces struggling over political representation, and thus their position within the state, which often leads to reductive and generalized cross-cultural interpretations of, say, 'popular culture,' 'popular music,' 'minority literature' or 'hybrid performance.' Martiatú's comments on the inverted power relations between majority and minority cultures in the Latin-American/Caribbean context are particularly provocative in view of the postmodern discourse on appropriation and border cultures that celebrates the circulating flows, the borrowing, quoting and interperformative relationships between styles of cultural expression, often without conscientiously marking the asymmetries of economic and cultural capital.

A transculturalist imaginary which posits the internationalization of culture under the 'post'-colonial conditions of capital and its mass markets must therefore project its own privileged, generalizing point of view of its hybrid local production onto the fetishized screen of the 'borderland,' the transnational currency of culture seemingly unmoored from any particular local or national system of value and exchange. Within only a few years, since the publication of Gloria Anzaldúa's book on *Borderlands/La Frontera* in 1987, her specifically situated depiction of herself as a *mestiza* has been expropriated, and 'borderland' today functions mainly as a metaphor for academic conceptualizations.

Such an imaginary projects 'virtual localities;' cultural objects presumed to be further and further detached from their sites of production operate on a market-driven logic of dislocation and dispersion (as in the global audiovisual markets of TV and film). A Hollywood movie or a *telenovela*, rap or salsa music, 'world literature' and dance, thus function as transitional objects in potentially unlimited, heterogeneous matrices of cultural reception. Such multidirectional and multifunctional objects would precipitate a mode of production design for the largest possible audience, appropriating the world, so to speak. Riding on this wave of transcultural exchange, questions of agency, interpretation, use value, or translatability fall behind, and speaking about global cultural markets cannot but bring the forgotten notion of imperialism back to mind. The pervasive hegemony of US-marketed cultural products (linked to financial and military might) is uncontested, and the effort of France to protect its audiovisual territory, during a recent GATT meeting of the rich and powerful nations, appeared to many like whistling in the dark. But fearing such unprecedented dominance may reflect not so much a reactive cultural chauvinism as rather a growing awareness of the failure of the politics of nationalism which reinforces the constant, nervous reconstructions of national identities we witness within the global processes.

The sarcastic and playful optimists among independent artists and multi-lingual/multidisciplinary producers, such as James Luna, Guillermo Gómez-Peña, Coco Fusco, Nao Bustamente, Carmelita Tropicana, David Avalos, Elizabeth Sisco, Louis Hock, or the Chicano Secret Service, would claim that if France and Britain have grown nervous about their 'postcolonial' national identity, so will the United States become uncomfortably aware of its decentering and borderization. Interpreting the conservative backlash against immigrants and black, Chicano, queer and feminist politics, or the hypocritical multiculturalist policy of the institutions, as clear symptoms of the center's anxious neuroses about where it is placed, these artists have captured the implications of Ortiz's notions of transculturation and disculturation: Anglo-American culture is noticing its losses.

The question of what is lost and who is gaining from the losses remains critical, since the asymmetries don't go away. We must always ask whether our differences are translatable, and where we position and speak ourselves in relation to the agents of the dominant class owning and controlling the major means of material and cultural production. For example, how do we view the relations of domination between the US media and entertainment industry's production/ commodification of 'legitimizing fictions' of its own and other cultures *vis-à-vis* marginalized or alternative producers, or – to use another example – between the high-cultural institutions' promotion of multiculturalism on the one hand, and their strategic cultivation of 'folklore' or the spectacular 'exotic' on the other? Does the cultivation of national patrimonies or technological achievements function differently in non-western cultures? How can we compare the Disney theme parks or the nostalgic production of fake authenticity for mass (tourist) consumption to the traveling medicine shows we nowadays encounter on the

international festival circuit (including the lavishly sponsored, upscale interculturalism of the productions of Robert Wilson, Peter Brook, Ariane Mnouchkine,
or the South African musicals touring the capitals of the world, etc.)? Why is
such disproportionate prestige and status afforded to the theater anthropology of
Euro-American directors such as Eugenio Barba, Jerzy Grotowski, Peter Brook,
or Richard Schechner, rendering practitioners in the Caribbean, Latin America,
Africa, Asia, and Australia marginal or non-existent in the Western discourse on
cross-cultural performance?

1 4

> I make art for Indian people.
> In this way I do not separate myself from my community.
> I explore conditions here on the reservation.
> (James Luna)

Given Luna's ironic stance throughout 'Meeting Grounds,' I take it that this
statement is true and not true. Luna also makes art that is being shown and
exhibited to others, to audiences outside of the Luiseno Tribe in southern California. His art and his performance-installations (such as *New Basket Designs: No
Directions Known*) are a mode of communication, trading with the other
locations (reservations, art worlds, symposia) where such exchange takes place.

At the same time, perhaps it is true to say that he explores comparative culture
in North American society while always using Native American culture as his
focal point. The experience of life on the reservation is the site-specific experience of domination and survival that mobilizes the work with which he confronts social issues of both the Native American community and so-called
mainstream society.

During his brief presentation at noon, he looked at us for a while, making us
conscious of our looking at him, our looking at our images of him, our look. In
the most gentle voice, he suggested:

> Let me say that I do not talk about things in my work that I do not know,
> have not experienced or am experiencing now. I want my art to be real for
> the viewer and for myself.
>
> I make my art for Indian people. This is also a way of knowing who my
> audience is. In doing work about social issues I use myself to explore
> conditions here on the reservation. It is not my place to tell people how to
> act, so I talk about my dysfunction and attempt to communicate and
> touch people in this way. I feel it is of utmost importance that we explore
> the roots of that dysfunction. I see this communication as the first step in
> the process of recovery.
>
> My appeal for humor in my work comes from Indian culture where humor
> can be a form of knowledge, critical thought, and perhaps used just to ease
> pain. I think we Indians live in worlds filled with irony and I want to relate
> that in my works.

15

As I listened to Luna, I had some flashbacks to the earlier presentation by Milford Nahohai and James Ostler, and I thought about the ironies of this day, and the intimate sense of belonging that Luna was creating with his description of an art that heals through humor and the subtle indirections of basket designs that incorporate certain icons of the popular culture surrounding the reservation, running through the reservation. But the flow of culture also runs the other way. The white man is searching for medicine.

Nahohai called his talk 'Negotiations in an Unmarked Playing Field' and gave a straightforward (untheorized) description of the day-to-day activities of 'marketing a culture.' A board member of the Museum of Indian Arts and Culture at Santa Fe and the Zuni manager of the Pueblo of Zuni Arts and Crafts, Nahohai introduced us to the work he does as a recognized Zuni potter, and he also displayed the work of several other Zuni artists by carefully unwrapping clay sculptures he had brought along. Interestingly, most of the slides he showed depict the men and women at work, their environment and studios, and the social and community life in the Pueblo. Mentioning that the Zuni are trading their pottery to major cities around the world, Nahohai matter-of-factly stated that 'the bottom line for us and our business of the Zuni Tribe is to be competitive with all other businesses which sell similar goods, to make as much money as we can, and to do it in such a way that is not detrimental to either individual Zuni craftspeople nor to the Tribe.' He then told us that they work under no real guidelines other than those they generate, and that there is nothing codified as to how they operate since there is no one they can turn to for guidance. The main reality check, he said, is always to test the ventures against public opinion, which in his Pueblo means 'testing against the Zuni gossip network.'

His partner James Ostler, who is an artist and trader, had joined him to be the business manager at the Pueblo of Zuni Arts and Crafts, and he has also written books on contemporary Zuni pottery and fetishes. Ostler's talk addressed the various ways in which a Zuni-owned enterprise presents some aspects of Zuni culture to non-Zuni in a commercial setting, and he gave a profile of the negotiations he practices with other traders. In the end, he said, 'Our legs are in the commercial business world of L.A., Tokyo, New York and Paris; our eyes are focussed on the trade network; our ears always in Zuni. Ultimately, it doesn't matter what outsiders say about us, it only matters what the Zuni say.'

Nahohai and Ostler's bio-politics of trading sounded refreshingly uncomplicated, perhaps anticlimactic in the particular setting of our politicized questions about domination and subordination. But Ostler also mentioned that he works for the Zuni Tribe as a kind of marketing director, an employee who is considered a guest/outsider. I wonder why the discussion afterwards did not take up this constellation insider/outsider, and the issues of commodification and the global trading in authentic craft artifacts ('insider art' or 'outsider art'?), especially since Ostler refused to comment on the apparent contradictions between market demands or marketing strategies and the imperatives (the construction) of Zuni public opinion. The nature and concern of this public opinion was not disclosed, although we were made to understand that the Zuni people appreciate it when their crafts are doing well and are desirable on the market, thus confirming local pride in the labor-intensive traditional craft. Sometimes such handicrafts are described as rare examples of non-alienated labor. If we assume the Zuni Tribe to be a small and cohesive community that negotiates private enterprise (among the collective group of artists) through consensus of public opinion and gossip, such a model of community-based art-making as a needed business venture would illuminate, and perhaps throw into sharp relief, the common cynicism we may feel toward so-called tourist or airport art (sometimes grouped under the category of kitsch), the mass-produced simulated pottery and jewelry we find in urban fairs, hotel or museum souvenir shops, or exploitative commercial markets and advertising in the larger, global space where the determination of the financial market value, say, of cultural objects/artworks often escapes our understanding (for instance, when a Van Gogh from a private collection is sold for 40 million dollars to a Japanese bank).

At the same time, perhaps we might also call the Zuni trading of their crafts a 'public art' that inserts itself into the international art-culture system, its museums and markets, while contesting the rules of the market's 'playing ground' by following its own improvisational logic of keeping the business always in sync with local knowledge, especially as these artifacts continue to have their social place and function (ritual and symbolic association) in native practices and cosmologies. Indigenous art thus also performs a political role, since its community has historically suffered enormous violence and damage, and the Pueblo continues to survive only through the constant contestation of the majority culture's imposition of its laws and technologies. The heated debate about the repatriation of cultural objects from national museums to tribal institutions in Canada and the USA reflects this ongoing struggle over self-representation. I did not feel qualified to comment on the economic and political entanglement that must be built into the Pueblo's cultural production, which functions both separately, within the ethnically separate reservation, and collusively, within the dominant national order and international market. And in fact the general reluctance of the audience to engage in critical discussion perhaps underlined the uncertainty many of us felt as to how tribal artifacts communicate cross-culturally and how historical, economic, political or aesthetic criteria would apply to tribal objects on sale. More importantly, the playing ground evoked by Nahohai involves different sets of criteria, and Anglo-American museums have had to confront and completely re-evaluate their own aesthetic or ethnographic bias toward the display, (re)contextualization, and narration of native culture as tribes have now asserted their own authority more radically after decades of land-claim movements.[7]

While the resonance I am describing casts me in the role of 'outsider,' one step removed from the intermediary role Ostler takes as knowledgeable 'outsider/manager' of tribal business, the 'insider' (Nahohai) in fact did not use the term 'artwork' at all but patiently recounted the traditional processes of making handicrafts (passed on from generation to generation within families) and connected each particular crafted object to a maker and thus to local histories of kinship, pride, aspiration, and ownership ('it only matters what the Zuni say') as if these histories were not so much beleaguered or damaged by the eradicating colonial violence of the past but were regenerating themselves, drawing on autonomous spiritual sources of tradition, creativity and identity. And the production of artifacts for trade vitally reappropriates the recognition Native American art had been granted by dominant museum institutions over the past sixty-five years (the first Exposition of Indian Tribal Arts took place in New York in 1931); it reappropriates the majority culture's increasingly patronizing 'salvage' and 'appreciation' of 'tribal art' by turning its craft production into a lucrative source of native power and revenue in the global marketplace, on its own terms and not on those of the philanthropists, collectors, or wealthy patrons of metropolitan museums that sought to regulate the aesthetic evaluation of 'authentic' Indian art.

Undoubtedly, however, these converse relationships have had mutual effects on each other, and the pueblo craftspeople, like other minority artists, may very well aspire to wider recognition and global participation in markets which will render their craft inevitably mixed up in the hybrid dynamics of local–global economies, even if the local meaning of Zuni pottery resists or contradicts commercial consumption. The exchange between local culture and global market may also facilitate a reverse collection effect, insofar as Zuni craftspeople will acquire new objects, influences, and design ideas; their buyers or outside traders may send back suggestions or demand one shade or brightness of turquoise over another, reinforce one traditional design while discouraging another. Even if the museums no longer stand by their natives to protect, salvage, and expropriate their handicrafts, the question remains whether independent tribal cultural production can escape the terms set by the commercial market of hobby collectors and the imperatives of the tourist trade catering to mass consumers often unfamiliar with the designs or particular identities of pueblo pottery, baskets, blankets, beadwork, jewelry, and sculptures. How will Zuni artifacts compete with African tribal art or Mexican or Guatemalan pottery, or with the imitations that Korean artists may create for local fairs in Singapore or Mallorca? The globalization of the traffic between cultural artifacts complicates any assumptions about traditional value or a cultural object's original ritual or ceremonial use-value as soon as the object is removed from the local practice. The effects of the tourist industry, as I indicated already, also lead to the inevitable self-exoticizing of local cultural practices, as I observed in the performances of the Cuban Conjunto Folklorico Nacional, which spiced up its presentation for tourists at Havana's International Hotel with '*motivos del encuentro de la religión yorubá*,' while the beach hotels in Varadero announce Monday nights as 'special *Santería*' nights, whatever that is. *Santería*, perhaps the most paradigmatic popular religious practice in Cuba whose ceremonies and effects are accessible only to initiates, has traveled in the same directions as Cuban music and visual art, mostly with Cuban expatriates who are practitioners, and the *Village Voice* reported in early 1996 that it has now successfully taken root in Brooklyn and Manhattan, alongside Haitian *vodun* rituals, as a resource for spiritual or New Age clients in search of stimulating nurturance.

In this slippery context of migration, self-exoticization, commercial kitsch, and ersatz culture, it is probably wholly illusionistic to speak of 'authenticity' except in the ironic sense of transcultural elaboration and refunctioning, and I would therefore argue that Nahohai's claim – 'we work under no real guidelines other than those we generate' – must be understood as a politicized claim of ownership which runs counter to the commodity market's operation of demand and supply, and its unstable, shifting value and price fluctuations. The value of native cultural objects in fact depends on 'guidelines' of distinction and is therefore controlled by the market, since both collectors and tourists know where to buy 'legitimate' artifacts or the cheaper junk. The pueblo craftspeople, historically, needed the anthropologists, museums, galleries, traders, and trade associations to 'provide terminology, frameworks, and classificatory schemes for making distinctions between objects and artists, art and trash – at least as much, nowadays, using indices of quality as of authenticity – and stress the labor-intensiveness of the art's production and its connections with culture, tradition, and regional history. Many buyers of Indian art, as with any art, would simply not buy . . . if they did not have curators, writers, and exhibition judges to help them be discerning in their purchases.'[8] The performances of legitimation, in our scenario of transculture, would be more equal if they were less clearly dependent on power and control over the categories. James Luna seems completely aware of this: his 'new basket designs' are informed by mainstream pop culture, hybrid and hyperauthentic, mocking the categories as such.

16

Sharon Stephens portrayed another dimension of this contest over control of the categories, and her testimony of the indigenous Sami communities' struggle to have the right to define and promote distinctive visions of cultural identity and 'the social good' was a harrowing reminder of the social and political realities in which marginalized peoples find themselves entrapped when not even existential rights of self-preservation are guaranteed. The Sami, whose main subsistence economy relies on reindeer-herding and whose cultural history is shaped by strong relations between people, place (herding pastures) and deer, were suddenly faced with the 'invisible event' of the Chernobyl reactor explosion and its radioactive fall-out in April 1987. The event had complex social consequences for the indigenous communities who only came to know of the dangerous fall-out through its often conflicting or manipulated representations by outside experts – health professionals, politicians, journalists, and environmental activists (whose intervention itself was triggered by the general confusion in Europe over the extent of the damage in the Ukraine and its transborder effects on European regions, water and earth, crops, human and animal populations, etc.). As diverse groups struggled to define the 'facts' of Chernobyl contamination, to

Figure 33 James Luna, *New Basket Designs: No Directions Known*. Chicago 1993.

assess its long-term risks and to develop appropriate responses, the Sami also had to assert their particular claims and perceptions *vis-à-vis* the majority culture's political response to Chernobyl (reindeer meat was declared contaminated and the people were asked to consume only 'outside'/imported meat, vegetables, milk, etc.).

I was deeply moved by Stephens's engaged critique of dominant 'reactionary' politics, which in this case, in reaction to the nuclear accident, quite literally exposed itself as operating according to inadequate categories of fixed and bounded national identities ('national security'), ignoring both the transborder implications of radioactivity (the 'outside' across central/western/southern Europe and the Common Market was potentially contaminated, too) and the distinctive concerns of an ethnic minority within the northern regions whose entire nervous system was threatened, and whose way of life had already been encroached upon by earlier government policies to rationalize herding, implement scientific breeding, and annex reindeer pastures for military camps or weapons-testing sites.

What surfaced here was the immediate connection between primarily political and socioeconomic crises and national policy-making conditioned and endangered by profoundly ambiguous and morally tenuous cultural representations, which led Stephens to argue that the Sami, lacking sufficient medical knowledge about radiation as well as sufficient political representation on the level of democratically elected majority government, were inclined to suspect or resist state policies, believing them to be a pretext and giving them new interpretations (defending their traditional herding practices and, idiosyncratically, consuming some of their own meat they considered safe while also buying imported 'safe' foods). Gradually, they felt urged to dramatize central aspects of Sami culture to confront bureaucratic governments, technical experts, and 'outside' media that displayed no knowledge of Sami cosmology and self-understanding. Aware of her own role as outsider-mediator, Stephens proceeded to delineate, without showing any visual 'documentation,' the Sami responses to state radiation policies crucially affecting the lives and livelihoods of the South Sami in heavily contaminated areas. She questioned facile democratic assumptions about majority-rule by pointing out that 'some Sami communities realized they could not even trust elected representatives from official Sami organizations, since it turned out that these organizations are largely run by Sami from *outside* the most irradiated area, and these groups have their own reasons for de-emphasizing the seriousness of Chernobyl fallout in Sami regions.'

Somebody 'standing for' somebody else: the South Sami's questioning of the existing representation of their claims in the 'representative' democratic government turned into a prolonged negotiation with state policies on behalf of their history and their rights, and Sami communities sought to counter the post-Chernobyl demoralization by starting a concerted effort to document and 'collect' evidence, memories, stories, and artifacts and to chart their cultural landscape as a way of preserving their threatened way of life – a process of 'objectification and museumization,' as Stephens calls it. Chernobyl thus became the catalyst for the new South Sami Cultural Center's construction of a unified narrative of Sami cultural history.

> While many Sami are critical of notions of a Sami museum culture depicting an unchanging Sami society engaged in ancient reindeer herding practices, other South Sami have also participated in the objectification and codification of Sami culture for their own purposes, contributing artifacts, traditional handicrafts, photographs of ancestors, and oral histories (now graphically illustrated on wall panels titled 'US' and 'THEM') describing the history of Sami-Scandinavian colonial relations. But while contributing to this construction of a unitary Sami cultural history, Chernobyl has also presented practical difficulties for maintaining a sense of unitary Sami identity, since markedly different levels of fallout in South and North Sami regions foregrounded differences and tensions between these groups characterized by different histories, dialects, and cultural traditions. Most of the tensions were economically motivated since the South Sami in the more heavily contaminated areas felt that selfish North Sami reindeer market interests led their politicians to disinform the majority population about the relative safety of reindeer meat, which corresponded to national government interests. Politically, the North Sami movement toward the establishment of an economically strong ethnic community with leverage was threatened by the Chernobyl confusion and the dependency on welfare and Norwegian state support claimed by South Sami in a period of crisis that made the South Sami feel like a minority within a minority.

These regional differences were exasperated by the new South Sami women's movement that emerged in 1990 to claim women's particular role in maintaining the family way of life and union with nature characteristic of the culture, while also defending their right to proper public health monitoring (cancer and radiation treatment; assessment of various effects of radiation on the immune and hormonal systems, etc.) *vis-à-vis* scientific assessments that were floated to downplay the risks of radiation – official discourses that women activists took to represent the interests of the bio-medical/military-industrial establishment. These activists, Stephens argued, thus shifted the political-economic debate over reindeer-herding to their expressed concerns over national health policy, information policy, and the newly fixed levels of 'acceptable radiation.' The Sami women activists formed coalitions with western feminists and alternative medical discourses to fight both Norwegian state agencies and North Sami-controlled ethnic-political representation of Sami herding interests, thus intervening into closed circles and the marginalization of the South Sami community which, as I described, had just begun to consolidate a consistent, imaginary cultural unity already internally contradicted by conflicting needs.

The portrait emerging from this constellation is very complex, as we see how needs and identities are expressed in relation to parallel, contradictory, and complementary collectivities in overlapping circles. The women's concern for their role in cultural practices and long-term physical and psychological health-care, although incorporative of international feminist ideas, is focussed locally on their particular Sami situation and world-view, including their criticism of male preoccupation with the economy and representative 'museum culture.' The Chernobyl effect, as an international crisis, has thus opened a range of new questions about contemporary community mobilization. The South Sami women's group demonstrates, in its politicized negotiation of different discourses and 'insider'/'outsider' knowledge and strategies, effective ways of vocalizing the understanding of how woman's life-roles have been affected, while also relativizing the separatist ethnic politics of their community leaders and, at the same time, forcing Scandinavian government agencies to rethink their risk management policy, the ways in which scientific 'truths' are produced (which are in fact also 'culture-specific'), and their relations to differentiated ethical minority protests.

In a conversation with Stephens I asked her to tell me more about the staging of the protests, since she had mentioned the theatricality of various Sami cultural self-representations, and the difficulties faced by governments and the media in figuring out whose cultural representations were to be considered 'representative' in *risk societies* (Ulrich Beck's term for late industrial societies) which, in the West, tend to be administered by scientific rationality. Her concrete example of a society at risk was so very illuminating that I thought it harbored tremendous potential as an analogy for local–global identifications across different social, political, and cultural situations, since the process described in fact moved the boundaries of the circles to open up dialogue among alternative groups, speakers, and agencies who could share their concerns and the knowledge that matters in their cultural life-experience. This movement implies a shift from technoscience to a science of social interests connected to people in living environments. The state-level discourses of administrative rationality are challenged to respond much more flexibly to local and anecdotal knowledge (indigenous knowledge) and alternative perspectives if we are to imagine a shared politics of multiculturalism not controlled by majority power.

Stephens responded by describing how difficult it has been for radiation victims, and for disempowered communities affected by radiation damages to their environment, to have their complaints taken seriously by the scientific community at national or international levels which devalues opinions not adherent to its standards of knowledge production and evaluation. This raises a crucial question about the kind of transmissions of knowledge and modes of communications that can 'stand for' and negotiate cultural or political representation, and this is also epitomized in the ambivalent process of a minority culture's self-objectification in ethnic museums. Stephens admitted that indigenous groups, in order to have a political presence at the state level, in a sense have to *produce themselves* in the image of what outsiders think of as 'indigenous,' and on such occasions of political meetings Sami representatives tend to appear in colorful Sami clothes on their reindeer-pulled sleighs, almost as if in a self-conscious parody of 'indigenism,' producing the politically accepted iconography of their ethnicity. The dialectics of these relations are full of ironies, since this production of the kind of 'primitivism' that modernist Western culture had always imputed to indigenous culture was accompanied by Sami arguments about the risk of radiation spread that were more sophisticated and reasonable than the conflicting Norwegian or Swedish national security policies that pretended to be able to manage the nuclear fall-out within sovereign state borders.[9]

When I asked Stephens about the non-visual documentation of her work in the Sami community, she gave a very poignant explanation:

> Many of the Sami people with whom I work are 'camera-shy.' After Chernobyl, the hardest-hit communities were for a short time inundated with journalists. Some asked Sami herders to stage mock reindeer round-ups for the camera. In one case, a woman looking out of her kitchen window saw someone filming her children. When she asked what he was doing, he explained that he was documenting the 'vanishing culture' of contemporary Sami, threatened by Chernobyl fallout. The nature of this situation made me conduct my fieldwork without audio-visual means.
>
> But there are other reasons to think seriously about the use of audio-visual representation. What is at stake for many Sami in the wake of Chernobyl, namely the sense of a certain kind of familiar bodily experience, certain kinds of tastes, tactile sensations and smells in everyday life, is not capturable on film or cassette. These sorts of cultural representations are more resolutely embodied and less easily commodified and transportable than visual or auditory representations. Not every cultural practice or landscape is as visible and available as every other for potential absorption outside the social context in which it is produced.

Stephens also told me that she was intrigued by the photographic and filmic materials shown by other artists and traders at 'Meeting Grounds,' but she insisted that the anthropologist's role as a mediator is ethically and politically compromised, since she is always aware of the fact that, when explaining the complexity of the social consequences of the nuclear fall-out in Sami culture to non-Sami audiences, some understanding of the Sami social world needs to be constructed. Her role as a mediator thus participates in a process of objectifying and transporting cultural images, artifacts, and experiences to other social contexts, and her portrayal of the minority culture's alternative vision and experience is subject to criticism and could also be appropriated for profit within the global marketplace. Her cautioning us about the transmission of cultural experience is an honest and accurate reminder of the consequences involved in doing ethnography or activist political work 'on' indigenous or minority peoples or human rights issues, since we always have to ask ourselves how cultural representations affect lives, and how their and our productions are consumed by others in the marketplace.

This most challenging problem of cross-cultural work has far-reaching implications not only for ethnographers but also of course for cultural producers, activists, and artists who claim to do collaborative work or build solidarity and intercommunal alliances across borders. Even the postmodern, self-reflexive fieldwork practice of 'participant observation' tends to be a quaint euphemism for collaborations that are most often politically and economically asymmetrical, since the ethnographer or producer is always implicated with the subject of her/ his study – and thus in the production of 'objectivity' or 'subjectivity' – together with the history of such power (colonial) relations. The history of visual anthropology or filmic documentation belongs quite centrally to this history of colonial relations, and 'participant observation' does not change the position of power arrogated by the Western producers to themselves, their motivations and desires, and their capturing of the other to produce themselves and offer the participating other for consumption. This is primarily a political process which involves material relations of production generally controlled by the producers, and it would be dishonest to argue that such production takes place in a shared cultural space or 'common border.'

If we gave up the control and our motivation to stage our project, we could more humbly imagine ourselves quite pragmatically to be working *with* others, or perhaps *alongside* others, as filmmaker-ethnographer Trinh T. Minh-ha conspicuously renames the 'outside-in-inside-out' relationship.[10] This idealization is perhaps a necessary political fiction if we want to maintain our passion and belief for cross-cultural communication and collaboration, for the discovery of political, social, cultural, spiritual, and expressive connections, affinities, and identifications that would empower communities of interconnectedness inclusive of multiple or discontinuous viewpoints and psychophysical experiences.

In the realm of cross-cultural performance or media production, these challenges have been recognized, but the implicated history of unequal power relations is not always acknowledged or productively engaged, and the introduction of so-called advanced Western technologies or technological aesthetics into other local indigenous or Aboriginal information economies needs to be scrutinized critically – from several angles – if we claim to act consciously toward community mobilization. On the one hand, as performers or producers we will have to become much more critically aware of the cultural codes or the codifications of the techniques (and their underlying assumptions) we use when we 'meet within the common borders' of our passion or profession, as Eugenio Barba describes cross-cultural collaboration in his *Guide to Theater Anthropology*, which delineates, in a richly metaphorical manner, the 'scientific objectivity' pursued in his research on the recurring principles of 'pre-expressive scenic behavior upon which different genres, styles, roles and personal or collective traditions are all based.'[11]

Whereas Barba and his collaborators study the practical craft of performers by observing how unique, individual performer-characteristics and the particularities of performance traditions in their contexts can be reduced or traduced to essential, transcultural principles of the *bios* (the use of body-mind upon which performance techniques are founded), other approaches to working within 'common borders' of performance or cultural practice have been less sanguine about the possibility of recovering or proposing such essentials that could be objectified in and across specific cultural contexts already always subject to complicated negotiations (and languages of negotiation) and to the *history/memory of contact* charged with traumatic experiences and fantasies. All processes of identification, in this sense, are hypercharged with psychological fantasies about self and other, sameness and difference, but the application of our techniques of practice and observation needs to be rigorously questioned as to the assumptions we bring to the 'common borders' of perception, and this involves, in my experience, the often unacknowledged closed-circuit of the self-reflexive implication of one's position *vis-à-vis* an other subject, an other reality, which tends to *confirm* one's position of power. I work alongside and with the other whose sameness I try to recognize and respect across the differences that I need to take into account as I distance myself from an uncritical assumption or imposition of sameness, equality, solidarity.

The entanglement of working alongside other workers or producers in 'post'-colonial or (as I would call them) neo-colonial contexts, specifically if such work introduces or implements new performance/media techniques and codes into local cultural contexts of minority groups, is depicted in all of its disruptive effects by the highly charged and honest account of Eric Michaels's participation in the Warlpiri Aborigines' 'invention' of video/TV technology in their remote Central Australian community, published posthumously in his *Bad Aboriginal Art: Tradition, Media, and Technological Horizons.*[12] While I don't wish to question the sincerity and importance of Barba's transcultural study of the practical craft of professional performers (generally conducted in elite workshops open to a select/invited number of European and Asian artists), I prefer to mention Michaels's work alongside the Aboriginal communities because it has an immediate connection to 'Meeting Grounds' and represents one of several cases of indigenous media production that have recently attracted much attention (apart from the Warlpiri and Pitjanjajari in Australia, there have been new media production projects among the Inuit and Yup'ik in Canada, and the Indians of the Amazon Basin).

'Indigenous media' is meant to refer to the use of video and TV technology for the cultural and political purposes of indigenous peoples; the producers, in this case, are also the receivers, although their videos have also been distributed and shown at festivals in the USA and in Europe. As a transcultural phenomenon, the emergence of Aboriginal media production, within and against Australia's technocratic government policies and broadcasting/VCR/video markets, created such a powerful dynamics of self-management for the Warlpiri, Michaels argues, that the particular accomplishment of their local community-access television-'sovereignty' in the age of global media presents an unusual opportunity (for him) to observe Aboriginal appropriation and adaptation strategies that may also be pertinent for others (like him) interested in developing alternative models of TV production, distribution, and reception.

Like Ostler's work for the Zuni, Michaels's contribution to the Warlpiri experiments with communal VCR/cassette sharing, pirate television transmission, and the eventual creation of their own permanent TV station at Yuendumu consisted in being a technical adviser, consultant, and activist on behalf of Warlpiri production rights. The development of Aboriginal telecommunications comprises a range of local decision-making processes during which the Warlpiri explored the content they wanted for their programming and the modes of adaptation they deemed appropriate for the integration of the new media and the 'social role' of the camera into their *Jukurrpa* (Law of the Dreaming) that informs human social relationships, rituals, ceremonies, reciprocal kin-based obligations, and spatiocorporeal relationships with the environment (especially significant are the interdictions, boundaries, and detours determined by taboos or sacred sites). Michaels vividly describes this arduous process, and the political complications involved, and concludes that Warlpiri videomakers have 'learned ways of using the medium that conform to the basic premise of their tradition in its essential oral form. They demonstrate that this is possible, but also that their efforts are yet vulnerable, easily jeopardized by the invasion of alien and professional media producers.'[13]

The motivations behind Aboriginal community video production and television transmission, Michaels observes,

> can be seen as basic issues of self-determination, cultural maintenance, and the prevention of cultural disruption that might have resulted from satellite broadcasts of alien programming, whether Australian, American, British, or 'ethnic' (most of the world). The strategies they have employed include control of incoming television signals, control of self-representation through local video production in local languages, refusal to permit outsiders to film, and negotiation of coproductions that guarantee certain conditions aimed at cultural maintenance. These developments have arisen from the Warlpiri politics of representation.[14]

Michaels is arguing a case of 'image sovereignty' in the local network of Warlpiri video production, and although this may appear contradictory in the context of global information flows and the homogenizing influence of media technology, I think it here addresses a crucial moment of a community's rehearsal with audio-visual media (in the politically active sense in which Augusto Boal uses the term 'rehearsal') *in order* to gain and maintain control over their production/reception in the face of the patterns of domination (re-)created by First World cultural transmitters/media. The question that resonates here is: who has the right to make films and videos about native peoples?

17

This brings me to the concluding, and for me most riveting, encounter staged at 'Meeting Grounds:' between Kayapo videomaker Kinhiabiëiti and Chicago anthropologist Terence Turner who has conducted fieldwork with the Kayapo in Brazil since 1962 and is currently involved in making documentary films with them about their resistance to exploitation by outside forces. Kinhiabiëiti, a member of the Metuktire community of Kayapo and the first one to be given a video camera, recorder deck, and monitor by Turner, had been taught to use the camera by Turner, and then proceeded to do his own recording of Kayapo traditional culture, above all the ceremonial performances, but also important events and actions such as the Altamira demonstrations against the construction of a hydroelectric dam, and other Kayapo transactions with the Brazilian government or the Bureau of Indian Affairs.

I felt puzzled and provoked by the presentation of the Kayapo Video Project, partly because the precise history of the foundation of this indigenous media project remained obscured (the initial steps were made in 1985 by Brazilian researchers from the São Paulo-based Centro de Trabalho Indigenista, and by independent filmmakers from the Mekaron Opoi D'joi Project in Rio de Janeiro), and partly because Turner mentioned only in passing that in 1987 he had been sent back to the Gorotire and Metuktire communities with film crews from Granada Television (Great Britain) to be a consultant for Granada's *Disappearing Worlds* series.[15] After briefly introducing the project, he proceeded to show excerpts from his own documentaries, and then several of the videos filmed and edited by Kinhiabiëiti.

It was hard for me to avoid the impression that Big Brother was introducing his Native Apprentice, although that is an impression I am sure Turner wanted to prevent by all means, since he sees his dedicated and helpful role as that of a facilitator who is now reporting to us how the Kayapo succeeded very quickly in seizing and exploiting the opportunity of video production as a way of defending their traditional culture and social institutions. Yet the first film he showed was one of his own, establishing his (ethnographic) involvement and authority in the matter, and I was trying to grasp the cross-cultural issues and translations at stake. The translation problem was most poignant here: Kinhiabiëiti was the only 'Meeting Grounds' participant who did not speak the 'universal' English used at the conference, and this had at least two dramatic effects on the audience. First, the flow of the conference was interrupted, since Turner naturally wanted Kinhiabiëiti to speak for himself (in the Kayapo Ge language and in Portuguese), as they were standing next to each other, Turner looming over the smaller-sized Kayapo filmmaker. I could sense that Kinhiabiëiti was very anxious to address the public in Chicago and did so in a very distinct and clear manner. Initially, I felt that people in the audience were impressed and moved by his dignified and poised address; but there were others, later on, who began to shuffle nervously, impatient with the delay in the translation back-and-forth between Ge, Portuguese and English, between the native from the Amazons and the white US American anthropologist/interpreter.

I think these time-lags or spaces in-between, these crossings and failed translations (especially when audience members asked pointed questions, and Turner tried to render the gist of the question to Kinhiabiëiti who sometimes did not understand the cultural bias from which the question originated), created a rather important distancing effect, perhaps a 'defamiliarization' in the Brechtian sense. This space of distance that suddenly opened up between the US metropolitan audience and the visitor from the Amazons was the most disjunctive event of the symposium, since it reminded me of the privileged space and First World predicament under which the whole event was organized. My Portuguese is not very good, but from what I understood I sensed that Turner was editing the questions.

Here the trading or exchange momentarily faltered, but at the same time another exchange was shown and framed for us, right there on the proscenium stage, in the subsequent presentation of Turner's and Kinhiabiëiti's own videos. Turner proudly explained that Kinhiabiëiti is now the most well-known and respected videomaker among the Kayapo, having recently started to train other members of the community in the use of video camera and editing techniques. After the first impact of this presentation of Kinhiabiëiti (with unfortunate resonances of the 'noble Indian,' ambassador and engineer of his native culture, standing there visibly 'othered'), Turner introduced his visual footage about the Kayapo Video Project (ostensibly constructed for grant-giving institutions in the West), and another *déjà vu* set in. Perhaps it was the recognition of something all too familiar (the documentary mode of low-budget ethnographic video; certain frame compositions and editing cuts I know all too well). Perhaps it was the intuition I had of the 'space between' – what Taussig refers to as the mimesis of our vocabulary, in a space permeated by the colonial tension of mimesis and alterity, in which it is far from easy to say who is the imitator (of 'our' technology) and what is the imitated. What was it my civilized high-tech eyes saw? These are the wrong questions.

Turner's voice-over (in English) explains the (his) introduction of electronic media into the Kayapo culture ('first contact' with Western technology), pointing to the Kayapo video operators at work, describing their editing process, and finally the video showed a sequence in which the Kayapo videomaker, in the frame, addresses the camera directly explaining in his own voice what he is doing, and why. The archive of tapes is shown behind him: the recording (recoding) of Kayapo culture has begun.

In terms of the political dimension of the work, it is also shown that Kayapo videomakers take their own journalism into their hands and record rallies, demonstrations and verbal encounters with Brazilian government officials (so as to have the equivalent of a legal transcript); they film dams that are built or loggers who intrude into their territory, and create activist videos that participate in their resistance against dominant culture and their struggle for autonomy and land rights.

When Turner explained the process of incorporation of videomaking into Kayapo culture, I recognized both the strategy of hands-on training (passed on between the members who then become trainers of the next group of community videomakers in an ever-widening spiral, as I had learnt it when I worked for Community Access Television in Dallas) and the activist mode of documenting one's protest while staging the documentation for the dominant media. The Kayapo did this very successfully when they made sure that they would be photographed and filmed, themselves filming their protest at

Altamira, by the large numbers of Brazilian and world media present at the event. Sensational images of the Kayapo with cameras on their shoulders later on appeared in *Time* and the *New York Times Magazine*, ostensibly featured for the strange effect this might create for our intimations of the high-tech natives of the global village.

Turner argued that video media for the Kayapo have become not only the 'means' of representing their culture, their actions, and the objectification of their meanings in social consciousness, 'but themselves the ends of social action and objectification in consciousness. The Kayapo have moved from the initial stage of conceiving video as a means of recording events to conceiving of video as the event to be recorded and, more broadly, conceiving events and actions as subjects for video.' In the activist context I discussed in the previous chapter, such tactical uses of video are the strategies used by ACT UP and Greenpeace demonstrations staged for media dissemination. The Kayapo undoubtedly have gained leverage and recognition by doing so, and the Brazilian government has shown its willingness to listen to their complaints and land-claims. Governments sometimes like to avoid bad publicity and care about their national image. (Such concerns were voiced repeatedly by conservative politicians in Germany in 1992, when the refugee asylums were fire-bombed by neo-Nazis, and the Foreign Minister complained that this might hurt the German export industry.)

18

Subsequently, Turner showed four video segments by Kinhiabiëiti that reflect some of the work being done in recording community culture, such as the *Memu Mebiok* (male naming ceremony) and *Menire Mebiok* (female naming ceremony) ritual performances that traditionally last up to three months. These video segments were immensely interesting, and I would have liked to watch them without Turner's introductory comments on how Kinhiabiëiti had mastered the technology of editing or created his point of view or a particular angle of shooting the ceremonies. The videos use real-time sound; there are no voice-overs, verbal narratives, or subtitles. In other words, these films once again plunge the Western eye into a distancing mode, where most of us won't understand the meaning or contextual significance of the content (the place, dance, play, headdresses, ornaments, and actions of the ritual event), and where we must interpret what we see according to conventions of ethnographic filmmaking we may know, and according to the specific ways in which the videomaker has captured the action, based on our prior knowledge of the filmic apparatus and the grammar of editing, shot composition, framing, focus, rhythm, etc.

The first two segments portray ceremonial and processional action; the third one is an extraordinary sequence of continuity depicting a soccer match between two villages ending in a joint ceremonial dance, in itself a remarkable example of the Kayapo having adopted Brazilian soccer practice and assimilated it into their own cultural practices. The last segment records the important political meeting between Chief Ropni and then President Collor of Brazil, during which the Kayapo chief exhorts and lectures the embarrassed-looking president about their land-rights. Turner had explained this scene as a Kayapo tactic of 'shaming' Brazilian politicians and agencies attempting to impose 'development' schemes that would disrupt Kayapo community life and their connection to their environment.

The critical issue here, which deserves discussion in much greater detail than I can offer, concerns the various discourses and interpretive actions that produce the boundaries of this screening and of the video document itself: Turner's explanatory comments on Kayapo video technique and the development of the Kayapo Video Project, which intermix anthropological translation and the technological expertise of the producer, and, furthermore, the native account of the Kayapos' understanding of their use of video technology. These accounts and comments enter into our context of reception and the different readings we as spectators bring to the representations and the represented, and this raises the question whether the indigenous filmmaker is able to objectify his meaning into the competing discourses for his film's reception. Even the question of ownership (whose film is it?) cannot be easily answered if the film records a traditional ceremony performed by the village community. Kinhiabiëiti argued that he and 'the Kayapo have a mind and a spirit, just like other peoples, that allow them to use the camera in such ways that they can preserve/record their cultural life as it really is, and as it can be passed on to their children and grandchildren.' These videos, he added, will represent Kayapo life to the Kayapo, but they can also be shown to other peoples.

19

One could also argue that the video does not represent Kayapo life but only a version of it. Earlier, Turner had refered to the Kayapo videomaker's handling of the camera and shot selection, commenting on how scrupulously Kinhiabiëiti had followed the rhythm and sequence of the ritual, its site-specific dances and the respective ornaments worn, in the same order in which they actually occurred. Pointing to the video images, he used a descriptive terminology that squarely represented familiar criteria of cinematic aesthetics (e.g. close-up function, movement, panning, editing/suturing, diegesis, etc.) but also the inevitable technological functions built into the apparatus itself (camera zoom, wide angle, etc.). I was puzzled by this, since such commentary cannot explain the meaning of the recorded ritual at the level of the natives. In his published explanation, Turner mentions that his 'main anthropological reason for launching the video project was to study the Kayapo approach to editing their own material.' He had surmised, he argues, that the Kayapo might be guided in editing videos of their culture by the same cultural schemata that guided the performance of the cultural activities in question. He then explains that Kinhiabiëiti's editing of the ceremony 'fully bore out [his] expectations.'

The ceremonies in question [the naming ritual imparting status on the name-receiver] were long and complex, involving some two months of continual ritual activity. This activity is organized in repetitive sequences of singing and dancing, in which the same dances, accompanied by the same songs, are performed in the same order but in a series of different places, beginning at a secluded area in the forest far from the village and then moving through several intervening sites to end with the climactic celebrations in the central village plaza. In the earlier performances, only a few decorations made from palm leaves are worn, but in the final dances in the village plaza, the full panoply of feather capes, headdresses and other special ornaments are worn. In editing his tapes of these sequences, Kinhiabiëiti meticulously included bits of every dance performance at every site that he had on tape, in the same order in which they occurred. Repetition was not only not avoided but emphasized. The aim was to make a full and faithful representation of the entire ritual performance, and to show that the ceremony had been fully and properly performed.

The schema of the ceremonial performance, in other words, was applied reflexively as the schema guiding the editing of its video representation. Nonrepetitive elements, for example special rites . . . , were also scrupulously shown. No significant particularity, in Kayapo terms, was omitted. There was, in sum, no editorial selection or emphasis of some segments or aspects of the scripted order of the ceremony at the expense of others.

Turner appears satisfied with the Kayapo's effort at cultural self-documentation. He commends Kinhiabiëiti's successful editing performance and leaves us with the impression that the Kayapo are 'excellent and assiduous ethnographers of themselves.'[16]

This, I believe, is a rather astonishing example of postmodern anthropological fantasy, ostensibly promoting a pluralist or relativist argument on behalf of 'aboriginality,' and emphasizing the 'authenticity' of the native recording of their orginal or traditional ceremonies, while asserting at the same time the Western anthropologist's correct hypothesis and empathetic understanding of the natives' social imaginary ('schema'). The contradictions are striking, not only in the choice of terms ('scripted order,' 'faithful representation'), but above all in the uncritical presumption of the transparency of the medium through which Turner proposes the Kayapos' preservation of the essential contours of the ceremonial culture.

The postmodern turn – the anthropological self-critique and the new discourse on 'participant observation' that grants the natives their own role as 'ethnographers of their own culture' or even as ethnographers of the intruding, dominant state bureaucracies, foreign anthropologists and tourists – here fails to acknowledge its (unintentional?) mediation or application of its critical theory to native subjects and their cultural activity or capacity for mimicry. In its implicit recuperation of such charged and contested terms as 'authenticity,' applied to the traditional communal ceremony *and* its purportedly accurate reproduction in the upgraded medium of video, Turner's judgement comes across as a romanti-cization of indigenous media in spite of itself. As the older positivism has come under attack, so the newer postmodern, 'post'-colonial critical theory has grown more complex and contradictory as it deconstructs coherent subject identities, nations, communities, origins, essences, and other ideologies of continuity or master narratives. Turner is undoubtedly aware of his 'salvage' operation, as he interprets the Kayapo Video Project in terms of the preservation of traditional ritual culture. But he never discusses Kinhiabiëiti's work as a culturally hybrid activity or as an intervention, although it should be clear from the examples that were screened that the Kayapo are negotiating the new video technology – in their oral culture in which social kinship relations, community spaces, and phys-ical geographies are most significantly expressed and re-enacted through long-durational ceremonial performances – as a method of cultural and political invention of their positions or claims against dominant culture, recombining and syncretizing elements from Brazilian culture with their local expressions. He also failed to comment on his desire for the manufacture of the Video Project and the building of the Kayapo 'archive,' for which he acts not only as a facilitator but also as the anthropological expert who will be able to trade in the knowledge of the other (for Granada Television, for the profession), building his own career on the project and the commodification of Kayapo culture for the international film circuits, where he is already competing with the documentaries produced by Brazilian videomaker Vincent Carelli (who works for the Centro de Trabalho Indigenista in São Paulo).

I don't want to become involved in the flame wars that have already been exercised between Brazil, Australia, and the USA (involving Turner, Eric Michaels, Fred R. Myers, and others), except noting that political struggle that is ongoing among the peoples described by ethnography, i.e. *their politics of location* and their rootedness in a world threatened by state or capital interests, drops out of the motion pictures staged by engaged anthropologists hailing indigenous media autonomy or 'post'-colonial theory's urbane celebra-tion of hybridity, deterritorialization, and dispersal in contemporary global processes.[17] The Kayapo have not yet published their theory in the First World journals.

20

What was not discussed by Turner was the effect of the videotaping/recording on the cultural performances themselves; at least it seemed to me that the issue of the *staging* (the production) of the 'real' cultural and ceremonial action for the camera was not taken up critically, partly out of respect for the guest, I believe. But it would have been very illuminating to hear Kinhiabiëiti comment on his choices for the editing cuts. After all, the ritual lasted for two months, and the video is condensed into thirty minutes. As in all films, documentary or fictional, the camera must select and compose, and the postproduction process involves a further construction and renarrativization of the image-movement. Video production, furthermore, as a process of image-making, cannot be seen in isolation. It always remains connected to other contextual modes of narrative or performative story-telling, and to the particular social agency, preference, and inclination of the videomaker.

These choices in the Kayapo mode of video production are a rather crucial issue if we want to examine the politics of production within and across the colonial space (the space between, which is now always also a technological space of mimesis/copying between), and the question of how culture is constructed/produced, re-invented (for camera/recordings) for the community itself and for the outside world/viewers, or, close by, for the majority culture in Brazil. Do we not have to assume that the Kayapo are now inventing a culture in filmic action? How is Kayapo performance transposed from one site (local forest and village) into another (the medium), translated/altered/postproduced by video technology and the limited aesthetic languages of video? How is the next Kayapo generation of viewers going to 'read' the video clips of the ancestors' dance? Especially if there is no verbal narrative included, or if the dance is watched as image/soundtrack, but cannot be taught (as embodied practice) in this way? How is culture-in-action then transmitted or, more correctly, mediated? Or will the traditional cultural practice continue as embodied practice, while the video archive serves as a 'local museum' or cultural information or entertainment center? Turner's film showed the Kayapo gathered together in the village plaza around one monitor, apparently in a tremendously joyful mood, watching their 'home movies.'

21

Turner in fact raised some of these questions implicitly when he made his introductory remarks:

> What role does media use play in self-conscientization, both of one's culture and one's creative powers of representation? To what extent may previous traditions of representation in a culture interact with new techniques of representation like video? And what specific role is played by play in these connections?

The questions thus formulated are abstracted from the actual power relations and dynamics between trainer and native student, technological expert and local community. Whereas Michaels describes in great detail the role of reciprocal obligations in Warlpiri culture, which structures the understanding of personhood and 'authorship' in creative production quite differently from Western notions of 'producer' or 'author,' Turner didn't comment on the position assumed by Kinhiabiëiti's role as filmmaker within the local political economy. But his last question was pertinent to the second video which showed what Turner refered to as 'traditional Kayapo play': ritual clowning and enactment of comedic skills. It was impossible to ascertain whether

Kinhiabiëiti's camera had provoked or 'asked for' some of the clowneries, but there were several scenes in which Kayapo members of the community played to the camera.

I think this reference to 'play' brings us very close to the critical transition that I implied when speaking of first contact and 'reverse contact.' It is entirely conceivable that the Kayapo indeed enjoy performing for the cameras, and are becoming self-conscious by beginning to theatricalize their 'traditional' cere-monies in a new or different way and by incorporating the new creative possi-bilities discovered in the interface between performance and video. The videos will be watched by the community: they are their first 'home movies,' and they will create a feedback effect.

It is not at all clear why Kinhiabiëiti didn't bring any of his experimental, narrative, or poetic videos to Chicago or why he, in other words, was content to show only the ethnographic and activist work he was doing. Or would it seem incongruous that the Amazon Indians are now working in diverse (Western?) aesthetic modes and genres? What is the disjunction created here? Did we, in fact, feel disappointed that the Kayapo videos looked 'authentic' in a weak ethnographic way, i.e. not inflected by the consciousness of self-reflexive First World visual anthropology (after Jean Rouch, Michael Oppitz, Trinh T. Minh-ha, and others; or after the vibrant debates among Latin American fimmakers of the 'Third Cinema' era who claimed an alternative *cinema-process* of becoming)? What is the difference between Third World Cinema and indigenous media? Did we take it for granted that the Kayapo are just at the beginning of 'modernizing' the culture? Had they watched *Trobriand Cricket*? Their passionate and ironic soccer matches seem to indicate that they had.

How much of their work depends on well-intentioned instruction by Turner, and at what point will they have to engage the political questions of access (to technology, television space, equal representation, distribution, sales, conserva-tion of tapes, upgrading, transfer systems, the Internet, etc.) or of horizontal communication (cf. women's access to equipment to produce their own versions of what constitutes valuable and preservable cultural action)? At what point will they begin to consciously manipulate and fabricate their cultural life or identity?

22

I would suspect, from all the evidence I have seen (in parallel work and in the history of the introduction and incorporation of new technologies and new relations of production), that the Kayapo have been encountering, processing, and absorbing video technologies into their lives, although it is too soon to make claims about the cultural future, nor do I know how the Kayapo account for or evaluate the process. This absorption will have profound effects on native image and self-image, inter-tribal relations, and relations with the dominant bureaucra-cies and populations in Brazil. If we are assuming, as many at the symposium did, that culture is processual and dynamic, and engaged in constant re-invention of tradition within as well as in relation to neighboring border cultures, then the Kayapo video culture will be part of this transformation and their political struggle for autonomy. It will bring contests and negotiations with it, as it will remain subject, to a certain extent, to the larger political economies determining the transmission, expansion, marketing, and trading of technologies and commodities. The problem with video production is that it creates 'packages' that can be utilized, for example, by governments and dominant commercial media for the purpose of their programming or national multicultural policy requirements. Once appropriated 'local production' is inserted into mass media or the traveling of images, the local transcultural process becomes unrecognizable. It cannot be transferred. If the Kayapo process and reproduce their subjective notions of community, as a viewer I remain outside, in the presence of the video trade, in the translocal space of media communications. Kinhiabiëiti's video resists my identification of the other; it communicates, but what the results of this exchange are it is not very clear. Does this resistance remind me of my irreconcilable difference, or of the need to redefine what I mean by 'difference'? Or has the (fantasy of) dialogue already taken place because it has provoked uncertainty, uncertain speculation on differences?

Some of the questions I asked are wrong, once again, because they unwillingly reinforce a dualism in the relations between postmodernity (my own situatedness as a producer in metropolitan culture) and 'modernization' among the indigenous producers. They reinforce the visualist impulse to compare or to think of technological 'effects' on a local indigenous culture in a linear and evolutionist mode. The questions of this spectator concerning the content of Kayapo production are curious and impertinent; my criteria are my tools, and why would my Western distinctions or classificatory schemata of documentary, ethnographic, fictional, poetic, or experimental film necessarily make sense to Kinhiabëiti, who may in fact have mixed all of these modes into his videos? Or his creative modes are different, and I have no language for them as we may not share the same *bios* of spatiocorporeal action, or the same transpositional processes. (*The body is a movement of boundaries.*)

If he has brought his camera and videotaping into the local 'law' of social reproduction, ceremony or performance, does his recording in fact 'counter-interpolate' the new medium to the traditional culture, as Michaels describes the process of 'restricted expression' among Warlpiri videomakers? In that case, I would need to understand, for example, what Kinhiabiëiti left out, what dances in the secluded forest sites he did not or could not film, and to what extent Kayapo culture does or does not regulate sensual-spatial access to men's or women's rituals and enclaved locales of ceremonial action. Since I lack this local knowledge, I am thrown back to interrogation, putting questions about the production of representation, which Trinh T. Minh-ha defends as a necessary step in a political reading toward the interruption of the commodifying process. She would insist that reading is a creative responsibility crucial to the breaking of encased knowledge or pre-formulated, codified resistance we may bring to any language other than those approved by dominant ideology. I need to read Kinhiabiëiti's video against or alongside with Turner's work and Turner's involvement in the *Disappearing Worlds* series of commodifications.

Perhaps what is at stake in my own political relation to indigenous media is not the question of ascertaining the hybridity or the technological transposition of a traditional culture; neither do I want to imply that my insistence on historicizing economic/colonial power relations suggests that the importation of video technology into Kayapo culture inevitably transforms local practices and social relations in the sense that it will have a negative or destructive effect, or that I will be able to judge the production process (the camera's technical codes) because of its recognizable signs of Westernization. I also have no business pondering the quality of Kayapo videos, since such judgements (technical, aesthetic 'standards') may be irrelevant to the Kayapo, or they will be decided, as Nahohai suggests, by the community. If these videos are shown at international festivals, that is another matter. My role, as I see it in cross-cultural relations of exchange, is primarily an experiential and self-critical practice; I become aware of the interdependences and disjunctions of local and global process, and if I cannot claim to understand what the Kayapo Naming Ceremony evokes, I can enter the video by addressing my own language of reading it and, therefore, my own representational action or subjectivity.

This reading of indigenous media and documentaries with/about indigenous peoples is complicated by comparative cultural interpretations which, I fear, heighten the incongruities and the gaps opened in the transcultural imaginary. My vantage point is slipping, because the real differences between Kinhiabiëiti's work and Turner's work indicate how important the oppositional or antagonistic concept of spatial practices (inside/outside, local/global) still is if we want to locate video production as a transformative political praxis.

The power of transformation in the local context of production is less visible to the marketplace of international festivals, where I encounter the exoticized surface of the spectacle of tribal ritual and inter-tribal 'first contact.' Vincent Carelli entered four short videos into the competition at the 1994 and 1996 Chicago Latino Film Festivals, and they also circulated at the Margaret Mead Film Festival in New York and at other exhibitions in Toronto, Houston, San Francisco, and Los Angeles. *Video in the Villages*, *The Spirit of TV*, *Meeting Ancestors*, and *Video Cannibalism* (the latter announced as 'sexually explicit') feature sensationalist ethnography that is exploitative precisely because it pretends to be directed not at outside spectators or voyeurs, but at the practical work that is being done among the Indians filming their rituals or trading information between villages. In *Meeting Ancestors*, Chief Wai-Wai is the protagonist recounting his visit to the Zo'e, another recently contacted group whom the Waiapi had only been aware of through video images. The Chief discovers that the two tribes speak the same dialect and share many traditions and myths. The Zo'e then offer to stage a few stories to offer their guest a glimpse of their ancestral history. Chief Wai-Wai seems troubled by the total nudity of the Zo'e, and the video humorously but calculatedly uses the distinctions in tribal customs to play up the embarrassment caused by gestures and horse-play that would appear sexually provocative to Western audiences.

Video Cannibalism is even more preoccupied with eliciting the spectator's fascination with uninhibited sexual play, but here I will suggest a different allegorical reading of the surface images. In this instance, Carelli's Video in the Villages Project travels to the isolated Enauene Naue Indians in the northern Mato Grosso region and solicits a performance during which the tribe stages an attack against intruding neighbors. In the course of the highly theatrical performance, the Indians capture the Brazilian filmmakers and threaten to kill them. It is not clear who is actually videotaping this scene. It doesn't appear that the video is ironically foregrounding excessive performance style or the pathetic colonial stereotypes of exoticized, 'savage' natives; rather, the prurient ethnographic fascination with indigenous sexuality and aggression is shifted into a homosocial register in which the colonialist trope of the *cannibal* is ambiguously re-inverted. The visiting camera men come to represent the hostile neighboring tribe (an incident that happened in the recent past) as well as the white colonizing intruders in this re-enactment, and the Enauene Naue steal the phallic camera to devour the force of the enemy. The video thus represents the 'cannibalist' turning-around of the camera-power, implying that the white man is feminized and sodomized while the natives produce their independence by seizing the power to film the allegory. It is conceivable that Carelli, who is of course the director within the scene of this fantasy of being beaten, is alluding to the Brasilian modernist *anthropophagy* (as it was developed by artists and poets in the *Revista de Antropofagia* and Oswald de Andrade's 'Anthropophagic Manifesto' of 1928) and its conversion of the trope of cannibalism into an aesthetics of insurrection, envisioning the devouring incorporation of the colonizer's technology in order to transform it. In a sense, the oral economy in this scene suggests the exchange of the camera-fetish, and the Enauene Naue rehearse a 'revolutionary' ritual which, perversely, re-enacts the compromised Brazilian poetics of a nationalist modernism which claimed, according to de Andrade, to synthesize the European avant-garde (futurism, surrealism) with the imaginary communal ethos of the indigenous Amerindian tribes. De Andrade's utopian vision of unproductive and unsubordinated playful-communal life in affluent nature, turning European industry and *negocio* (business) inside out, conjured a very nostalgic ideology, since his dream of anticolonial 'primitivism' invents, so to speak, an indigenous Brazilian culture meant to supply a better social model than the European one, namely one founded upon the full enjoyment of leisure.[18] De Andrade's tropical utopia is not an ethnography, of course, but an aesthetic theory imagining the possibility of creation within a culturally dependent situation, and Carelli's Video in the Villages negotiates the anthropophagy for humorous, perhaps cynical effect, since the natives' performance of 'cannibalism' is shown to be playfully naive, and there are no contextual references to their actual conditions of existence and their history. On this level of political interaction with the owners of the camera, the natives are utilized, tricked into a pantomine which is then authored and signed by Carelli, to be sold to the international festival and video databanks.

The commodification is one part of the problem. Another disturbing aspect of the staged fantasy, in fact making it more interesting than Turner's videos that are too hungover from the anthropologist's institutional kinship with colonialism, is Carelli's apparent fascination with the playful politics of mimicry within the Latin American/Brazilian context. Homi Bhabha, in his surprisingly influential psychoanalytic discourse theory of 'mimicry,' draws attention to a Freudian reading of the ambivalence of colonial mimicry and mockery as repetition:

> Colonial mimicry is the desire for a reformed, recognizable Other, *as a subject of a difference that is almost the same, but not quite* . . . Mimicry emerges as the representation of a difference that is itself a process of disavowal. Mimicry is, thus, the sign of a double articulation; a complex strategy of reform, regulation, and discipline, which 'appropriates' the Other as it visualizes power. Mimicry is also the sign of the inappropriate, however, a difference of racalcitrance which coheres the dominant strategic function of colonial power, intensifies surveillance, and poses an immanent threat to both 'normalized' knowledges and disciplinary powers.[19]

When Bhabha, whose theory is historically focussed on the colonial relations between the British Empire and India, writes about the menace of mimicry in the fetishized other capable of mocking colonial power and destroying narcissistic authority, he could be describing the 'other scene' of Carelli's *Video Cannibalism*. With 'other scene' I mean to suggest that there are (at least) two processes happening simultaneously in the video, splitting the overtly playful performance so that 'two attitudes toward external reality persist; one takes reality into consideration while the other disavows it and replaces it by a product of desire that repeats, rearticulates 'reality' as mimicry.'[20]

On the one hand, Carelli's project implies handing over the camera to the Indians and encouraging them to perform a fantasy scene in which they enact their aggressive mastery of a threatening situation. They expertly stage-manage the antagonistic scene by capturing the Brazilian videoartists. Their 'cannibalism' is shown to be a sexualized fantasy which upsets the 'normal' strategic function of the producer. On the other hand, Carelli properly produces a fictional confrontation in which the real Other, as Frantz Fanon would argue, is always the 'black man,' perceived on the level of the unassimilable, homosexualized inappropriate body-image – the Indian warriors who are simultaneously innocent in their nakedness but also flamboyant, exotic, and knowing in their sexuality and potency. Inadvertently, Carelli's production thus invites the viewer to apprehend the primary function of fantasy in such a *mise-en-scène*, which offers a multiplicity of identifications with the desire for what is prohibited.

According to Freud, we never give up a pleasure we have once experienced (as children); in fact we never give anything up but only exchange one thing for another. *Video Cannibalism* makes us ponder, in our relations to the images, whether the structure of cross-cultural power relations in a conflictual field of confused identification with (and envy of) the other can be altered, and whether Fanon's demand for equality between black and white can be imagined 'beyond the pleasure principle' (Freud). Such an imaginary would have to reconsider what it means to hand over the camera, giving up the rights of production to the pathological scene of transferences where an objectified other is either fetishized or subsumed under a myth of equality. The syncretic articulation in the relational system of the video is inconclusive; I can only speculate on the relations between Carelli and the Enauene Naue, or between international audiences and the video. Carelli's playful suggestion that the threatening natives in their creative madness may very well devour the benevolent master plays into the hands of paranoid fears in the West, expressed in many contemporary racial discourses based on the fantasy of the 'alien,' the 'enemy,' the 'immigrant,' the 'illegal other,' and even more hideous distortions that surfaced during the wars in Iraq and Bosnia. At the same time, the 'cannibalism' of the Enauene Naue could be received as an inspiring trickster performance by all those non-Western or Western spectators who don't assume the logic of hierarchized difference, operating in terms of clearly identifiable oppositions (black/white, poor/rich, subordinate/dominant, etc.), to be immutable.

At the bottom of this discussion lies the unresolved ambiguity of the anthropophagic scene in the colonial and 'post'-colonial relations I have tried to illuminate through these examples of cultural transferences or, rather, transformational processes that constitute what I described as 'transculturation.' The transcultural imaginary, as I understand it, is always a local process, but it is a syncretic process that transcribes both a historical/political reality (referring to specific colonial, economic, and ideological dominations) and a psychic (fantasy) reality, and in projecting itself into history and specific cultural productions, it is also interconnected with global transactions and the transnational economy of commodification and communication. *Meeting Grounds* presented an opportunity to listen to, and to look at, a model of multivocal collaboration between artists, traders, and researchers mostly positioned in the First World but engaged with the very question of the productive conditions and possibilities for non-Western, minority, or native local communities to participate in the debates on globalization and cultural identity. In a sense, the Chicago event was a kind of charity, a world music concert conducted with a progressive multicultural rhythm that sought to dance around the fact that a dominant legitimizing framework of postmodern liberal humanism was already in place that sees itself in sync with the forces of globalization and cross-cultural communication. I would argue that producers like Kinhiabiëiti or James Luna know that they are invited to express themselves through their difference, and if their racial, ethnic, or cultural difference is desirable (to the putative center), then the issue of the affirmative globalization of cultural contacts must be criticized as a blind

Western infatuation with its own system of legitimation. It is all too obvious that this desirability is limited. For a long time Aboriginal writers, producers, actors, and artists have felt enormous frustration regarding the barriers facing them in producing their work and selling it in the marketplace (this was articulated very forcefully during the 1992 'First Nations Dreamspeakers/Film Festival' in Canada); the participation of black, Latino, and Asian artists in the US mainstream media and art worlds has always been and still is curtailed. As recently as the late 1980s, the vociferous protests of the Guerrilla Girls and the Women's Action Coalition against institutionalized gender-biased exclusion, discrimination, and homophobia reminded us of long-standing traditions of inequality. It is not very convincing, either, that the academic left, wielding its privileged discursive position, tends to rhetorically project an ethos of marginality or romanticize the border.

A number of Third World writers have pointed out that these projected boundaries between center and margin become blurred when celebrated postcolonial intellectuals and artists benefit from their new market-value in the Western metropoles but avoid attacking the inequalities that global capitalism reproduces. 'Well-meaning liberals', Guillermo Gómez-Peña observes, 'have learned the correct termimology to not offend us, but they remain unwilling to give up control and stop running the show. Politicized artists who work directly with troubled communities such as the homeless, prisoners, migrant workers, or inner city youth are seen as opportunistic, and their intentions are often questioned by people who do absolutely nothing for those communities.'[21]

On the other hand, *Meeting Grounds* was particularly intent on aggravating any romantic notions of the margin; its explicit concern with material culture, artifacts, and social actions encouraged the participants to explore how cultural production and trade are linked to the transformations in social and economic structures, and precisely how the place (or representational space) attributed to a producer's work functions in relation to visual systems of communication, media, and public spheres. David Avalos's contribution was vital, in this respect, although his provocative notion of 'economic communities' did not find the echo it deserved in the discussions. This reluctance to enter into a political and economic analysis of the production of the conditions of inequality reflects also the weakest side of all those contemporary cultural theories, exemplified by Bhabha's conversion of Frantz Fanon's political critique into a psychoanalytic reading of colonialism's hybrid discourses, which accept the status quo and abandon the dialectic of liberation that anti-apartheid and revolutionary movements insist on believing in.[22]

23

Avalos spoke about his experience as a member of the Border Arts Workshop and his activist work in a wide range of community-based projects about issues of cultural identity in the San Diego/Tijuana border region. In particular, he described his recent collaboration, with Elizabeth Sisco and Louis Hock, on an urban project called 'Arte Reembolso/Art Rebate,' which got them into trouble. The furore that broke out this time was not too different from earlier controversies that had surrounded their installation, media and public poster works, such as the billboard project they had designed in 1988 ('Welcome to America's Finest Tourist Plantation') to coincide with San Diego's preparations to host the Super Bowl. Avalos's collaborations are designed to attain maximum public visibility, and their use of posters, billboards, bumper stickers, and photographic murals mimics and subverts advertising strategies that create commercial messages for citizen-consumers. In re-inventing the 'mural' as a site for 'public service announcements' specifically addressing social ills (unemployment, discrimination, racism, homelessness, the plight of migrant workers), Avalos and his colleagues dramatize the volatile political realities of a multiracial border city by stepping outside of the safe art arena to promote public dialogue. In a sense, such political art/activism is also a strategy of grass-roots politics that invites participation in a shared process of healing the ill social body.

The 'Arte Reembolso' project, commissioned by the Centro Cultural de la Raza and the San Diego Museum of Contemporary Art as part of its 'La Frontera/The Border'exhibition (partly funded by the NEA), took a different conceptual turn but again sought to intervene immediately into the urban space of civic life. Employing a kind of situationist actionism that seeks to trigger public debate about social issues, 'Arte Reembolso' directly addressed the role of illegal immigrants as unacknowledged taxpayers in the US economy. During the performance of the project, Avalos, Sisco, and Hock 'reimbursed' tax dollars to taxpayers, specifically to undocumented immigrant workers, by handing over to each undocumented taxpayer they met a $10 bill signed by the artists (they gave out $4.5000 of a $5.000 commission). Avalos explained that the project 'conceptually traces the network describing our economic community as it follows the circulation of rebated $10 bills from the hands of the documented to the undocumented, acknowledging their role as vital players in the community.'

Protests were raised almost immediately by conservative California Congressmen, local politicians, and the local and national media; the NEA rescinded their funds, and the project had achieved the public visibility and debate it had wanted to set in motion. The project also took place at the right time and the right place, since Governor Wilson and Senator Feinstein had just launched their new 'get tough on Mexican immigrants' campaign (Proposition 187) and were staging press conferences at the border to advocate severe border control legislation. As a conceptual provocation and practical intervention into the silence surrounding the issue of the undocumented workers' contribution to the local economy, 'Arte Reembolso' in fact not only highlights a sensitive sociopolitical issue that has divided public opinion, but brings marginalized or 'invisible' people themselves out of the hidden ('illegal') sphere of labor exploitation and *maquiladora* industries into the public space of debate. It links the issue to the embattled discourse on rights that has been at the forefront of the Chicano Civil Rights movement since the 1960s, and it also links it to the newly revitalized immigrant labor union movements in southern California (CIWA, UNITE, LAMAP). LAMAP, for example, has recently sought to build coalitions with community organizations throughout south-east L.A. and has built upon the network of organizations among Latino and other immigrant workers themselves, many of whom belong to labor clubs based on those from their home in Mexico or Central America. Avalos told me that LAMAP organizers meet regularly with church organizations in the immigrant community and have also reached beyond Latino immigrants to organizations in the Korean community. The media, he told me, have a mistaken view of illiterate and poor immigrants coming from rural areas; they will have to realize that there is a rich history of activism and Mexican trade unionism here in the USA Evoking the history of César Chávez's United Farm-workers movement, LAMAP has started the largest organizing drive since the 1960s to fight Proposition 187 and the falling immigrant wages, and to demand job safety, social benefits, and an end to discrimination in the workplace.

As a creative mode of street activism, denounced by media commentators as a perversion of the idea of 'art' and an abuse of public funds, 'Arte Reembolso' brought the issue of what constitutes the 'public domain' (who pays for it, who shares in it, who is excluded and demonized) into sharp focus. Avalos and his collaborators, who are part of a larger network of border artists, did not remain alone in their protest, since it appealed to a communitarian spirit that has a strong base in both mainstream and subcultures. In his carefully constructed documentation of the public responses to 'Arte Reembolso,' Avalos pointed out that his idea of 'economic community' was meant to have a symbolic effect, and that it indeed mobilized a broad range of vigorous responses in the city. In fact, during Avalos's slide presentation he almost assumed the role of a reporter who analyzed the concept of the project and its resonance in the response-behavior of the public. The shift in the role of the artist as producer is apparent; as a form of politicized or activist art, projects such as 'Arte Reembolso' cannot claim to offer solutions or to effectively contribute to a socioeconomic analysis of late capital-ism's globalization process and reconfiguration of the whole infrastructure of jobs, or of the Californian corporations' tendency to exploit the border region as a safe investment paradise for *maquiladoras*. But it can act as a symbolic catalyst for intervention and the building of public awareness for cultural forms of repre-sentation ('public service announcements') that can engage communities in the defense of its more vulnerable economic actors and disenfranchised citizens. Public art, in this sense, takes to the streets and reimagines symbolic processes that concretely speak up for issues of 'public interest.'

Such a task clearly exceeds the limited appeal of a dadaist action-event like 'Arte Reembolso.' Since we don't have any clear measuring tools with which to evaluate the impact of local art-activism, we need to emphasize the syncretic process of catalysis it represents as a method of building public opinion and controversy. It thus represents a transcultural production process during which socioeconomic and cultural issues are taken up which demonstrate the volatile relations between social demands and the violence written into systemic dis-enfranchisement. If the current economic globalization process in fact under-mines the very notion of a local 'economic community' by superseding the state's guardianship-role as an *integrator* of social relationships, citizenship and welfare rights, forms of knowledge, and cultural practices, then the question of 'economic community' is fundamental if we posit that actors (such as migrant workers or the un/underemployed) who are excluded from the public space of negotiation also find themselves excluded from the public sphere of cultural/ political representation. The absence of an international working-class movement therefore problematizes the actual process of transculturation, since cultural production – as we experience it in the embattled field of identity politics – cannot at all ensure the *syncretization or integration of differences* that are experienced as an effect of social exclusion, deprivation, or stigmatization.[23]

The deterioration of social relationships, aggravated by racial tensions, which is linked to the disintegration of spaces for concrete expressions of the working classes and covered up by the indifference of wholesale consumer behavior in the assimilations of the middle classes, tends to be viewed today in light of the fragmenting 'culture wars.' It should be obvious that popular consumer culture and mass media do not in fact produce a national or global homogenization at all. If we look at large border cities like San Diego/Tijuana, or any other major city in the world, we can in fact observe immensely vibrant processes of transculturation that produce conflictual pluri-culturalist diversity (in ways that Fernando Ortiz could not have imagined). If we think of Avalos's notion of 'economic community,' it becomes a difficult task to imagine what kind of cultural production could meet and express demands by social actors whose identities are distinctly socially conditioned either by downward mobility, economic difficulties, discrimination, and exclusion, or by other differentialist mobilizations (cf. Queer Nation, Afrocentrism, New Age groups, religious fundamentalism, etc.). If cultural production, linked to social processes, articulates the internationalization of culture in terms of identity politics, it will contribute to conflictual social relations, and most radical art and performance, I think, tends to assume that such a conflictual process is necessary in order to change the relations of domination. The ideology of popular culture production more benignly (and thus falsely) pretends, as Madonna claims in her *Vogue* song, that consumers can escape conflicts and 'it makes no difference if you're black or white, if you're a boy or a girl,' since you can 'be anyone you want.' This particular illusion is not available to many social actors, many of whom may not agree with the proposal that there is one 'economic community' or an identifiable 'public interest' in societies where civic rights are eclipsed and often dominated by private interests. Healing the social body and imagining participatory processes that can integrate cultural differences for a framework in which to fight for civic rights – this is our most radical challenge, and it is a challenge that connects local mobilizations in all areas of the world.

24

The most demanding aspect of 'Meeting Grounds' remains this open question of how we are to understand the economic processes in which cultural productions and performances take place. This symposium illuminated a great deal of work that is currently done in specific reference to ethnic, racial, sexual, and national identity and in reference to the necessary alliances that are being forged among feminist, multiculturalist, subaltern, ecologist, and human rights activists or cultural workers in many parts of the world. One of the unsettling paradoxes of the political struggle remains the issue of identity, since the essentializing and exclusionary dimensions of claiming a particular identity (or centricity) tend to reproduce technologies and ideologies that repress others or that misrecognize the fact that others are part of this identity formation (this involves, of course, the complex historical problematic of shared colonial space and differently shared temporalities).

I left the symposium feeling inspired and drained. The 'meeting ground' in Chicago was an opening to other perspectives and to shared concerns over the politics of production and reproduction, and I would like to hear more languages, other accents represented at such meetings. Or I would like to hope that the translations between the ethnographic and empirical work and the artistic/ media work proved a productive opening for further 'Meeting Grounds,' in other places, where the Western eyes and ears are attuned to the comfortable irony that our language (like Luna's basket designs) is not the only one and/or doesn't even belong to us.

5

LA MELANCOLÍA DE LA JAULA

1. THE SKY BELOW

In reviewing contemporary perspectives on art and performance, I notice the particular influence that Latin American and Latino/Chicano cultural productions have had on my work and my thinking. Mostly through personal contact, and the transcultural contexts in which I perform, I am learning to explore a dialogue across borders and in more than one language. The learning process is slow, and I cannot claim the competence with which Coco Fusco, Gerardo Mosquera, Diana Taylor, Juan Villegas and others have begun to redefine the terms of the postcolonial debates on cultures here and there, both 'outside' and 'inside' North America, and within the shared space of the cities in which we live.[1] But there is no question that we are living on these borders, thriving on the dynamics of diversity and the processes of our inevitable transformations.

The vitality and complexity of the relations among the performative cultures in *América latina*, and between these cultures and their migrations to, and presences in, the North will be considered here in the context of local developments in Chicago and Havana which are symptomatic for their transnational and intercultural significance. First, I will describe Chicago's Mexican Performing Arts Festival (April–May 1994), the first of its kind dedicated to a broad exploration of Mexican music, theater, dance, and performance art from both sides of the Rio Grande/Río Bravo. I will add a few comments on the Chicago Latino Film Festival and its extraordinary growth and visibility within the Latino and multicultural landscape of the city. I will also comment on the particular contributions of Latino performers to the annual International Theater Festival in Chicago.

In the second part, I will contextualize the workshops held at the CONJUNTO 94 in Havana's Casa de las Américas – a traditional meeting ground for gatherings of theater artists and critics from all over Central and South America. CONJUNTO 94 took place during the last week of May and overlapped with the fifth Havana Bienal which, even more so than the São Paulo Bienal, is an exhibition self-consciously committed to the global exchange and communication among the contemporary visual arts of the *tercer mundo*. Some very interesting parallels emerged between the energies and concerns of many of the younger visual artists in the bienal and the Cuban performances shown during the CONJUNTO 94. These parallels and confluences illuminate the contemporary conceptualization of cultural and political expression. Interwoven with these observations are my personal reflections on the new Cuban film, *Fresa y chocolate*, and my memories of the new queer expressions on the island.

2. DEL CORAZÓN

The Mexican Fine Arts Center Museum, founded in 1982 and located in the Pilsen barrio southwest of downtown Chicago, has gained a reputation for its innovative exhibition programs. Now considered one of the most important museums in the USA dedicated to Mexican culture, it plays the role of *agent provocateur* in Chicago not only by taking an explicit stand in serving its community but also in interpreting the culture of a bilingual community and its relations to the multiethnic urban population. Over the past few years, the museum has also co-sponsored exhibitions and live performances at other locales, both mainstream and alternative, and it was a logical step to involve other venues in the presentation of over two dozen performances, workshops and lectures during '*del Corazón*.' The title for the first Mexican Performing Arts Festival means 'from the heart' – an obvious iconographic reference to a powerful symbol in Mexican culture (the festival's publicity design displayed the blood-red heart with a knife stuck inside), but also to *Aztlán*, the imagined community of Mexicans in the heartland of the USA. If the mythic concept of *Aztlán* served as a symbol for the defiant ethnic self-assertions of *la raza* in the early Chicano movement, today's economic and social reality has supplanted the myth. Without its more than 500,000 Mexican/Mexican-American citizens, Chicago would clearly be dysfunctional. The Latino cultural presence in the city makes itself felt in so many diverse and dynamic ways that it would be a melancholy mistake to expect the museum to create only a backward-looking populist festival celebrating *la raza*. Deliberately shifting the emphasis away from the preservational ideology of museums that manage cultural patrimonies, the young festival directors, Encarnación Teruel and Pablo Helguera, instead chose to concentrate on *performance* as the pulsating, emotional, and expressive force linking a crazy bilingual quilt of traditional and avant-garde, folkloric and experimental, classical and contemporary mixed-media genres. They took some obvious risks, given the fact that the museum depends on donors as well as government agencies who often have their own skewed understanding of what constitutes multicultural or 'ethnic' art. However, *del Corazón* succeeded precisely because it ignored stereotypical categories of cultural and authentic identity, allowing the conjunctures of heterogeneous styles and performance genres to generate a truly dialogic scenario that attracted diverse audiences of all age-groups and social strata. Ranging from traditional folkloric music and dance (Tlen-Huicani; The Mexican Folkloric Dance Company of Chicago, performing to the music played by Cuerdas Clásicas) to classical recital music (María Teresa Rodríguez), and from popular song and ballad music (Oscar Chávez), popular dramatic and children's theater (Teatro de la Esperanza; Latino Chicago Theater Company) to experimental dance theater and performance art (Asaltodiario; Jesusa Rodríguez; Maris Bustamante; Lorena Orozco and César Martínez; Guillermo Gómez-Peña and James Luna), the festival dramaturgy created both a continuum (the postmodern-traditional) and a provocatively self-reflexive recontextualization of the historical depth and the transcultural contingencies of Mexican performance. This was perhaps captured most suggestively in the ironic postmodern mysticism of Jesusa Rodríguez's *Cielo de Abajo*, her 'pre-Hispanic cabaret' becoming a graphic stage for erotic fantasies about *calaveras*, the queer body, and Aztec gods.

The relationship between 'traditional' folkloric music, originated in Mexico and connected to a specific region or rural culture, and contemporary bilingual Chicano performances created in the USA is crucial for our analysis. Presented together, the latter recontextualizes the former and exposes both the sentimentalism and the radical, dynamic features in popular culture. Although folklore neither is a static form of indigenous culture nor exists outside the international economies of the mass cultural industry, the code-switching and the fluidity between languages and media in Chicano poetry and performance are particularly characteristic of the dynamics of evolution and transformation. Contemporary urban artists, both here and there, reinterpret or write back Mexican, pre-Columbian, or postcolonial history – and all the various layers of popular-cultural mythology and iconography. Their work thereby illuminates how specific traditions of expression (or repertoires 'traditionalized' for world-wide commercial consumption) have been invested in the ideology of national culture.

The Mexican Folkloric Dance Company of Chicago, like the Jalapa-based group Tlen-Huicani (meaning 'the singers' in the indigenous Nahuatl language), came closest to filling the role of 'faithful' interpreters of tradition, 'using authentic choreography, music and costumes,' as the program indicated. However much the visual reconstruction of 'authentic' traditions may be fraught with ambiguity, the company's joyous performance of pre-Columbian and Mexican dances (with European influences) primarily addressed a communal spirit of celebration and affirmation. Using romantic music and well-known Mexican *rancheros* to sustain a celebratory sense of collective memory, the dance company appealed to an unquestioned identification of the folkloric with the national heritage. Since both the dance and Tlen-Huicani's opening gala concert proved hugely successful with the Latino families in the audience, one could consider the celebration of memory as an emotional, nostalgic ritual necessary for the self-recognition of the community-in-the-audience in the first place. The all-embracing strategy of the *cantores* was remarkable, in this respect, because under the superb musical direction of Alberto de la Rosa, Tlen-Huicani not only played the most popular *Jarocho* and *Huasteco* music of their home region (Veracruz), but also interpreted numerous *canciones* from other Latin American regions in Colombia, Venezuela, Paraguay, Chile, and Argentina. Greeted by sighs and cheers of recognition, these *canciones* allegorically traced a circle of dis-placement from home for an audience acutely aware of its shared projection of such imaginary/lost homes or nations.

As a reservoir for collective remembrances, the folk melodies played on the *arpa jarocha* thus offered the immigrant audience a backward-looking glance at the ghosts of its Mexican or Latin American identities, whereas the reproduction

Figure 34 Marís Bustamante. Chicago 1994. Photo courtesy of The Mexican Fine Arts Center Museum and Encarnación Teruel.

of local tradition (Tlen-Huicani's recorded music on cassette/CD was on sale) already always takes part in the contemporary mass markets of conversion and distribution. In Celeste Olalquiaga's cool analysis of the progressive 'Latinization of the United States,' such dissemination and consumption of ethnic music belong to the level of first-degree emotional kitsch that is already absorbed or extended by further degrees of transcultural recycling.[1] Noting that nostalgia for the homeland or the politicized ethnocentrism of the Chicano movement both responded to alienated identities and the struggle for social and economic integration, Olalquiaga argues that contemporary conversions of traditional and modern, local and foreign, popular and high cultural sources have already led to the formation of hybrid (Chicano, Nuyorican, US Cuban, etc.) cultures. If we follow her argument about the mutual transformation of dominant mass and ethnic cultures to the point where the melancholia of identity is left behind, we would have to travel the distance from Tlen-Huicani's traditional 'La Bamba' to, say, a young urban Latino rapper's parodic sampling version of an 1980s punk-rock version of Ritchie Valens's late 1950s 'La Bamba.'

The festival traveled this distance from emotional investment in origins to the detachment of cynical postmodernity, without ever imposing upon the differing expectations and class-specific tastes of its audiences that wanted to listen to Oscar Chávez's legendary political ballads or watch the young street-theatre-dancers of the punk group Asaltodiario (Mexico City) or the California-based Teatro de la Esperanza (performing the family play *Rosario's Barrio* with a Latino spin on the TV sitcom *Mister Rogers' Neighborhood*). Both groups produce works that are completely hybrid and interreferential with other contemporary mass or popular-cultural media. Jesusa Rodríguez, performing jointly with Liliana Felipe in her stunning visual production of *Cielo de Abajo*, posed an enormously complex scenario of (false) clues leading us from contemporary power relations between high-tech advanced culture and low-tech indigenous culture into the landscape of a cosmogony where rational and mythic time, Eros and Thanatos, the sacred and the secular, are inextricably conjoined. Known for her irreverent and satirical work, Rodríguez directs the small alternative La Capilla theater and El Hábito cabaret-bar in Coyoacan (Mexico City), attracting international attention in the mid-1980s when she staged an outrageously erotic 'conversion' of Mozart's opera, *Donna Giovanni*, with her all-female cast of 'Divas.' Her new *cabaret prehispanico* is adapted from Alfredo López Austin's book *Cuerpo humano y ideologia de los antiguos Nahoas* which reinterprets the myths of Amerindian civilizations, and especially the legends containing ritual beliefs transposed from everyday reality into creation myths and sacred cosmogonies.

Already in 1990 Rodríguez had started to work with the figure of Coatlicue, earth-mother, womb of the warrior god Huichilopochtli, goddess of water, whose frighteningly powerful statue, excavated from the Sacred Precinct of Tenochtitlan, now resides in the National Anthropological Museum. Since Rodríguez has built a moveable rubber replica of the stone statue, it's worth pointing out that the original bears terrifying aspects – a divided head, another centrally placed mouth that is fanged, claws, hands of flayed skin, and serpents entwined all around her body – which associate this Aztec mother of the gods with an 'origin' so horrific that it often remains concealed, rejected, unmentionable.

Consequently, Rodríguez's performance in *Cielo de Abajo* follows a backward-looking but unashamedly parodic strategy of excavating precisely the distanced and silenced 'Mesoamerican aesthetics' of Coatlicue, connecting the mother-image to the cultural mythology of the continuous life–death–rebirth cycle and Mexico's baroque preoccupation with death. After a prologue in a dark, computerized TV control room, Rodríguez is first seen, under a spotlight, kneeling alone in a brilliant white shroud, a bride of death ready to 'go under,' to enter the voyage of the deceased through the nine places of the underworld toward the final region, called *Mictlán*. Most Amerindian myths of katabasis follow this model of the voyage of the soul toward *Mictlán*, yet there are variations on the kinds of hazards and trials encountered by the dead or by the young men (in Huichol mythology) who undergo shamanic initiation. The descent into the underworld is always also a myth of the completion of a cycle, of the emergence/birth of men (in Huichol myth, the underworld is the place where the sexual act takes on its complete meaning), and of the return to one's ancestors, to one's origins. In Aztec, Chichimeca, and Purepecha mythology, the underworld is also associated with dreams or with woman's uterus.

Including references to the symbolism of the Mayan *Popul Vuh*, Rodríguez puns on all of these archetypal cosmogonies. Her achievement lies in the poignant inversions and humorous metamorphoses she enacts through her female-centered re-telling of the shamanic journey – the journey of her body and souls (the Nahoas believed in three souls). In the process of her memory-journey, she becomes a *nahual* (a sorcerer), so to speak, able to constantly change her appearances and to appropriate the power traditionally reserved to men. After her disappearing through the trap-door, what we first see of Rodríguez's reappearance behind a black curtain are body parts, a breast, a hand, a foot: figments (and fetish objects) of our imagination. They are false, artificial limbs. Next we see her, now accompanied by her guardian spirit Felipe, carrying a skeleton on her back, ready to brave the trials of the crossroads, the wind of rocks, the stone knives, the wild animals, and finally the hilarious, carnal and less-than-frightening encounter with the rapacious mouth and tongue of Coatlicue. Sprawling on the footsteps of Coatlicue's temple, a naked Jesusa – her body painted green and seductively positioned in a cruciform, sacrificial pose – awaits to be licked by the mother-goddess. Felipe, who is inside the rubber statue, begins to dance in joyful anticipation, heightening our delight in this extraordinary scene of sexual foreplay and 'martyrdom.'

Throughout the performance, the homoerotic overtones and the assertive nakedness of the two soulmates are instrumental for Rodríguez's and Felipe's rediscovery of their places in the mythical universe that palpitates underneath the veneer of official Mexican Catholicism and bureaucratic state censorship. This postmodern-anachronistic 'descent' into the underworld of 'origins' taps into taboo regions of maternal and sexual roles, and of the identity of the mother (the legend of Malintzin/Malinche standing in between Coatlicue/the native goddess

Figure 35 Jesusa Rodríguez performs in *Cielo de Abajo*. Chicago 1994. Photo courtesy of The Mexican Fine Arts Center Museum and Encarnación Teruel.

and the Virgin Mother/Guadalupe), which since the Conquest have suffered misogynist interpretations in the historical emotions of Mexican life and the formation of national consciousness. Unlike the paternal-literary revisions of the mother/traitor figure by Octavio Paz or Carlos Fuentes, Rodríguez primarily embodies herself, not a mythic figure. Hers is a visual theater that moves, dances, and plays havoc with the languages and transvestisms of ideology. Her virtuoso transformations of literary metaphors, religious and mythical symbols and popular buffooneries during the course of her epic journey toward ecstasy/death/rebirth are enacted in the spirit of what I would call 'magical camp.' It is a feminist camp that also inverts the transvestism of gay camp drag shows or the cultural/ethnic transvestism of the *pachuco*, since her deliberate nakedness makes her rely on her body's power of expression precisely against the trappings of the faux symbols and props she quotes and discards. Rodríguez's and Felipe's parodic transgression therefore can be said to take place on the level of the real physical bodies of women who travel the journey of convoluted historical/mythical narratives backward and forward, projecting a lesbian subjectivity which neither renounces the 'origins' nor hides under the superficial redemption of national, cultural, or gender identity. Rather than trying to revise the myth of Coatlicue or the melancholic-archaic figuration of a patriarchal 'labyrinth of solitude' (Octavio Paz), *Cielo de Abajo* suggests that women's uncensorable bodies and self-visualizations need not be controlled by religious, political, and cultural boundaries of identity. They can cross over.

Rodríguez as well as Maris Bustamante, the latter concluding *del Corazón* with her lectures and *Naftaperformances*, admits to the difficulties of their calling themselves feminist/lesbian artists in the Mexican context. When I asked Bustamante about this, she told me that she has worked as a visual artist-performer-writer for over twenty years and in 1983 founded Polvo de Gallina Negra, the first feminist art collective actively seeking to modify the existing image of women in the mass media and in academic discourse. 'The *machismo* in our country is so very strong,' she explained. 'It's hard to be a woman in such a society, and it's even worse to be a woman artist. So we chose this name for our small group, which refers to a certain mysterious powder sold in the market-square by older women who know witchcraft. It's a powder that protects us against the evil eye.'

In-between her performances in Chicago, Bustamante also lectured on her new book project, a wide-ranging 'History of Performance in Mexico' which examines the manifold performative dimensions and expressions of popular culture and public art. Many of her examples illuminated a history of performance understood as a continuous refashioning of the cultural cross-overs and inter-references between Mexican iconographies, folk art, urban mural art, ceremonies, *retablos, historietas*, music, dance, graffiti, fanzines, and other print or audiovisual media. Her own show consisted of a bewitching mixture of conceptual art, spicy monologues, magical tricks, and ironic commentaries on the latest stage of cultural exchange we have reached with NAFTA. In one sense, what she calls the 'end-of-century syndrome' may refer to the dominant globalizing power of technocratic capitalism as it reopens in Latin American popular memories the traumas of the first invasion. In another sense, her *Naftaperformances* are dangerously sarcastic and playful, as she tells us that she enjoys the 'terror of the dying borders' and the challenge to find out what it means to be an 'intercontinental artist.'

Her constant manipulation of visual associations and physical props is astounding. Her visual actions are like embodied *historietas* or *revistas continuadas* as they are known in the Mexican vernacular culture of serial comic books that always focus on current events, tragedies, natural disasters, romance and sex. But her graphic humor and dead-pan poetic style of deflating the illusionism of objects provoke very complex questions about how we create our/other realities. The disappearing borders are a reality (of transnational capital) and a horrific illusion (cf. the blockade against Cuba, the Rio Grande/Río Bravo and California's Proposition 187, the so-called 'Save our State' initiative). Bustamante's 'terror' has to do with the experience of uncertainty at a moment when technological and economic systems have reconfigured the boundaries that define our bodies and cultural identities, our hearts, memories, and intercontinental languages. Performance, for Bustamante, is 'an art of thinking (this) reality.'

Hearing her definition of performance art, I thought of the other border-crossers who had performed at the festival a week earlier. Guillermo Gómez-Peña and James Luna, in collaboration with Roberto Sifuentes, had joined forces for a two-day investigation of cultural and racial prejudices in precisely that space (the 'ethnic' museum) normally dedicated to the exhibition of minority culture. Their performance, *The Shame-Man, El Mexi-Cant & El Cyber-Vato Come to Chicago in Search of their Lost Selves (or The Identity Tour)*, was a mixture of site-specific action-performance, lecture, incantation, improvisation, and interactive TV talk show – a 'tour' inspired by the delight they take in mocking the 'evil eye' and the obvious or unacknowledged racial and ethnic projections people drag onto others. On one level, their strategy was to *perform* ethnic signifiers, to put on the costumes and external markers of ethnicity in order to highlight their transvestite aspects and thus to reveal the ambivalent construct of identity. On another level, their visual and verbal puns addressed the mutuality/mixture of US and Mexican clichés, parodying the corrupted dualism of inside/outside; such cultural transvestism precisely challenges today's right-wing fears which promote a nationalism and cultural patriotism with a racially exclusive notion of difference.

The solos and duets that ensued after their opening 'ethnic fashion show' created a constantly shifting mixture of *verbal*, multilingual transvestisms moving from an audience poll on NAFTA to 'confessions of a shame-man' and other exorcisms. While Luna confides to us that he's willing to sell a Native American blessing, Gómez-Peña tells racist jokes, creates his own bizarre version of aural poetry in Nahuatl or fakes a heavy Mexican accent. As the ironic *double-entendres* of 'Fashion Show' and 'Regression Session' slowly begin to sink in, the performers continue their interrupted make-up sessions, casually exchanging costumes and asides about their 'scripts' and probable failure to be believable, eventually bracing up for their 'Seminar on Race Relations.' Their interactions with the audience are always friendly and apologetic, while they in fact display a marvellously understated sense of authority as *les enfants de la chingada* who would gladly act as our 'spiritual advisers.' After a final question-and-answer period ('has anyone ever wanted to change his or her ethnicity?'), Luna erupts into a visionary re-formulation of Martin Luther King's 'I have a dream' speech, with Gómez-Peña standing behind him in a wrestling mask, translating the vision back into fake Nahuatl.

The performance of *Identity Tour* epitomizes the immense difficulties we face, all across our diverse communities and social classes, in confronting the mystifications of cultural identity, and especially the Western mystification of non-Western cultures within and without. The *del Corazón* Festival, like Chicago's Latino Film Festival, drew attention to an ongoing process of *descubrimiento*, a discovery of new identities, for which there are no more sanctioned roles, either within the memory of Latin American struggles for modernity and independence, or in the dense and politically contested context of the multicultural United States. That context of exploding cultural modernities must now be seen as a space in which white North America faces its own postcolonial history as an immigrant society having lost its post-war assurance of self-identification through homogenizing consumption-capitalism. Today's reality, not least its mass cultural construction, is defined by diversity rather than homogeneity; the borderlands of Western metropoles have problematized older geopolitical models of center–periphery/global–local relations, as they embody the transnational circulation of populations and the continual transcultural flow of information which make 'ethnicity' much more a dynamic construct than an inherited fact. Such borderlands demand that we view cultural production from several perspectives at once in order to recognize in which direction it moves, how it is received and converted, and how it is positioned within the dialectic of economically dominant and subordinate classes.

Cuban anthropologist Inés María Martiatu, writing about the dialectic of 'ethnic majority and cultural minority' in the Latin American and Caribbean context, points to the paradox that ethnic and cultural majorities have been dominated by ethnic and cultural minorities (identified with European/Western, or Universal culture) since colonial times. In his book *La jaula de la melancolía* (Mexico City, 1987), Roger Bartra criticizes the emprisioning myths of national character promoted by official majority culture in Mexico, arguing that popular culture in fact plays no active part in these 'myths of national character' that have become a debilitating and self-perpetuating net in which Mexicans and foreigners get tangled.[3] When he mentions the distorting images of 'Mexican emotiveness and sentimentalism,' he is refering to literary and mass media stereotypes. If we follow the argument that Western metropoles are hybrid extensions of other (home) communities and are increasingly less Western, then *del Corazón* or the Latino Film Festival mark the relentless vibrancy of cultural production beyond the closed circuit of the stereotypes.

3. FAMILY HISTORIES

Before I turn to the films, it is encouraging to note that other borders of prejudice are breaking down in popular performance when the International Theatre Festival, not generally known for its radical programming, can announce Marga Gómez to the mainstream media as 'one of the most impressive comedians in the burgeoning field of lesbian comic entertainers.' *Marga Gómez is Pretty, Witty & Gay* took its cue from a song in *West Side Story*, and the work owed its huge audience appeal to the riotous and irresistible humor, honesty, and directness with which its protagonist talked about her life and contemporary lesbian experiences in a cross-over culture. What this actually means became even more poignantly clear in *Memory Tricks*, her other show presented in Chicago. Marga Gómez is the daughter of a Cuban vaudeville impresario and a Puerto Rican 'exotic dancer'; after growing up in Spanish Harlem she moved to San Francisco in the 1980s, joining a feminist theater ensemble, Lilith, and the San Francisco Mime Troupe before becoming a founding member of the very popular Latino comedy group Culture Clash. It is significant that *Memory Tricks*, her first solo performance, can thus be located in a continuum of alternative, feminist, and Chicano theater emerging from an earlier, much less familiar and recorded history of first generations of Latino popular performance and entertainment. In fact, Gómez's *recuerdo* of her parents is a direct tribute to her predecessors' struggle to pass, to cross-over, to have success in the entertainment world of New York City in the 1950s. That world, the pre-history of the 1960s movements, often imposed painful limits to her parents' aspirations, and Gómez's memory is filled with ironies when she recounts the pathetic or humiliating defeats of assimilation. But Gómez's autobiographical performance of her childhood and early adult life gradually becomes a sharply contoured portrait of her mother and her own contradictory socialization. The tricks she plays on our empathy come to haunt us in the course of the evening, as the comedy grows dark and the mother's destiny unperformable.

In the beginning, Gómez enters untheatrically in jeans and T-shirt to tell her family story from the point of view of a daughter who sees her mother, the Puerto Rican belly dancer, as someone who hilariously combines all the unflattering clichés of femininity, vanity, and self-delusion that young Marga abhors. For quite some time, *Memory Tricks* tells of Marga's failed acculturation, with the comic effects slowly building up to a whole panorama of affectionately parodied gender and kinship roles in a Latino family trying to hold on to community values and their American Dream. However, as she portrays her manipulative, selfish mother and her pathetic father, Gómez slowly begins to shift more and more frequently into impersonating her mother's instructions and attitudes, her efforts to teach her how to walk like a lady or carry a pocketbook, care about her hair and make-up, and flirt with a man. Holding up Elke Sommer ('that great Swedish actress and role model to many Latinas') as an icon to emulate, her mother insistently poses her own constructed femininity (sexy appearance, bleach-blonde hair, perfumes, flirtatious body language) as a mirror for Marga:

¡Mírame, mírame! And watching her, Marga begins to understand the script her mother is performing in her effort to succeed in an overdetermined patriarchal and heterosexual world, straddling the lines between Latino *machismo* and the dominant white society.

There are numerous ironies, not the least of which is Gómez's own linguistic preference: she speaks English and 'quotes' her 'mother tongue' only when she mimes her mother's instructions to act like a desirable Latina assuming a white mask or lady-like behavior in order to pass (the family eventually moves from Spanish Harlem to Long Island). But young Marga doesn't want to 'pass,' in the sense that she rejects the social scripts for acceptable sex/gender roles and thus the normative economy of domination and otherness. Since we know that she opts to go away and assume a lesbian subjectivity, Gómez seeks to accomplish the remarkable feat of deconstructing gendered identity, displaying it as a perform-ance by performing the codes through which identities are socially visible and intelligible. She performs being her mother but not becoming (like) her mother, thus conceding that lesbian identity is also apparitional *vis-à-vis* the straight world's refusal to visualize/accept her desire.

If I read her as a lesbian daughter refusing to accommodate her mother's lesson, the disruptive ironies of Gómez's initial mimicking performance – send-ing up her mother's body-language, intonations, gestures, and mannerisms – gradually identify her difference, only to be transformed at the end when Marga becomes a mother and caretaker to her incapacitated mother diagnosed with Alzheimer's. At this point in a greatly moving finale, Gómez acts as mother and daughter simultaneously, her body now remembering and dignifying her dead mother in the final years of literal psychic delusion, when the earlier admonition ¡Mírame, mírame! would come back to haunt the survivor.

Gómez's choice to write and embody autobiographical material shares its focus on the demystification of female cultural identities with many of the currently produced performance art pieces and films/videos. During the film festival I also noticed that the somber earnestness of some of the documentary films paled in comparison to the more humorous and enticing fictional treat-ments of social criticism. In their video *Ramona: Birth of a mis-ce-ge-NATION*, David Avalos and Deborah Small employ comic strategies of quotation/misquotation and hilarious voice-over repartees to create an astonishing pastiche of 'memory tricks' by re-assembling various scenes from popular movies like *Flaming Star*, *West Side Story*, and *The Last of the Mohicans*. The off-screen couple, HIM (a multicultural tourist) and HER (a tourist guide for the multi-culturally impaired), engage in a mock film analysis of Hollywood's melo-dramatic portrayal of *mestizaje* and its vicarious projection of the forbidden desire for, and inevitable horror of, miscegenation. In the process of their camp reading of white America's fear of racial mixing, the video pokes fun at 'central casting' (cf. Charlton Heston playing Ramon Miguel 'Mike' Vargas in *A Touch of Evil*) while speculating with great poignancy on the anxiety and denial of 'multi-cultural voyeurism' projecting itself into the other and affecting a sentimental affiliation blind to its own narcissism.

The self-reflexive meditation on media and the representation of cultural and sexual difference finds another twist in the work of Cuban-American filmmaker Ela Troyano. Her short films are experimental cross-over poems mixing comedy-musical-cabaret styles with performance art and rap music, defying the labels that distributors would give them ('women's film,' 'lesbian and gay films,' 'Latino film'). Defiance is the motivating engine behind a work that is often outrageous, campy, funny, and sexy while being deeply involved in the reclamation of 'local' communities of women and artists of color, and in the bridging of cultural activism and aesthetic production. How heterogeneous and fluid the notion of 'community' can be is dramatized in both films. *Once Upon a Time in the Bronx* features the rap group Latin Empire in midst of a chaotic and burlesque montage of fragments from urban street life in the Bronx. *Carmelita Tropicana: Your Kunst is Your Waffen* features Troyano's sister playing herself (Carmelita is a well-known lesbian cabaret/performance artist) and the character of a superintendant from the Lower East Side who receives strange phone-calls from her Cuban father, gets mugged on the street, jailed for helping to defend an abortion clinic against right-wing fundamentalists, and bailed out by her woman lawyer after staging an inspirational 'prison musical' she bases on the melodramatic story of Cukita, her great-aunt who was murdered by her lover in Cuba. While in prison with her lover and her sister, she befriends another woman, Dee, who turns out to be her mugger. Dee is addicted to drugs and HIV+, and she explains that she probably wouldn't even be alive had she not been adopted by a Puerto Rican family when she fell upon hard times. The film's crazy-quilt narrative joins all the colorful women together in the magical prison number toward the end in which they sing and dance their vision of an empowering community of women who will act up and fight back.

4. THE REPEATING ISLAND

The Cuban entries into the Chicago Latino Film Festival were two older films, Tomás Gutiérrez Alea's *Memorias del subdesarollo* (1968) and Humberto Solás's masterpiece, *Lucía* (1964). The new Cuban feature film by Alea and Juan Carlos Tabío, *Fresa y chocolate* (1993), highly successful and much debated on the island, was not presented at the festival – a striking omission in an otherwise exemplary and exciting panorama of newly released and classic Latin American films and public discussions. Having expanded in its ten-year existence from a small neighborhood activity to a city-wide cultural event that attracts a huge, passionate following, the Latino Film Festival (organized by Chicago Latino Cinema under the direction of Pepe Vargas) provides an important window on the diverse national cinemas of Latin America, Spain and Portugal while also espousing a very inclusive philosophy of showcasing multinational Latino cultures (incorporating Chicano/Nuyorican films and coproductions with other countries).

Its most important role lies in featuring Latin American films/videos that would not otherwise be distributed in the Hollywood-dominated world market.

It often owes the selection of its Latin features to the preceding Festival del Nuevo Cine Latino-americana at Havana, which in December 1993 celebrated its fifteenth anniversary with the premiere of *Fresa y chocolate*. The Havana Film Festival has been crucial for the aesthetic development of the New Latin American Cinema, for the continuing construction and interpretation of Latin American cultural and national identities, and the distribution/marketing of films that are created under the depressed economies of the regional film industries. This leading role of the Havana Festival, and of the Cuban Institute of Cinematographic Art and Industry (ICAIC) founded immediately after the Revolution in 1959, gives testimony to the significance placed on the development of an independent, national cinema designed to participate in the popular movement of revolutionary social transformation. The Cuban Revolution of course held symbolic value for other liberation movements in Latin America, and its cultural institutions, such as ICAIC and the Casa de las Américas, were instrumental in generating artistic and intellectual debates, exchanges and collaborations between countries.

During its enormous output of the first fifteen years, Cuban cinema produced many documentaries directly engaged in diverse aspects of the revolutionary social process and the specific features of Cuba's syncretic history as it has also been captured in the literature and ethnology of 'transculturation' (Fernando Ortiz, Alejo Carpentier) or, even more immediately, in the ever-present popular music, dance, and religious practices of Afro-Cuban traditions. Many of the documentaries also emphasized collective creativity and participation, while feature films experimented with techniques of radical synthesis mixing conflicting visual styles, subjective and objective points of view, archival footage, interviews and dramatic re-enactments. The preponderance of the historical genre illuminates the difficulties that became noticeable in the last twenty years of Cuban cinema, when the focus shifted to contemporary realities and contradictions, and when several films created controversy over their treatment of taboos such as sexism, racism, intergenerational conflict, and the exile community (cf. Pastor Vega's *Retrato de Teresa*, Alea's *Hasta cierto punto*, Jesús Díaz's *Lejania*, or the collectively produced five-part *Mujer transparente*).

The satirical allegory *Alicia en el pueblo de maravillas*, created by Daniel Díaz Torres in 1991, offered such a scathing, ironic view of the increasingly tense and disorganized situation during Cuba's 'Special Period' that it was banned after the Havana premiere. However, Torres (a documentary filmmaker in his mid-forties who only recently started to create fiction features) is a kindred spirit with a new generation of filmmakers exploring personal visions or critical strategies outside the parameters of a strictly national or anti-imperialist cinema. Interestingly, the international dimension of such new film and video work, and the broad range of political, cultural, and spiritual issues it addresses, have in fact been indirectly promoted by the official establishment in 1986 of the International School for Film and Television near the township of San Antonio. Nicknamed the School of Three Worlds, it houses students from Latin America, Africa, and Asia who are trained by a faculty of distinguished Latin American media professionals.

When I visited the school and saw the creative energies of the young students and their valiant struggles with scarce supplies and shrinking resources, I felt anger at the tragedy of the Cuban economic crisis even as the hardships may have facilitated paradoxical opportunities for the students' artistic work. Some of their short films, which probe the contradictions in the history of generations divided by revolution and exile, are now shown on Cuban television or enter international festivals. They are symptomatic of a confluence of critical motivations that also drive the unexpectedly revealing, even riveting treatment of the oppression and the exclusion of homosexuals from the Revolution depicted in *Fresa y chocolate* ('Strawberry and Chocolate') – the film that everyone talked about during my first visit to Havana, and that was shown to the participants of the CONJUNTO 94 on the opening night of the theater conference.

The film entered the public at a truly critical moment of Cuba's political and economic struggle for survival, as the culture faces far-reaching questions about the future of the nation and the meaning of a socialism now condemned to dabbling in restricted free market 'concessions' (to the tourist industry and foreign investment). After the disintegration of the Soviet Union and the socialist bloc (Cuba's main trading partners), the long-term effects of the US blockade against the island are now pushing its economy to the brink of collapse. All the measures taken by the Cuban leadership during the 'rectification' campaign, and now during the post-Soviet 'special period,' have created no viable answers to the structural economic crisis and to the even more crucial question of the future of Cuban socialism. The conditions on the island are desperate: austerity, shortages, hunger, power failures, housing decay, lack of medical supplies, dysfunctional public transportation, and a growing threat of social collapse that is mostly the combined result of material suffering, unemployment, and an overwhelming sense of isolation. The resiliency of the Cuban people notwithstanding, many on the island are aware of the crisis of socialism, or revolutionary ideology itself; Castro's intransigence has illuminated the absence of democratic socialism at the moment when economic reforms through foreign investment and entrepreneurial capitalists are made, dollars circulate around tourist hotels, and uneven distribution of wealth becomes visible.

In fact, such international events as the Havana Film Festival or the bienal expose this inequality in an immediate way; some of the main locations of the bienal's exhibitions are tourist sites with steep admission charges (the Wilfredo Lam Center, the El Morro and La Cabaña fortresses, and the Crafts Center, all near the Cathedral Plaza in Old Havana), and the hotels or restaurants are privileged enclaves for tourists only, surrounded by an impoverished population waiting in long lines for rationed food. All around one sees huge painted slogans and murals: ' *Socialismo o muerte,*' '*100 % Cubano*' or '*No penetraran*' ('they will not penetrate'). But foreign investors are needed, and *Fresa y chocolate* was made possible only as a co-production of Cuba, Mexico, and Spain. The bienal was also supported by foreign governments and by a donation from German industrialist and art collector Peter Ludwig. Such contradictions have become obvious to Cuban artists; many strove to be selected for exhibition at the bienal because visibility is a means of selling work and obtaining dollars. Most of the generation of important young artists who came of age in the 1980s have actually been 'exported,' as Gerardo Mosquera observed; up to a hundred artists have lived abroad temporarily or permanently, and some who helped to give the 'Cuban Renaissance' since 1981 its critical, aggressive and ironic edge, have now emigrated to the US (including most recently José Bedia, Carlos Cárdenas, Consuelo Castañeda, Arturo Cuenca, and Quisqueya Henríquez).

In the previous biennials, Cuban mixed-media and installation artists had concocted an explosive mixture of 'ideological realism' (Third World Marxist critiques of First World imperialism) turned inside out to emphasize transnational references through the *mestizaje* of local ethnic hybridization, social criticism, and appropriations of home-made kitsch, unofficial religion (*Santería* and *Yorubá*-derived ritual tradition), and Western pop culture. The critical and aesthetic edge of this work made it successful in the international art world; official Cuban government policy supported exhibitions abroad and sales that would return dollars to Cuba. Painters and art students of the 1990's, the current generation, are both influenced by the aesthetics of their elders and aware of the export value they had before the exodus of most of them. Since the 1991 bienal, Cuban galleries are more concerned with sales than with supporting experimental or overtly critical art, which creates another contradiction since there have been several incidents of censorship recently (including the removal in 1991 of the 'Arte Cubano Actual' and, in 1994, of several works by Tania Bruguera, Fernando Rodríguez, and invited artists Marcos Alvarados and Lourdes Groubet), whereas some Cuban exhibits curated abroad were allowed to show off the kind of 'dissident art' that the West likes to see emerging from Communist countries, often without understanding what it means by dissidence.

I was therefore not surprised by the cynical or ironically opportunistic way in which several Cuban artists in the 1994 Biennial courted controversy and censorship by adapting the themes of tourism, export, and Western patronage or media hype for their work. Such irony, indeed, addresses an incontrovertible reality, as in the painting series by Eduardo Ponjuán and René Francisco entitled 'Dream, Art, and Market,' which conjures up their future success (in *Art in America* and with collector Peter Ludwig), or in the prints by Abel Barroso which depict dollar bills raining from the sky while a young prostitute awaits her tourist customers (titled '*Carpeta de grabados para resistir y vencer*'). Even more fantastic are the narrative pieces by Fernando Rodríguez – ten painted wood reliefs with varying titles – which show a couple (Fidel Castro and the Virgin of Charity, Cuba's patron saint) getting married and going off on a shopping tour in the Crafts Palace. The latter piece, '*Comprando artesania*,' was hung in the Crafts Palace itself.

The most persistently repeated, haunting, and archetypal image that has emerged over the past years, however, is that of the *balsas*, the floating rafts or boats that have carried so many Cubans away from the island toward 'The Other Shore,' as one theme exhibition at the 1994 Biennial was unexpectedly called. Although various foreign artists were asked to address the impact of migrations and the diaspora on cultural transformation, the most urgent representations of exodus, emigration, exile, and desertion or betrayal of the Revolution were created by Cuban artists such as Tania Bruguera, Sandra Ramos, Rolando Rojas, Ricardo Brey, and Kcho. Some of these works had a lyrical or fantastic dimension, others were sarcastic and bitter or lamented the dead *balseros* who never made it to the other side. Kcho had several installations at Galeria Habana (joining Ibrahim Miranda and the superbly sardonic cartoon drawings by Tonel), one of which showed fragile oars made out of crutches. At the Morro he had built an entire 'Regata,' dozens of tiny rafts made out of driftwood, shoes, plastic and toys. Bruguera performed her work on opening night: she silently lay in a boat for several hours, embodying the *balsa* in an ambivalent ritual of affirmation and uncertainty, perhaps linking the floating *balsa*, potential savior or coffin, to the principles of Eleguá – beginnings, openings, chance, indeterminacy.

The actual flood of Cuban refugees trying to leave the island in August 1994 drew new attention to the plight of people suffocating from the embargo and from their discontent with a stagnant political system that in its failure to renew socialism and its institutions undermines its legitimacy. The political inability to process both the international and the internal transformations puts all its revolutionary gains at stake. Contemporary Cuban society is thus forced into a painful reflection on its own *resistencia*, its spiritual, psychological, and emotional connection with and defense of the popular Revolution.

When we were shown *Fresa y chocolate* at the CONJUNTO 94, I was sitting next to Teresa Cárdenas, a black Cuban dancer from Matanzas who had already seen the film several times. I noticed how elated she was about the film's many visual allusions to the cultural practice of *Santería*, but I also sensed how puzzled she was by the sensuous, almost decadent milieu depicted in it. I vividly remember the thousands who had lined up in front of Havana's movie theaters, passionately coming together in the public space of the film screenings to recognize – in the difficult and tragically unresolvable love-affair between a gay man and a straight young communist activist – a story of their own national, revolutionary, and socialist past. As an unresolved proposition to the present, the film is centered on Diego (Jorge Perugorría), an openly gay artist and intellectual who loves his culture and lives through the contradictions of a revolution that identified homosexuals as 'undesirable,' thus isolating and humiliating many of them or driving them into exile (thousands left with the Mariel boatlift in 1980). The subject of this oppression had never been dealt with within Cuban revolutionary cinema, although Néstor Almendros's testimonial documentary on gays in Cuba, *Mauvaise conduite* ('Improper Conduct,' 1984), caused a stir when the exiled cinematographer (co-directing with Orlando Jimenéz Leal) initially released the film in France, Spain, England, and the USA. Several of the witnesses in *Mauvaise conduite* had been imprisoned for a number of years, others such as writer Reinaldo Arenas had been forced to work in the UMAP labor camps of the 1960s. Castro always denied that there existed such repression, and when I saw *Mauvaise conduite* in Houston in 1988 I noticed that the film was clearly intended to be a revelatory indictment of Castro's regime, and it was utilized as anti-Castro propaganda by conservative US-Cuban factions. In fact, the oral testimonies are so harrowing that left-leaning critics in Britain and the USA were prepared to criticize the anxious transparency of the film's documentary form, faulting it for its one-sided ideological slant against the revolution and arguing that homosexuality is only a pretext for its agenda.

I don't want to enter into the controversy over Almendros here, but the conflicted responses *outside* of Cuba to the documentary film's form and content are illuminating since *Fresa y chocolate* is certainly not Alea's strongest film in formal terms; on the contrary, it is a thoroughly traditional, naturalist melodrama designed to have a broad popular appeal to audiences. This is not a coming-out film, nor could it be perceived as a gay film in terms of the identity politics familiar to Anglo-American culture, although it may be the very first Cuban feature that treats homosexuality openly and unflinchingly. *Fresa y chocolate* goes much further in its critical treatment of the conditions that structurally make homosexuality (in)visible: by examining Cuban culture, incarnated in an out-of-the-closet queen, it traces back revolutionary social history and decades of prejudice and internal contradiction, of intolerance and dogmatism, *vigilancia* and self-censorship. And in challenging this very history of revolutionary dogma, the film raises the question of national destiny and of a future in which sexual difference, intellectual dissidence, and diverse religious beliefs and practices can be openly acknowledged and appreciated in the culture. If the Revolution and the nation are intimately linked, and if 'Cuba' is identified by a social revolution which now no longer corresponds to the needs and desires of its people, then it is vitally necessary to ask how the island-nation (split off from the US Cuban and other exile communities) can continue to reproduce itself as a nation. Although it leaves representation of gay sexual pleasure and of direct political repression off-screen, *Fresa y chocolate* transparently dramatizes, perhaps even sentimentalizes, the splitting and the schizophrenic tensions and double standards endured by the characters in the film who identify with Cuban revolutionary culture and its struggle for independence and survival. Diego's melancholia and his many ironic and tender efforts to seduce David (the sexually repressed and initially homophobic communist youth from the countryside) manifest a powerful moment of self-critical consciousness at the end of the unity the national revolution once symbolized. The illusions of sexual and national identity are exposed, and Diego's longing gently and fatally subverts the inflexible ideological preferences on which the Cuban revolution was and is based. It is almost as if the film marks *la hora del cambio*, the time of change. At the end of the film, Diego prepares for his departure. He cannot live in the culture he identifies. In their last cathartic scene together, David accepts the friendship and affection he has come to feel for Diego, and he gives him a long and emotional hug. I believe that this final embrace of reconciliation has already become such a potent symbolic image that it has affected the Cuban theater community which in its own way is seeking to find new directions and to reconcile with its suppressed past. There were clear indications that this new openness is also officially encouraged, since the programs at the Casa de las Américas are funded by the Ministry of Culture. As in the case of José Lezama Lima, one of Cuba's greatest lyrical poets who was ostracized for the international success of his homoerotic novel *Paradiso*, the playwright Virgilio Piñera is now considered the most important Cuban writer for the stage in the twentieth century, after having been forced into silence and internal exile before his death. What is left of this period of suppression, reaching its height in the 1970s when many theater directors and actors were fired, silenced and marginalized, are shameful and bitter memories and, in the case of Piñera, his unpublished writings that have now appeared under the title *Teatro inedito*.

The CONJUNTO 94 made a symbolic statement of re-evaluation by dedicating two seminars to the past, to Virgilio Piñera and also to playwright José Triana (*La noche de los asesinos*, 1966), inviting testimony from some of the most prominent theater critics and directors of the older generation, including Rine Leal, Graziella Pogolotti, Abilio Estévez, Roberto Gacio, Vincente Revuelta, Adolfo de Luis, and Carlos Díaz. Also present were Luisa Piñera, Virgilio's sister, and the younger playwrights Alberto Pedro and Eugenio Hernández Espinosa among many other artists and writers who joined the week-long workshop, organized by Rosa Ileana Boudet and Vivian Martínez Tabares.

The Casa became a space hospitable to all of our different expectations, open for frank discussions, reunions, and the exchange of sad memories with anxious critical debates about the future. The *testimonios* of the older and younger artists created a bridge not only between the different generations of the Revolution, but also between the main established institutions and recently emerging de-centered theater groups and projects as well as between the various facets of a national dramaturgy (Stanislavsky or Brecht-based realism centered in texts) and the popular or experimental performance practices. Adolfo de Luis, for example, had studied with Piscator and then worked in New York and Havana in the 1950s, at a time when Cuban theater productions had adapted Euro-American modernist/realist conventions and predominantly featured foreign plays, regularly including Arthur Miller and Tennessee Williams. Vincente Revuelta became the most important director and mentor of Cuban theater in the 1960s, after he had helped to found Teatro Estudio and declared its support of the revolutionary movement.

With a much stronger emphasis on Cuban playwrights and new plays, Teatro Estudio became the leading theater in the country, remembered for its critically successful productions and the enormous influence it exerted on the professionalization of acting, before and also after it had become officially conjoined with the Instituto Superior del Arte (ISA, formed by the Ministry of Culture in 1976). Revuelta, Roberto Blanco, Berta Martínez and other directors from the Teatro Estudio became the main theater instructors at the ISA. A reorganization of artistic institutions took place in 1989, when the Ministry of Culture gave greater autonomy to the individual arts divisions, and theater is now taught and funded by the Consejo Nacional de Investigaciones de las Artes Escénicas.

Outside of the centralized professional system of theatres, national ballet and modern dance companies, there were efforts by younger Estudio actors in the late 1960s to explore more independent formal experiments (such as the group Los Doce) or to break away and find a more activist cultural and social role in the Revolution. Teatro Escambray represents such an effort to move from Havana to the mountains and develop collective work directly connected to social and economic issues of development in the rural areas. Similarly, the Cabildo Teatral Santiago focused on the development of a popular theater based on Afro-Cuban religions and cultural sources mixed with other historical and Catholic traditions; their work over the past twenty years has become known as *teatro de relaciones*. As a method of anthropological and popular performance research, their work could also be seen in the context of the interest that Cuban theater scholars and practitioners awarded to European theater anthropologists/directors (Jerzy Grotowski, Eugenio Barba) who traveled to Latin America and crossed paths with the influential ideas of the Theater-Pedagogy of the Oppressed (Paulo Freire, Augusto Boal).

It is symptomatic of the state's rigid political and economic central planning policies that it sought to control the center/off-center relations by promulgating a 'Teatro Nuevo' movement in the regions during the late 1970s. The forced creation of a regional movement failed, and there was a general sense of stagnation and dissatisfaction in the early 1980s that reverberated through the Cuban theater journals. More recently, a younger generation of actors and directors has begun to form its own groups and develop projects and aesthetic visions of its own in Havana, perhaps inspired by the sudden success of an independent group, Teatro Buendía, which had created a performance acutely aware of the crisis of uncertainty among Cuban youths. Staged in a converted church in their neighborhood, Buendía's *Lila: La Mariposa* (1986) was in fact a radically revisionary treatment of a pre-revolutionary play by Rolando Ferrer; but as in its more recent creations, *Las perlas de tu boca* and *Las ruinas circulares*, which also dissect cultural rituals and family traditions, the group addressed young audiences in a highly visceral and emotional way, inventing strong visual languages and choreographies.[4]

In the context of Buendía's performance work one can also think of the Teatro Verdun, a converted cinema where Eugenio Hernández Espinosa directs an experimental group, Teatro Caribeno, and an open space for spontaneous music and poetry events. There is Marianela Boán's group Danza Abierta, founded in 1988, or the dance-theatre group Retazos, and the *acciónes plasticas* created by visual artists in the late 1980s and early 1990s. Another radical departure from official dramatic theater has been tested in the small private spaces in which Víctor Varela's Teatro del Obstáculo performs its intimate, intensely physical and ritualized experiments with new body languages.

I listened to lectures on 'The Actor and Ritual in Latin-American Theatre' by Ileana Azor and on 'Ritual and Magic in Caribbean Theatre' by black anthropologist Inés María Martiatú, and then saw a performance-lecture by Jamaican dancer Fatima Patterson who has been collaborating with Martiatú on a project of ceremonial processions/musical dances involving larger community groups in Santiago de Cuba. Their work explicitly reconnects with the celebration of popular religious, spiritual, and mythological expressions that mark the vital and constantly flowing and ebbing rhythms of lived culture, which could be considered as a *concrete utopia* on the other end of the spectrum from Teatro del Obstáculo. Varela gave me a statement he had formulated for his group's programmatic *estetica de la dificultud*, which also includes references to Chinese Taoism, and to Mishima and de Sade:

> In principle the concept of 'obstacle' has been connected to the idea of CONVERTING OBSTACLES INTO CREATION. This means: if you face a wall you don't have to break it. If it is strong and consistent, then you don't want to destroy it but embrace it, in a way that it is no longer an empediment but an ally . . .
> THE THEATER is the leap into the abyss; against every principle of gravity and practical reality, it meets an OBSTACLE and challenges death.

Varela also told me that he believes in the theater as a 'space of freedom,' where everything can be built and where material objects need not exist: 'There is nothing. The only obstacle is loneliness. The unexistent. So I can be a creator.' Varela, together with Barbara Barrientos and Alexis González, performed *Segismundo ex marqués* as the study of an internal kinesis of oppositions that always exclude and complement each other. Metaphorically, this means a search for a center or a resolution that is impossible to reach, and in this sense their performance research is also a kind of *concrete utopia* in the process of struggling with the contradictions of Cuban reality. Varela and his actors have made this struggle against obstacles their own in a special way. The group has now consistently worked together for almost ten years (cf. Chapter 2).

Noticing the separate efforts of younger theater groups to find and define their own performance work and space, and responding to the necessity for structural economic changes in the 'special period,' Cuban cultural policy once again changed in 1990 and has since then allowed for further decentralization by supporting *proyectos* instead of institutions only, thus making resources available for creative ideas that are developed in the communities or by independent groups themselves. During the CONJUNTO we were shown a wide range of performances encompassing a folkoric dance concert by the Conjunto Folklorico Nacional, dedicated to motifs drawn from Yoruba religion; two theatrical monologues; a new play by Alberto Pedro; two large-scale productions (one based on a García Lorca play, the other adapted from Patrick Süskind's novel *Perfume*); and the experimental work of Teatro del Obstáculo. In addition, I spent two days in the countryside at the Cultural Center of Alamar observing the independent group La Jaula Abierta rehearse several monologues written and directed by Felipe Oliva.

Monologue performances are very popular in Cuba, and Oliva's prose has an emotional and poetic texture that can be quite demanding for an actor, as in the case of his story *La reencarnación de Mateo el Reprimido*, which asks for the embodiment of split personae and different presentational styles by the same actor. Similarly, Adria Santana's solo performance of *Las peñas saben nadar*, based on a text by Abelardo Estorino, was done on the bare stage at Sala Hubert de Blanck, with a telephone and chair as the only props. Santana's rendering of a difficult, painful long-distance relationship was a feat of the imagination, pulling the audience along on a journey beyond the confines of theatrical realism. The young student actress María Elena Espinosa Plutín presented a recital of a story by Guadalupean writer Simone Schwartz-Bart, *Tu bello capitan*, and even though she may have lacked Santana's professional experience, her performance was visually captivating. She had turned the stage of the Sala Antonin Artaud into the distinct metaphorical space of an island; in front of the circular island, close at our feet, there stood a tiny, miniature replica of a ship, suspended outside of time. At the end of the recital, she lit the boat with a match, and it slowly burned to ashes.

A few hours later, on the mainstage of the Gran Teatro de Habana, Grupo La Colmena together with students from the ISA mounted their large-scale, almost overbearingly baroque and melodramatic adaptation of Süskind's *El perfume*, directed by Josué Martínez. Stylistically meandering between fairy-tale, *teatro bufo*, and grand guignol opera, the production did not impress me as anything

Figure 36 Adria Santana performs in *Las peñas saben nadar*. Havana 1994. Photo courtesy of Adria Santana.

more than spectacular entertainment. A very large audience in attendance seemed to enjoy every moment of it.

It was not the same audience reaction I had witnessed a few days earlier, however, when Teatro Mío, under the direction of Miriam Lezcano, performed Alberto Pedro's new one-act play *Manteca*, a subtle, poignant, and choking family drama describing the divisions between two brothers, Pucho and Celestino, and their sister, Dulce, who live in the here and now of Cuba's 'special period' facing the final decomposition, the existential and moral collapse of the long-standing stability of values represented by *la familia* and *la casa* in Cuban culture. Portraying Cuba's economic and psychic disintegration in a painstakingly exact naturalist manner, with an audience responding emotionally to almost every single scene of (self-)recognition, *Manteca* both questions the mythology of the home and the nation by depicting them as a decaying island ghetto filled with amputated families and broken revolutionary dreams, while at the same time appealing to the ethos of a spiritual *resistencia* and to the re-creation of family unity as the only hope of redemption left for a society that needs to rebuild itself. Perhaps too obvious and stereotypical for my taste, the vision of *lo principal es la familia* is articulated by the nurturing, sweet, and conciliatory female character, icon of self-sacrifice and endurance. Dulce's depressed and aggressive brothers carry the burden of acting out the schizophrenia of a situation in which life itself has become insupportable. *Manteca* surely reaches into many deep layers of the collective psyche, layers that I could not have been aware of as I sat among a profoundly moved audience many of whom stayed afterwards to wander around the *casa*, the little wooden house on the stage, talking to the playwright and the superb actors: Celia García (Dulce), Jorge Cao (Celestino), and Michaelis Cué (Pucho).

A few days later, there was also a public discussion between cast, playwright, and participants of the CONJUNTO, moderated by Vivian Martínez Tabares who wrote the critical introduction to the text of *Manteca* published in the *revista de teatro latinoamericano* (no. 95/96) that has appeared, since 1964, under the same title as the conference. *Conjunto* means 'ensemble' or 'confluence', coming together: for the Casa de las Américas this idea symbolizes a cultural mission extending to all of América Latina and all those theater artists and scholars committed to an exchange of ideas and information. Each year the Casa organizes numerous symposia, lectures, and cultural events in the areas of literature, theater, music, and the visual arts; it sponsors several important publications, and houses its own library that is open to the public and visiting scholars who help to decrease the distances between the various Latin countries, and to illuminate the differences or communalities among their theater cultures. Seeking to stimulate communication and solidarity among theater professionals, the Casa has also participated in the ambitious project of forming an international ensemble of editors and writers: the Espacio Editorial de la Communidad Iberoamericana de Teatro (EECIT).[5] Regular publications and meetings of this ensemble at conferences and festivals (such as the international theater festivals in Havana, Bogota, Cadiz, Caracas, Mexico City, São Paulo) assure the continuity and growth of a network of ideas, plays, and performance theories that now travel more quickly back and forth between the Spanish- and Portuguese-speaking arts communities. Many of the editors and prominent writers from the Espacio Editorial had come to the CONJUNTO 94 to take part in the workshops, present the latest issues of their journals, and propose their viewpoints on the tendencies in the theater of their countries during the last decade (1980–90). Featured speakers included Osvaldo Pellettieri (Argentina), Maria Elena Kühner (Brazil), Rodolfo Obregón (Mexico), Pilar Romero-Javier Vidal (Venezuela), and Victor Viviesco (Colombia). Magaly Muguercia (Cuba), former editor of *Conjunto*, distributed some of her new writings on '*Teatro y utopia*,' and Cuban sociologist Esther Suarez addressed the subject of *Investigacion y práctica teatral*,' while Lillian Manzor-Coats, representing *Gestos* (published at the University of California-Irvine), gave a provocative and stimulating introduction to '*El cuerpo y la memoria histórica: performance de latinas en los Estados Unidos.*' The most vigorous and polemical discussions followed after such critical exposés, as well as after the penetrating analyses of ritual performance, offered by Ileana Azor and Inés María Martiatu, and of the emergence of a new Cuban dramaturgy, sketched out by Vivian Martínez Tabares.

Attempts to summarize the most important theatrical events and trends in countries as vast as Argentina or Brazil seemed rather more futile and presumptuous to me, especially when a single perspective, usually from the center/capital of the so-called national theater, stood in for the diversity and heterogeneity of hybrid cultures, and for those manifestations that resist a central/national ideology – or the ideology of texts and canons – in the first place. Nevertheless, such overviews of theatrical events in the different countries are valuable as information that can be shared and examined; they can also be instrumental in bringing about more frequent, direct encounters between performers, directors, writers, and cultural critics, especially in light of the daunting realization we all had, namely that the idea of a shared editorial space of a *communidad iberoamericana* (bridging the European continent with the former colonized continent and stretching north along the axis of NAFTA) remains a utopia, and an ambivalent global concept at best. While the global transnational flow of mass media and consumer products may be guaranteed as the century is turning, theater takes more time to travel, and the economic conditions and sociocultural/historical roots in their particular local contexts determine different processes of theatrical invention.

It was admitted in our discussions that a critic or director in Salvador, Brazil, may not know what kind of performance ideas take shape in South Brazil, northern Peru, or Canada. It is tantalizing to imagine that the exchange of journals, and the translation and publication of work across the Portuguese, Spanish, English, French (or other) language borders, could indeed foster a *communidad* of creative and critical research that would illuminate the ensembles of cultural and political factors that, say, led to the repression of the subject of homosexuality in Nelson Rodrigues's play *Beijo no asfalto*, and to the enormous cathartic effect that Senel Paz's story about Diego and David has had on Cuban theater and film, and their reception there and elsewhere.[6]

The space of dialogue is open and unpredictable, in spite of blockades and central planning, First World economic hegemonies and self-assertive national culture industries in the South. In fact, cultural expressions and forms always move across geographical or social boundaries, and the openings I've described here remind me of the Caribbean flows, polyrhythms, and improvisational unfoldings that Antonio Benítez-Rojo so beautifully evokes in *The Repeating Island* and in his poetic effort to write a song of an 'island' without center and without any one reality that can be fixed or explained. When he speaks of the continual flow of paradoxes in the fictions of this 'island that is impossible to reach,' I am reminded of the obsessive melancholia, bitterness, and longing for a lost home that often pervade the literature of exile. Benítez-Rojo himself is writing from an other shore, and like his generation of exiles (Jesús Díaz, Severo Sarduy, Reinaldo Arenas, Octavio Armand, and many others) or the younger generation of Cuban American writers who now publish their novels and poems in English (cf. Cristina García's *Dreaming in Cuban*), he is forever imagining realities grounded in the fictions of memory.

The contemporary situation in Cuba as I experienced it seems to have shifted the ground between the generation empowered by the Revolution and the one that is coming of age during its 'special period' of disintegration at a tragic moment when dogmatic political intransigence, both toward the internal formation of a new civil society and the necessary reconciliation with the exile community, is clearly paradoxical in light of the openings that young artists are creating. La Jaula Abierta, Danza Abierta, Teatro Mío, Teatro El Público, Buendía, Varela's Teatro del Obstáculo and many of the young paint- ers and performers I saw are living and working on the edge of existential survival, and their pushing against obstacles and the problems of scarcity shows no sign of melancholia or resignation. On the contrary, what CON- JUNTO 94 and the Espacio Editorial seek to build on a transnational level of exchange and dialogue, the young generation of Cuban artists articulates in their own creation of alternative spaces, performance projects, and ironically provocative *refracciones* of scarcity. This expresses itself in the Taoist aesthetics of the Teatro del Obstáculo, and the spiritual will to survive that propels the creative determination of Felipe Oliva's actors who rehearse for five hours in a dark building without electricity or running water. Or it receives an outra- geous and parodic twist, as in the deliberate nudity shown off in the high camp performance of García Lorca's experimental play, *El público*, with which the young actors of the Teatro El Público (named after the play) created a space for their presentation of homoerotic theater. This very stylized and beau- tifully choreographed production, directed by Carlos Díaz, recuperates the explicit homosexuality in *El público* which has been silenced or disguised behind the surface surrealism and poetic language often foregrounded in the history of the play's stagings. It also thereby projects its transgressive intention into the public realm of contemporary Cuba, using the complex and intricate meta-play (Lorca's parody of theater, theatrical reality, and the 'truth' of love or 'love' of truth) as a means of pushing the masquerades and constant

Figure 37 *El Público*, performed by Teatro El Público. Havana 1994.

mutations of its characters/names/roles/costumes to the edge where the question of homosexual relations, between one (Director) and the other (First Man), between Second Man and Third Man, and so forth, becomes a haunting allegory for the reversibility of one's position. I am an other: there is no other truth beneath the masks. This production plays dangerously with fundamental ethical dilemmas, in fact, posing an unanswerable question about Cuban identity or sense of itself.

5. EMBRACING DIEGO

That night at the theater I met 'Diego' (Jorge Perugorría), and with him I want to end this chapter. Jorge had helped to found the group El Público, and when I asked him whether the success of *Fresa y chocolate* had made theater productions such as *El Público* possible and acceptable, he explained that the film is based on Paz's story, *El lobo, el bosque y el hombre nuevo*, of which several versions had already been adapted for the theater in 1993, before it became the script for the film. Jorge liked the story so much that he planned to transform it into a monologue for himself, but when the film was cast he went to audition for the role of David, feeling that the character was closest to him and his generation, and worrying a little about the huge responsibility of playing Diego. Alea decided to cast him as Diego, and then they worked together on building the role of the older, gay character. When he comments on the film's objective, he is practically echoing the crucial scene from *Manteca*, with a difference:

I think we have a lot of work to do. Maybe we don't persecute homosexuals in Cuba any more, but we still don't have the political maturity to give equal opportunity to everybody regardless of political, ideological or any other kind of difference. Society still doesn't give gays and lesbians a chance to help save our homeland. The Cuban problem is complex; the film is about intolerance, it argues for a reconciliation of all Cubans, and the embrace between Diego and David sends a message to all Cubans, here and abroad, in any part of the world: it's time to join together, to accept our differences because only by uniting and accepting our differences will we be able to save our country from this economic crisis.[7]

We continue talking for a long time, since I feel the need to understand how the body politic of homosexuality is inflected in Cuba, and how it was perceived to clash both with Latin American *machismo* and with Cuban revolutionary, Marxist doctrine. Why was homosexuality considered counterrevolutionary? What are the relations between homosexuality and nationality? I am particularly uncertain about the function of silence and 'closeted' homosexuality in Cuba, since I gather from reading Reinaldo Arenas's autobiography, *Antes que anochezca* (1992), that he is dismayed, even disgusted, by the excessive visibility and ostentation of queer life-styles in the US and remembers with great melancholy the *paradiso*-like freedom of anonymity and sensuous fluidity experienced during his childhood in revolutionary Cuba where the ecstatic eroticism he evokes seems dependent on a 'compulsory heterosexuality' that always ambivalently includes homosexuality. In other words, Arenas evokes a fluidity that would be broken if 'gay identity' articulated itself as a separate minority as we have experienced it in the West and in the recent emphasis on coming-out/outing narratives in the USA.

Jorge admits he doesn't know much about the queer movement in the USA and feels it has little relevance for Cubans.

It's really difficult for me to give you a valid answer because I am not gay, nor do I understand the thinking of those who say that homosexuals have neither the right to contribute to the country nor to represent it. I don't know what excuse they can come up with. I think that in the first years of the revolution, they wanted to create this 'New Man.' It was this new man who was the model, the prototype that society wanted, and they couldn't accept that he be homosexual, wouldn't even accept that he be religious. What happened? A lot of people became marginal, especially homosexuals . . . which is really a bit illogical. In my opinion homosexuality is quite simple: you are talking about two people of the same sex who love each other. But they are men, like others, like us. And so I don't understand, nor am I aware of the excuse or justification for creating anti-homosexual policies.

I ask Jorge about the relationship between Diego and *la vigilancia*, and between homosexuality and religion; for example, Nancy's practice of *Santería*?

'All of this is changing now,' he argues, and his explanation indicates that voluntary silence among gays resembled the camouflage practiced by the *santeros*.

> At the beginning of the revolution, in the early 1960s and 1970s, what happens is that along with the aspect of society that involved the formation of the new man through Marxism-Leninism and materialism, religious beliefs were also denounced. That was also the stage during which people didn't show their religious beliefs. Now it's accepted and now society tolerates religious people and believers, whether they believe themselves Catholics or *santeros*. In this way government policy has changed, but it was different in the beginning. People kept their saints hidden, and then at some point they said, no, this has nothing to do with the political thinking that was part of our culture and heritage, and everybody went outside with their necklaces. What you see now, people in the street with their necklaces or white dresses or whatever, you never saw this before. People always believed, but kept quiet about it. Now, in a time when the crisis has become more acute, people have had to grasp for something that gives them some faith, no . . . something that lets them believe in something to help them get over these bad times in Cuba. All beliefs and religious tendencies are on the rise. Even the Catholic Church is seeing an increase in the number of young people attending church.

'Is the practice of Afro-Cuban religion or saint worshipping a subversive act?' I ask. 'Is the connection between homosexuality and religion subversive?' Jorge does not answer immediately, but I know we are both thinking about the politics of camouflage and the predicament of a sexuality that is too visible or is *made too visible* by political repression that cannot tolerate resistance that is invisible, lying behind the official mask of ideology, silent and unedited like Piñera's ambivalent theatrical silence.[8] In the film, Diego is 'hiding' the religious sculptures of his artist friend Germán in his apartment while negotiating with a foreign embassy to show the work outside of Cuba. Jorge suggests that 'yes, it's noteworthy that many gays – something I've seen all my life – seek refuge in religion.' He pauses.

> Look . . . at one point here, when revolutionary policy was very intolerant toward homosexuals, many gay theater directors and writers got married and had children as a cover-up in order to be able to continue working and living in the society. In that way they couldn't come and tell you that you can't do this or that work because there was no official law permitting persecution of homosexuality. People are still very much aware of that period of our history; it's still very hard for people to come out of the closet. So, you see, for example a group like Carlos Díaz's is doing a production of Lorca which already comes from another generation of creativity of people who didn't live through the 1960s or 1970s and who are not afraid to produce plays without constraints. Besides, this is a generation with another point of view, and what they are doing is exposing that

point of view, trying to be provocative. This is especially so with the homosexual content, or let's say with two actors kissing on stage, two men, something which in Cuba had never been done before.

I'm aware that Jorge keeps referring to the regime as 'they.' Castro and the regime he identifies are the unspeakable secret, the transparently obvious *extrañamiento* (alienation) that cannot be acknowledged in political terms but must be sublimated, in *Fresa y chocolate*, by the seductive decadence of Diego's highly cultured and discreet, private milieu which is the critical scene inside of the 'obscene' outside: Havana's decrepit, crumbling economic and social infrastructure. 'Old Havana is sinking into shit,' Diego tells his young communist friend when he takes him on a tour to some of the architectural landmarks while the camera silently dwells on the peeling grandeur of buildings and, finally, on a structure that has collapsed, dogs roaming in the garbage.

Jorge meanwhile has followed his train of thought; he becomes agitated now, his eyes light up when he speaks about his theater group: 'Gay identity in Cuba also manifests itself more extensively. We called ourselves "El Público" after Lorca's play, and we find a strong connection to his work.' He laughs. 'But it's a very difficult text, for a lot of critics it's an unperformable text, which it also was for Lorca himself. He kept it hidden.'

I think about revolutions and repetitions. And about paradoxes. About the 'wolf' and the 'new man.' I remember hearing stories about Lorca's visit to the 'forest,' to Havana, about the many lovers he had on the island at the time he started to write *El público* in 1930. I look at Jorge and know he's reading my thoughts. 'Yes, our production of *El público* is about unmasking ourselves, showing ourselves. I think the whole wave of transvestisms and gay sensibilities is connected to the development of society, to the possibility of tolerance. Here it has been very hidden, and now it's developing.' I am trying to follow Jorge's sonorous, rhythmic Spanish, and listen to the pauses he makes. He seems very calm, relaxed, but throughout our conversation he becomes passionate when we speak about the theatre. 'I love the *mise-en-scène in El público*,' he adds. 'All these masks, the theater as mask. I think the double standard of morality has been one of the most damaging effects of the Revolution.'

I think of the scene in the film where Diego arranges a festive dinner party for David and Nancy in the high style described in Lezama's *Paradiso*. The scene self-consciously eroticizes a culinary pleasure no longer available under current conditions of scarcity, but it also epitomizes the melancholic collapse of the film's critical relations to the historical moment of the revolution: the banquet ends in Nancy's seduction of David (he loses his virginity), and Diego abandons his sexual desire for him and prepares to leave Cuba. The heterosexual romance, no doubt ironically, masks the impossible *resistencia* of the homosexual who cannot shift the borders of the cage, who cannot re-create the fluidity of the *Paradiso*. I ask Jorge why the film equates homosexuality with aesthetic melancholy instead of with a possible political transformation of the borders:

This is a complex phenomenon. Nowadays there is a terrible crisis of values. After the fall of socialism, after the intensification of the economic crisis in our country people are very disoriented, and they react to this disorientation with fatalism and with this passive *resistencia*. Because in reality the situation in Cuba is very complicated, and so what happens? You can't see the solution to the problem, the way out of the contradictions. You stop because you don't know which way to walk nor whom to fight against or for what reason you got into the contradictions because you don't know where the truth is. Because up to now the ideal model of society was the Soviet Union and the Socialist bloc because we were raised for thirty-five years in this model of society. Now the ideal is destroyed, and when you destroy the ideal of a human being, people get lost and it's very hard for them to find another road to follow. As long as people are like that, they don't know what to do. We have a problem which makes this conflict even worse, which is the Cuban community in the USA Unfortunately a lot of Cubans think they can solve their problems by going abroad, which is something that seems absurd to me. It seems like a big mistake. So that's something that affects our society a lot. I believe we Cubans have to solve Cuba's problems, and by that I am referring especially to us who live on the island. It's difficult because every day Cubans . . . I think that there are two extremist tendencies, among Cubans here and among Cubans who live in the USA. I think that the US blockade is causing us a lot of harm; it's very, very unfair. The blockade is unjust in a lot of ways, but most of all it is a justification for the Cuban leadership, with all its economic power and its politics. It's also a justification for the Cubans in Miami who for thirty-five years have made a political career out of Fidel Castro. So all these factors make Cuban reality very complex right now at the very time we are trying to discover the truth.

I thank Jorge for speaking his mind and for raising the ethical dilemma of struggling for the truth in the hour of change. It's already getting dark when I make my way home. During the long walk along the Malecón, I try to listen to the sounds of the water as they mix with the music that drifts out of the dark houses. If I walk close enough to the edge, I can feel the moist breeze on my skin, the blue-grey-pink colors of the edges of sky and water shore begin to blur, and for moments on end I am dreaming in Cuban.

6

LOVERS FRAGMENTS

NOTES TOWARD

A NEW PERFORMANCE EROS

Film/video production for Lovers Fragments *started in December 1994; stage rehearsals began in March, and ACT I was premiered at the Cleveland Performance Art Festival in mid-April 1995. Film versions were shown at dance and theater festivals in London, Helsinki and Montréal (April–May 1995). The completed ACTS I–III premiered at Northwestern University's Barber Theater during 5–15 May. A new version (ACT IV) was staged for the Blue Rider Theater Festival in Chicago in December 1995, and entirely different reconstructions were performed, first with collaborators in Cuba in late December 1995, then in collaboration with Gruppe RU-IN, at the Deutsche Hygiene Museum in Dresden in August 1996 as part of a European tour.*

And yet we are still at the beginning, asking questions about the stories and fantasy-images we are telling each other as they fade out. So we meet in a dance/photo studio and summon up stories while we dance and shoot film.

[PROLOGUE] POSTCARDS FROM THE HOMELAND

The failure of love is a most intense autoerotic experience. The latter inspires me to rethink eros in the era of AIDS and panic sex at the end of the century, as memories of the remembered flash up, in their endlessly proliferating associations. The rethinking is here like a fade-out of performance relations, here just language.

Yet the following rehearsal notes actually point toward concrete experienced work, and not to the lover's discourse alone. They are not about the determination to fail and the extreme solitude that Herbert Blau has explored so fondly and hauntingly in Beckett or in Barthes. I don't want them to fail, or fall prey to speculation alone.

Rather, *Lovers Fragments* is a work in progress stimulated by what I would call an economy of erotic relations that seeks to make them politically productive within our experience of loss or mourning and the work or techniques we create to transform the experience. Our physical process began in December 1994 after an intensive weekend spent in the snow-landscape surrounding a friend's pottery farm in Wisconsin. Our personal relations, passions, and fantasies motivated the questions our project raises about collaboration, sexuality, queer consciousness, bodily pleasure, and a new performance eros based on the desire to live through those who love us and to work with those whom we love.

It was not the first time members of our ensemble had retreated to this isolated 'winter camp' in the vast midwestern countryside, getting lost during our excursions into endless white regions of snow, retracing our steps back to the hot kiln that waited for us in the night. In 1992 we prepared ourselves there for rehearsing *Orpheus and Eurydike*, a feminist opera project designed to challenge the Orphic gaze, its built-in male fantasies of looking at the silent female body, and its phallic constructions of the power of voice and narrative. We decided to eliminate Orpheus altogether, altering the myth and queering Eurydike's voices, her many voices and overlapping stories which set the subject of opera off-center. [The eliminated Orpheus was watching, I guess.]

In 1993 we met there to explore the possibilities of crossing the boundaries of cultural difference, testing the limits of our various languages, conceptions, and artistic prejudices, getting lost in the labyrinth of identity politics. That intercultural collaboration, *From the Border*, turned out to be a small nightmare of emotional struggles over the gender-polarizing and distorting strictures of the performance apparatus within the institutions where some of us occasionally earn our living (the university/the theater), where the production of cultural, racial, and sexual others tends to get normalized or accommodated by a benevolent liberal multiculturalism pretending to appreciate difference. The space and context for our production, the university theater, became obstacles in the creation of new working methods, since the regulating

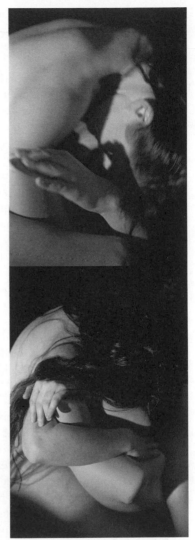

Figure 38 Photographic performance, *Lovers Fragments*, 1995.

pressures of academic discourse, the proprieties of technical production, and the current obfuscations of political correctness can be particularly debilitating to physical rehearsals that attempt to unravel the sexual and racial border relations in production.

I should add that the piece I performed in, *AlienNation*, subsequently traveled to other locations and crossed-over into other predicaments, not all of which can be subsumed under the problematic of translation or cultural difference, or what Blau, in 'Universals of Performance,' has described as the displacedness of performance as such, most moving because essentially always 'a testament to what separates.'[1] On the other side of my homeland where we performed it (in East Germany), our gently paranoid parody of the failed union/unification of the heterosexual couple moved our audiences only insofar as they considered it obscene and intimately infuriating because of its depiction of the neo-colonial sexual politics within inter-German relations. Our experience in Slovenia was more traumatic, in a different way, because we became so immediately aware of the perverse denial (within all of us) of the war that was being waged against Bosnia a few miles away. We knew, without speaking, that we were watching, with the impotent gaze of the impassive witness of televised fascist/racist aggression, a violent war against bodies and cultures of human relations. To put it differently, my speaking about, or any rational critique of, the monstrosity of the aggression, is possible only if I maintain some minimal distance to reality and hide, hysterically, the unspeakable fantasy in myself. Slavoy Žižek, in a conversation at his mother's house in Ljubljana, translated the unspeakable to me as 'guilty fantasy,' divided between fascination with the enjoyment (of the other) and utter repulsion at it.

I was still trying to reflect on this confusion of the impotent 'eye of prey' with the guilty fantasy, when a few days later I encountered the unexpected, Bosnian version (in the Serbo-Croatian language) of Lucky's mad cacophony of quaquaquaquaqua blasting its frenzied path through the documentary film *MGM* ('Man, God, The Monster'), which Ademir Kenović, Ismet Arnautalić, Mirza Idrizović, and Pjer Žalica had brought with them from Sarajevo. The image of the Sarajevan actor rehearsing Lucky's speech in 'Godot/Sarajevo' became the *punctum*, the ripping, piercing movement-image, that spoke to me of love's body, of the most vulnerable love expressed by that actor's face refusing to let go of his besieged city and his memory of what once was, refusing to utter anything but a truth betrayed by the horror yet clinging to an ethos that is, of course, afflicted with pain. In the actor's face I read the destruction of community and the indestructibility of memory.

This film collaboration is a most stubborn, most deliberate survival guide, full of sound and fury, yet signifying in content and production mode the very phenomenon of creative cultural intermixing for which the ancient city of Sarajevo historically stood as a cultural crossroads where Catholic, Eastern Orthodox, Islamic, and Jewish religions and diverse ethnic traditions converged. Its visual scenes both confirm and protest the burning fears described in Juan Goytisolo's *Cuaderno de Sarajevo* ('Sarajevo Notes'):

The city lying before my eyes is now nothing but a wasteland. Injuries, mutilations, entrails, festering wounds, scars that make one want to avert one's eyes . . . High-rise buildings with sparkling glass soar like beehives with plugged openings. The sight of glittering windows reflecting light, intermingled with windows here and there whose glass has been knocked out, suggests the socket of an eye that has been gouged out or the cross-tempered look of a one-eyed person. The burned-out automobiles and buses make manifest the fears fanned by fire in the middle of the street.

When I asked Ademir Kenović about the description of the visiting Spanish writer, he shrugged and urged me to look at another book, the *Sarajevo Survival Guide* compiled by a Sarajevan artist collective called FAMA. This book is no less poetic, but eschews the voyeuristically elegiac descriptions of death and waste. Rather, with a stunning sense of irony it mimics the practical form of a guide-book yet offers very real strategies for survival, for obtaining water, food, medical help, and nurturance, to residents who live in the diminished reality of an urban battlefield. FAMA gathers information for civil defense and black humor, giving spiritual sustenance to the immediate and metaphysical needs of the human self whose customary boundaries are broken and whose survival depends on cooper-ation with others even as the fiction of a multi-ethnic, multilingual community seems destroyed. The problem with Goytisolo's elegy is the distance it creates through the imaging of the conflagration (wishing to avert the eyes). His images are eccentric to the human experience and the differences among women and men in Bosnia; they do not collaborate with the existential challenge of needing to see through the crisis and its affect on the physical memories of women, men, and children. If memory could be destroyed by military force, it would spell the end of any ethics of survival and resistance, and of the work that needs to be done to create safe spaces and to recover what the body remembers.

I saw 'Lucky,' in the wildly choreographic (e)motion of this angry protest-film, as a survivor and an activist, in midst of the Sarajevan funeral rites that reminded me of personal experiences with mourning rites as political demonstra-tion (during the past nine years of participating in AIDS activism, attending funerals or exhibitions of the Names Project Quilt, and the processionals staged on each first day of December), gesturing toward the not-forgetting of lost friends and lost lovers. More importantly, the performance of such mourning interventions has transformed our sense of community over the years, even as the relations (in performance) of community will always remain unstable, shifting, and vulnerable, since the fantasy of community itself is not shared by all in the same way. It is perhaps also a guilty fantasy, a blind extension of the narcissistic self.

When we worked on *Lovers Fragments*, we also tried to examine these impulses that seem to connect or, sometimes, disconnect us over the re-enactment of the scenes of loss or desire, our identification with absence. As I implied earlier, we became particularly interested in the role of images that incite and move (us), that move us *forward* together, when we began shooting film and video back in the winter snow, extending some earlier footage or dreams we created/re-created in Cuba when our company was working there in December. Tara Peters's entire drawing/painting and writing process in fact has been based on her dreams. Her performances in our group consistently inspire us to improvise with the fragmentary associations we can all make between her dreams and our rememberings, her remembering and our dreams, exploring the flow of otherness in the imaginations inside our own bodies.

It is not possible to avoid looking back, even if such looking can have unexpected or undesirable consequences. I had lived in the United States for ten years when the Wall in Berlin fell, and in 1990 I returned to Germany and to the border-land in Berlin to trace the ghostly contours of a division that had only yet begun again. The repetitions are painful, as they sometimes are in rehearsal. And the past is a foreign country one visits as a guest or a former lover who is not always welcome. In Cuba we were welcome precisely because of the pathological divisions prolonged by a disastrous embargo which humiliates the desire to exchange, to relate, to return. Crossing into forbidden territory made the politics of *AlienNation* more easily readable for audiences there, as they touch upon the amputated concept of 'family' or 'nation' and on the feminization of the one who waits and suffers from waiting, experiencing the 'horror of being split off not only from the loved one but from any conception of himself, self-banished, betrayed, abandoned.'[2]

Looking forward, then, for me assumes an attitude different from the tired and exhausting reflections of Roland Barthes's broken heart in *A Lover's Discourse*. It assumes, for example, the necessity of reconstituting relations with the self and with others not identified with the 'demand for love' or with the 'homeland' of family and nation or any of the dominant ideologies of white heteronormativity and their reproductive fantasy structures. Addressing heteronormativity means to relocate the focus of gay, lesbian, and bisexual theory away from categories of sexual identity (as well as from a fantasized 'queer nation') toward the cultural production of the hetero/homosexual code that frames knowledges and practices and the ways we organize social and personal experience. Contemporary queer theory has started to attack the compulsory order, cruising the 'performative' (i.e. picking up Judith Butler's thread into the theoretical maze) and rediscovering the politics of camp. But cruising may not be enough, and many artists now also realize that they had better react to the conservative backlash in the US that threatens to wipe out the ground on which the new social movements could articulate their terms of the debates. The code operates in our performance spaces, of course, and I believe we need to rehearse and disseminate critical techniques of understanding the normative pressures that create the social conditions and institutional policies within which we rehearse whatever it is we rehearse (including the much-talked-about 'subversive parody' and gender-burning drag).

The dissemination I have in mind is indebted to Foucault's political critique of the disciplinary regimes of power/knowledge, and above all to his idea that resistance is an ethical, transformative, and thus *creative process*. As creative experiments, performance art and activist media can test their eccentric or hybrid technologies and positions (outside of the mainstream and capital-intensive means of self-representation) to envision, as David Halperin suggests, 'a variety of possibilities for reordering the relations among sexual behaviors, erotic identities, constructions of gender, forms of knowledge, regimes of enunciation, logics of representation, modes of self-constitution, and practices of community – for restructuring, that is, the relations among power, truth, and desire.'[3]

The exhibition *Ecstatic Antibodies*, which I saw in London in 1988, did precisely what Halperin suggests, and along with Marie-Françoise Plissart's photo-scenario *Droit de regards*, Kiss & Tell's photowork *Her Tongue on My Theory*, and the films, videos, dance and performance works of many contemporary activists and queer artists, it has been more profoundly encouraging than the occasionally intoxicating rhythms of rhetorical claims (Sister Sledge notwithstanding) that we are here, and that we are here to stay, as some sort of 'family,' however happily dysfunctional.

On the practical level, I think we need to be honest enough to realize that the marginality we might claim, or the lack of social security we might experience anyhow, are both relative to other marginalized experiences and contingent also on the extra-discursive elements of our practice as performance personae *vis-à-vis* the fantasmatic center. Most of the dancers, musicians, composers, and visual artists I work with rehearse techniques or explore sensibilities of expression that are not 'formated' by Foucaldian or deconstructionist theory. Changing our residual habits or bodily techniques will take time, and the evolving hybrid and syncretic processes of contemporary artmaking, in a social arena subject to many simultaneous and conflicting influences, have hardly been conceptualized, nor do I think it is possible to write a theory of improvisation, appropriation or collaboration able to adequately capture the physical and psychosexual dynamics of our corporealities, gestures, movements, voices, moods, emotional anxieties, interrelations, and all the (sub)cultural codes of particular locales into which they enter and cross over to be seen or not seen.

Perhaps this is a good moment to insert my acknowledgement of Herbert Blau's considerable impact on my thinking about leaving the theater before I had entered it, or perhaps I should say that I am greatly indebted to his retrospective, lovingly combative, libidinal deconstructions of theater work and the appearances of performance. When I arrived in the USA to encounter poststructuralist theory and deconstruction at Yale, on the other side of the street from the Drama School where they still reproduced the canon of conventions unthinkingly, I was instantly drawn to the intellectual passion with which he reflected on performance and the subject of desire in performance, at a point when he had withdrawn from his practice as a director (cf. *Take Up the Bodies: Theater at the Vanishing Point*; *Blooded Thought*). His writings presented such a challenge and provocation, throughout the 1980s, that I am hardly embarrassed to say that they encouraged me to start performing again, rehearsing, directing, and trying to keep up with the unnerving zig-zag of contemporary theoretical voguing that now circulates in the North American academy, more so than in other spaces of the world. I am even less embarrassed to admit that existential experiences, and my deepening commitment to dance and performance art practice, have exhausted my interest in theoretical discourses. I still wonder sometimes what they do and how they work, and perhaps Blau's *The Eye of Prey* is my favorite among his books because its chapters on the birth of his daughter, the memory of his mother, and his aversions to homosexual politics ('Disseminating Sodom') seem to me the most personal and most vulnerable writings, even as they stubbornly suture certain fascinations or aversions with literary citations (Barthes, Beckett, Genet, Proust, *et al.*) that make these texts, for me, nearly impenetrable. So I wanted to return to them here, just momentarily, in order to resist my own sense of foreboding (when do we stop performing with a broken heart?), and to wonder aloud, in the context of these notes on *Lovers Fragments*, about Blau's peculiar insistence, when he wrote the piece in 1986, on referring to homosexual practices as 'sodomy' and as potentially monstrous behaviors whose politics or theory are 'threatened by AIDS.'[4] I think we have learnt, after ten years of 'mourning and militancy,' as Douglas Crimp suggested with similar passion, that the epidemic has only strengthened the politics and increased our sexual imagination, necessarily so in the face of death and our justifiedly paranoic rebellions. The dissemination of our strengths contributes to our social security and the social imagination subjected to the perverse ideologies of the conservative civil rights agenda.

Let me return to the winter camp. With *Lovers Fragments* we felt that our challenge to role-playing and the normal operations of production codes rested in the initial decision to remove ourselves from the institution, the city, and the theater altogether. For some of us, the starting-point in the winter landscape, and the first outdoor shoots, represented a quite radical transition to a different mental geography, since we had just returned from a collaborative project in Cuba, in the tropical climate of a socialism on the brink of collapse. Two of our closest friends, Teresa and Nara, gave us a special gift on our last night: since they cannot leave the island, they wanted us to take their poetry along with us to the North.

Perhaps this is how my story began, with Teresa's and Nara's poems that speak of their desires and fantasies, confounding the boundaries (the blockade) between us, our ideologies and genders, affirming our erotic communion, dancing on the waves of our wet dreams, conjuring another time, that time outside of the categories of inside/outside, that time when our moving across borders does not reconstitute the border, once again.

As I walk in the snow, feeling my hands grow stiff and frozen around the camera, I know that boundaries can be moved but they can't be unthought. We always live in geographies of borders, our bodies running up against the relations of space and its (in)visible limitations, against the intersecting connotations of gender, sexuality, race, age and class that they perform or reposition. These borders cross us. As we started running into the snow immodestly, dragging our instruments with us (camera, saxophone, a few found objects, gloves, fantasies), we did not know yet how to get outside the cultural scripts and saturated textures of the erotic, but we were ready to explore the geographies and processes through which images of our erotic fantasies would be produced. We trusted our passions and the seasons, the lack of a controlled environment. I am not sure whether this is the same as 'trying on,' in the sense in which Blau recalls, in 'Disseminating Sodom,' the many attempts he made in 'over thirty years in the theater – and not only in plays by Genet – . . . [to explore] as an occupational hazard every sordid emotion or seeming perversion or enticing deflection of gender, . . . exercises that have involved not only discreet couplings by members of the same sex or trans-vestite versions of the self, but some as free-flowing and polymorphous as Love's Body or as garish as anything bargained for in a leather-and-buckle bar.'[5] In fact, if there's a theatrical predicament in such 'trying on,' I'd wish Blau had elabor-ated on the bargain, as I'd wish to have experienced him in rehearsal, and not in writing.

We became interested in boundary relations, and after shooting film and video in the snow we kept returning to several specific locations during the course of the winter and spring, moving our process of continuously 're-scripting' the images along with the arrival of another season that slowly melted the frozen surfaces, changing the sight-lines, as we relocated the work into the interior, the darkroom, the dance studio, the labyrinthian corridors of an old abandoned hotel in Cleveland, and the editing suite in Chicago. The following refractions of *Lovers Fragments* can be read as 'inserts,' like the ones we use in the editing of our video tracks, assembling the different versions of our dance, our music and the rhythms of our promiscuous fantasies. These inserts are like frames that slip by, phantasms, potential scenes between us that may (not) have taken place.

1. BORDERS OF PHOTOGRAPHY

Greywhite sensitive thin plastic, translucent skin, all the different kinds of hair on the body turned white, the dark mass must be the snow in reverse. Dark snow. Negative tonalities: the shimmering hues of uncanniness.

One of our rehearsal motifs was inspired by Roland Barthes's late writings (*Fragments d'un discours amoureux*; *La chambre claire*), namely his idea of *locating the elusive love object in the photograph* (of his mother).

'I had no hope of "finding" her, I expected nothing from these photographs,' writes Barthes. Shortly after the death of his mother, Barthes finds himself peer-ing into images of a woman 'who was alive *before me* . . .'. 'Did I *recognize* her? . . . According to these photographs, sometimes I recognized a region of her face, a certain relation of nose and forehead, the movement of her arms, her hands. I never recognized her except in fragments.'[6]

Is he suggesting that he could never grasp her full image, or that it is too late now, in retrospect? The scene of a lost scene.

History's divisions, a familiar scene. Barthes speculates that 'history is hyster-ical: it is constituted only if we consider it, only if we look at it – and in order to look at it, we must be excluded from it. As a living soul, I am the very contrary of History, I am what belies it, destroys it for the sake of my own history.'[7]

In our rehearsal process, we are interested in such divisions, and in the performer as a figure or referent of photography as well as of the scenography, the choreography of a presence that is still, moving, or both, always on the borderline between what is here, in the space, and what has been, elsewhere. The intermediary, Barthes suggests, is Death.

> To make oneself up [is] to designate oneself as a body simultaneously living and dead . . . [T]he whitened bust of the totemic theater, the man with the painted face in the Chinese theater, the rice-paste makeup of the Indian Kathakali, the Japanese No Mask . . . Now it is this same relation which I find in the Photograph; however 'lifelike' we strive to make it (and this frenzy to be lifelike can only be our mythic denial of an apprehension of death), Photography is a kind of primitive theater, a kind of *Tableau Vivant*, a figuration of the motionless and made-up face beneath which we see the dead.[8]

Actors/figures in the stage images: they also experience, become aware of images of actors/figures (in the film/projected photography). Which controls which (movement)?

> It all begins with two planes – one black, one white, one positive, one negative. Time stops and starts, shifting the spaces in a slow, segmented motion off-screen. Gradually, the image identifies itself, spatializes. Planes become bodies, fragments of bodies, body parts; space is embodied. A scene of eroticism materializes . . . and dissolves. A confusion of body parts, of caresses, of genders is cast in an aura of mystery and suspense. Framing devices and suspended action hint at in-visible pleasures.[9]

I please myself in pleasing myself.

After the first 'apparition,' it's all about the return of the departed. It is there in black and white . . . At once immobile and cursive, the

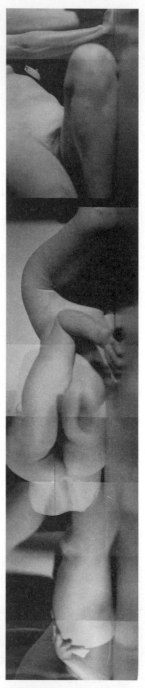

Figure 39 Photographic performance, *Lovers Fragments*, 1995.

question of *genre* takes bodily form, becomes a body which moves about other bodies, the bodies of others. It gives rise, in so many places, to the folly of all desires, without or almost without a word . . . spoken.[10]

Photography articulates the permanent possibility, or the structural necessity, of inversion. Derrida would call it parergonal, with a missing *Mittelglied*. A very unclear genre.

Images refer to each other. The real is only one element among them. The dead, the lost, the distant, the former lover, the 'past' (image) can appear.

Photography's irony: it is a memory/reference to that which is not. 'It' was there, it is not here. Afterimage, temporary hallucination. That has been. . . . And yet, in our performance many of the referents (our bodies our selves) are there and here, will be here, after the image and over the image. Superimpositions, double exposures, triple exposures. Video is a good prosthesis since time doesn't seem to lapse. Video time is *mudunza*, (in)constant and moving, coming back.

The cinema has a power which at first glance the Photograph does not have: the screen is not a frame but a hideout; the man or woman who emerges from it continues living: a 'blind field' constantly doubles our partial vision . . .

The presence (the dynamics) of this blind field is, I believe, what distinguishes the erotic photograph from the pornographic photograph. Pornography ordinarily represents the sexual organs, making them into a motionless object (a fetish), flattered like an idol that does not leave its niche. . . . There is no *punctum* in the pornographic image.

The erotic photograph, on the contrary, does not make the sexual organs into a central object; it may very well not show them at all; it takes the spectator outside its frame, and it is there that I animate this photograph and that it animates me . . .

The *punctum*, then, is a kind of subtle *beyond* – as if the image launched desire beyond what it permits us to see: not only toward 'the rest' of the nakedness, not only toward the *fantasy of a praxis*, but toward the absolute excellence of a being, body and soul together.[10]

A subtle beyond? In our rehearsals we are becoming obsessed, perhaps not (only) with the beyond, but with the relations between the images we made or fantasized, with the perplexing objects before us who are our own bodies, the uncertain memories or half-developed parts of ourselves in the love stories we wanted to compose or recompose. We started the composing in an empty mansion where we met to begin shooting film, not knowing each others' stories or memories.

After shooting still photography and film scenes based on these personal fantasies and memories, we later on began the dance rehearsals, trying to figure out where our stories were moving, where they had begun, and how our differences became intertwined and our fantasies complementary. Figuring the other in the self.

The space (the mansion) itself participates in the fantasy production, [*fantasy of a praxis?*], the recollection of first rooms of love, of imaginary homosexual encounters, of departures and arrivals, of the divided house after the divorce, of events that might have happened, before/below/behind/off the screens of memory.

Zoom in. My gaze tries to fix the image of (my lover/my fantasy).

The figure/actor frames himself/herself. (Identifies with his/her part, or projects it onto another actor, or focuses attention to the edges, the 'off.') The dancer moves too fast, his arms are blurs, seemingly sliding into another body.

We look at our 'footage.' At the negatives, the contact sheets, the prints. The potential development of a possible love story. Photographs as evidence? Of what?

'When I look at you, do you look at me?'

'I'm over it now.'

The body is caught by the camera. Image transfer.

Relations: of body to image, of movement to image movement, of movement to still. Body takes in the image (of itself, of the other, of sexuality-in-terms-of-the-image).

Self-love: an ethical necessity. Playing the part(s) of ourselves in the love story.

Image: it has the power to eroticize (objectify?) the body (against itself?). What if we like being eroticized feeling eroticized, moving, constantly on that edge that animates us (an erotics of transgression: 'the knowledge *between us*'?).[12] The imaginary relations between us, the performers, the filmmakers and dancers and musicians, camera rotating around being exchanged, theater-within-the-studio, the performers performing themselves performing themselves, 'modeling,' taking turns behind the camera, taking layers of clothes off, hiding less than before, laughing at the idea that the image is the means for the alienation of the living body, the other bodies and my own. The bodies have never felt so close, so immediate, in the performance of 'modeling' in the exposure of fantasy. The camera mediates bodily relations. Camera composer. Can one play the camera like an instrument making music to which we move or with which we move?

The animating border is a duplicitous one, that edge where the dominant, proper discourse on performance or acting method tends to break down or become sweaty, where the cultural order that pretends to distinguish between performance/art and pornography (or, as Barthes wants us to believe, between eroticism and pornography), between immobility and the dynamics of the 'blind field', becomes blurred, where we lose, between movement and movement, control over our images and our paradigms. Where the camera becomes unfocussed.

The love story, of course, is our saddest, most mythical and ideologically overburdened paradigm. In the old *Orpheus* operas, the myth is rigidly upheld and also deeply invested in a virulent narcissism and male sado-masochism. Its narrative machinery revolves around the interdiction, the prohibition against looking (back) at the love-object, against touching her [a prohibition which

Atom Egoyan brilliantly recaptures in his last film, *Exotica*, where the bourgeois clients of a striptease bar rehearse their own private (public) sexual and ritual therapies by paying for the 'intimacy' of a table-dancer who remains taboo, inaccessible even if exceedingly close to the gaze, a breath away, always a breath away from loss. In Egoyan's films, video used by the characters often functions as a pathological means of controling the sight/memory of bodies, the arousal and satisfaction of voyeurism, yet the real, tactile body is separated from the visual body that can be seen and manipulated by video technology. Egoyan's Orphic characters seem to have lost the ability to touch other bodies even if video images are there to mediate. Ironically, the video images themselves are always a breath away from fading out, from loss.]

But it is an endlessly repeatable loss, and the music continues, as in Orpheus's unending masochistic lament caught up in the mourning and the production of music, a prototypical production system (fantasies of loss). If you read the old stories to the end, you will find the autoerotic/homoerotic inversion. Mourning transforms.

I remember the comments Elizabeth Wood made a few years back after seeing our *Orpheus and Eurydike* production, namely that one of the more ironic aspects of Orpheus's role in historic opera, his appropriation of siren vocal authority, has been its characterization by a literally unsexed singer, a castrato, who is forever deprived of male potency. And by a delicious redoubling or reversed revoicing, Elizabeth argued, his characterization as the castrato-embodied voice, dismissed by later history, becomes one of the female contralto, the *female Orpheo*. The castrato, the 'borderline male' as Marjorie Garber calls 'him' in *Vested Interests: Cross-Dressing and Cultural Anxiety*, is the artificially constructed non-male representing the female who is a singer. In Orpheus, as myth and opera, a castrato, a transvestic voice, is hiding in the story/score. The castrato-Orpheus oscillates between signifying male and female. The transvestic or castrato voice is an otherworldly sonic androgyny of brilliant, strong, piercing sounds that communicate a sense of danger, an emotional excess, a thrilling readiness to take risks, to go beyond reasonable limits.[13]

What attracted Elizabeth to Orpheus is the shift in performance to the female Orpheo, from castrato contralto to what she calls the 'Sapphonic voice,' the sonic space of lesbian desire. If you remember, Orpheus is killed by an angry vengeful group of women and dismembered, at the end the mythic legend, because they resent him in his demand for love, his preoccupation with his homosexual 'broken heart,' or his 'erotic pessimism' (as Miller describes Barthes's melancholia). The 'Sapphonic' action reclaims voice through resentment, confirming the end of the couple that opera insists in reinvoking with its S/M rituals. This reclaiming transforms into a voice of defiance and desire. Like the castrato, Elizabeth explains, this female voice has a huge vocal range from low chest to high head and falsetto, integrating an exceptional range of registers across the boundaries of different voice types to challenge social and vocal polarities of both gender and sexuality as these are socially and vocally constructed. This refusal of categories and the transgressive risks it takes have a seductive impact on listeners.

Visually, however, this would also unveil a new politics of interpretation and performance. I already mentioned Egoyan's *Exotica* which keeps its family secrets or traumatic core hidden until the end; and in the previous chapter I hinted at the heterosexual blindness in *Fresa y chocolate* that keeps the political obscenity hidden behind its preoccupation with domestic homosexuality. Even more interestingly, we can see this in Patrick Conrad's film *Mascara*, with its continuous and open scenes of queer unmasking, male transvestites costuming as female opera characters who lip-sync their favorite roles, and the masquerade of Pepper dressed as Eurydike who is revealed as a biologically transient, M2F transsexual, who is killed by her enraged male lover. Like Eurydike, she dies when her lover gazes upon her and sees her for whom she really might be.

Examining the soaring music of loss, the 'physiology of opera singing' becomes a 'set of metaphors,' as Wayne Koestenbaum has suggested in his wonderful book *The Queen's Throat: Opera, Homosexuality, and the Mystery of Desire*: 'When we hear an opera, we are listening not only to the libretto and to the music, but to a story about the body, and the story of a journey: the voyage of "voice," traveling out from hiddenness into the world.'[14]

This story is also the story of sexuality. As Koestenbaum would argue, 'voice uplifts and degrades us as forcibly as sexuality does. Voice is a system equal to sexuality – as punishing, as pleasure-giving; as elective, as ineluctable.'[15] I would reconnect the listening experience to the tactile experience of dancing and touching, and of our kinetic identification with the dance. The dance, like the voice of the body, *cures* as it ecstatically reminds us of pleasures and wounds in touching, being touched. The erotic touch confuses and melts the boundaries of the body. In our rehearsals with the musicians, Brazilian composer André Marquetti introduces the saxophone as a transgendering voice, a sound-movement reaching into the most fragile regions of our acoustic perceptions, violating bodily limits. In the act of listening and following the movement of voice and body, we cannot know precisely where an emotion or a sensation begins. Yet our bodies are always coming out, incoherently, in spite of the cultural control systems and psychic economies of denial or repression.

This *incoherence* interests us in the rehearsal process, during the shooting, the dancing, the posing, the pretending, touching and grappling for the images (images of self, images of others, of our love for . . .), during our hectic or sustained debates over the frames (that guarantee the image/memory?), the recordings, the music and the voices. There is no photograph of the voice of the saxophone except if we were to assume that it is mirrored in the bodies' movements. And these movements constitute the comfort of our pleasure-seeking organism, the arousal and endurance of our ever-changing debates leading to new *mudanzas*.

Transfer: from medium to medium, body to body, part to part. Bodies (lovers) are exchangeable, but we don't know that or don't want to know it. If we understand it, we grow to like it.

The other is enclosed (in my fantasy). Rewind image. In the video studio, the sound-track races back with the image-track. It's a high piercing sound.

Figure 40 Photographic performance, *Lovers Fragments*, 1995.

Figure 41 Photographic performance, *Lovers Fragments*, 1995. All rehearsal photographs by Patricia Sotarello.

I am enclosed (rewinding image). But the video is running, frame-by-frame, always in two directions, and thus implies questions about the relationship between video recording and our memory. The running images are always in excess of what I can see, at the moment. What does my body know of video?

I cater to the images others have of me. My 'lover' plays for/in my fantasy, my story, my script (still/moving?) (still moving). I play for his and for hers.

Reciprocal and complicitous. The exchange of looking exchanges the images. A game of criss-crossing. I enjoy it, I enjoy my bisexuality, I can come out with it, it comes out with me. It cannot be adjusted.

Perhaps we are not used/trained to speak about our fluid sexualities in rehearsal, on the stage. We don't have erotic training sessions, although erotic engagement is bodily movement and attentiveness, and thus a vital part of rehearsal, of being fully attentive to the others with whom we are in collective contact. If fluid movement excites us, why would we seek to deny that arousal? What is this unspoken *discours amoureux*? How do we make our body visible to desire? A little less tense and rigid? Hiding or producing differences? '*A would-be prudent silence about the other's body never means that the differences . . . cease at any moment being thought, fantasized, eroticized, spoken.*'[16]

Our preoccupation with differences is incoherent. It is like our sad quests for lost loves, our crossings into otherworlds or back into our own worlds. Voyage of bodies.

> Opera can't achieve the coherence it seeks. This failure makes opera queer, because culture has cast homosexuality (like femininity) as the condition of loss, forgetting and fragmentation.[17]

We collaborate on our fragmented stories, on our incoherence and the pleasure of exceeding the bounds of heterosexual paradigms. This is not a lost scene. It's a sign of health to be mutually interested in each other's wild incoherence. Common assumptions break down, including those about inherent power relationships in film production. Camera does not equal active control, performer does not equal passivity. The excitement about the pleasure of exchange implies that we grow sensitive to the process of shooting and performing with each other, learning to play with closeness and distance and the time it takes to repeat or reframe a scene. The reframing allows us to try out different, alternative scenarios, becoming aware of certain gestures, movements, and the affect of touch, voice, silence. As a group, we grow more confident in exploring various imaginable and unimaginable dimensions of our fantasies and narratives.

We meet in the dance studio or the photo studio and show/tell each other our stories, often without words. In our rehearsals we try to remember what it was that developed, and how we can un-develop the images. Or how we might interpret the filmic images of ourselves, at a later stage, on-stage, off-stage, as figures of our love lives and the strange logic of the rituals we create to explain emotions to us or others. There is an even stranger logic in the way we repeat ourselves, not knowing why we feel love, why we feel loss, and why sexual intimacy or the erotic appear dangerous once we lose control over the projections we make of ourselves.

Is the film the recording or does the dance or the music record something else? Simultaneity of tracking devices? What is the whole story, and can there ever be one story when we stumble, blindfolded, over so many different desires and sexual possibilities?

> It was a game at first. I can't remember now how it began. Perhaps I shed my dress. Perhaps she tore it as we fought. Perhaps we were naked over dinner. Like all games, it was a licence of sorts – a licence to touch. A licence to hurt. A licence to struggle, to resist, to restrain. To keep holding. To cry out. To feel fear. Did you see it happen? The circling, the clinch, the rocking and slaps of flesh. It was real enough at the time. Time after time. Because it never had to stop. No one ever won. No one ever came. No one ever got married, or paid the mortgage. The children never left home, or died in car wrecks. Like in a story, or in memory.

Margaret Werry's monologue (later repeated by Tara) comes half-way through Act I; she has been seen standing on the edge between the abstract, asymmetric steel sculpture (which represents perhaps the real forest we discovered in Wisconsin, or another kind of labyrinth of dreams or entangled threads of stories) and the white screen that closes one side of the upstage area.

She carries a dark coat in her arms, a piece of clothing that is shared by other dancers in the performance, worn by others, used by others to cover their nakedness or their uneasy memory. When she speaks of 'licence' in games and in fiction/memory, she's of course also commenting on the freedom we took to invent or re-create the various individual choreographies of the body's memory. We also saw them as geographies of memory, each particular one connected to an experience of a lover and place in time – reconstituted through the gestures of longing and loss, of irony and reflection, of disavowal and impassioned insistence. Chronicles of places.

> Cada dia regreso a esta playa donde por primera vez me besaste debajo de la luna llena y con el sonido de las olas golpeando contra las rocas y acariciando la arena blanca. Te espero . . .

Catherine Satterwhite, Venezuelan-born actress, reads from the letter she is writing at her little table where she patiently plays a poker game with herself, enacting perhaps what Barthes, in *A Lover's Discourse*, has described as the extreme solitude of the one who loves and waits, engulfed in fantasies fending off the absence of the other. She seems cheerful, her table is the beach.

> Absence can exist only as a consequence of the other: it is the other who leaves, it is I who remain.[18]

Figure 42 Stage rehearsal, *Lovers Fragments*, 1995.

Our performance moves into another direction, deeply into that absence which is not caused (only) by the other but by our own fortunate narcissism, our stubbornness which clings and drives us into the many stories we invent and act out, the scenarios of sexual pleasure that turn us on and cannot be written but are sensed, in the contact of skin and breath, hands sliding over sweat-drenched body muscles nerve-ends nipples, curves of flesh.

Sex for its own sake. Movement born out of passion or a desire too frightening or unexplored or tender to express in words, still grappling with absence and waiting for emotion to be recognizable. How do we know our emotions? Is it a certain rhythm or the lightness or heaviness of touch, weight upon weight, or gravity floating in an invisible color, tasting like the juices of wet tongue savoring tropical fruit? Margaret returns to the stage with a large pineapple, her 'vegetable love,' luscious secret seated inside the mouth, *peso del sabor* ('weight of taste'), yet also carried as a concrete metaphor of displacement, the deviation of her desire, centerpiece of the table at the dinner she later stages for her male and female lovers. A Lezamian banquet filled with operatic splendor. The music she chooses for the banquet is an aria from Johann Strauss's *Die Fledermaus*. It ends with the eruption of boisterous laughter.

Dance for the sake of loving or translating the body into incestuousness: the body cannot be alone. And it blurs all the lines of sexual and gender identities others worry about in their theory or soulless hatred of what they call obscene, dirty, perverse, shameless, imperfect, abject. Or not theoretically rigorous enough for their high standards. Dance for the sake of loving and embracing culturally degraded projections of forbidden love: sweet licence to delve into our own images, nothing to hide except our own awkward force, a strength that allows us to set our own rules, when we dance the tango or invent a triple *pas de deux* or wrestle with each other and the ghost images of our film personae. Our films have become strange mirrors, we are inside and outside at the same time. No mere duplication or refraction but breaks and silences, in the simultaneity of all our stories crossing and departing and never identical. Our kinematics moves like the spurts of the saxophone, a frozen still-image, a sudden turn, a backward glance, hands touching eyes, a fluttering of fingers, a sequence of quick kisses on the ear, the rubbing of necks against each other, the frozen images sliding. Sharing the stage with three other women, Shannon Steen stands alone and sings an old blues song by Billie Holiday, 'I'm gonna love you like no one', and at this point I'm not sure any more how to explain the visibility of touch, since her voice reaches inside us in a way I had never felt before. On our bodies: traces left by voice, the film goes black.

If I can't forget, is that because it never happened?

2. REFLECTIONS IN THE DARKROOM (ACT II)

At first, there are only two males in a group of women with whom I work. We create a piece together, but it's not my piece. The other man, slightly younger than me. I can see myself in him, or should I say that I have tender feelings for him? I can understand how he feels. I'm trying to decipher his movements when I watch him work with the others.

I know the feeling/the illusion of being flattered (being the only man or reduced to being only a man). Feeling desired or desirable or desiring. But what exactly? Desiring without remembering the antagonistic difference between desiring the same and the different? Desiring without possessing. Forgetting what was promised by the image. What was the cause of the image?

Then I begin to see myself as a woman in this strange, slightly older body, enjoying the company and erotic intimacy of the other women. I feel like a lesbian, wish that they would love or desire me as a woman. I imagine the contact of skin, the flesh and the wetness and I desire to be taken or to lose control.

(so what are these lovers fragments we are creating?)

when i wake up i try to imagine the film of that loss of control – how blurred the images would be – how all contours would be hard and blurred at the same time – soft and creamy like skin

Figure 43 Stage rehearsal, *Lovers Fragments*, 1995.

like tongue like dark color – hurt me she said – i couldn't quite do it – then it became a fantasy in reverse – hurt me i would hear myself say – playfully & excitedly.

straight men's awkward sexiness reassures me. there's something completely disarming about certain men trying to be emotional, tender, confessional, intimate. rare event. so we play these even more awkward games. we get drunk. we plan revolutions or new art works. we don't write to each other. we don't admit that the women we fuck don't turn us on. so what exactly is it that turns us on?

what is it about that saxophone (in the forest scene we shot) that became such a crucial object for three people to struggle over, blow into, put into their mouths?

john cook's ghosts in the snow . . . why are these fantasies or memories so hard to film? is it possible to create a composite fantasy in which all congeals? snow looks like a white blur on the screen, without contours. when we project it onto the large screen in the theater, we see nothing.

it's a matter of imaging that which stirs our little destructive and sadistic will which we have been trained to sublimate, deny or compensate (in our impotence). i still love my mother, try forever to evade her disapproving look, her mild, forgiving empathy. being cared for. so i struggle to reject it in any other way. but there are contradictions. i wouldn't like not being cared for. but i've developed this sense of narcissistic balance which i can only keep up when i am feeling the freedom of intimate solitude.

intimacy is the desire to give pleasure.

the pleasure of those who moan or twist their bodies like dancers on a wave rolling over me burying me. so my solitude is actually twisted. i practice dancing every day. how can i lose myself let myself fall let myself drift toward abandonment, while i can still see the control track (safe sex!), while i want nothing more than the risk or the danger of not knowing the consequences, of not knowing where it will go or end, knowing the fascination will end inevitably and begin again inevitably. perhaps. twice behaved behavior (repeating what i know but not always knowing what i repeat and then wanting the unknown or only faintly fantasized. can one desire that which is not fantasized?).

share your fantasies with me.

is this what our film/performance is trying to do? giving the audience something (that's missing and that they have to put into the interrupted scenes) to wrestle with? i am really beginning to like catherine's soft whispered voice, as she is writing this hopelessly romantic love-letter . . . to someone who may or may not exist. meanwhile, we introduce wrestling firmly into our dance rehearsals. margaret is our teacher, but most of us remember how to wrestle since it comes along with childhood. how many boys did I wrestle with?

the soft whispered voice. perhaps that is a form of love. they do this commercially (never had much phone sex, but enjoy voices on the other side of my closed eyes, feeling the skin of touch but not always wanting too much of it, watching myself reacting, waiting for my nipples to harden, sensing my body all over, enjoying my body, loving my body being moved). like dancing, a form of self-sufficiency. while knowing that i'd die if i couldn't touch someone else. my body's fantasies are almost infinite, but i also know that i have lived quite some time not knowing it very well or not allowing it to be whatever it can do. i'm wondering why everybody avoids talking about the erotic in dance. is it undiscussable?

Figure 44 Public performance, *Lovers Fragments*, 1995.

so i observe and learn from others, the dancers with whom i work, whose abandonment and hard passion i know but still experience anew, each time, when the tension rises and the energy spills over and i sense the rush of vulnerability and how that excites me. there's such enormous strength and satisfaction in vulnerability. the unspoken.

i've learnt to wait, because everything happens.

but yesterday i was impatient because i wanted us to work more physically, more concentratedly, full of attention to all there is. a lot is unspoken, between us, and we have tip-toed around the question of how much we'd be willing to do/reveal on stage, right there, in front of everyone, in the light.

film is easier. it seems to have this distance/illusion built in, and we also seem to be more comfortable being naked in front of a camera (strangely so) than in front of each other. why? does the camera (focused on you) turn you on?

so let's talk about pornography and why we like it (or why we still, often, retreat into the evasive theory of the politics of it all, and why we can't risk it, in this context or on that stage, that customary environment of viewing, making spectacles of ourselves, cringing when the laughter comes or the awkward, tense silences.

her tongue on my theory – i love the work of these three canadian artists (kiss & tell), their collaborative coming together to discover their unpredictable bodies interacting to contest prescribed roles and counter the risk of rejection. i love the films of isaac julien, and the visual art work and photography of pratibha parmar, rotimi fani-kayode, lyle ashton-harris, teiji furuhashi, and joel-peter witkin. we need art that promotes the erotic in all of its exuberant, disturbing, riotous and different dimensions. in performance, its collaborative creation is all the more crucial in affirming our choices to lay down our bodies and dances on the line, taking responsibility for what we show in public and under public constraints, for the images we make, own, and disown, and for the fluid, unstable relations between our corporeal bodies and the images we play back. for several years now i've come to understand why i find a certain academic language boring, that correctness of pretended distance/superiority, covering up (the 'coat' image that we like so much) the exhibitionism it shares with much of popular tv culture, the talkshows spilling the guts out, in another coded version of controlled manipulation.

so can we create this strange, intermingling fantasy piece in which our fantasies cross paths, almost inevitably or accidentally, like hilary cooperman's stumbling blindfolded into the two men who just began making love. she wouldn't let go of them. so andré ended up walking away, without his saxophone.

why am i wanting to do this piece at this point in my life? starting out, i wanted to create a work that would be totally affirmative, perhaps even ecstatic, about love and sexuality, the dark bright streaming of the erotic in our movements, our moving the boundaries.

bodies are movement of boundaries. if consciousness of movement is performance, then how conscious are we of those movements we don't know how to do, or don't dare to do, or wish to do but can't? which are those we have abandoned, feel ashamed of, guilty of? and which are the ones we do because they feel guilty?

i like it when men fall in love with me or find me attractive. i like to be in intense creative energy fields, and i enjoy danger. walking a thin line, blurred line, operating on the assumption that sexuality (not alignment) is everywhere. the more experienced one becomes sexually, the more elaborate one's erotic fantasies must get. sex is not a rebellion any more, nor a self-fulfilment or self-empowerment. it's a way of working but that's not the whole story. what is the whole story? i don't know, and i can't afford to be sentimental. sometimes i think that my life is many stories running backward and forward simultaneously. they all make sense.

why is it that in *lovers fragments* i am trying to work backwards? from the end to the beginning? why did we shoot the images first, before knowing what we were doing? so the film is 'developed' (we have photography, for example patricia sotarello's wonderfully slow, careful, increasingly more daring work, and her superimpositions, double-exposures). the other footage on video is 'recorded' and yet *developed* also, because we keep reshooting, adding/ changing situations and spontaneous impulses. i also remember how much i had to laugh when i noticed the 'vampire' scene with mariko ventura, when her image wouldn't show up in the mirror, although i pointed the camera directly at where it should have been. kiss me with those red lips, i'm waiting.

like vampires, our ideas of what we are doing there have no clear, objective boundaries, we mistake them for others. how did we get into this picture! so can one re-develop a picture, un-develop it? why are we setting the clock forward on april 1? why is the time always wrong, and what matters in performance is the timing, as it does on the tbc in video? but the actions cannot be timed yet, we don't really feel ready yet to break down the defenses, the deferrals. we have trouble finding the organic links in the development, between the stories. *are* there any organic desires that intersect when working together, or are our fantasies always strangers?

how come the photographer gets the 'model' to do things that begin to look exciting? can the performer get the photographer to do things that excite the performer, or is the performer always already enjoying the voyeur's illusion. so what are we pretending? why do we revel in our losses? should our piece end with the broken shard that mariko smashes onto the floor? what will happen when margaret slices the pineapple (her 'embryo') and passes out the pieces to the audience?

is all love nostalgia, too sweet like pineapples? do we remember any happy moments of fulfilment, or is that a fantasy too, reaching backwards, because we already know the future won't keep any promises. john brings his collection of tea bags, and writes the names of his lovers on them.

we shoot my wrestling with john, long, extended movement sessions, first they make us breathless, then we enact them with style, as if we were kabuki actors. do i like wrestling because i can pretend to 'lose', and what am i losing? why do i like the strength of the other body so much? i find strength creatively exciting. it's the only way to get used to dying.

3 OUT OF THE FOREST (ACT III)

Recuerdo. El mundo alucinante. La loma del angel. Nadie parecia.

Imma begins her solo dance, on the edge of the stage, accompanied by Weldon Anderson's double bass. He is naked, standing quietly at his instrument, holding it and creating an irregular rhythm, a music that is a series of questions, tones pointing to the images on the screen or to the small steps he sees Imma making. Perhaps these tones come from his body, partly hidden by his instrument. Or has he begun to dance with the bass? The screen images were shot in the abandoned mansion, ghostly corridors, empty rooms with some rubble that was left behind whenever the owners or occupants left. When we were shooting, we found some old newspapers from 1959, and some wedding photographs, smiling faces, uptight body postures. The couples look uncomfortable in their tight festive outfits. The smiles look posed.

Imma's tall body looks twisted, as if in sleep or in dream. Slowly she begins to move, down the slope of the raised stage, across the shadows that are thrown onto the ground by the arms and legs of the forest-sculpture, spider-web. Her lips are painted black.

Her solo touches me in a place I had not even known, but it's not an unpleasant or sad emotion; perhaps that place houses the melancholy warm motion of solitude, the lover's solitude, that I didn't find reading in Barthes's book. His book leaves me cold, because I don't share his sense of dispossession, even as I recognize it as a defense. Imma's dance, which intimates a similar sense of dispossession, of the breaking of the heart, sings to me full of tenderness, the small gestures of her hands signal the caress and the touch we remember as we remember our body. That body is defenseless.

The music slowly dissolves, and the dance ends in stillness. During this gradual fade-out, we hear Imma's voice (recorded) reading Teresa's letter, which took two months to travel from Cuba to the United States, across a surreal border of mutual misunderstanding, intolerance, hysteria, and longing, in search for a shareable memory. During the silence at the end we see Teresa on the filmscreen as she is leaving her house in Alamar, walking toward the beach and into the water. She's here now, with us, and nothing is lost. And nothing is lost.

'La loma del angel' is Reinaldo Arenas's reference to the lost Cuba, insisting that a gay Cuba always existed: *nadie parecia porque todos eran.* In his last book before his death, *Viaje a La Habana,* he returns there, meeting a young man with whom he makes love on the beach, discovering afterwards that he was his son. The voyage home shatters the anxious secret fantasy so obsessively disowned in Egoyan's *Exotica.*

Teresa. Her body caught by the camera, on the edge of the water, standing in the waves under a pink-blue sky, 30 miles east of Havana.

She sings to the ocean, to Yemayá, her goddess of the water. She has a dream. She has forgotten the camera.

Figure 45 Videostills of *La lógica que se cumple*, Alamar (Cuba) 1995.

My desire is swept away by the waves, returning, intensified, making me forget, like in a trance, the sharp-edged rocks on which I balance my feet as I walk further into the ocean, my camera tilting, the sky merging with the surface of the water. Everything becomes a blurry motion in the viewfinder.

My indiscreet narcissism. Cuba is hardly a mirror (of East Germany, of my fantasies of a lost home, a forgotten land, of a memory of my mother, of lost lovers), nor is it a graveyard. I make love with the enemy, our lusts need no translator.

I cannot sustain a gaze, everything begins to blur dangerously, and I am in a kind of trance walking further into the water, the sharp rocks cutting into my naked feet, I don't feel the blood or the pain. Disoriented, I feel that time and duration are erased, I am aroused by a certain pain that feels pleasurable, guilt without recognition, no guilt, a perfect confusion of sense. The problem of eroticism, our initial starting-point, is best solved through further complications; I am in a trance, my imagination thrown off-balance, my skin does not match the body.

The remainder of my ecstasy on the rocky beach in Cuba lives in me throughout the *Lovers Fragments* process A year later we continue our collaboration right in that place where Teresa stood in the waves. Everything is allowed to evolve, the organism of community needs the nourishment of our fluid erotic imaginations, especially in these times of extreme scarcity of hope. Our fragments become *La lógica que se cumple*. During the process of composition, we imagine the beach as undivided territory, space of fantasy in which our performance incorporates the borders that would separate us. The beach is our survival guide. In this space of production we protect and enjoy each other, moving through our stories, literally on the side of a failed utopia, and imagining our physical/emotional sense of solidarity to take on a life of its own. We focus on our relations in performance and the existential situation itself, namely the responsibility all members feel toward the collective process as a unique opportunity of collaboration politically denied to us. Our joint working process becomes a bridge across which we carry our ideas and care for each other. The passion which has characterized this work is precisely born from the need and the will to struggle with the political and geographical obstacles and to show each other our capability to disregard territorial thinking, the spatial separation and its ideological reproductions of a particular violence of displacement, dismemberment, disillusion. The separating border thus becomes the expansion of subjectivities and the transformational re-collection of our bodies and histories. The bridge as a border is the space of transaction and transfer of energies.

The starting-point for the physical work arises from a sequence of twenty-four imagined filmic scenes; each member of the group works as her/his own scriptwriter/performer on the drawing board, imagining scenes in which others from the group could become integrated to produce the actions or narratives. All of these 'personal narratives' are initially conceived without a common ground-plan. Almost simultaneously, however, emerges our interest in moving our subjective images into a circle that includes the earth, the ocean, the flight of birds.

Manuel Avila's poem 'La lógica que se cumple' inspires us to give a more defined shape and direction to our ideas. Gradually, the poem becomes a guide for our creative process and a source of self-reflection on our roles, positions, and perspectives.

The next step consists of the exchange of ideas and proposals; sometimes these ideas are vague, sometimes very concrete, sometimes we develop different versions of the same potential action. This constant process of discussion, feedback, and criticism helps our individual materials to become richer and to gain texture.

We work on location and interact with the different places surrounding the village of Alamar, the seashore, the highway bridge over a river, the vegetation, abandoned industrial sites, ruins and unfinished housing projects. Our interactions with the environment are like small rituals, sensual recognitions of our bodies within the body of nature and the ruins and derelictions of the social. The work gains a spiritual dimension it did not have in Chicago. One day Ana Vega discovers the cadaverous carcass of a dog on the side of the highway, and she incorporates its putrefying remainder into her ceremonial body-paintings. Manuel is constructing a new 'city' on the beach with driftwood and rocks, while Imma composes another image of the remainder of the body/time, turning herself into a human pendulum suspended upside down from the bridge. Felipe Oliva takes up residence in an abandoned, unfinished house to compose new music for the Russian songs Lourdes Vásquez remembers from her days in revolutionary school.

These locations and re-memberings imprint themselves on our imagination, feeding us new ideas for our actions or suggesting ties and threads between the 'characters' we are becoming in our stories. The physical environment gives concrete shape to specific actions or moods. The places of Alamar become subjects in the stories themselves, and our contingent desires grow more fantastic as they resonate with the immanent world which seems crowded with arrested time and signs of a decomposing past. Little by little, and mostly on an imaginary or intuitive level, the collective film 'script' starts to gain shape in a poetic, if not linear or logical, manner, growing larger and more detailed until the day the shooting starts.

We complete the shooting of all twenty-four scenes-on-location in two days. Following a tightly organized shooting schedule, the eight performers prepare the costumes, make-up, and props and work on the physical creation of each scene during an exhausting process that requires a very high concentration and intuitiveness, since all of the actions are created in real time and often in relationship to the others and the demands of the physical environments. Many of the actions, although conceptually based, are driven by spontaneous, highly visceral reflexes or kinaesthetic and emotional explorations of the bodies' relationships both to the immediate and the imaginary landscape of Alamar, Cuba, the ocean. *La lógica que se cumple*, a new 'Lovers Fragments,' in its fragmentary wholeness, manifests the concretized metaphors of a compelling story. It's our story of love collected from touching each other, and from remembering a shared history of unfulfilled possibilities.

NOTES

INTRODUCTION

1. Richard Bolton, ed., *Culture Wars* (New York: New Press, 1992). For the censorship-in-the-arts controversy, see Steven C. Dubin, *Arresting Images: Impolitic Art and Uncivil Actions* (New York: Routledge, 1992).

2. Francis Fukuyama, *The End of History and the Last Man* (New York: Free Press, 1992).

3. Héctor Calderón and José David Saldívar, eds., *Criticism in the Borderlands: Studies in Chicano Literature, Culture and Ideology* (Durham, NC: Duke University Press, 1991); Denis Lynn Daly Heyck, ed., *Barrios and Borderlands: Cultures of Latinos and Latinas in the United States* (New York: Routledge, 1994); bell hooks, *Teaching to Transgress: Education as the Practice of Freedom* (New York: Routledge, 1994); Catherine Ugwu, ed., *Let's Get It On: The Politics of Black Performance* (London: ICA, 1995). Among the growing body of 'border theory,' see José David Saldívar, *The Dialectics of our America* (Durham, NC: Duke University Press, 1991); Neil Larsen, *Reading North by South* (Minneapolis: University of Minnesota Press, 1995); Juan Flores, *Divided Borders: Essays on Puerto Rican Identity* (Houston TX: Arte Público Press, 1993); Emilie L. Bergmann and Paul Julian Smith, eds., *¿Entiendes? Queer Readings, Hispanic Writings* (Durham, NC: Duke University Press, 1995); Rodolfo F. Acuña, *Anything but Mexican: Chicanos in Contemporary Los Angeles* (New York: Verso, 1996); Carl Gutiérrez-Jones, *Rethinking the Borderlands* (Berkeley: University of California Press, 1995); Asunción Horno-Delgado, Eliana Ortega, Nina M. Scott and Nancy Saporta Sternbach, eds., *Breaking Boundaries: Latina Writing and Critical Readings* (Amherst: University of Massachusetts Press, 1989); Ileana Rodríguez, *House/Garden/Nation* (Durham, NC: Duke University Press, 1994); and Carlos G. Vélez-Ibáñez, *Border Visions: Mexican Cultures of the Southwest United States* (Tucson: University of Arizona Press, 1996).

4. John Champagne, *The Ethics of Marginality: A New Approach to Gay Studies* (Minneapolis: University of Minnesota Press, 1995).

5. Guillermo Gómez-Peña, *Warrior for Gringostroika* (Saint Paul, MN: Greywolf Press, 1993), p. 29.

6. Laleen Jamayane and Anne Rutherfod, 'Why a Fish Pond? An Interview with Trinh T. Minh-ha,' *The Independent* (December 1991): 22.

7. Cf. Susan Leigh Foster, ed., *Choreographing History* (Bloomington: Indiana University Press, 1995), pp. 3–21. I am also indebted here to Allen Feldman's ethnography on the victims of political terror: *Formations of Violence* (Chicago: University of Chicago Press, 1991), pp. 6–7. My companion book to the present text was published as *Media and Performance: along the border* (Baltimore, MD: Johns Hopkins University Press, 1998).

8. Judith Butler, *Gender Trouble: Feminism and the Subversion of Identity* (New York: Routledge, 1990), p. 33. Butler's careful attempt to revise her theory of performativity through even more abstract ideational and psychoanalytical models of phantasmatic identification with constraining discursive norms is delineated in *Bodies that Matter: On the Discursive Limits of 'Sex'* (New York: Routledge, 1993).

9. The 'Connected Body?' workshop/conference took place 21–8 August 1994. The event was organized by Scott deLahunta and Ric Allsopp and hosted by SNDO in Amsterdam. The main ideas and workshop discussions were published by Allsopp and deLahunta in *The Connected Body?* (Amsterdam: Amsterdam School of the Arts, 1996).

10. Cf. Slavoy Žižek, *For They Know Not What They Do: Enjoyment as a Political Factor* (New York: Verso, 1991), and Renata Salecl, *The Spoils of Freedom: Psychoanalysis and Feminism after the Fall of Socialism* (New York: Routledge, 1994).

CHAPTER 1: AFTER THE REVOLUTION

1. Citations are from the catalogue, *The River Pierce: Sacrifice II, 13.4.1990*, published by the River Pierce Foundation (San Ygnacio: 1992) and distributed by Rice University Press, pp. 58, 29.

2. Christa Wolf, *Kassandra* (Darmstadt: Luchterhand, 1983), pp. 5–7 (my translation).

3. Catherine Clément, *Opera, Or the Undoing of Women*, trans. Betsy Wing (Minneapolis: University of Minnesota Press, 1988); Susan McClary, *Feminine Endings: Music, Gender, and Sexuality* (Minneapolis: University of Minnesota Press, 1991); Elizabeth Wood, 'Sapphonics: Desire in a Different Voice,' in Philip Brett, Elizabeth Wood, and Gary C. Thomas, eds., *Queering the Pitch: The New Gay and Lesbian Musicology* (New York: Routledge, 1993), pp. 27–66.

4. Klaus Theweleit, *Male Fantasies*, 2 vols., trans. Stephen Conway, Erica Carter, and Chris Turner (Minneapolis: University of Minnesota Press, 1987–9).

5. Trinh T. Minh-ha, *When the Moon Waxes Red: Representation, Gender and Cultural Politics* (New York: Routledge, 1991), p. 107.

6. Homi K. Bhabha, ed., *Nation and Narration* (New York: Routledge, 1990), p. 310.

7. Gloria Anzaldúa, *Borderland/La Frontera: The New Mestiza* (San Francisco: Spinsters/Aunt Lute, 1987), p. 3.

8. Trinh, *When the Moon Waxes Red*, pp. 107–8.

9. Ibid., p. 108.

10. See also Avanthi Meduri, 'Western Feminist Theory, Asian Indian Performance, and a Notion of Agency,' *Women & Performance* 5:2 (1992): 90–103.

11. Theo Angelopoulos, quoted in Andrew Horton's review of 'Ulysses' Gaze,' *Cineaste* 22:1 (1996): 43.

12. Anzaldúa, *Borderlands/La Frontera*, p. 195.

CHAPTER 2: DIALOGUES AND BORDER CROSSINGS

If not otherwise indicated, all direct quotations are transcribed from my recorded (videotaped) conversations.

Prologue: border media

1. Néstor García Canclini, *Culturas híbridas: Estrategias para entrar y salir de la modernidad* (Mexico: Grijalbo, 1990). The book has now appeared in English as *Hybrid Cultures: Strategies for Entering and Leaving Modernity*, trans. Christopher L. Chiappari and Silvia L. López (Minneapolis: University of Minnesota Press, 1995). See pp. 206–63.

2. Homi K. Bhabha, *The Location of Culture* (New York: Routledge, 1994), p. 1.

3. Gloria Anzaldúa, *Borderlands/La Frontera: The New Mestiza* (San Francisco: Spinsters/ Aunt Lute, 1987), p. 78.

1. Fronteras: from the local to the translocal

2. performing postcolonial history

1. Stuart Hall, 'What Is This "Black" in Black Popular Culture?', in Gina Dent, ed., *Black Popular Culture* (Seattle, WA: Bay Press, 1992), p. 32.

2. See Chapter 5.

3. Celeste Olalquiaga, *Megalopolis: Contemporary Cultural Sensibilities* (Minneapolis: University of Minnesota Press, 1992), pp. 53–4. For recent discussions and appropriations of the border topos, see George Yudice, Jean Franco and Juan Flores, eds., *On Edge: The Crisis of Contemporary Latin American Culture* (Minneapolis: University of Minnesota Press, 1992); Bhabha, *The Location of Culture*; Mae Henderson, ed., *Borders, Boundaries, and Frames* (New York: Routledge, 1995); Henry Giroux, *Border Crossings* (New York: Routledge, 1992); Paul Gilroy, *The Black Atlantic: Modernity and Double Consciousness* (Cambridge, MA: Harvard University Press, 1993). For a study of postcolonial consciousness in the Caribbean, see Antonio Benítez-Rojo, *The Repeating Island* (Durham, NC: Duke University Press, 1992). For the Mexican context, see also Canclini, *Culturas híbridas*.

4. Coco Fusco's trenchant critique and ethnographic reading of audience reactions to the cage performance have now been published, together with other essays and interviews, in her book *English Is Broken Here: Notes on Cultural Fusion in the Americas* (New York: The New Press, 1995).

5. For a critical assessment of transnational corporatism hidden behind the smoke-screen of current debates over 'multiculturalism' or 'the postcolonial experience' (Bhabha), see Masao Miyoshi, 'A Borderless World? From Colonialism to Transnationalism and the Decline of the Nation-State,' *Critical Inquiry* 19:4 (Summer 1993): 726–51. For a brilliant discussion of the complex issue of citizenship in the new Europe, see Michel Wieviorka, 'Violence, Culture and Democracy: A European Perspective,' *Public Culture* 8:2 (1996): 329–54. This entire issue of *Public Culture* is dedicated to local/global approaches to 'Cities and Citizenship' from different international perspectives.

Additional References

Luis Camnitzer, *New Art of Cuba* (Austin: University of Texas Press, 1994).
Coco Fusco, 'Hustling for Dollars,' *Ms.* VII: 2 (1996): 62–70.
Guillermo Gómez-Peña, 'The Free Art Agreement/El Tratado de Libre Cultura,' in *The Subversive Imagination*, ed. Carol Becker (New York. Routledge, 1994).
——, *Warrior for Gringostroika* (Saint Paul: Greywolf Press, 1993).
——, 'The New World (B)Order,' *High Performance* 58/59 (1992): 58–65.
Gerardo Mosquera, 'Modernidad y Africania,' *Third Text* 20 (1992): 43–68.
Celeste Olalquiaga, *Megalopolis: Contemporary Cultural Sensibilities* (Minneapolis: University of Minnesota Press, 1992).

3. Grenzland

4. transcentrala

Rabia Ali and Lawrence Lifschultz, eds., *Why Bosnia? Writings of the Balkan War* (Stony Creek, CT Pamphleteer's Press, 1993).
Jean Baudrillard, *Fatal Strategies*, trans. Philip Beitchman and W. G. J. Niesluchowski (New York: semiotext(e), 1990).
Johannes Birringer, 'The Utopia of Postutopia,' *Theater Topics* 6:1 (1996): 143–66.
——, 'Transcentrala – Na sončni strani Alp,' *Canadian Slavonic Papers/Revue canadienne des slavistes* 36:3–4 (1994): 449–66.
Ales Debeljak, *Twilight of the Idols: Recollections of a Lost Yugoslavia* (New York: White Pine Press, 1995).
Bogdan Denitch, *Ethnic Nationalism: The Tragic Death of Yugoslavia* (Minneapolis: University of Minnesota Press, 1994).
Ales Erjavec and Marina Gržinič, *Ljubljana, Ljubljana: The Eighties in Slovene Art and Culture* (Ljubljana: Zalošba Mdladinska knjga, 1991).
Marina Gržinič, 'The Alternative Scene and Civil Society in Slovenia.' Unpublished paper, 1994.
Emil Hrvatin, 'The Reterritorializing Gaze,' *Maska* V: 1–3 (1995): xxi–xxv.
Irwin-NSK Embassy Moscow Project: How the East Sees the East, ed. Eda Čufer (Koper: Loža Gallery, 1992).
Branka Magas, *The Destruction of Yugoslavia* (London: Verso, 1993).
Tomaž Mastnak, 'A Journal of the Plague Years/Dnevnik kužnih godina,' *Lusitania* 5 (1993): 83–92.
David Rieff, *Slaughterhouse: Bosnia and the Failure of the West* (New York: Simon & Schuster, 1995).
Paul Virilio, *Estetica de la desaparición* (Barcelona: Editorial Anagrama, 1988).
Slavoy Žižek, *Tarrying with the Negative* (Durham, NC: Duke University Press, 1993).

5. bloqueo/resistencia

I would like to thank the Cuban artists for permission to quote from their texts and our conversations, and for their helpful comments. For reasons of space limitation, it was not possible to publish all of the conversations and notes I exchanged with Cuban writers, directors, filmmakers and visual artists participating in the Havana Bienal and the Havana International Film Festival. I established a close association with documentary filmmaker Rigoberto López, whose films are not generally accessible in the USA He has asked me to help distribute them. I would like to share the Cuban materials, and if you have down-link capabilities, please contact me via email. There are two possible addresses. The first is: orpheus@rice.edu The second is: birringer.1@osu.edu

Víctor Varela's play, *El Arca*, has now been published in the USA, with introduction by Alicia del Campo, in *Gestos* 22 (1996): 123–60.

Additional References:

Ruth Behar, ed., 'Puentes a Cuba/Bridges to Cuba,' 2 vols, special issues of *Michigan Quarterly Review* 33:3–4(1994).

Antonio Benítez-Rojo, *The Repeating Island* (Durham, NC: Duke University Press, 1992).

Johannes Birringer, 'Homosexuality and the Nation: An Interview with Jorge Perugorría,' *TDR* 40:1 (1996): 61–76.

Luis Camnitzer, *New Art of Cuba* (Austin: University of Texas Press, 1994).

Néstor García Canclini, *Culturas híbridas: Estrategias para entrar y salir de la modernidad* (Mexico: Grijalbo, 1990).

Coco, Fusco, *English is Broken Here* (New York: New Press, 1995).

Guillermo, Gómez-Peña, *Warrior for Gringostroika* (Saint Paul: Greywolf Press, 1993);

——, *The New World Border* (San Francisco: City Lights, 1996).

Lillian Manzor-Coats, 'Performative Identities: Scenes between Two Cubas,' *Michigan Quarterly Review* 33·4 (1994): 748–61.

Randy Martin, *Socialist Ensembles: Theater and State in Cuba and Nicaragua* (Minneapolis: University of Minnesota Press, 1994).

Gerardo Mosquera, 'Modernidad y Africania,' *Third Text* 20 (1992): 43–68.

——, 'The 14 Sons of William Tell,' in *No Man Is an Island: Young Cuban Art*, ed. Marketta Seppälä. Exhibition catalogue (Pori: Pori Art Museum, 1990), 42–49.

——, 'The New Art of the Revolution,' in *The Nearest Edge of the World: Art and Cuba Now*. Exhibition catalogue for Massachusetts College of Art (Boston, MA: Polarities Inc., 1990), pp. 8–11.

——, *Exploraciones en la plástica cubana* (Havana: Editorial Letras Cubanas, 1983).

CHAPTER 3: MAKROLAB: A HETEROTOPIA

1. Michel Foucault, 'Of Other Spaces,' *Diacritics* 16:1 (Spring 1986): 23–4. See also *Politics-Poetics: documenta X – the book*, ed. documenta (Kassel: Cantz Verlag, 1997), pp. 262–83.

CHAPTER 4: THE TRANSCULTURAL IMAGINARY, OR STANDING WITH THE NATIVES

1. Quoted from the official program invitation to the 'Meeting Grounds' symposium, Chicago Cultural Center, 12–13 November 1993, organized by Robert Peters and produced by Randolph Street Gallery in conjunction with Sculpture Chicago. I wish to thank Bob Peters and Peter Taub for their encouragement. All quotations from the symposium are drawn from the program or my notes and video transcripts. I was invited by the organizers to document the event and to respond to the discussion. My videotapes of *Meeting Grounds* are freely accessible through RSG and are in the public domain.

2. Michael Taussig, *Mimesis and Alterity: A Particular History of the Senses* (New York: Routledge, 1993), p. 1. For Taussig's impressive writings on terror, violence, resistance and the fetish-power of the nation-state in the aftermath of colonial conquest, see his *The Nervous System* (New York: Routledge, 1992). For an incisive interpretation of the collecting and performing of 'authentic culture' for tourism, see Barbara Kirshenblatt-Gimblett, 'Objects of Ethnography,' in *Exhibiting Cultures*, ed. Ivan Karp and Steven D. Lavine (Washington, DC: Smithsonian Institution Press, 1991), pp. 386–443.

3. Cf. Alberto Pedro and Rogelio Martínez-Furé, quoted in Ivor Miller, *Belief and Power in Contemporary Cuba: The Dialogue between Santería Practitioners and Revolutionary Leaders*, PhD dissertation, Northwestern University (1995), pp. xviii–xx. I am in Miller's debt for his richly inspiring observations of contemporary Cuban culture and for his introducing me to the *ambiente* of the old neighborhoods in Havana. For a rigorous feminist reading of the ideologies of the Cuban national multiculture, see Vera M. Kutzinski, *Sugar's Secrets: Race and the Erotics of Cuban Nationalism* (Charlottesville: University Press of Virginia, 1993).

4. Cf. Diane Taylor, 'Transculturating Transculturation,' in *Interculturalism and Performance*, ed. Bonnie Marranca and Gautam Dasgupta (New York: PAJ Publications, 1991), pp. 60–74.

5. Fernando Ortiz, *Cuban Counterpoint: Tobacco and Sugar*, trans. Harriet de Onís (Durham, NC: Duke University Press, 1995[1947]), pp. 97–103.

6. Interview with Inés María Martiatú during the CONJUNTO 1994 meeting of theater researchers at the Casa de las Américas in Havana [my translation]. Her interpretation of the elite nationalist ideology of transculturation is also expressed in 'Mayoria étnica y minoría cultural,' *Tablas* (1993): 44–59. For a strong critique of the privileging of a general postcolonial cultural theory that abandons historical questions of specific determinations of domination, see Aijaz Ahmad, *In Theory: Classes, Nations, Literatures* (New York: Routledge, 1990); Román de la Campa, E. Ann Kaplan, and Michael Sprinker, eds., *Late Imperial Culture* (London: Verso, 1995); and Arif Dirlik, 'The Postcolonial Aura: Third World Criticism in the Age of Global Capitalism,' *Critical Inquiry* 20:2 (1994): 328–56.

7. See, for example, James Clifford, 'Four Northwest Coast Museums: Travel Reflections,' in *Exhibiting Cultures*, ed. Karp and Lavine, pp. 212–54. For a provocative new investigation of the relation between art and anthropology and the politics of displaying/consuming difference, see George E. Marcus and Fred R. Myers, ed., *The Traffic in Culture* (Berkeley: University of California Press, 1995).

8. Molly H. Mullin, 'The Patronage of Difference: Making Indian Art "Art, Not Ethnology,"' in Marcus and Myers, *The Traffic in Culture*, p. 183.

9. Ulrich Beck maintains in *Die Risikogesellschaft* that late industrial society is characterized by the 'over-accumulation' of risks, from which nobody is ultimately immune. It can no longer explain environmental threats or genetic harms through the paradigm of economic or class analysis; while hunger or poverty is hierarchical, nuclear contamination is not. Chernobyl exemplifies the transborder effects of technological accidents, disregarding national sovereignties or political-military policies of the old nation-states. If risk societies indicate global phenomena, this will necessitate new trans-state security systems, while the local Sami protests point precisely to their disagreements over how 'risk management' is constituted by administrative rationales or cost-benefit analyses. See *The Risk Society: Towards a New Modernity*, trans. Mark Ritter (London: Sage, 1992).

10. Cf. Trinh T. Minh-ha, *When the Moon Waxes Red: Representation, Gender, and Cultural Politics* (New York: Routledge, 1991), pp. 65–78.

11. Eugenio Barba, *The Paper Canoe: A Guide to Theater Anthropology*, trans. Richard Fowler (New York: Routledge, 1995), pp. 47, 9.

12. Eric Michaels, *Bad Aboriginal Art: Tradition, Media, and Technological Horizons*

(Minneapolis: University of Minnesota Press, 1994). See especially his breathtaking essay/
performance in 'Aboriginal Content: Who's Got It – Who Needs It?', pp. 20–46.

13. Ibid., p. 120.

14. Ibid., p. xxxvi.

15. Granada Television, part of the UK's Independent Television Network, initiated the
    Disappearing Worlds series of anthropological documentaries in 1970, and by 1992 it had
    produced more than fifty one-hour programs which enjoyed large popular success in
    Britain. Ethnographers played important roles in the production of the series, shifting its
    initial bias from social documentary toward an anthropological *cinéma verité* style
    ostensibly influenced by Jean Rouch and the Malinowskian tradition of presenting the
    non-Western world from the native's point of view. For a special selection of essays on
    Disappearing Worlds, see *Visual Anthropology Review* 8:1 (1992). I also found out that
    Brazilian and European camera teams had visited the Kayapo region already in the 1970s
    to extract images of indigenous culture and sell them commercially. The Kayapo stopped
    cooperating in the late 1970s, and drew attention to their struggle against the invasiveness
    of devastating development projects in the Amazons by staging the so-called 'Raft War' in
    1984, portraying themselves as aggressive and dangerous to capture the interest of Brazil-
    ian media. The Kayapo's resistance also explains the circumstances of Turner's gifts to the
    Kayapo (the communities demanded cameras, VCRs, monitors, and tapes as the *quid pro
    quo* for their cooperation with the British film crews). Shortly afterwards, Chief Ropni and
    another Kayapo leader, Payakan, established the 'Kayapo Foundation' with the objective
    of establishing a program to document, on videotape, traditional knowledge of the forest
    environment and other aspects of cultural history and myth, ceremonies, and oratory by
    community leaders. These tapes were to be used as education for the young people, as a
    method of preserving cultural knowledge and also of sharing the ecological concerns with
    Brazilian and international scholars or interested audiences. Turner returned several times
    to the Kayapo communities to help out with equipment and with providing access to
    editing facilities in São Paulo; some of the equipment was sponsored by grants from the
    US-based Spencer Foundation. Turner more extensively describes the process and his
    interpretation of the Kayapo use of media in 'Visual Media, Cultural Politics and Anthro-
    pological Practice,' *The Independent* 14:1 (1991): 34–40. For a praxis-oriented, political
    analysis by Brazilian independent filmmakers from the Mekaron Opoi D'joi [He Who
    Creates Images] Project, see Monica Frota, 'Taking Aim: The Video Technology of Cul-
    tural Resistance,' in *Resolutions: Contemporary Video Practices*, ed. Michael Renov and
    Erika Suderburg (Minneapolis: University of Minnesota Press, 1996), pp. 258–82. Frota's
    account differs from Turner's, especially since she is more directly concerned with the
    interactive relations of production and the social role of the camera (as a tool belonging to
    the male sphere).

16. Turner, 'Visual Media,' p. 39.

17. Arjun Appadurai, in addressing the 'central problematic of cultural processes in today's
    world,' argues that the 'world we live in now seems rhizomic (Deleuze/Guattari), even
    schizophrenic, calling for theories of rootlessness, alienation and psychological distance
    between individuals and groups, on the one hand, and fantasies (or nightmares) of elec-
    tronic propinquity on the other.' See his 'Disjuncture and Difference in the Global
    Cultural Economy,' *Public Culture* 2:2 (1990): 1–24. While native peoples like the
    Kayapo or the Australian Aborigines would precisely insist on not being displaced, critical
    theory, ethnography, and the Western art world have complemented each other in the
    recent incorporation of Aboriginal culture into the metropolitan exhibition and promo-
    tion of 'Aboriginality.' The first major controversy arose over the 1984 MoMA exhibit on

'"Primitivism" in 20th Century Art: Affinity of the Tribal and the Modern,' and James Clifford has examined the débâcle at length in *The Predicament of Culture*. (Cambridge, MA: Harvard University Press, 1988). In 1989, Paris followed suit with its global 'spectacular primitive' exhibition, *Magiciens de la terre* (Centre Pompidou), which celebrated the mystical or spiritual affinities of works brought in from all over the world and put together side by side. The controversy over the construction of a global postmodern 'magical primitivism' is well documented in several issues of the London-based journal *Third Text*. For some of the major positions in the ongoing theoretical arguments against a facile 'post'-colonial theory of hybridity and global culture, see especially Michaels, 'If "All Anthropologists are Liars . . ."', in *Bad Aboriginal Art*, pp. 126–40; Fred R. Myers, 'Representing Culture: The Production of Discourse(s) for Aboriginal Acrylic Paintings,' in Marcus and Myers, *The Traffic in Culture*, pp. 55–95; Faye Ginsburg, 'Indigenous Media: Faustian Contract or Global Village?', *Cultural Anthropology* 6:1 (1991): 92–112; Anne McClintock, 'The Angel of Progress: Pitfalls of the Term "Post-Colonialism,"' *Social Text* 31/32 (1992): 84–98; and Ruth Frankenberg and Lata Mani, 'Crosscurrents, Crosstalk: Race, "Postcoloniality" and the Politics of Location,' *Cultural Studies* 7:2 (1993). See also Kwame Nkrumah, *Neo-Colonialism: The Last Stage of Imperialism* (London: Nelson, 1965); John Tomlinson, *Cultural Imperialism* (Baltimore, MD: Johns Hopkins University Press, 1991); Peter Ian Crawford and David Turton, eds., *Film as Ethnography* (Manchester: Manchester University Press, 1992); Ella Shohat and Robert Stam, *Unthinking Eurocentrism* (New York: Routledge, 1994); Homi K. Bhabha, *The Location of Culture* (New York: Routledge, 1994); Partha Chatterje, *Nationalist Thought and the Colonial World* (Minneapolis: University of Minnesota Press, 1993); Rey Chow, *Writing Diaspora: Tactics of Intervention in Contemporary Cultural Studies* (Bloomington: Indiana University Press, 1993); V. Y. Mudimbe, *The Invention of Africa* (Bloomington: Indiana University Press, 1988): and Gayatri Chakravorty Spivak, *Outside in the Teaching Machine* (New York: Routledge, 1993).

18. Cf. Oswald de Andrade, *Do Pau-Brasil e Antropofagia as Utopias* (Rio de Janeiro: Civilizacao Brasileira, 1972). I am indebted to Bruno Campos for this reference. For a more extensive contextualization of the Brazilian aesthetics of 'cannibalism,' see Shohat and Stam, *Unthinking Eurocentrism*, pp. 302–18.

19. Bhabha, *The Location of Culture*, p. 86 [italics in original].

20. Ibid., p. 91.

21. Guillermo Gómez-Peña, 'From Art-Maggedon to Gringostroika: A Manifesto against Censorship,' in *Mapping the Terrain: New Genre Public Art*, ed. Suzanne Lacy (Seattle, WA: Bay Press, 1995), p. 108.

22. Contrary to the notion, propagated by 'post'-colonial theorists, that we have reached the end of history or ideology in the global moment of the expansion of capitalism and neoliberalism, the Chiapas uprising in1994 was only the most dramatically effective political mobilization among a range of Latin American indigenous movements. A recent issue of *NACLA: Report on the Americas* (March/April 1996) describes growing political grass-roots movements in Chiapas, Bolivia, Colombia, Ecuador, Chile, Guatemala, and Brazil.

23. My argument here is indebted to the online discussion in the *Public Culture* Cyber-Salon, in response to the issue on 'Cities and Citizenship' and especially to Teresa P. R. Caldeira, 'Fortified Enclaves: The New Urban Segregation,' *Public Culture* 8:2 (1996): 303–28, and Michel Wieviorka, 'Violence, Culture and Democracy: A European Perspective,' *Public Culture* 8:2 (1996): 329–54.

CHAPTER 5: LA MELANCOLÍA DE LA JAULA

I would like to thank the Cuban artists for permission to quote from their texts and our conversations, and for their inspiring comments. I would especially like to thank Rosa Ileana Boudet and Vivian Martínez Tabares for inviting me to CONJUNTO 94, and Maris Bustamante for sharing her insights into Mexican performance.

1. See Coco Fusco, *English Is Broken Here: Notes on Cultural Fusion in the Americas* (New York: New Press, 1995); Gerardo Mosquera, 'Modernidad y Africania,' *Third Text* 20 (1992): 43–68; Diana Taylor and Juan Villegas, eds., *Negotiating Performance: Gender, Sexuality, and Theatricality in Latin/o America* (Durham, NC: Duke University Press, 1994), and Paul Gilroy, *The Black Atlantic: Modernity and Double Consciousness* (Cambridge, MA: Harvard University Press, 1993). For a study of postcolonial consciousness in the Caribbean, see Antonio Benítez-Rojo, *The Repeating Island* (Durham, NC: Duke University Press, 1992).

2. Celeste Olalquiaga, *Megalopolis: Contemporary Cultural Sensibilities* (Minneapolis: University of Minnesota Press, 1992), pp. 76–91. See also Néstor García Canclini, *Culturas híbridas: Estrategías para entrar y salir de la modernidad* (Mexico: Grijalbo, 1990).

3. Inés María Martiatú, 'Mayoría étnica y minoría cultural,' *Tablas* (1993), 44–59; cf. William Rowe and Vivian Schelling, *Memory and Modernity: Popular Culture in Latin America* (London: Verso, 1993), pp. 164–5.

4. This brief overview is indebted to conversations I had with artists at the CONJUNTO, to the lectures and writings of Rosa Ileana Boudet and Vivian Martínez Tabares, and to the research published by Randy Martin in 'Cuban Theater Under Rectification,' *TDR* 34:1 (1990): 38–59.

5. The idea for EECIT originated in the collaboration of the members of CELCIT (Centro Latinoamericano de Creacion e Investigación Teatral), an association whose main office is currently located in Spain (after a residency in Venezuela) and directed by Luis Molina. EECIT constituted itself in 1988 during a reunion meeting at the Festival Internacional de Teatro in Bogota. At the present time, EECIT includes the following journals: Espacio, *Teatro 2, Teatro-CELCIT* (Argentina); Revista de *teatro* (Brazil); *Gestus* (Colombia); *Conjunto, Tablas* (Cuba); *ADE, Entreacte, Primer Acto, Puck* (Spain); *Gestos, Latin American Review, Ollantay Theater Magazine* (USA); *Mascara, Repertorio* (Mexico); *Cuadernos* (Portugal); *Theatron, Yanama* (Venezuela).

6. Cf. Melissa A. Lockhart, '*Beijo no asfalto* and Compulsory Heterosexuality,' *Gestos* 17 (1994): 147–58, and Lillian Manzor-Coats, 'Performative Identities: Scenes between Two Cubas,' *Michigan Quarterly Review* 33:4 (1994): 748–61.

7. Interview with Jorge Perugorría, Havana, 29 May 1994. A fuller version of our dialogue titled 'Homosexuality and the Nation' appeared in *TDR* 40:1 (1996): 61–76. Reinaldo Arenas's autobiography, *Antes que anochezca*, is now available in English as *Before Night Falls*, trans. Dolores M. Koch (New York: Penguin, 1994). For the passages on his childhood, see esp. pp.1–65.

8. In his preface, 'Piñera teatral,' Virgilio Piñera introduces his plays (*Teatro completo*, 1960) by ironically speaking of the 'unveiling' of his 'masks' while referring to himself as a character in the massive 'theatricality' of the new social revolution. For a provocative reading of Piñera's later silence on the repression of his homosexuality, see José Quiroga, 'Fleshing Out Virgilio Piñera from the Cuban Closet,' in Emilie Bergmann and Paul

Julian Smith, eds., ¿Entiendes? Queer Readings, Hispanic Texts (Durham, NC: Duke University Press, 1995), pp. 168–80.

CHAPTER 6: LOVERS FRAGMENTS: TOWARDS A NEW PERFORMANCE EROS

All illustrations in this chapter are taken from the rehearsal photography and production videos of *Lovers Fragments*, created by AlienNation Co. in 1995. Photos/videostills: Craig Roberts, Mariko Ventura, Imma Saries-Zgonc, Patricia Sotarello, Johannes Birringer. (c) AlienNation Co. 1995. Verbal citations from the performance refer to Margaret Werry and Catherine Satterwhite.

1. Herbert Blau, *The Eye of Prey: Subversions of the Postmodern* (Bloomington: Indiana University Press, 1987), p. 183.

2. Blau citing Roland Barthes, *The Eye of Prey*, pp. 93–4.

3. David M. Halperin, *Saint Foucault. Towards a Gay Hagiography* (New York: Oxford University Press, 1995), p. 62.

4. Blau, *The Eye of Prey*, p. 106.

5. Ibid., p. 131.

6. Roland Barthes, *Camera Lucida: Reflections on Photography*, trans. Richard Howard (New York: Hill & Wang, 1981), pp. 63–5.

7. Ibid., p. 65.

8. Ibid., p. 31–2.

9. Jonathan Milder and Margaret Werry, 'Lovers Fragments: A Re-presentation.' Unpublished manuscript, 1995, p. 1.

10. Jacques Derrida and Marie-Françoise Plissart, 'Right of Inspection,' trans. David Wills, *Art & Text* 32 (1989): 34.

11. Barthes, *Camera Lucida*, pp. 55–9.

12. Cf. D. A. Miller, *Bringing Out Roland Barthes* (Berkeley: University of California Press, 1992), p. 6.

13. Elizabeth Wood, 'The Future of Opera,' Transcript of a symposium, coordinated and edited by Johannes Birringer, Northwestern University, 1992, pp. 9–12.

14. Wayne Koestenbaum, *The Queen's Throat: Opera, Homosexuality, and the Mystery of Desire* (New York: Poseidon, 1993), p. 155.

15. Ibid.

16. Miller, *Bringing Out Roland Barthes*, p. 42.

17. Koestenbaum, *The Queen's Throat*, p.179.

NOTES

277

18. Roland Barthes, *A Lover's Discourse: Fragments*, trans. Richard Howard (New York: Hill &
Wang, 1984), p.13.

Additional References

Reinaldo Arenas, *El mundo alucinante* (Mexico: Diógenes, 1969).
——, *La loma del angel* (Miami: Mariel, 1987).
——, *Viaje a La Habana* (Novela en tres viajes) (Miami: Universal, 1990).
Roland Barthes, *Incidents*, trans. Richard Howard (Berkeley: University of California Press, 1992).
Leo Bersani, *Homos* (Cambridge, MA: Harvard University Press, 1995).
Herbert Blau, *Take Up the Bodies: Theater at the Vanishing Point* (Urbana: University of Illinois Press, 1982).
——, *Blooded Thought: Occasions of Theater* (New York: PAJ Publications, 1982).
Judith Butler, *Bodies That Matter: On the Discursive Limits of 'Sex'* (New York: Routledge, 1993).
Douglas Crimp, 'Mourning and Militancy,' *October* 51 (1990): 3–18.
Jacques Derrida, *The Truth in Painting*, trans. Geoff Bennington and Ian McLeod (Chicago: University of Chicago Press, 1987).
Michel Foucault, *The History of Sexuality*, Volume I: *An Introduction*, trans. Robert Hurley (New York: Pantheon, 1978).
——, *Power/Knowledge: Selected Interviews and Other Writings, 1972–1977*, ed. Colin Gordon (New York: Pantheon, 1980).
Marjorie Garber, *Vested Interests: Cross-Dressing and Cultural Anxiety* (New York: Routledge, 1992).
Juan Goytisolo, *Cuaderno de Sarajevo* (Madrid: El Pais/Aguilar, 1993).
Deborah Hay, *Lamb at the Altar: The Story of a Dance* (Durham, NC: Duke University Press, 1994).
Kiss & Tell, *Her Tongue on My Theory: Images, Essays, and Fantasies* (Vancouver: Press Gang Publishers, 1994).

INDEX

abstraction, 107
ACT UP, 194
Afrika, Sergei Bugaev, 58
AIDS, 15, 17–8, 30, 38, 68, 133, 240, 246;
  and activism, 14, 18, 38, 68, 243, 246;
  and performance, 38; and video, 68
Alamar, 127, 264–6
Alea, Tomás Gutiérrez, 124, 169, 222–3,
  227, 235
AlienNation Co., 6–23 passim;, 33–4, 55–8,
  63, 240–66; AD MORTEM, xiii, 17;
  AlienNation, 45–6, 53–4, 89, 94, 97, 101,
  128, 244; *Before Night Falls*, xiii, 61;
  Between the Places, 62; *bewegungen in der
  mitte der dritten stadt (ort 1)*, 59–61;
  Border-Land, xvi, 8, 10, 24–8, 39, 53, 59,
  65, 89; *La lógica que se cumple*, xiii, 57, 61,
  265–6; LBLM, 58, 62; *Lovers Fragments*,
  xiii, 21, 54–5, 58–9, 61, 240–66; *migbot*,
  xii, 62–3; *North by South*, xiii, 62; *Orpheus
  and Euyrike*, xiii, 28–33, 241, 251;
  Parachute, xiii, 62–6; *Parsifal*, xiii–xiv,
  55–8; *Vespucci*, xiii, 63–4
Allsopp, Ric, xii, 21
Almendros, Néstor, 226–7
Alvarez, Pedro, 81
Angelopoulos, Theo, 64–6; *Ulysses' Gaze*,
  65
anthropology, 73, 165, 188, 196–7; and
  postmodern ethnography, 23, 72, 78,
  164–5, 188–9, 196, 209
anthropophagy, 202–3
Anzaldúa, Gloria, 34, 65, 69, 78, 177–8
Arenas, Reinaldo, 234, 236, 263–4; *Antes que
  anochezca*, 236
Armand, Octavio, 234
Arnautalić, Ismet, 111, 242
art, 19, 38, 48–53, 71–3, 79–80, 85, 109,
  135–6, 149–59, 175, 180–3, 208, 211,
  224-, 6; and economy, xvii, 74–5, 80,
  163, 180–3, 205–8; indigenous, 181;

installation, 48–53, 82; interactive
  technologies, xv, 64; and politics, 38,
  48–9, 85, 109–23, 174–5; and trade, xvii,
  79, 163–5, 180–3, 225; *Volumen I*, 79,
  135
Asaltodiario, 211, 214
Ashton-Harris, Lyle, 262
Avila, Manuel, 57, 265
Avalos, David, 165, 178, 205–8, 221; 'Arte
  Reembolso/Art Rebate,', 206–8; *Birth of a
  mis-ce-ge-NATION*, 221
avant-garde, the, 5, 45, 106, 119, 154, 202
Azor, Ileana, 229, 233

Baker, Josephine, 44
ballet, 96, 105–8, 133, 228; and
  Cosmokinetic Cabinet, 106–08; *See also*
  dance
Barba, Eugenio, 44, 179, 189–90, 229; and
  third theatre, 189–90
Barrientos, Barbara Maria, 138, 142–3, 145,
  230
Barroso, Abel, 79, 225
Barthes, Roland, 240, 244–51 passim, 256,
  263
Bartra, Roger, 219
Baudrillard, Jean, 104
Bausch, Pina, xiii
Beck, Ulrich, 187, 272n9
Beckett, Samuel, 112, 240, 246
Behar, Ruth, 135
Benítez-Rojo, Antonio, 80, 130, 234
Benjamin, Walter, 169
Berlin Wall, the, xv, 5–6, 24–7, 33, 59–60,
  89, 98, 244
Beuys, Joseph, 51, 146
Bhabha, Homi, 34, 69, 78, 203
bharatha natyam, 47
bisexual, 244, 255
Blanco, Roberto, 228
Blau, Herbert, 240, 242, 245–7